A Law of Peoples for Recognizing States

A Law of Peoples for Recognizing States

On Rawls, the Social Contract, and Membership in the International Community

Chris Naticchia

LEXINGTON BOOKS
Lanham • Boulder • New York • London

Published by Lexington Books
An imprint of The Rowman & Littlefield Publishing Group, Inc.
4501 Forbes Boulevard, Suite 200, Lanham, Maryland 20706
www.rowman.com

Unit A, Whitacre Mews, 26-34 Stannary Street, London SE11 4AB

British Library Cataloguing in Publication Information Available

Library of Congress Cataloging-in-Publication Data

Names: Naticchia, Chris, author.
Title: A law of peoples for recognizing states : on Rawls, the social contract, and membership in the international community / Chris Naticchia.
Description: Lanham : Lexington Books, [2017] | Includes bibliographical references and index.
Identifiers: LCCN 2016034875 (print) | LCCN 2016040893 (ebook) | ISBN 9781498526135 (cloth : alk. paper) | ISBN 9781498526142 (ebook)
Subjects: LCSH: Rawls, John, 1921-2002. Law of peoples--Influence. | International law--Philosophy. | International relations--Philosophy. | Recognition (International law) | State, The. | Social contract. | International law and human rights.
Classification: LCC KZ1256 .N377 2017 (print) | LCC KZ1256 (ebook) | DDC 320.51--dc21
LC record available at https://lccn.loc.gov/2016034875

∞™ The paper used in this publication meets the minimum requirements of American National Standard for Information Sciences Permanence of Paper for Printed Library Materials, ANSI/NISO Z39.48-1992.

Printed in the United States of America

To my parents

Flory Naticchia

Dolores Naticchia

I believe that, as time goes on, *A Theory of Justice* will stand out with increasing clarity as by far the most significant contribution to political philosophy produced in this century. Only one thing threatens to obscure that achievement: the publication of *Political Liberalism*.

—Brian Barry, 1995

Contents

Acknowledgements	ix
Part I: Critique and Diagnosis	**1**
1 Introduction	3
2 The Law of Peoples: Act I	29
3 The Law of Peoples: Act II	55
4 The Communitarian Concession	67
5 From Justice to Recognition	93
Part II: Solution	**119**
6 The Justice-Based and Pragmatic Theories	121
7 The Critical Mass Principle	159
8 The Justifiable Secession Principle	181
9 The Economic Development Principle	201
10 An Appraisal of International Law	215
Epilogue: Brian Barry's Encore	235
Appendix 1	245
Appendix 2	247
Appendix 3	253
Appendix 4	257
Bibliography	269
Index	275
About the Author	281

Acknowledgements

Like many who began their study of moral and political philosophy in the 1980s, I came to a field heavily influenced by John Rawls. From his criticisms of utilitarianism to his derivation of the difference principle, from his rejection of libertarianism to his defense of reflective equilibrium, from his setup of the original position to his use of the veil of ignorance, Rawls and his ideas dominated much of the agenda in moral and political philosophy. Impressed by the precision, elegance, comprehensiveness, and force of his arguments, I, like many others, embraced his now famous principles of justice enthusiastically. As my knowledge of moral and political philosophy continued to grow, so did my appreciation for Rawls and his contributions—an appreciation which continues to this day.

So when I entered graduate school in the 1990s, it was hardly surprising that I would champion, in my dissertation, Rawls's political liberalism as the best strategy for defending liberal principles of justice—better, that is, than competing views, such as natural rights liberalism, consequentialist liberalism, or perfectionist liberalism. By then, the ideas of an overlapping consensus, public reason, and justice as fairness as a political conception had circulated widely, and I found the ways in which Rawls had integrated them to defend a principle of toleration to be as powerful and as compelling as the ways in which he had earlier combined notions of freedom and equality in defense of his principles of justice. Then, one sweltering morning in July, I defended my dissertation. Exhilarated and proud, I began preparing for my move from Charlottesville to California, where a tenure-track position awaited me.

But in the three or four weeks that it took me to say my good-byes, pack my belongings, load the truck, and steel myself for the drive across the Rockies, something awful (or perhaps fortuitous) happened: something that would rock me out of my dogmatic (Rawlsian) slumbers.

It started innocuously enough. It arrived in my mailbox, just as it had many times before. The subscription wasn't cheap—not for a graduate student. But there, in thin, clear, plastic covering, was the item that would forever change the way I would view Rawls and his work. Admire him—that would endure—no question about that. But now such admiration would be coupled with a dose of sobriety. Slowly, I opened the plastic covering and scanned the titles of the articles in the journal it contained. Immediately, one of them caught my attention. I began to read it—with pleasure at first, followed shortly by concern—and then with alarm. As the gravity of the situation sank in, I experienced a sense of dread. *My dissertation was completely wrong*.

The first person I would like to acknowledge (whether to thank or to blame him, I'm still not sure), therefore, is the philosopher whose review of *Political Liberalism* shook my worldview: Brian Barry.

How this would all affect a book on state recognition and *The Law of Peoples* I will describe later. But back then it appeared to me that I was faced with a moral quandary quite unlike any found in textbooks on moral philosophy. Should I tell my dissertation advisor, John Simmons, that I was disavowing the dissertation that I had successfully defended only a couple of weeks before—that I wanted to go back, start it from scratch, and give it another try? Should I call my future colleagues and tell them that I changed my mind, that I was declining their tenure-track position so that I could write another dissertation? Normally, a moral quandary like this would require days or weeks of reflection and agonizing, but in my case, fortunately, the answers came in an instant. Lured by the promise of my first real paycheck in years, I climbed into the truck, turned the ignition, and headed for California.

As I crossed the Shenandoah mountains, I cleared my conscience by resolving to draft a revision within a year or two.

As with any book whose gestation period lasted longer than the time it took Odysseus to find his way home, this book has incurred many debts of gratitude along the way. Like Odysseus, I eventually did reach Ithaca, where, thanks to David Lyons, my love of learning was transformed into a love of learning philosophy in particular. It was primarily David who taught me how to think precisely and to write concisely, and it was he who challenged me to stretch my limits by encouraging me to take some graduate classes as an undergraduate. Nicholas Sturgeon, Gail Fine, Allen Wood, Harold Hodes, and Robert Stalnaker (who, without complaint, essentially tutored me during his office hours in a graduate logic class) also deserve thanks for their contributions to my philosophical development.

Although my stay at NYU was brief (this was back when it had just a master's program), I want to thank the professors there with whom I took classes—Thomas Nagel, Ronald Dworkin, Derek Parfit, Peter Unger, Hiram McClendon—and David A.J. Richards, with whom I wrote my thesis.

I will always have a special fondness for Charlottesville—it's the most beautiful place I've ever lived—and my four years at the University of Virginia were memorable in ways academic and nonacademic. Special thanks, clearly, go to my dissertation advisor, John Simmons, who freed me from much of my muddled thinking about political obligation and other matters. If only I had listened to him more carefully about the pitfalls of hypothetical contractarian accounts of political obligation and legitimacy, I might have been spared my years of reflective disequilibrium caused by the Barry bomb. John Marshall, James Cargile, Cora Diamond, Dan Devereux, George Thomas, and Paul Humphries also deserve credit for helping to launch my academic career.

In the years since then, I have incurred other debts of gratitude too. The National Endowment for the Humanities supported me with two Faculty Research Awards and provided me with stipend support for two NEH Summer Seminars. I am grateful to the organizers of those seminars, Alvin Goldman (social epistemology), and Andrew Altman and Christopher Heath Wellman (political obligation, democratic legitimacy, human rights), for their generous support both during and after those seminars—truly above and beyond the call of professional duty. I am also grateful to Thomas Pogge and David Miller for their advice on papers that were later published and that are included in this book (revised) as chapters 2 and 6, respectively. On the subject of international recognition, I am indebted to Brad Roth and members of the International Law Association's Committee on Recognition and Nonrecognition (on which I serve) for what I have learned from them. I am particularly indebted and grateful to Hsu Hahn and Ser-Min Shei of the philosophy department at National Chung Cheng University in Chiayi, Taiwan, for their generosity and hospitality while hosting me as a visiting scholar and for arranging such a phenomenal audience for my presentation there (the feedback from which forced wide-ranging changes to this book). Three stellar students of mine, Donovan Rinker-Morris (who went on to graduate from Harvard Law School), Michael Stieg (who went on to graduate from the Georgetown School of Foreign Service), and Joel Miller, class of 2016, also supplied invaluable research assistance. My department colleagues—Jill Buroker, Matt Davidson, Susan Finsen, Tom Moody, and Tony Roy—gave me useful feedback at various stages as well.

Of all these debts, perhaps the greatest, though, is owed to the Law and Philosophy Discussion Group of Southern California, the works-in-progress group to which I belong that has forced me to stay on top of my philosophical game for the more than decade-and-a-half that I've been a member. Through their careful guidance and support, they sustained my professional development from early- through mid-career. Without their commitment, this book simply would not have been possible. While the group's membership has fluctuated over the years, at its fullest glory it included Marshall Cohen, Herb Morris, Barbara Herman, Andrews Reath, Seana Valentine Shiffrin, David Dolinko, Aaron James, Pamela Hieronymi, Michael Cholbi, John Davis, Craig Ihara, Thomas Morawetz, Margaret Gilbert, Calvin Normore, John Linarelli, Kory DeClark, Steve Munzer, Carl Cranor, and Sharon Lloyd. Among these, Steve Munzer, Carl Cranor, and Sharon Lloyd deserve special mention for their years of dedication in organizing the group, hosting meetings, and offering fantastic feedback.

Finally, I must thank my family for their support throughout the years. I must thank my wife, the illustrious professor (of communication studies) Rueyling Chuang, for her enduring encouragement and contagious enthusiasm as I slaved over these pages; our daughter, Elisea Chuang-Naticchia, for giving me the opportunity to experience the joys of parenthood, for being my most precious student, for letting me read Plato's dialogues to her at bedtime, and for reminding me through her very presence that there are more important things in life than writing a book; and the two people who created my love of learning in the first place, my parents, to whom I dedicate this book.

San Bernardino, California
2016

Portions of this book (in revised form) appeared previously as "Human Rights, Liberalism, and Rawls's Law of Peoples," *Social Theory and Practice* 24 (1998), 345–74 (chapter 2); "The Law of Peoples: The Old and the New," *Journal of Moral Philosophy* 2, no. 3 (November 2005), 353–69 (special issue on Global Justice) (reprinted in Thom Brooks and Fabian Freyenhagen (eds.), *The Legacy of John Rawls* (London and New York: Continuum, 2005), 177–94) (chapter 3); "Recognition and Legitimacy: A Reply to Buchanan," *Philosophy & Public Affairs* 28, no. 3 (Summer 1999), 242–57 (chapters 6 and 7); and "Recognizing States and Governments," *Canadian Journal of Philosophy* 35, no. 1 (March 2005), 27–82 (chapter 6).

Part I

Critique and Diagnosis

Rawls, the Social Contract, and the Law of Peoples

ONE

Introduction

1.1 THE SOCIAL CONTRACT

Writing anything fresh today on John Rawls promises to be more daunting than ever. Even in the early days (the 1970s), the saturation of the field with works on Rawls, followed by the inevitable Rawls fatigue, led one reviewer to quip: "Like a chain letter, *A Theory of Justice* was an opportunity for those of us who got in early and a trap for those who came along later."[1] Decades later, another reviewer noted that "[o]ver the course of the last half-century, roughly three thousand articles that discuss the work of John Rawls have been published in journals of philosophy, law, economics, political science, and related fields."[2] How much more daunting it must be today, then, to offer something different and interesting.

Yet I believe that Rawls's work continues to teach us new lessons about our moral and political universe, and therefore my main task in this introduction will be to lay out the case for my optimism that the present work will defy the Sisyphean cycles of interest and fatigue.

Encountering Rawls for the first time, we get the argument advanced in *A Theory of Justice*: the original position, the veil of ignorance, the presentation of the alternatives, the rejection of utilitarianism, the selection of justice as fairness, reflective equilibrium. Whether or not we agree with its conclusion, we recognize at once that Rawls's argument, with its precision and sophistication, merits our serious attention. Rawls teaches us how to be precise.

Upon engaging with him repeatedly, we notice something further. Rawls teaches us to be precise about a particular subject matter within moral and political philosophy. He teaches us to be precise about the *social contract*—and contractarian reasoning more generally. "My aim," he announces in the opening pages of *A Theory of Justice*—and reaffirms in *Political Liberalism* and *The Law of Peoples*—"is to present a conception of justice which generalizes and carries to a higher level of abstraction the familiar theory of the social contract as found, say, in Locke, Rousseau, and Kant."[3]

Part of the enduring fascination with Rawls, I believe, comes from the combination of his precision with his devotion to the social contract tradition. As a result, many critics and defenders alike, whether discussing his domestic contract in *A Theory of Justice* or his international contract in *The Law of Peoples*, tend to focus on a common set of questions. How should the social contract be structured? How should the parties be characterized? What are their interests and motivations? How should they be situated and how much knowledge should they be allowed to possess? Which alternatives do they consider? How do they reason?

Defending answers to these questions requires discipline, but once we have defended them, we will have, Rawls suggests, "the most philosophically favored interpretation" of the original position—the one from which our principles of (domestic or international) justice should be derived.[4] Another part of the enduring fascination with Rawls, I believe, therefore, is this: the structure of this social contract, this "most philosophically favored" contract, might not match the one Rawls himself employs.

Once we acknowledge this possibility, we are no longer considering Rawls's theory alone as he himself presents it but Rawls*ian* theory more broadly—that is, the best version of Rawls's theory, one similar enough to Rawls's own to deserve that description, but which improves upon it by deviating from it when its underlying assumptions are indefensible or poorly motivated. Yet however far we may wish to push the limits of the Rawlsian (and the present work is one of them), no view can plausibly count as Rawlsian that sacrifices this central commitment to the social contract. Taking Rawls seriously requires taking the social contract seriously. Nowhere does this matter more than in *The Law of Peoples*.

1.2 THE LAW OF PEOPLES

Even Rawls's defenders will concede that, in *The Law of Peoples*, Rawls's argument requires assistance. As in *A Theory of Justice*, in *The Law of Peoples* Rawls derives principles of justice from a hypothetical social contract. Rather than representing individuals, though, as the parties to his domestic contract do, the parties to his international contract represent peoples, a collective agent; and rather than choosing principles of domestic justice, the parties choose principles of international justice. Rawls's argument therefore possesses three main features:

1. A social contract
2. Collective agents
3. Principles of international justice

Now among these principles, the most important ones for our purposes will be the duty of nonintervention and the duty to honor basic human rights (especially the latter). Rawls has been roundly criticized for taking a narrow view of what rights count as basic human rights. They include "minimal" rights to life and liberty (so individuals have rights to physical integrity and against forced slavery, for example) and to "a measure" of freedom of conscience and association (rights against persecution, essentially), but they exclude rights familiar from the liberal tradition, such as freedom of speech, equal liberty of conscience, democratic political rights, and rights to nondiscrimination. Rawls argues that peoples whose societies respect this narrow view of basic human rights deserve to be tolerated internationally.

In the first part of this book, I examine this argument by taking Rawls seriously as a social contract theorist and asking whether the international original position, as he constructs it, or with modest modifications that preserve the overall spirit of his view, can generate something like the basic human rights as Rawls conceives them. What we find, however, is that, no matter how much painstaking care we take in formulating alternative constructions, no matter how much charity we use in evaluating their assumptions, and no matter how much precision we employ in determining their outcomes (all of which I attempt to demonstrate in chapter two), Rawls's argument for basic human rights not only fails, but fails at a most fundamental level. The international original position cannot generate any restrictions on internal sovereignty at all—not just ones requiring respect for basic human rights, but ones requiring respect for any rights at all—for the simple reason that the principles that the parties must agree to can govern only their relations with one another, not their relations with their own members. As long as the parties are collective agents, the contract will be powerless to regulate what goes on within the groups they represent. Call this the *idle-contract* objection.[5]

Since Rawls's main objective is to establish the limits of international tolerance, and since the international contract is unable to produce those limits, the idle-contract objection seems quite damaging. What is most surprising about this inability, though, is that Rawls either *knew* about it already, or should have known about it. As far back as 1977, he was aware of Jane English's claim that, "By making the parties in the [domestic] original position heads of families rather than individuals, Rawls makes the family opaque to claims of justice"—and Susan Moller Okin's later elaboration of that claim.[6] After all, it was these (feminist) criticisms that led him to abandon the supposition that the parties to his domestic contract were heads of families and to seek some other basis for defending a just savings principle (one that assumed that the parties in the original position were individuals).[7] Can it really have escaped Rawls's notice that, just as the collective agents in the one case (heads of families) render members of the groups they represent (families) beyond the reach of justice (since the principles apply only to the contracting agents), so too do they in the other (international) case? Perhaps Rawls simply assumed that this was not the case domestically, since his principles protecting individual family members were already "on hand," having already been chosen in the original position (this would also explain his remarks on the family in "The Idea of Public Reason Revisited").[8] But this assumption itself presupposes that individuals rather than collective agents do the choosing in a domestic original position—a presupposition that he expressly rejects as a condition for entering his international original position (most notably for "decent," nonliberal societies).

However, the idle-contract objection can be stated even more strongly than this. The objection is not merely a variant of the standard nonparticipant objection: that animals, nature, and individuals who, through accident, injury, or misfortune, lack the two moral powers are not represented in the contract, and are therefore unprotected by justice. Rawls acknowledges that there are other virtues besides justice, and perhaps the interests of nonparticipants can be covered by one of them. This case is different. In this case, Rawls specifically sets out to establish the limits of tolerance using the social contract, and yet, the social contract cannot deliver the goods.

In addition to the idle-contract objection, there is another objection that is best brought out by considering Rawls's argument chronologically, as he himself developed and revised it. Rawls produced two versions of the law of peoples: an article, published in 1993, and the book by the same title, published in 1999.[9] While some of Rawls's changes are merely cosmetic, one of them is strikingly substantive: the set of basic human rights expands to include a requirement of equal justice for women (even for cultures whose traditions reject it). Clearly, this seems to be a response to the criticisms he faced earlier with making the set of basic human rights so narrow. As I argue in chapter 3, however, this requirement seems to imply a right to nondiscrimination on the basis of gender (otherwise it would be an idiosyncratic use of "equal justice")—but also, in isolation, it seems ad hoc. Why afford women a right to nondiscrimination on the basis of gender, but not, say, adherents of minority faiths a similar right to nondiscrimination on the basis of religion? The logic of Rawls's apparent concession to his critics seems to push him toward granting a more robust right to nondiscrimination, one broad enough to require equal liberty of conscience for all individuals rather than the mere "measure" of it that he had earlier defended for members of minority faiths. But now the set of basic human rights begins to look more and more liberal, and—despite the inability of the contract to generate them—

the limits of international tolerance get drawn much more narrowly, so that only nearly-liberal societies qualify. Call this the *almost-liberal* objection.[10]

Considering the idle-contract and almost-liberal objections together, many defenders of Rawls respond by sacrificing the second of the three features we previously identified. Substituting individuals for collective agents, they retain the social contract (the international original position) and argue that parties so situated would choose principles of international justice that are recognizably liberal—ones that include the standard package of liberal rights and freedoms (as well as a more egalitarian distributive principle)—just as they do in Rawls's domestic contract.[11] If Rawls is driven toward more liberal limits on internal sovereignty anyway, why not make it official and justify it by enabling the social contract to generate them?

Although this response is natural enough, its sheer obviousness, I believe, counts against it. Rawls could have taken the cosmopolitan route but decided to reject it.[12] How could he have bungled things so badly by constructing an idle contract when he had such a clear and direct contractual path to defending basic human rights (and more)?

Recognizing this difficulty, other defenders of Rawls respond by sacrificing the first of the three features we identified. Retaining the collective agents but detaching the social contract from any role in justifying basic human rights, they instead rely on notions of public reason to determine the core of an overlapping consensus among such agents on principles of justice—principles that include restrictions on internal sovereignty, principles that require respect for basic human rights.[13] Conceding the idle-contract objection, these defenders deny its force.

If we are going to rely like this on ideas from *Political Liberalism* to support Rawls's argument for basic human rights, however, we must also remember that Rawls there reminds us that his argument proceeds in two stages.[14] In the first stage, parties to a social contract select principles of justice. In the second stage, those principles are tested to see if they can be the focus of an overlapping consensus. The problem with this response, in short, is that it ignores the first stage—the social contract—and in so doing fails to take Rawls seriously as a social contract theorist. Call this the *two-stages* objection.

I will say more later in this introduction about each of these two strategies for handling the difficulties Rawls encounters in *The Law of Peoples*. For now, though, their initial weaknesses should be sufficient to motivate the search for an alternative strategy. What appears to cause Rawls's difficulties is his insistence on using collective agents. We might begin, then, by asking why he decided to use collective agents in the first place: in a concession, so it seems, to his communitarian critics.

1.3 THE COMMUNITARIAN CONCESSION

Conceding nothing to Michael Sandel, and little of significance to Charles Taylor and Alasdair MacIntyre, Rawls nonetheless makes a substantial concession, in *Political Liberalism,* to Michael Walzer—creating a precedent for *The Law of Peoples.*[15]

Powerfully reformulated in the works of Will Kymlicka and David Miller, the communitarian criticisms, combined with this precedent, then find expression in the international contract in the form of collective agents. As I also argue in chapter 4, they suggest a different way of construing the question Rawls seeks to answer, too.

To Sandel's criticism that the parties to Rawls's domestic contract represent noumenal selves, "prior to and independent of purposes and ends," unencumbered by any constitutive ties, unable to see themselves as so deeply committed to any project that "turning away from it would call into question the person I am,"[16] Rawls replies that, far from resting on Kantian metaphysics, the conception of the self that the parties presuppose is "political not metaphysical": it rests on ideas found in the public political culture, ideas like freedom and equality, which get "modeled" in the original position.[17] To Taylor's assertion that, without a thriving political community, the capacity for freedom that liberals value cannot maintain its worth, Rawls replies that his view does embrace the good of political community, just not one organized around a comprehensive doctrine. Against MacIntyre's charge that, in the absence of a shared commitment to a human telos and the virtues that comprise it, Rawlsian liberalism offers an impoverished sense of community, Rawls claims that his view does allow for a shared commitment to virtues that are instrumentally valuable for maintaining a just society. However, justice is established independently, the virtues derivatively, without relying on a human telos.

Walzer meets a different fate. Whereas Rawls rejects or deflects Sandel's, Taylor's, and MacIntyre's criticisms, he appears to accept Walzer's. For Walzer, principles of justice are pluralistic in form, and they depend on shared understandings of the goods being distributed.[18] "Social goods have social meanings," he argues, "and we find our way to distributive justice through an interpretation of those meanings."[19] Since "the political community is probably the closest we can come to a world of common meanings," the implication is that we are to interpret the meanings shared within each political community in order to find the principles of justice appropriate for that community.[20] Otherwise, Walzer suggests, we risk running "roughshod over local understandings and decisions."[21] Apparently influenced by such reasoning, Rawls concedes that "justice as fairness is framed to apply [only] to . . . a modern constitutional [liberal] democracy"[22] and proceeds to defend that position at length in *Political Liberalism.* So rather than deriving justice as fairness from a comprehensive doctrine that aspires to universal truth, he explains, justice as fairness "starts from within a certain political tradition"—the liberal political tradition—and works up "ideas . . . implicit in the public political culture," like the essential freedom and equality of its citizens, in an effort to identify its principles of justice.[23] By relying on a liberal democracy's shared understandings and circumventing what he regards as deep disagreement among its citizens over the true comprehensive doctrine, Rawls limits the scope of his principles.

One clear implication of this apparent concession to Walzer is that political communities without liberal traditions might appropriately have different principles of justice—ones faithful to their own traditions. Another implication is that, if we want to justify principles of international justice, we will first need to seek some area of commonality between liberal and nonliberal political communities.[24] These implications combine to present the main challenges in *The Law of Peoples*.

If we can credit Walzer with persuading Rawls to appeal to shared understandings, we can credit Kymlicka and Miller with helping him to identify their international content. Reformulating the communitarian criticisms, Kymlicka argues that, while often overstated, they contain an important insight: that without a strong sense of cultural membership, individuals will lack a secure context of choice that gives them the confidence and self-respect required for meaningfully exercising their capacity for choice.[25] For this purpose, it is not necessary to exaggerate and to claim that some ties seem so inescapable that we cannot imagine ourselves without them. Even communitarians who make such claims acknowledge that we should have the freedom to reexamine those ties.[26] Rather, it is only necessary to show that, in judging for ourselves the worth of alternative ways of life, a strong sense of cultural membership provides us with the options that serve as our starting points and the resources with which to make them vivid. Liberals who value individual freedom should therefore value membership in cultural communities. As Kymlicka observes, however, "for a culture to survive and develop in the modern world, given the pressures towards the creation of a single common culture in each country, it must be a societal culture"—that is, a culture with its own social institutions—and these societal cultures, he notes, tend to be *national* cultures.[27] Kymlicka defends the ethical significance of *nationalilty*.

Like Kymlicka, Miller defends the ethical significance of nationality, but whereas Kymlicka defends its instrumental value[28]—its value for individual freedom—Miller defends its fundamental (nonderivative) value. Resisting the tendency to view the moral subject "as an abstract individual, possessed of the general powers and capacities of human beings . . . but not fundamentally committed to any particular persons, groups, practices, [or] institutions," Miller (echoing Sandel) instead argues that we should view this subject as "partly defined by its relationships," such that, "[t]o divest oneself of such commitments would be, in one important sense, to change one's identity."[29] Otherwise we get "an implausible account of ethical motivation," one where "[n]o considerations about who I am, where I have come from, or which communities I see myself as attached to are . . . allowed to influence my ethical reasoning."[30] Once we reason from this particularist perspective, though, we can defend the value of national attachments without needing to go through the universalist detour. "The particularist defence of nationality," he claims, "*begins* with the assumption that memberships and attachments in general have ethical significance." It is "*[b]ecause* I identify with my family, my college, or my local community," he adds, that they hold value.[31] The same applies to national attachments. All else equal, attachments to national communities will hold value *as such*, without any need to justify such value by reference to (for instance) their instrumental value for individual freedom.

Whatever we think of the merits of these arguments, Kymlicka and Miller provide Rawls with a viable candidate for linking liberal and nonliberal political communities together: an agreement on the value of national groups, a collective agent. Whether endorsed for the liberal individualist reasons that Kymlicka offers or the more particularist, communitarian reasons that Miller defends, that value can be supported by both kinds of political community in much the same manner that Rawls imagines adherents of different comprehensive doctrines supporting the conception of the person used in his domestic contract. Call this reliance on collective agents *the communitarian concession*.

Representing these collective agents in the international contract seems easy enough: they are the parties to the contract. But Rawls seems uncertain about the exact collectivity that they represent. They do not represent states with traditional powers of sovereignty like the right to wage war—that much is clear—as Rawls explicitly rejects that position.[32] But whether they represent peoples or societies is unclear. Taking the title of the book, numerous direct references, and the statements of the principles themselves (along with the fact that *nations* is roughly synonymous with *peoples*),[33] we have ample evidence for claiming that they represent peoples. The implication, in that case, would seem to be that all peoples everywhere, regardless of whether they are organized into political societies, possess the rights, powers, and duties that Rawls defends.[34] On the other hand, Rawls does seem to use *peoples* and *societies* interchangeably, and the powers that he ascribes to peoples would make no sense unless they were organized as political societies—indeed, as states, albeit ones with more constricted powers than the traditional powers of sovereignty—evidence for claiming that they represent societies.[35] In that case, the implication would seem to be that *only* peoples who are organized into political societies possess the rights, powers, and duties that Rawls defends.[36] In the one case, Rawls appears to offer a "radical" theory that "ascribes many of the powers of sovereignty, including that of self-determination, to hundreds, if not thousands, of groups that exist within state boundaries but which do not have states of their own."[37] In the other, he appears to offer a conservative theory that grants these same powers to the national group that happens to control the state apparatus but then ignores all the other minority nations or peoples in its midst.[38]

Read against the backdrop of Kymlicka's and Miller's concerns with multinational states, minority nations, and national self-determination, though, Rawls's law of peoples can split the horns of this dilemma. Hardly unaware of these intellectual crosscurrents, Rawls, I argue, neither idealizes away the problems posed by minority nations nor does he ignore them. If we construe the collective agents as representing societies without knowing whether, or to what extent, they contain minority nations, as surely Rawls must have allowed, then we can at least acquit Rawls of having failed to address them.

Beyond this interpretive reason, though, there is a theoretical one as well. Just as Rawls claims in his domestic theory that, for theoretical purposes, domestic societies should be considered closed for individuals (as ones "we enter only by birth and exit only by death"),[39] so too, in his international theory, should we consider them closed for minority nations. Like individuals, minority nations simply find themselves in a domestic society—"born into" it irrespective of their voluntary choices—and the possibility of seceding no more makes it voluntary for minority nations than the possibility of emigrating makes it voluntary for individuals, given the costliness of both. We have additional reason, then, for construing the collective agents as representing societies without knowing whether, or to what extent, they contain minority nations: it is necessary for identifying principles appropriate for a society given the general infeasibility of secession.[40]

Understanding the roots of Rawls's communitarian concession, therefore, I argue, not only enables us to appreciate why he uses collective agents in his international contract. It also enables us to see *how* best to interpret the collectivity that they represent. Still looming is the formidable idle-contract objection, but if my conjecture about Rawls's concession is correct, then it will also provide us with the resources to answer it. The first step to seeing this is to recast the question that Rawls seeks to answer in terms not much different from his own—terms already implicit in the original—terms suggested by our analysis. Instead of asking, as Rawls seems to ask, which nonliberal societies should liberal societies tolerate, we can ask, which societies (liberal or nonliberal) with minority nations should we tolerate? The next step is to notice that Rawls will occasionally add: "as a *member* in good standing of the Society of Peoples" (my emphasis).[41] As we will see, this focus on *membership* provides the key to our answer.

1.4 FROM JUSTICE TO RECOGNITION

Armed with the preceding analysis, we may begin to develop an alternative to the two strategies that we previously identified for handling the difficulties Rawls encounters in *The Law of Peoples*. One of those strategies, recall, the cosmopolitan strategy, essentially denies that Rawls needs to make any communitarian concession at all. It insists that liberal individualism is defensible, and that this fact ought to be reflected in the international contract by having the parties to that contract be individuals. As a result, the cosmopolitan strategy substitutes individuals for collective agents, retains the international contract, and generates principles of international justice. According to this view, if Rawls errs by constructing an idle contract, he has only himself to blame for making a concession he ought not to have made. I will say more about this strategy momentarily. For now, what I would like to suggest—by recasting Rawls's question so as to emphasize his concern with international membership—is that Rawls may have had a different ambition in mind than the one this strategy seems to assume.

The other strategy, the political liberal strategy, is to retain the collective agents, but draw on ideas from *Political Liberalism*—like public reason, a political conception, and an overlapping consensus—to justify his principles (particularly restrictions on internal sovereignty) instead of relying on the international contract to generate them. As we observed earlier, though, this strategy fails to take Rawls seriously as a social contract theorist.

Not only does it fail to take Rawls seriously as a social contract theorist, I argue, it relies on an assumption that we ought to reject: that the justification for principles of justice should depend on their ability to be the focus of an overlapping consensus. So if the rationale for denying the contract a role in justifying principles rests on the claim that ideas from *Political Liberalism* can pick up the slack—that Rawls is mistakenly regarded, first and foremost, as a social contract theorist—then that rationale, I maintain in chapter 5, is indefensible.

Clearly, this will require me to discuss the Brian Barry bomb that I referred to in my acknowledgements: the article that convinced me that my previous embrace of political liberalism (not to mention the dissertation that I had defended just two weeks before the article arrived in the mail) was completely wrong.[42] Barry's review is more wide-ranging than what I focus on, and I elaborate his main argument perhaps in ways he would not accept, but I take his central claim to be that the inability of principles to be the focus of an overlapping consensus should not be sufficient reason for rejecting them. Public reason, a political conception, the burdens of judgment, reasonableness—all of these ideas (and others), arguably, are instrumental toward achieving what is central to that work, an overlapping consensus—so any effort to undermine the claim that we need to achieve one would seem by implication to undermine the work as a whole. Although I doubt that I will persuade everybody of this position—attempting that would seem to require, not just a different book entirely, but an entire book itself—I am confident that I will present considerations sufficient for determining the intellect.

Whereas the cosmopolitan strategy retains the international contract but substitutes individuals for collective agents, and whereas the political liberal strategy retains collective agents but substitutes ideas drawn from political liberalism for the international contract, the third alternative—the one that I defend in chapter 5—retains *both* the international contract and collective agents but denies that Rawls's ambition was to generate principles of international justice (the third of the three features we identified). Given the liabilities with the other strategies, I argue, this third strategy represents the best way of handling the difficulties Rawls encounters.

Admittedly, the very first sentence of *The Law of Peoples* and many references throughout the book suggest that Rawls does indeed seek a theory of international justice. At other times, however, he suggests that he is after something much more pedestrian: a liberal *foreign policy*. This latter way of characterizing his aim makes much more sense when we consider Rawls's concern with membership. One aspect of foreign policy is determining who counts as a member of the international community of states. Members of the international community of states possess rights to nonintervention. So if we take Rawls's concern to be with determining the class of entities that possess a right to nonintervention, then we can construe him as aiming to establish criteria for determining which entities belong to that class. Entities belonging to that class will constitute member states of the international community.

Under international law, the criteria for determining which entities count as member states, with the rights, powers, and immunities of statehood, are referred to as the criteria for *recognizing* states. Accordingly, we may construe Rawls as aiming to defend, on normative grounds, such criteria. In *The Law of Peoples*, Rawls's aim is not to defend principles of international justice, but a theory of international recognition.[43]

Now as a distinct issue in political philosophy, international recognition has received little sustained, systematic attention. The reasons for this lack are unclear. However, one reason stands out as a plausible candidate: that questions of recognition are covered, implicitly, under the heading *secession*. When we decide that a political entity has a right to secede from its parent state, for example, what we are deciding, implicitly, is that if it desires international recognition, we ought to grant it. Hence, a theory of secession is implicitly a theory of recognition: a theory for when we ought to grant recognition to *new* states and admit them as new members of the international community. Secession, of course, has received much philosophical attention.

Nonetheless, we should not assimilate international recognition to secession. While a theory of international recognition will share one important feature with a theory of secession, it will also possess one crucial feature that a theory of secession lacks. Like a theory of secession, a theory of international recognition takes as its starting point the status quo—meaning, in this context, the current array of internationally recognized states. But whereas a theory of secession is forward-looking only, concerned with determining which entities to add, from that point forward, to the international community of recognized states, a theory of international recognition is both forward-looking and backward-looking, concerned not only with which entities to add, but also with which ones to subtract: with which currently recognized states to derecognize.

This difference, I argue, is not a mere difference in scope or ambition—as if we could limit or expand a theory at will, to serve narrower or broader theoretical purposes. Theoretical consistency *demands* it. Theoretical consistency demands that the same standards that apply for recognizing new states also apply for recognizing (or continuing to recognize) existing states (or else some justification be given for the asymmetry). In limiting their scope to cases involving new claimants for recognized statehood, theories of secession seem to assume that all currently recognized states ought to *continue* to be recognized, even if they fail to meet the criteria or standards that they set for new claimants. But just as we can ask whether this or that future political entity ought to be recognized as a state, so too can we ask whether this or that current political entity ought to have been recognized as a state—that is to say, we can ask whether its standing, as a recognized member of the international community, ought to be *revoked*.

We need to be able to ask these questions. Representatives from political entities who are denied recognition ask them. Why are we denied recognition according to such-and-such criteria, applied prospectively, when, applied retrospectively, there are so many entities that fail to meet them too, yet are granted recognition? Besides reasons of theoretical consistency, then, there are reasons of moral consistency for defending criteria that are both forward-looking and backward-looking. Just as a dog can tell the difference between being tripped over and being kicked, representatives from entities denied recognition know the difference between being rejected and being snowed.

Reading Rawls as defending a theory of international recognition is the next step in answering the idle-contract objection. We still need to develop that theory, and in doing so on his behalf we will depart in significant ways from the content of his view. However, if the argument up to this point is sound, we will not be straying too far from its spirit.

1.5 THE FOUR-STAGE SEQUENCE

Following the selection of justice as fairness, the parties to Rawls's domestic contract, using gradually increasing amounts of information about their society, adopt a constitution, enact legislation, and then, with the veil of ignorance completely lifted, establish administrative and judicial rules. Rawls calls this process the *four-stage sequence,* with the outcome of each stage constraining the options available at each subsequent stage.[44] In developing a theory of international recognition, I will follow a similar sequence, except that I will use a full veil at each stage.

Reinterpreting Rawls's claims about international justice as claims about the conditions for international recognition, we get a view like the following. Respecting basic human rights is among the minimum requirements of justice ("minimum" signifying their being capacious enough to include liberal and nonliberal societies). Also among those requirements is peaceful foreign relations. Meeting these minimum requirements of internal and external justice is necessary and sufficient for recognizing political entities as states. Thus, political entities ought to be recognized as states if and only if they meet minimum requirements of internal and external justice. Call this the *justice-based* view of international recognition.

In chapter 6, I argue *against* the justice-based view. We should reject any attempt to include minimum requirements of justice as a condition for recognition, for one simple reason: doing so may prevent us from making moral progress.[45] Achieving such progress does not happen on its own. It requires the collective efforts of many countries working together under difficult circumstances, attempting, in some cases, to overcome decades (or centuries) of hostilities. This requires that enough political entities work together as recognized states—as recognized members of the international community, participating in the international bodies that formulate, adjudicate, and implement international law. Call the number that constitutes enough political entities a *critical mass*. Since a plausible minimum might prevent us from recognizing this critical mass, I argue, we should reject including one as a condition for recognition.

Rather than have moral progress depend on whether enough entities happen to satisfy this or that criterion of minimal justice, I argue, we should embed this commitment into the first principle of the theory. So far, the argument here is exactly parallel to Rawls's argument against utilitarianism, in which he claims that our basic liberties are not sufficiently well protected if their protection is left to how the balance of utilities happens to turn out—to contingent empirical circumstances. In response, Rawls argues for embedding a commitment to our basic liberties in his first principle of justice as fairness.[46] Using this same strategy, we can show that the first principle of any adequate theory of international recognition will claim something like the following: a political entity ought to be recognized as a state if and only if it belongs to the critical mass of entities which, working together, is necessary for making at least some moral progress toward the ideal. Call this the *pragmatic* view of international recognition.

Defending a pragmatic rather than justice-based theory represents one departure from Rawls's own view. A second departure is this. Earlier I mentioned that a theory of recognition will take as its starting point the current array of internationally recognized states and establish criteria for determining which entities to add as recognized states and which currently recognized states to derecognize. The idea is that, by starting with the status quo and making adjustments, we progress in steps toward the targeted state of affairs. Just what is this state of affairs? In Rawls's terms, the targeted state of affairs is the *ideal*, it is the outcome of ideal theory, it is established through ideal theorizing, and it is expressed in terms of *justice*. Its aim is "to guide the course of social reform" as we approach it through "transition cases."[47] It assumes strict compliance with its requirements, the ideal being *satisfied* as a result. In contrast, when we face situations involving partial compliance, the ideal state of affairs, for that reason, is not satisfied. We fall short of it, to a greater or lesser degree, depending on the extent of noncompliance. Although the ideal provides us with the ultimate target toward which we should move (our guide to social reform), we still need principles to govern the transition. There is no assumption that we must move toward it directly. If we need to, we can take one step back in order to take two steps forward.[48] In the conduct of foreign policy, a theory of recognition supplies us with such transitional principles: ones governing identification of the international community's member states. We will need further principles to cover other aspects of foreign policy, and principles concerning things other than foreign policy, in transitioning to the ideal. But principles governing international recognition will form one important class of principles in that set. In short, a theory of recognition, I argue in chapter 7, belongs to *nonideal* theory.[49]

Here, then, we have our second departure from Rawls as we develop the best Rawlsian view, for Rawls himself conceives of his law of peoples as supplying principles that identify the target at which we should aim—as belonging to ideal theory.

Obviously this leaves entirely open what the ideal is, which is to be established at the first stage in the sequence. Here I simply make an assumption in the alternative. On the one hand, we can assume that the ideal is a *universal liberalism* and take no position as to how it gets established. It can be a liberal comprehensive doctrine (not established by a social contract). It can be the outcome of Rawls's domestic contract, justice as fairness, applied to all societies. It can even be the outcome of a global original position with individuals as parties to the contract, as cosmopolitans argue. The basic point is that, if we read Rawls's law of peoples as an attempt to defend a theory of recognition, then we will be developing, on his behalf, a nonideal theory, in which case the ideal to which such a theory is joined must be established independently. Although this does not require a universal liberalism as the ideal, having it be the ideal is clearly the simplest and most straightforward solution to the almost-liberal objection, and Rawlsians in particular will be at no loss to imagine how to defend liberalism. Rawlsians who are inclined to push Rawls in a more universal direction (myself included among them) can then read the present work as an attempt to detail a Rawlsian account of international relations under the assumption of a universal liberalism.

On the other hand, for Rawlsians (and others) who are not inclined to push Rawls in this direction, the argument involving the second and third stages can still go through if one replaces a universal liberalism with an ideal that is broad enough to include some nonliberal societies. Only the argument involving the fourth stage will be affected.

Either way, we get a contractarian defense of a theory of recognition, a result that will interest philosophers, legal academics, and international relations scholars alike.

In the rest of the book, I turn to the main challenge, which is to argue systematically for the pragmatic view. The pragmatic view, I show, can be defended as the outcome of a hypothetical social contract among collective agents—three stages of it, in fact.

As I show in chapter 7, in which I construct the second stage of the four-stage sequence, the pragmatic view relies on *the necessity of moral progress,* which holds that, necessarily, in matters moral, we are permitted to make moral progress toward the ideal. This assumption is so fundamental to nonideal theorizing that it deserves the name of *regulative principle* of nonideal theory, for without it, nonideal theorizing simply cannot get off the ground. However, absolutist prohibitions of any sort seem to deny this regulative principle, and so the challenge is to find a way to adjudicate this dispute in a way that avoids dead-end appeals to contrasting intuitions. Arguing that parties to a suitably constructed international contract would affirm the regulative principle and reject absolutist prohibitions, I show by implication that they would accept the pragmatic view of international recognition.

The challenge now is to expand upon that result to add other principles to the first principle of the theory. In chapter eight, in the third stage of the sequence, I argue that the parties to the international contract would choose a principle guaranteeing the right of *secession*—and that this principle belongs, not to ideal theory, but to nonideal theory—as a remedial principle, a transitional principle, one that aims to bring us closer to the ideal. While this is not a blanket right of secession (there are conditions), neither does it merely reaffirm the status quo under international law, which appears to deny a right of secession, even as a remedial right: that is, as a remedy of last resort for persistent and grave human rights abuses at the hands of the government's security forces. The agreement would extend at least a remedial right of secession, and possibly beyond it as well.

Taken together, the second and third stages generate a theory that begins with the status quo, the current array of internationally recognized states, and then adjusts it according to the first principle, adding entities as recognized states, or derecognizing some existing states, as the case may be. For reasons explained more fully later, with the first principle the emphasis will be on existing states, whether recognized or unrecognized. An entity that satisfies the international law definition of a state, but which is currently unrecognized internationally—like Taiwan—might well qualify for recognition according to this first principle. In contrast, a currently recognized state whose inclusion is not necessary for progress toward the ideal (and whose inclusion may well be a positive impediment) might qualify for derecognition. With the second principle guaranteeing a right of secession (with conditions), the focus changes to entities (such as minority nations) that typically do not satisfy the international law definition of a state. The concern then is solely with adding to the adjusted array of member states.

With the fourth stage, we confront the question of whether the first principle is too narrow despite the fact that it enables us to make progress toward the ideal. Although that principle authorizes the recognition of a critical mass, and although that critical mass enables us to make moral progress, one may reasonably wonder whether progress is progress enough. Might not the parties to the international contract have an interest in *accelerating* such progress beyond what they could achieve with that critical mass? Arguing in chapter 9 that they do, I nonetheless show (drawing on Rawls's observations about the just savings principle) that they would not choose to make such progress as rapidly as possible. As a result, the parties to the international contract choose a third principle that claims the following: further political entities (beyond the critical mass) are to be recognized as states if and only if recognizing them hastens the economic advance of the least well-off entities so that they come closer to the point at which they would no longer seriously countenance tradeoffs between economic goods and liberal freedoms.

As I hope to show, then, these three principles—the critical mass, justifiable secession, economic development principles—can be defended as the outcome of three consecutive stages of a hypothetical international social contract among collective agents, with each principle adding to the set of recognized states, and their disjunction stating the necessary and sufficient conditions for state recognition. Combining the results of the second, third, and fourth stages thus generates a robust theory of international recognition, one that can serve as a normative guide in evaluating answers to a foundational question in international relations: who counts as a member of the international community, and why? No longer idle, the social contract generates an answer and provides a defense.[50]

1.6 APPRAISING INTERNATIONAL LAW

Finally, chapter 10 takes the critical mass, justifiable secession, and economic development principles and uses them to evaluate the criteria that states and other international bodies currently use to decide which entities to recognize as member states of the international community. While the criteria are contested (and inconsistently applied), the dominant view, it seems to me, is that the recognition of *new* states requires the consent of the parent state (sometimes with extra conditions), while the recognition of *current* states requires nothing more than their continued acceptance by the other members of the international community, whether or not they themselves meet the criteria required for recognizing new states. Taken together, these positions seem to imply that under current international law there is no unilateral right to secede—not even as a remedy of last resort for persistent and grave human rights abuses at the hands of the government's security forces. Instead, the right to territorial integrity held by existing states takes precedence.

Now of course whether there is such a remedial right to secede under international law is a matter of dispute among international legal scholars. We find scholars like Rosalyn Higgins, Donald Horowitz, and John Murphy denying it, while others, like Antonio Cassese, James Crawford, Hurst Hannum, and Steven Ratner, claim that there is such a right under highly restricted circumstances.[51] We can trace the dispute to UN Resolution 2625, the *Declaration on Principles of International Law concerning Friendly Relations and Cooperation among States in accordance with the Charter of the United Nations*, which declared both:

1. "By virtue of the principle of equal rights and self-determination of peoples enshrined in the Charter of the United Nations, all peoples have the right freely to determine, without external interference, their political status and to pursue their economic, social and cultural development, and every State has the duty to respect this right in accordance with the provisions of the Charter;" and
2. (a) "Nothing in the foregoing paragraphs shall be construed as authorizing or encouraging any action which would dismember or impair, totally or in part, the territorial integrity or political unity of sovereign and independent States. . . ." (b) ". . . conducting themselves in compliance with the principle of equal rights and self-determination of peoples as described above and thus possessed of a government representing the whole people belonging to the territory without distinction as to race, creed or colour."[52]

The question, familiar by now, is whether (2b) establishes a remedial right of secession when states either persecute or deny participatory rights to peoples in their territory—a remedial right held by peoples whose rights to self-determination have thereby been violated. Advancing arguments of principle, policy, and legislative history, and according them various weights in relation to one another, we find, not surprisingly, different scholars defending different interpretations, with some insisting that the right to territorial integrity is inviolable (as Resolution 2625 itself states at one point), others maintaining tight exceptions.

What leads me to claim that the dominant view requires parent state consent for recognizing new states, and thus for suggesting that the status quo under international law appears to deny remedial rights to secession, is the way states themselves have interpreted their international legal responsibilities under Resolution 2625. State practice itself evidences a decided tendency to deny remedial rights to secession even where it would seem most justified, and to uphold rights to territorial integrity of even the worst state offenders, as Mikulas Fabry shows.[53] While it always remains open, of course, to argue that these states mistake what international law requires, the fact that state practice displays the tendency it does should be sufficient to support the claim that the status quo under international law at least appears to deny remedial rights to secession. In any case, my argument is meant to challenge the way state practice has evolved under Resolution 2625 by insisting that, on the contrary, there ought to be such a remedial right—and that this "ought" represents not some lofty ideal, but is firmly grounded in sound nonideal theorizing. If it should turn out instead that—contrary to how states themselves interpret their international legal responsibilities—there is such a remedial legal right after all, then my argument will supply a contractarian grounding for that conclusion, which will be of theoretical interest in its own right.

Were this book just about secession, this conclusion would be significant enough on its own, but the book is about far more than that, since it deals with recognition more generally. And this is where it offers an even sharper critique of the status quo, despite disavowing aspirations to ideal theorizing. As noted, current international law seems to embrace an *asymmetry* between the standards it employs for recognizing new states and the standards it employs for continuing to recognize current states: the recognition of *new* states requires the consent of the parent state (sometimes with extra conditions), while the recognition of *current* states requires nothing more than their continued acceptance by the other members of the international community. The pragmatic view of international recognition, however, challenges this very asymmetry, as it entertains the possibility of revoking recognition of some currently recognized states should they fail to meet the standards required for recognizing new states.

Now in one perfectly natural sense of the term *pragmatic*, it is clearly pragmatic, politically, to accept this asymmetry, on the plausible ground that current members of the international community would likely reject any proposal calling for the potential derecognition of one of their members. In that case, one might construe one's role as a philosopher to be to offer a theory for recognizing new states alone, with the implication that all currently internationally recognized states will continue to be recognized even if they fail to meet the standards that the theory requires for recognizing new states. We might call this an *asymmetric pragmatic* theory. In contrast, we could offer a *symmetric pragmatic* theory consisting of the three principles that I defend, or something similar, applied prospectively and retrospectively, so that they countenance the possibility of derecognizing some currently recognized states. To judge between them, presumably, we would need to ascertain which view is best designed, in the long run, to reach the ideal presupposed by the theories.

But if this is how we conceive of the matter, then it is no longer clear what special contribution philosophers have to make to the decision, for now the theories appear not just pragmatic but purely *strategic*. The term *pragmatic*, as I am using it, indicates that, if we are to make moral progress, we must regrettably recognize some states that do not even meet minimum standards of justice. Both views are pragmatic in that sense. However, conceived in this way, they are both now strategic as well, in that their justification depends solely on how well suited they are, as strategies, to making moral progress. That strategic decision, though, seems to fall within the disciplinary expertise of other fields (like law, international relations, and political science) and not within the special province of philosophy.

The approach taken by this book insists that philosophy does indeed have a distinct contribution to make, and it makes it precisely by demanding that even strategic decisions be embedded in a deeper level of normative justification. This deeper level of normative justification is the nonideal theory that issues from the social contract. It requires submitting the asymmetry to its tribunal, and it delivers a verdict against it. Because of this, we must confront some difficult questions that the asymmetry enabled us to avoid, such as what to do with derecognized states. But in my view this beats compromising the normative advice that we as philosophers would offer by surrendering prematurely to perceived political feasibility. On the contrary, if we get politicians and diplomats to think more expansively, to consider new possibilities, or reconsider old ones anew, then we are not only fulfilling but honoring the philosopher's distinct role.

Finally, in combination, these two findings—the acceptance of remedial secession, the possibility of derecognition—have important implications for what is arguably the historically dominant criterion of recognition: effective statehood, the view that a political entity's effectively establishing itself as an independent state is either necessary, sufficient, or necessary and sufficient for international recognition. Although as I have formulated the pragmatic view, neither new nor existing states require effective statehood for recognition, surely effective statehood plays a large role in *explaining* their recognition. After all, the continued recognition of (most) existing states largely rests on their being in effective control of their territory, population, and government, and the recognition of new states would seem to require, in addition to parent state consent, their establishing their effective independence. We might then propose, as an alternative to my formulation, that effective statehood is a sufficient condition for continuing to recognize existing states, and a necessary condition for recognizing new states. To the extent that we value stability and want to avoid reopening old battles, we might then regard this result as enjoying normative backing.

If my argument succeeds, however, this result must be received with some caution, for once we reject asymmetry, we find that effective statehood can serve neither as a necessary nor as a sufficient condition for recognition. The possibility of derecognition shows that effective statehood should not be a sufficient condition. The acceptance of remedial secession shows (I will argue) that it should not be a necessary condition either. While effective statehood and the stability it promises nonetheless remain valuable, the argument to follow will suggest a more nuanced understanding of the value it offers.

1.7 COMPARISONS WITH REALISM

Naturally the pragmatic theory of recognition invites comparisons with realism in international relations, but despite some superficial resemblances, the views are not (and are not meant to be) equivalent.

Without attempting to distinguish the various types of realism, let's say, provisionally, that realism in international relations consists in a family of descriptive, explanatory, and normative views that roughly go as follows. States are the key international actors. Because there is no effective supranational authority over them, the international system is anarchic. States always act so as to advance their national interests. And this is as it should be, since moral criteria do not apply under anarchy. No doubt this does not do full justice to the full range of realist views, but it should be enough to make some initial comparisons.

Like realism, the pragmatic theory of recognition does assume that states are the key international actors at this point in time (we'll see this in chapter 6). It does not assume that they are the exclusive international actors, however, nor does it preclude the existence of other prominent international actors (such as nongovernmental organizations and multinational corporations). All that it assumes is that, today, states are important enough international actors to motivate the need to defend a theory of international recognition—an assumption that it shares with its rivals.

Beyond that resemblance, though, the pragmatic theory differs substantially from realism. First, it does not assume, nor is it committed to, the view that, because there is no effective supranational authority over states, the international system is anarchic. In fact, it regards existing processes for formulating, adjudicating, and implementing international law as crucial for achieving international peace and justice, and so seems to imply both their effective authority over states and the denial that the international system is anarchic. Second, it does not assume, nor is it committed to, the view that states always act so as to advance their national interests. In fact, the pragmatic view implies the denial of that claim, since its principles assert requirements (such as recognizing or derecognizing this or that entity as a state) that hold independently of their national interests. If states were incapable of acting any other way than to advance their national interests, then principles requiring any other sort of conduct would be indefensible. Strictly speaking, the pragmatic theory of international recognition is a *normative* theory—and it is perhaps for this reason (paradoxically) that one might want to assimilate it to realism. After all, not only is it a normative theory—it is a *nonideal* normative theory. In a nod to the realities of international politics, it rejects pursuit of ideal principles, even ones that make the most modest demands, such as requiring minimal justice for recognition. Insofar as realism in international relations is often juxtaposed with idealism, this rejection of ideal theorizing seems to imply an embrace of realism.

However, realism does not follow from the rejection of ideal normative theorizing, as we can see from the following argument. Call the view that normative criteria do not apply to international affairs *moral skepticism about international affairs*. Realists frequently assert moral skepticism about international affairs and infer from it *realpolitik*, which holds that states, in their foreign policy decisions, should consult only their national interests. (These two claims are essentially the normative claims of realism stated above.) A long line of realists—from Thucydides, Machiavelli, and Hobbes to Carr, Morgenthau, Hoffman, and Kennan—are claimed to have held one or both of these views.[54]

Hobbes offers us perhaps the clearest statement of them: "To this warre of every man against every man," he argues, "this also is consequent; that nothing can be unjust. The notions of right and wrong, justice and injustice have there no place. Where there is no common power, there is no law: where no law, no injustice. Force, and fraud, are in warre the two cardinall vertues."[55] For Hobbes, this characterizes the state of nature, and since he also holds that the international realm is a state of nature,[56] he implies that moral criteria will not apply there either—and suggests that states, in their foreign policy decisions, should only consult their national interests. Thus, Hobbes seems to embrace both moral skepticism about international affairs and realpolitik.

Clearly, the pragmatic view of international recognition denies both realpolitik and moral skepticism about international affairs. It asserts three normative requirements—the critical mass, justifiable secession, and economic development principles—as morally binding upon states regardless of whether the recognition decisions they require advance a state's national interests. So if moral skepticism about international affairs and realpolitik are essential features of realism, it follows that the pragmatic view, far from assuming the truth of realism, entails its falsity. From the rejection of ideal theorizing, therefore, realism does not follow.

Similarly, from the rejection of ideal theorizing, the denial of idealism does not follow either. If we understand idealism as the view, roughly, that states in the conduct of their foreign policy may pursue a normative ideal (either the one that grounds their domestic institutions, or, alternatively, the one that is valid for all states), then, as we have seen, the pragmatic view is consistent with idealism, for it is consistent with a universal liberalism defended at the first stage of the four-stage sequence. In that case, a universal liberalism would define the ideal at which we should aim, and the pragmatic theory, as a nonideal theory of transitional justice, would articulate the principles that we must follow in pursuing it.

1.8 CONCLUDING REMARKS

All of these assertions must be defended, and in the rest of the book I hope to defend them convincingly. If I am successful, I hope also to establish my earlier claim: that Rawls continues to teach us new things about our moral and political universe, and in particular, about the resourcefulness of the social contract tradition.

If we stay true to its ideals, it will guide us in reaching them.

NOTES

1. See Brian Barry's review of J. H. Wellbank, Dennis Snook, and David Mason, *John Rawls and His Critics: An Annotated Bibliography* (New York: Garland Publishing, 1982), in *Ethics* 94, vol. 2 (January 1984): 353, 351–3 (referring to the period 1975–1979).

2. Anthony Simon Laden, "The House That Jack Built: Thirty Years of Reading Rawls," *Ethics* 113, vol. 2 (January 2003): 367–390, p. 367 (reviewing Henry Richardson and Paul Weithman, eds., *The Philosophy of Rawls: A Collection of Essays* (New York: Garland, 1999)).

3. Although the quote comes from John Rawls, *A Theory of Justice* (Cambridge, MA: Harvard University Press, 1971), p. 11, he first mentions the idea in the opening paragraph of the book. See also John Rawls, *Political Liberalism* (New York: Columbia University Press, 1993), pp. xv–xvi; and John Rawls, *The Law of Peoples* (Cambridge, MA: Harvard University Press, 1999), p. 4.

4. Rawls, *A Theory of Justice*, p. 18.

5. See Chris Naticchia, "Human Rights, Liberalism, and Rawls's Law of Peoples," *Social Theory and Practice* 24 (1998): 345–74.

6. Jane English, "Justice Between Generations," *Philosophical Studies* 31, no. 2 (1977): 95. Susan Moller Okin, *Justice, Gender, and the Family* (New York: Basic Books, 1989), ch. 5. Will Kymlicka makes a similar observation on pp. 59–60 of his *Liberalism, Community, and Culture* (New York: Oxford University Press, 1989).

7. Rawls acknowledges this at *Political Liberalism*, p. 274, and John Rawls, *Justice as Fairness: A Restatement* (Cambridge, MA: Harvard University Press, 2001), p. 160.

8. John Rawls, "The Idea of Public Reason Revisited," section 5, originally published in *University of Chicago Law Review* 64 (Summer 1997): 765–807, and reprinted in Samuel Freeman (ed.), *John Rawls: Collected Papers* (Cambridge, MA: Harvard University Press, 1999), ch. 26.

9. John Rawls, "The Law of Peoples," originally published in Stephen Shute and Susan Hurley (eds.), *On Human Rights: The Oxford Amnesty Lectures, 1993* (New York: Basic Books, 1993), pp. 41–82, and in *Critical Inquiry* 20 (1993): 36-68, and reprinted in Freeman (ed.), *John Rawls: Collected Papers*, ch. 24.

10. See Chris Naticchia, "The Law of Peoples: The Old and the New," *Journal of Moral Philosophy* 2, no. 3 (November 2005): 353–69 [special issue on Global Justice] (reprinted in Thom Brooks and Fabian Freyenhagen (eds.), *The Legacy of John Rawls* (London and New York: Continuum, July 2005), pp. 177–94).

11. See, e.g., Brian Barry, *Theories of Justice* (Berkeley: University of California Press, 1989); Charles Beitz, *Political Theory and International Relations* (Princeton, NJ: Princeton University Press, 1979); Darrel Moellendorf, "Constructing the Law of Peoples," *Pacific Philosophical Quarterly* 77, no. 2 (June 1996): 132–54; Thomas Pogge, *Realizing Rawls* (Ithaca, NY: Cornell University Press, 1989); and David A. J. Richards, "International Distributive Justice," in J. Roland Pennock and John W. Chapman (eds.), *Ethics, Economics, and the Law: Nomos XXIV* (New York: New York University Press, 1982), pp. 275–99. In fairness to most of these authors, however, it should be mentioned that they wrote well before *The Law of Peoples* was on the scene.

12. Rawls, *The Law of Peoples*, p. 82.

13. Examples include Mitchell Avila, "Defending a Law of Peoples: Political Liberalism and Decent Peoples," *The Journal of Ethics* 11, no. 1 (March 2007): 87–124; Alyssa Bernstein, "A Human Right to Democracy? Legitimacy and Intervention," in Rex Martin and David Reidy (eds.), *Rawls's Law of Peoples: A Realistic Utopia?* (Malden, MA: Blackwell Publishing, 2006), chapter 16; and David Reidy, "Political Authority and Human Rights," in Rex Martin and David Reidy (eds.), *Rawls's Law of Peoples: A Realistic Utopia?*, chapter 10.

14. Rawls, *Political Liberalism*, pp. 140–41, and p. 140, n. 7.

15. With Sandel and Walzer, the evidence will be more direct than with Taylor and MacIntyre. With Taylor and MacIntyre (and again later with Kymlicka and Miller), I take Rawls up on his invitation to explain the apparent changes to his theory by offering "an analytic view of how they fit into" his later works. See Rawls, *Political Liberalism*, p. xvii, for the reference.

16. Michael Sandel, "The Procedural Republic and the Unencumbered Self," *Political Theory* 12, no. 1 (February 1984): 81–96, p. 86. Such selves, he adds, are "wholly without character, without moral depth" (p. 90).

17. Rawls, *Political Liberalism*, 27 and section 5 generally.

18. See Michael Walzer, *Spheres of Justice* (New York: Basic Books, 1983), ch. 1.

19. Walzer, *Spheres of Justice*, p. 19.

20. Walzer, *Spheres of Justice*, p. 28.

21. Walzer, *Spheres of Justice*, p. 30.

22. See John Rawls, "Justice as Fairness: Political not Metaphysical," *Philosophy & Public Affairs* 14 (1985): 223–52, reprinted in Freeman (ed.), *John Rawls: Collected Papers*, pp. 388–414. The quotation appears on p. 389.

23. Rawls, *Political Liberalism*, pp. 13–14.

24. "We should be prepared to find that the deeper the conflict," Rawls claims, "the higher the level of abstraction to which we must ascend to get a clear and uncluttered view of its roots." See Rawls, *Political Liberalism*, p. 46.

25. Kymlicka, *Liberalism, Community, and Culture*, ch. 8.

26. Kymlicka, *Liberalism, Community, and Culture*, ch. 4.

27. Will Kymlicka, *Multicultural Citizenship* (New York: Oxford University Press, 1995), p. 80.

28. Avishai Margalit and Joseph Raz offer a similar argument in their "National Self-Determination," *Journal of Philosophy* 87, no. 9 (Sept. 1990): 439–61.

29. David Miller, "The Ethical Significance of Nationality," *Ethics* 98, no. 4 (July 1988): 647–62, pp. 649–50.

30. David Miller, *On Nationality* (New York: Oxford University Press, 1995), p. 57.

31. Both quotes come from Miller, *On Nationality*, p. 65 (emphasis added).

32. Rawls, *The Law of Peoples*, sec. 2.

33. Here I follow Kymlicka's usage. See Kymlicka, *Multicultural Citizenship*, pp. 11, 18.

34. This is how Kok-Chor Tan reads him. See Kok-Chor Tan, "The Problem of Decent Peoples," in Rex Martin and David Reidy (eds.), *Rawls's Law of Peoples: A Realistic Utopia?* (Malden, MA: Blackwell Publishing, 2006), pp. 76–94.

35. This is how Allen Buchanan reads him. See Allen Buchanan, "Rawls Law of Peoples: Rules for a Vanished Westphalian World," *Ethics* 110, no. 4 (July 2000): 697–721, p. 698.

36. Buchanan, "Rawls Law of Peoples: Rules for a Vanished Westphalian World," p. 699.

37. Buchanan, "Rawls Law of Peoples: Rules for a Vanished Westphalian World," p. 699.

38. Buchanan, "Rawls Law of Peoples: Rules for a Vanished Westphalian World," pp. 716–20.

39. Rawls, *Political Liberalism*, pp. 135–36, elaborating the claim at p. 8 of *A Theory of Justice*, that we are to conceive of society "as a closed system isolated from other societies."

40. It will not be sufficient, though, due to the idle-contract objection.

41. Rawls, *The Law of Peoples*, p 67.

42. Brian Barry, "John Rawls and the Search for Stability," *Ethics* 105, vol. 4 (July 1995): 874–915.

43. The claim is not that Rawls consciously had in mind the aim of establishing a theory of recognition. The claim is that, however vaguely and inchoately, Rawls may have had this aim in mind, and more importantly, the best Rawlsian position is to attribute this aim to him.

44. Rawls, *A Theory of Justice*, pp. 195–201.

45. See Chris Naticchia, "Recognizing States and Governments," *Canadian Journal of Philosophy* 35, no. 1 (March 2005): 27–82.

46. See Rawls, *A Theory of Justice*, section 26.

47. Rawls, *A Theory of Justice*, pp. 245, 248.

48. A. John Simmons, "Ideal and Nonideal Theory," *Philosophy & Public Affairs* 38, no. 1 (Winter 2010): 5–36, p. 23.

49. See Chris Naticchia, "Recognition and Legitimacy: A Reply to Buchanan," *Philosophy & Public Affairs* 28, no. 3 (Summer 1999): 242–57.

50. A full statement of the principles, given in chapter 10, contains riders to ensure their mutual consistency. The intuitive idea is that the first principle establishes an initial array of recognized states, which the second, and then the third, sequentially adjust through further additions.

51. Antonio Cassese, *Self-Determination of Peoples: A Legal Reappraisal* (Cambridge: Cambridge University Press, 1995), pp. 101–29; James Crawford, *The Creation of States in International Law* (Oxford: Oxford University Press, 1979), pp. 247–66; Hurst Hannum, "Rethinking Self-Determination," *Virginia Journal of International Law* 34 (1993):

1–69, pp. 42–65; Hurst Hannum, "The Right of Self-Determination in the Twenty-First Century," Washington & Lee Law Review 55 (1998): 773–77; Rosalyn Higgins, *Problems and Process: International Law and How We Use It* (Oxford: Oxford University Press, 1994), pp. 119–25; Donald Horowitz, "The Cracked Foundations of the Right to Secede," *Journal of Democracy* 14, no. 2 (2003): 5–17; Donald Horowitz, "A Right to Secede?" *Nomos* 45 (2003): 50–76, pp. 60–64; John Murphy, "Self-Determination: United States Perspectives," in Yonah Alexander and Robert Friedlander (eds.), *Self-Determination: National, Regional, and Global Dimensions* (Boulder, CO: Westview Press, 1980), pp. 43–61; Steven Ratner, *The Thin Justice of International Law: A Moral Reckoning of the Law of Nations* (New York: Oxford University Press, 2015), chapter 5. Bruno Simma is a bit more tentative, calling the existence of such a remedial right "arguable." See Bruno Simma, *The Charter of the United Nations: A Commentary* 3d. ed., vol. 1 (Oxford: Oxford University Press, 2012):, p. 330.

52. General Assembly Resolution 2625 of 24 October 1970, *Declaration on Principles of International Law concerning Friendly Relations and Cooperation among States in accordance with the Charter of the United Nations*, A/RES/25/2625.

53. Mikulas Fabry, *Recognizing States: International Society & the Establishment of New States Since 1776* (New York: Oxford University Press, 2010), chapter 6. Fabry also notes that, despite Crawford's initial claim that there was a remedial right to secede, he later admitted that it was hardly reflected in international practice. See Fabry, ibid., p. 177, note 98.

54. See Thucydides, *History of the Peloponnesian War* (431 BC); Niccolò Machiavelli, *The Prince* (1532); Thomas Hobbes, *Leviathan* (1651); E. H. Carr, *The Twenty Years' Crisis 1919–1939* (London: Macmillan, 1939); Hans Morgenthau, *Politics Among Nations* (New York: Knopf, 1948), p. 12; Stanley Hoffman, *The State of War* (New York: Praeger, 1965), p. 14; George Kennan, *Realities of American Foreign Policy* (New York: Norton, 1966), p. 49. The realist interpretation of Thucydides, Machiavelli, and Hobbes is not undisputed. See, for example, L. M. Johnson, *Thucydides, Hobbes, and the Interpretation of Realism* (DeKalb: Northern Illinois University Press, 1993), esp. p. 91; Noel Malcolm, "Hobbes's Theory of International Relations," in ed. Noel Malcolm, *Aspects of Hobbes* (New York: Oxford University Press, 2002, pp. 432–56, esp. pp. 436–43, 499; and David Armitage, "Hobbes and the Foundations of Modern International Thought," in eds. Annabel Brett and James Tully, *Rethinking the Foundations of Modern Political Thought* (New York: Cambridge University Press, 2006), pp. 219–35.

55. Thomas Hobbes, *Leviathan*, XIII.13. (1651), ed. C. B. Macpherson (Penguin Books: New York, 1985). References to *Leviathan* are given by chapter and paragraph number.

56. *Leviathan*, XIII.12.

TWO

The Law of Peoples

Act I

2.1 SKEPTICISM AND DISAPPOINTMENT

Even before Rawls published *The Law of Peoples*, critics expressed skepticism about extending his principles to other societies. Whether it is apartheid in South Africa or communism in Eastern Europe, claimed one of them—reacting to what was then his latest work—"Rawlsian principles of justice will provide no basis for communicating criticisms of their political institutions or practices to nonliberal societies" since "members of those societies [do not] share 'our' conceptions of citizenship and of fair procedures of cooperation."[1] Rawls's principles are "of little relevance," said another, "in those situations where the justification of liberalism matters most: that is, where liberalism is confronted by, and must engage with, societies whose traditions and practices are not liberal."[2] The reason, they suggested, is that for Rawls, "justification is addressed to others who disagree with us, and therefore it must always proceed from some consensus."[3] So if citizens within liberal societies agree that their society ought to be a fair system of cooperation between free and equal citizens, then the justification of their political principles should proceed from that consensus and not from any positions on which they disagree, such as the best way to balance liberty and equality or which (if any) conception of the good is true. But if citizens within nonliberal societies reject that liberal idea—if they find it foreign to their own traditions and values—then it follows, argued the critics, that the justification of *their* political principles must begin elsewhere, so it will likely end elsewhere too.

If the critics were skeptical before, they must have been doubly disappointed after *The Law of Peoples* appeared. Gone was the aggressively egalitarian difference principle, replaced by a kinder and gentler distributive principle requiring only that nonliberal societies meet the basic needs of their own citizens. Gone too was the equal liberty principle, replaced by one that allowed inequalities in liberty of conscience and freedom of expression as long as they respected basic human rights. Thus, in their internal affairs, nonliberal societies were permitted to meet standards much weaker than justice as fairness. But Rawls also maintained that his principles did not apply to some liberal societies either. As long as a society protected the rights, liberties, and opportunities familiar from democratic regimes, said Rawls, it would qualify as liberal. But it need not underwrite the fair value of the political liberties, or of fair equality of opportunity, or satisfy the difference principle.

If the critics were pessimistic about extending Rawls's principles to other societies, they were more optimistic about extending them to the basic structure of the world as a whole.[4] So here, perhaps, *The Law of Peoples* caused even greater disappointment. Although it prohibited external aggression and required helping the poorest countries meet the basic needs of their citizens, the more affluent—usually liberal—nations otherwise were entitled to all of the economic benefits from natural resources they happened to control. They were not expected to fulfill the demands of anything like a global difference principle. Given the rather modest demands imposed on the internal affairs of nonliberal societies, one could not help wondering whether the underlying message was something like this: we affluent liberal societies will tolerate the unequal freedoms of your nonliberal societies if you don't claim too much of our wealth. To his critics, therefore, Rawls offered us, on the one hand, an initially appealing statement of liberal tolerance, extended into the international realm:

> We recognize that a liberal society is to respect its citizens' comprehensive doctrines—religious, philosophical, and moral—provided that these doctrines are pursued in ways compatible with a reasonable political conception of justice. . . . Similarly, we say that, provided a nonliberal society's basic institutions meet certain specified conditions of political right and justice and lead its people to honor a reasonable and just law for the Society of Peoples, a liberal people is to tolerate and accept that society.[5]

Yet on the other hand, this initial appeal, they maintained, was illusory. Was Rawls's proposal truly worthy of being deemed a political philosophy of international justice, or was it just an unprincipled compromise?

These criticisms raise important and interesting questions, and here I focus on two of them. I first consider whether Rawls has an effective reply to the charge that his law of peoples strikes an unprincipled compromise with nonliberal regimes. Then I consider whether, in his desire to avoid imposing liberal principles in a world that contains nonliberal regimes, Rawls undermines his defense of human rights.

2.2 THE INTERNATIONAL CONTRACT

A just law of peoples, Rawls argues, is the outcome of two separate international sessions of the original position. In the first, only delegates from liberal societies are represented; in the second, only delegates from nonliberal societies are represented. In both cases, the outcome is the same. From behind a veil of ignorance that excludes knowledge of the size, population, military strength, natural resources, and economic development of their society, they select principles that guarantee the freedom and independence of their peoples, impose a duty of nonintervention, allow a right to wage war in self-defense, place limits on the conduct of war, enable them to ratify treaties, bind them to observe the ones they make, require them to assist peoples living under unfavorable conditions, and obligate them to protect human rights.[6]

Although Rawls does not describe the delegates' reasoning in any detail, his intent is fairly clear: principles of international justice are to be the outcome of a fair procedure of construction. A fair international procedure is fair among peoples. Different peoples have different ways of well-ordering their societies.[7] Treating these peoples fairly means situating their delegates equally in the original position, letting them represent their society's conception of domestic justice. In the first session, for instance, we find liberal societies organized around political liberalisms (such as justice as fairness) represented, but also other liberal societies, less egalitarian ones, even ones organized around comprehensive liberalisms.[8] In the second session, we find delegates representing nonliberal (what Rawls calls *decent hierarchical*) societies—nonexpansionist states, usually organized around comprehensive religious doctrines, that privilege the state religion over other sects but otherwise protect dissidents from persecution and respect human rights.[9] Among these rights are minimum rights to life (to personal security and means of subsistence), to liberty (to freedom from slavery, serfdom, forced labor), to personal property, to "a sufficient measure" of liberty of conscience, to formal equality (treating like cases alike), and to emigration.[10] In both cases, each society has one vote and the agreement must be unanimous.

2.3 POGGE'S CRITICISMS

Thomas Pogge raises several forceful criticisms against this way of proceeding:

1. *Why is the veil of ignorance thinner?* That is, why does Rawls allow the delegates to his international original positions to know their conceptions of domestic justice but prevent the parties to his domestic original position from knowing their particular conception of the good? Rawls says nothing to justify the disanalogy.[11]
2. *Why does Rawls assume that each people's sole fundamental interest is that their domestic institutions satisfy their conception of domestic justice?* Surely, Pogge argues, they must have an additional interest in the well-being of their individual citizens beyond that needed for their institutions to be just—surely each people would rather have a higher than a lower average standard of living.[12] Besides, the affluence of one's country of birth is "a difference that, on the face of it, is no less morally arbitrary than differences in sex, in skin color, or in the affluence of one's parents."[13] To remedy the profound impact of this morally irrelevant contingency, Pogge proposes an egalitarian principle of international distribution. In contrast, Rawls balks at adopting such a principle, fearing that it would impose liberal values by resting on an individual's, rather than a people's, interest.[14] Such hesitancy, Pogge argues, is problematic for Rawls. His treating peoples rather than persons as the ultimate units of moral concern allows him to accommodate the communitarian values of decent hierarchical societies, but it does so at the expense of sacrificing the liberal values of liberal societies.[15]
3. *What guarantee is there that delegates representing decent hierarchical societies would be motivated to protect human rights?* If the "dominant end" of decent hierarchical societies is advancing their comprehensive religious doctrine, won't they recognize human rights only if, and only to the extent that, such rights are instrumentally valuable for securing that end? Whether decent hierarchical societies recognize human rights is entirely contingent—hardly a result Rawls could welcome given his criticism of utilitarian societies on the same ground.[16]
4. *Why wouldn't delegates representing liberal societies be motivated to protect more rights than the ones that appear on Rawls's list of human rights—a list that excludes freedom of speech, equal liberty of conscience and thought, and democratic political rights?* Since liberal and decent hierarchical delegates are likely to be working at cross-purposes, there is no assurance that their agreements would converge.[17]

The source of Rawls's error, according to Pogge, is that he tries to accommodate decent hierarchical societies by "express[ing] liberalism's own principle of toleration for other reasonable ways of ordering society"—a principle the decent hierarchical societies reject anyway.[18] But an accommodation between these two positions, he argues, is impossible to achieve.

> While our society can contain many different kinds of communities, associations, and conceptions of the good, some liberal in character and others not, it can be structured or organized in only one way. [Similarly, if] the Algerians want their society to be organized as a religious state consistent with a just global order and we want ours to be a liberal democracy, we can both have our way. But if the Algerians want the world to be organized according to the Koran, and we want it to accord with liberal principles, then we can *not* both have our way. There is no room for accommodation here.[19]

Instead of courageously championing liberal political philosophy in the new world order, Pogge argues, Rawls strikes an unprincipled compromise.

2.4 THE PRELIMINARY RAWLSIAN REPLY

Pogge's criticisms do sting, but there *is* a reply on Rawls's behalf. Suppose Rawls had made his international methodology parallel to the domestic. What changes would need to be made? The first would be to thicken the veil of ignorance. If "the fact that we affirm a particular religious, philosophical, or moral comprehensive doctrine with its associated conception of the good is not a reason for us to propose, or to expect others to accept, a conception of [domestic] justice that favors those of that persuasion," then similarly, the fact that we affirm a particular conception of domestic justice is not a reason to propose or to expect others to accept a law of peoples that favors our view.[20] But if this consideration warrants excluding knowledge of conceptions of the good in the domestic case, then it should also warrant excluding knowledge of conceptions of domestic justice in the international case.

This first change forces a second. If the delegates no longer know their own society's conception of domestic justice, then they can no longer know the conceptions held by their fellow delegates either. If they can no longer know the conceptions held by their fellow delegates, then they can no longer assume (as Rawls enables them to assume) that all the delegates must represent either liberal or decent hierarchical societies. Since only liberal and decent hierarchical societies are nonexpansionist states that protect human rights, the delegates can no longer assume that they all represent such regimes. If Rawls had made his international methodology parallel to the domestic, in other words, he would have to allow that some of the delegates might represent *outlaw regimes*.[21]

Allowing delegates to represent either liberal, decent hierarchical, or outlaw regimes, and making his international methodology parallel the domestic, Rawls would also have to allow the delegates to select principles together, in a single session of the contract, just as their domestic counterparts do.

Now the question arises whether they should reason as representatives of peoples or individuals. Pogge contends that there is no room for accommodation here. A choice must be made that will favor either liberal or nonliberal societies. There is no neutral position, no middle ground. This would be a persuasive point if it were as unfair for citizens of liberal societies to have their delegate reason as a representative of a people as it would be for citizens of nonliberal societies to have their delegate reason as a representative of persons. But the situations are not equivalent. Since it is accepted in both liberal and nonliberal societies that associations (families, churches, and so on) have claims, while it is accepted in liberal but not nonliberal societies that individuals have claims, it would be more unfair for citizens of nonliberal societies to have their delegate reason as a representative of persons (individuals) than it would be for citizens of liberal societies to have their delegate reason as a representative of a people (an association).[22]

Reasoning as representatives of peoples, unsure of whether any of their neighbors are expansionist outlaw regimes, and aware that the stakes for their societies are enormously high, the delegates now have as much reason to apply *maximin* to their choice as the parties in Rawls's domestic original position have to theirs. "So," they would ask, "what is the worst that can happen to us, and how can we insure against it?" Is it worse to be: (a) a nonexpansionist regime conquered by, at war with, or intervened in by an expansionist outlaw regime; or (b) a regime with expansionist tendencies—one that might spread its comprehensive religious doctrine (or exploitative economic policy) by force—required not to attack its neighbors?

The former situation is much worse, and delegates could insure themselves against it by adopting principles guaranteeing the freedom and independence of their peoples and imposing a duty of nonintervention—banning expansionist outlaw regimes from the international moral community.[23] But then, with outlaw regimes banned, the delegates, using similar (maximin) reasoning, would conclude that it is worse to be: (c) a society forced to conform to principles incompatible with its conception of domestic justice—a liberal society forced to advance some comprehensive religious doctrine, or a decent hierarchical society forced to embrace liberal freedoms and a liberal distributive principle—than (d) a society required to tolerate the existence of different kinds of societies. For that reason, the delegates would require no more than the protection of human rights and the meeting of citizens' basic needs, since that is compatible with both liberal and decent hierarchical societies.

So if Rawls had made his international methodology parallel to the domestic, he could have generated his law of peoples anyway. Assuming that these changes to the original international position make it as fair as the domestic version was, then the outcome should be fair principles of justice too—a *principled* political philosophy, in other words, not an unprincipled compromise. Call this answer to Pogge's criticisms the *preliminary Rawlsian reply*.

2.5 THE FULL RAWLSIAN REPLY

Notice that the preliminary Rawlsian reply makes an important assumption: that once the delegates eliminate expansionist outlaw regimes from consideration (in the choice between [a] and [b]), their maximin reasoning need only compare the worst outcomes for decent hierarchical and liberal ones (in the choice between [c] and [d]). Why are *non*expansionist outlaw regimes—those that violate the human rights of some of their citizens—not included in this latter choice? Does their exclusion affect the outcome?

It would be a mistake to think that a nonexpansionist outlaw regime had to be devoted to a senseless reign of domestic terror. It could be just like a decent hierarchical society except that its comprehensive religious doctrine denies certain human rights. Assume the doctrine requires forced labor from members of a certain ethnicity. It specifies a dominant end to guide its domestic policy. The rational pursuit of that end mandates limited violations of human rights consistent with social stability. Advancing the doctrine is what its conception of domestic justice involves.

If regimes like this had to be considered, the delegates' reasoning would be different. Since forcing a society to conform to principles incompatible with its conception of domestic justice would still be worse than requiring it to tolerate the existence of different kinds of societies, maximin would require tolerating this kind of regime too. Therefore, instead of requiring the full array of human rights, as they did before, the delegates would only require a partial array (all but the right against forced labor), since only the partial array is compatible with all three kinds of society. Protecting the full array would be optional, not mandatory. Clearly, excluding nonexpansionist outlaw regimes does affect the outcome, and unless we can justify their exclusion, we cannot use the preliminary Rawlsian reply.

One possible justification comes from Rawls's characterization of human rights. When he says that the law of peoples should "fit" the view that they ought to be protected, it resembles his description of considered moral judgments in *A Theory of Justice* as "provisional fixed points which we presume any conception of justice must *fit*."[24] If human rights are considered moral judgments, that would explain why the law of peoples should fit them. That would also explain why he calls human rights "not politically parochial," which suggests that they are judgments that "avoid excessive attention to our own interests" and are likely to be impartial—other ways that he describes considered moral judgments in *A Theory of Justice.*[25] In addition, considered moral judgments are those in which we have confidence because they have been formed under conditions that minimize distorting influences such as bias and other sources of error.[26] Apparently Rawls thinks that our view of human rights has been formed under such conditions, and the fact that these rights are widely recognized and not "peculiarly liberal or special to the Western tradition" reinforces our confidence in that view.[27] Some countries would dissent, of course, but they represent a small minority—not enough to shake our confidence. So it seems as though Rawls regards human rights as a kind of considered moral judgment.

But the law of peoples won't completely fit this judgment (since it won't bar forced labor) if the delegates have to consider the possibility of being a nonexpansionist outlaw society. In *A Theory of Justice* any discrepancies like this between principles and judgment force a choice; presumably the same choice holds for the law of peoples. "We can either modify the account of the initial situation," Rawls says, which in this case would be the *international* original position, "or we can revise our existing judgments."[28] Assuming our unwillingness to revise the judgment, we must modify the original position. This does not license making direct changes to the principles so that they can form a better fit with our judgments. We must produce those changes indirectly, working through the original position, "altering the conditions on the contractual circumstances . . . [until] we find a description . . . that both expresses reasonable conditions and yields principles which match our considered judgments duly pruned and adjusted."[29] Changes to the principles must be yielded by the contract, and the altered contractual circumstances must have a plausible rationale. Only then will we have achieved reflective equilibrium.[30]

Rawls seems to handle this predicament by introducing preconditions for entering the original position. He does not *call* them preconditions, even though they do set a substantive moral bar to entry. Nor does he explain that they're needed in order to establish reflective equilibrium. Most of the time, he simply explains that they stipulate necessary conditions for being a member in good standing in a reasonable law of peoples.[31] Now one would have thought that all that was needed for being a member in good standing was to obey the law of peoples—indeed, that would seem sufficient too. But the conditions he stipulates are not identical to the law of peoples, which implies that these are additional requirements of some sort.[32] Since only liberal and decent hierarchical societies meet them, and only liberal and decent hierarchical societies have a voice in constructing a law of peoples, it is natural to interpret them as preconditions on the contract.

The preconditions are that: (1) "the society does not have aggressive aims, and it recognizes that it must gain its legitimate ends through diplomacy and trade and other ways of peace," (2) it "secures for all members of the people . . . [basic] human rights," and (3) its domestic law is "guided by a common good conception of justice."[33] Immediately we see that there is no need to include (1) among the preconditions for entering the contract, since the contract is capable of deriving principles against external aggression without relying on any such precondition (as we saw in the preliminary Rawlsian reply in the choice between [a] and [b]). Further, if we include (2), we would be making the protection of human rights a precondition for entering a contract from which we hoped to derive a principle mandating their protection. But then the principle's emergence from the contract would contribute nothing to its justification: the contract argument would be circular.[34] So we cannot include (2) as a precondition either. Besides, Rawls considers it to be a consequence of (3): human rights are secured "*in accordance with* [society's] common good idea of justice."[35] If that is right, then we can bar regimes that violate human rights from entering the original position without making respect for such rights a precondition. We just have to insist on using (3) as a precondition instead.[36]

So it looks as though (3), the idea that societies must possess a common good conception of justice, must do all the philosophical work. But what does this vague idea amount to? Rawls lists some institutional requirements. A society must at least contain some kind of "decent consultation hierarchy"—institutions that hear different voices, respond in good faith to dissent, and look after the fundamental interests of all elements of society.[37] But these are clearly procedural mechanisms that are supposed to help realize a substantive moral minimum. What enables a society to meet the precondition is the realization of that substantive moral minimum, not the inclusion of certain procedural mechanisms. In order to realize that minimum, he says that the legal system must "impose bona fide moral duties and obligations . . . on *all* persons within the people's territory."[38] But that is not enough to guarantee the protection of human rights, since all people might only have duties "to do God's will," in which case whether those duties correlate with human rights will depend on what God wills (or to be more exact, on what those in power claim God wills). The only other comment that provides a potential basis for giving (3) more concrete content is Rawls's claim that a common good conception of justice "takes into account what it sees as the fundamental interests of everyone in society."[39] It is in virtue of this understanding of such a conception, presumably, that societies protect human rights.

The notion of a common good, however, is open to competing interpretations. It could mean that the common good is to be ascertained in some collective way, so that it represents the good of the people as a whole (as in teleological comprehensive doctrines, which define the good independently of the right and the right as that which maximizes the good).[40] But Rawls apparently does not mean this, since it is quite compatible with that description for a nonexpansionist outlaw society to advance its dominant end, and hence maximize the good of its people as a whole, by violating some human rights and generally discounting what it regards as the nonfundamental interests of some of its members.[41] Alternatively, it could mean that the common good is to be ascertained in some individualist way, so that it furthers the good of each and every individual over some understood baseline (that's what makes it *common*). But Rawls apparently does not mean this either, since it implies that individuals have claims apart from being members of societies or associations within societies and that nonliberal societies must recognize not just the content of these claims, but their source. If nonliberal societies must recognize individual as well as associational claims, though, this removes the basis for having delegates represent peoples rather than persons. Having the delegates represent peoples was thought to be fairest to both liberal and nonliberal societies, since both recognize associational claims, while only liberal societies recognize individual claims. But on the individualist interpretation, that would no longer be true: both kinds of society would have to recognize both kinds of claims.

Rawls probably intends the common good to be interpreted in a way that furthers the good of each subgroup or association over some understood baseline—a position intermediate between the collective and individualist interpretations. That would explain his notion of a consultation hierarchy, "a family of representative bodies whose role [is] . . . to look after what the people's common good idea of justice regards as the important interests of all [its] members"—interests they have as associations or groups.[42] Decent hierarchical societies could meet the precondition by furthering the good of their internal associations. Liberal societies could meet it by counting individuals as associations with one member, effectively collapsing the distinction between the individualist and associationist interpretations. For Rawls, then, a society possesses a common good conception of justice just in case its legal system promotes the common good interpreted in this associationist way. Call these common good conceptions *associationist* conceptions, and the other common good conceptions *collective* and *individualist* conceptions.

If a society promotes the common good, understood as the good of its various associations, will it protect human rights? Rawls thinks so and it is hard to disagree. Assuming that a consultation hierarchy takes seriously the voices it hears (those of association leaders, presumably), it is difficult to imagine it denying rights to security and means of subsistence on the grounds that these are not necessary to further the good of each association. Equally difficult is imagining it denying rights to freedom (rights against slavery, serfdom, and forced labor), or to some personal private property (instrumental to achieving security and subsistence) on the same grounds. Certainly some degree of liberty of conscience and freedom of association must be granted if membership in an association is to have any meaning at all (beyond ensuring bare survival). Requiring a right to formal equality seems unproblematic enough too if, following Rawls (who follows Hart), we regard it as part of the "natural" minimal content of a bona fide legal system.[43] The right to emigration is a bit harder to defend, if only because it seems unnecessary if all the other human rights suffice to further the associationist common good. But a case can be made, perhaps, if we regard nonemigration as a sign that the good of each association is indeed being furthered, a sign that carries weight only where emigration is an effective option. I will say more about this later. In the meantime, I want to grant that the full array of human rights can be supported by an associationist conception of justice. Given that an associationist conception supports the full array, it follows that nonexpansionist outlaw societies are properly excluded from the original position, since they fail to meet the precondition for entry. Just as they did in the preliminary Rawlsian reply, then, the delegates will choose a principle protecting human rights and thereby establish reflective equilibrium.

Call the combination of the preliminary Rawlsian reply (which assumes the exclusion of nonexpansionist outlaws) with the argument just presented (which attempts to justify that assumption) the *full Rawlsian reply*. I believe that this is the strongest answer to Pogge's criticisms that can be offered on Rawls's behalf. But before we can accept it, we must see whether the contract it defines is "the most philosophically favored interpretation" of the original position.[44] The outcome of the original position is only as good as the rationale that can be offered in support of each of its features,[45] and in the case of the international original position, these features include the precondition on entry. So we have to examine the rationale for the precondition. We might begin by asking why Rawls resorts to using one at all. He doesn't set any substantive moral limits on the conceptions of the good that the parties in the domestic original position may represent. They all emerge from the contract in the form of his first principle of justice.[46] So why does he place substantive moral limits on the conceptions of domestic justice that the delegates in the international original position may represent?

2.6 INTERNAL SOVEREIGNTY AND ORIGINAL POSITIONS

Compare two hypothetical contracts. In contract A, there are no preconditions limiting a society's internal sovereignty. In contract B, a precondition requires societies to possess an associationist conception of justice. For this fact to have any influence on the delegates' deliberations, contract B allows the delegates to know that only such societies are parties to the agreement and that such societies protect human rights.[47] Now in contract A, the delegates first protect their societies from external aggression, then agree that because forced conformity is worse than tolerance, they must tolerate the existence of nonaggressive societies whose conceptions of justice differ from their own. This tolerance places no limits on a society's internal sovereignty. In contract B, the delegates begin as they do in contract A, protecting their societies from external aggression first. Then they continue as the delegates in contract A do, agreeing that forced conformity is worse than tolerance, and therefore that maximin requires them to tolerate the existence of nonaggressive societies with conceptions of justice different from their own. But then, realizing that their veil, unlike that in contract A, allows them to know that they must represent a society with an associationist conception, the delegates recognize that they can limit the tolerance required of them by "locking-in" what these societies have in common, the protection of human rights. By requiring the protection of human rights, they limit the kinds of regimes they have to tolerate without risk of imposing principles incompatible with their conceptions of domestic justice. We have, then, two contracts, one that places no restrictions on a society's internal sovereignty (contract A), and another that does (contract B). The one that places no restrictions had no preconditions limiting a society's internal sovereignty to begin with. The one that does place restrictions had a precondition which entailed those very same restrictions. Clearly, the difference in preconditions is what accounts for the difference in restrictions on internal sovereignty. In both cases, no society is required to introduce any *new* limits on its internal sovereignty after it enters the contract. Unlike external limits on aggression, which the contract, not a precondition, introduces, all of the internal limits are entailed by the preconditions on entry. The contract merely reaffirms and ratifies whatever restrictions the preconditions require.[48]

In order to impose any limits on a society's internal sovereignty, therefore, we have to resort to using preconditions on entering the contract, since the contract itself is incapable of imposing them. The reason for this seems fairly straightforward: as long as an agent in the original position represents groups of individuals rather than individuals, the resulting principles will be silent on what goes on within each group, since the principles the agent must agree to are supposed to govern the relations of the groups with one another, not their relations with their own members.[49]

Not all contracts between representatives of groups are powerless to restrict the internal practices of groups. Bank A may agree to lend money to business B contingent on B's reorganizing—a contract that lacks preconditions but does restrict B's internal practices, its relations with its own employees. The restrictions affect A's interest in getting repaid. But the societies in the original position have no similar interest sufficient for requiring internal restrictions. They only have an interest in realizing their conception of domestic justice. And to the extent that societies have an interest in occupying a world in which others share their conception of domestic justice (to the extent that others' sharing it is part of realizing it), their interests have already been taken into consideration by the maximin preference for tolerance over forced conformity, a preference that leaves their internal sovereignty intact.

This is not to deny that the internal practices of societies may spill over borders and affect other societies' interests, in which case those internal practices should he subject to contractual regulation. Too often societies send their pollution—or refugees fleeing human rights abuses—across the border, or they build armies larger than necessary for defensive purposes—internal practices that affect the interests of other societies. Adopting a principle protecting human rights, however, would be an inappropriate remedy for these externalities. For one thing, that principle would be far too narrow—such externalities have causes ranging far wider than human rights violations. For another, it would be too broad. Not all regimes that violate human rights send refugees fleeing over the border. The delegates need a more flexible approach and they already have several. They have principles guaranteeing the freedom and independence of their peoples and imposing a duty of nonintervention. These principles require interpretation, as Rawls himself acknowledges, and there is no reason to prevent them from being interpreted in a way that shields societies against externalities.[50] No new principle mandating the protection of human rights is specifically needed for this task.[51]

There is, however, one exception to the general rule that when agents in an original position represent groups rather than individuals, the contract cannot impose new limits on internal sovereignty not already imposed by preconditions on the contract. That exception arises if we think of the individuals in the domestic original position as representing groups of person stages and construe paternalistic principles as restrictions on an individual's internal sovereignty over his or her person stages. When Rawls says that "[t]he principles of paternalism are those that the parties would acknowledge in the original position to protect themselves against the weakness and infirmities of their reason and will in society," he implies that such restrictions can be derived from a contract.[52] Such principles stipulate "when others are authorized to act in their behalf and to override their present wishes if necessary." But the warrant for paternalistic intervention, Rawls cautions, is quite narrow. It is justified only to protect ourselves against irrational acts that harm our interests, and these interests are to be determined by our more permanent aims and preferences, not by what others construe to be our good in some thicker sense inconsistent with such aims and preferences—even if we are later guaranteed to accept the intervention. "Paternal principles are a protection against our own irrationality, and must not be interpreted to license assaults on one's convictions and character by any means so long as these offer the prospect of securing consent later on."[53]

But we would be hard pressed, in the international case, to require the protection of human rights on these narrowly paternalistic grounds. Nonexpansionist outlaw societies that commit limited human rights violations cannot be accused of irrationality if, as we have stipulated, they are able to maintain social stability and rationally pursue a comprehensive doctrine that mandates such violations. Paternalism *would* justify overriding the present policies of nonexpansionist outlaw societies that commit extreme human rights violations if the violations create civil strife that threatens the survival of the society or makes the pursuit of any recognizable aim virtually impossible. But while paternalistic intervention would be justified in that case, there is no warrant for requiring, as part of that intervention, the protection of the full array of human rights. All that is required is enough reform to allow the rational pursuit of some recognizable aim, and as we have seen with nonexpansionist outlaw societies that commit limited human rights violations, that does not require protecting the full array. Any stronger intervention would constitute the kind of "assault on the character" of the society that falls outside the scope of justifiable paternalism.

So we cannot exploit Rawls's remarks on paternalistic intervention to justify the *contractual* imposition of limits on a society's internal sovereignty that require the protection of human rights.[54] Rawls may be right in claiming that the law of peoples "will restrict a state's internal sovereignty . . . its alleged right to do as it wills with people within its own borders," but the restrictions issue from the precondition on entering the contract, not from the contract itself.[55]

2.7 THE RATIONALE FOR THE PRECONDITION

The preceding argument shows that because a contract among societies is unable to restrict their internal sovereignty, we must use a precondition to do that instead. But what is the rationale for the specific precondition Rawls imposes (i.e., possession of an associationist conception of justice)? Obviously, Rawls cannot use a separate contract among societies to defend a precondition that limits internal sovereignty. That would merely reproduce the problem whose solution required a precondition in the first place.[56]

Perhaps that explains why Rawls seems inclined to offer the next best thing: a *procedural* defense that uses a consultation hierarchy instead of a contract as the procedure.[57] Just as the domestic contract's procedural and formal features are supposed to justify its outcome by incorporating "generally shared and preferably weak conditions,"[58] so are the consultation hierarchy's procedural and formal features. In the domestic contract, those features include certain procedural items (such as situating the parties symmetrically and placing them behind the veil) and formal constraints (generality, finality, publicity, and so on), and the outcome is justice as fairness. With the consultation hierarchy, they likewise include procedural items (such as consulting association leaders and responding in good faith to dissent) and formal constraints (imposing legal duties on all residents), and the outcome is supposed to be an associationist conception of justice (the content of the precondition). In both cases, if the procedure is based on weak stipulations and the outcome is a certain conception of justice, that conception, according to Rawls, is justified. The consultation hierarchy procedure, though, does seem to be based on weak stipulations. It amounts to a concession that a minimally decent government should inquire into the effects of its policies by consulting, and responding to, those leaders who are most likely to know; and that no one in its territory should be altogether exempt from legal duties (for example, no Austinian sovereigns). Who could argue with that?

But this procedure cannot guarantee an associationist conception as its outcome. The formal requirement that legal duties be imposed on all residents says nothing about their content. They could be duties to do what those in power claim God wills, and that does not necessarily mean that human rights will be protected or that the good of each association will be promoted. Requiring the government to consult and respond to associations does not guarantee this either. It could reply in good faith that although its policies violate human rights, this is necessary in order to advance its dominant end to the fullest—to promote the collective, not associationist, common good. Because these weak procedural and formal features cannot guarantee the outcome Rawls wishes to defend, a consultation hierarchy provides, at best, imperfect procedural justice, unlike the pure procedural justice that his domestic contract provides.[59] When a procedure provides imperfect procedural justice, there is an independent criterion for the right outcome, a criterion defined separately from and prior to the procedure, which, when followed, does not always produce it. But that implies that his defense of the precondition must rest on grounds independent of the consultation hierarchy procedure.

Stripped of its procedural defense, the claim that a society must possess an associationist conception of justice must itself be a stipulation, since Rawls offers no other argument for it. To be sure, it's a different kind of stipulation now—a substantive instead of procedural or formal one. But as long as it's "generally shared and preferably weak," that should present no problem.

This substantive stipulation, however, is not weak enough to be generally shared. Remember that in order to be admitted to the original position, a society must meet a certain level of minimal decency, a level that the precondition establishes by setting limits on internal sovereignty. But those substantive internal limits are precisely in controversy. Although there is general agreement that societies must protect human rights, that only shows agreement on what is necessary for being a minimally decent society: it must possess a conception of domestic justice which accounts for the generally shared view that such rights ought to be protected. But because that generally shared view underdetermines the conceptions that can account for it, there will still be controversy over what counts as a minimally decent society. Rawls apparently hopes to avoid this controversy by insisting that societies possess associationist conceptions, a precondition that both decent hierarchical and liberal societies can meet.[60] This assumes, however, that both decent hierarchical and liberal societies would not object to the inclusivity of the precondition. Why wouldn't liberal societies object that the lack of democratic political rights in hierarchical societies renders them unfit for admission to the original position, or decent hierarchical societies that the separation of church and state in liberal societies renders *them* unfit? If there is a significant rift here between liberal and decent hierarchical societies, as seems likely, then the stipulation is not weak enough to be generally shared.[61]

So Rawls cannot offer a contractual defense of his precondition. He cannot offer the next best thing, a procedural defense using a consultation hierarchy. Nor can he defend it as a weak and generally shared stipulation. This does not necessarily mean that it lacks a plausible rationale. It only means that we must look elsewhere for one. We will return to this issue in § 2.9. In the meantime, we need to examine the right to emigrate, too, for its inclusion as a human right, I want to suggest, requires further adjustment to the contract argument.

2.8 THE RIGHT TO EMIGRATE

Failing to exercise a formal right to emigrate is not a reliable sign that one's good, or one's good as an association member, is being furthered. As we have just seen, if that holds at all, it holds only where emigration is an effective option. But under what conditions is emigration an effective option? I propose the following as necessary conditions: (i) emigration to another country must be financially feasible; (ii) that country will admit the emigrant; (iii) that country does not treat members of the emigrant's religious association unjustly.

Why these three? (i) and (ii) simply insist that one not be financially or politically trapped in the country where one happens to reside—certainly a modest stipulation if we are to construe nonemigration as a sign that one's good, or one's good as an association member, is being furthered. But even if (i) and (ii) are met, we still cannot construe nonemigration as such a sign if one's only viable options are to emigrate to countries where one's religious association is treated unjustly. For that reason, we must include (iii) as well.

Notice what happens to Rawls's argument, though, if we insist on making the right to emigrate effective. As we have already seen, whatever precondition we defend must account for the full array of human rights. The full array, according to Rawls, includes the right to emigrate. But if this right is to be effective, it must be a right to emigrate to a country where one's religious association will be treated justly, as condition (iii) requires. Therefore, whatever precondition we defend must account for the right to emigrate to a country where one's religious association will be treated justly. But that means that before we can defend a precondition, we must know what the (minimally) just treatment of a religious association involves—otherwise, we would not know what the precondition must account for. However, knowing what the (minimally) just treatment of a religious association involves presupposes an account of the proper limits on internal sovereignty: those limits tell us (among other things) how just governments may treat the religious associations that are in the territory they govern. And of course once we know the proper limits on internal sovereignty, there is no longer any need to use a precondition to determine them, for we will have already determined them independently of a precondition. Not only will a contract be irrelevant to determining those limits, so will a precondition. Rawls's entire argument, in other words, will become irrelevant to determining the proper limits on internal sovereignty if we insist on making the right to emigrate effective.

It is interesting to note that Rawls himself almost appears to render his own argument irrelevant. When he says that "in view of the possible inequality of religious freedom, if for no other reason, it is essential that a hierarchical society allow and provide assistance for the right of emigration," he seems to suggest that any nonmember of the state religion who emigrates from a decent hierarchical society to a liberal one will receive just treatment in virtue of the latter's *equality* of religious freedom.[62] But then, if he is assuming that this is an effective right to emigrate (that everyone who wants to be a member of some liberal society can become a member), he seems to imply—without appealing to the contract or his precondition—that the proper limits on internal sovereignty are liberal ones. Even worse (from his point of view), he seems to imply that liberalism is the universal standard of domestic justice (the standard that everyone is entitled to), although individuals may voluntarily sacrifice some of their liberty for other ends (by remaining in a society where they are nonmembers of the state religion), or voluntarily join societies where their religion is the state religion (should any exist and be willing to admit them).[63]

So if we want to avoid making Rawls's argument irrelevant, and defending, contrary to his announced aim, a universal liberalism, we must assume that the right to emigrate is not an effective one. We cannot justifiably construe nonemigration as a sign that one's good is being promoted, in that case, and since this is what initially motivated including the right to emigrate as one of the rights guaranteed by associationist conceptions, we may wonder what motivates including it now. But these difficulties are not as serious as rendering his argument irrelevant. Besides, theoretically, it seems more interesting to construct principles for a world in which emigration is not a feasible option than for one in which it is. If changing countries were as easy as changing churches, we'd be living in a much different world. But, as Hume writes: "Can we seriously say that a poor peasant or artisan has a free choice to leave his country, when he knows no foreign language or manners, and lives, from day to day, by the small wages he acquires?"[64] If we stipulate, then, that for the purpose of constructing international principles, we should regard societies as closed systems—as places "we enter only by birth and exit only by death," as Rawls regards them when he constructs his domestic principles—then the principles we construct will apply in circumstances of justice much more like our own.[65]

2.9 THE SEARCH FOR A RATIONALE CONTINUED

As we saw in § 2.5, if we accept Rawls's precondition, only liberal and decent hierarchical societies may enter the original position. But we still have to decide whether to accept it, and that will depend on the strength of its rationale. However, none of the rationales surveyed in § 2.7 suffice. There seems to be just one other possibility: associationist conceptions can account for our considered judgment about human rights without requiring societies to be liberal.[66] Isn't that reason enough to accept it?

If a conception of justice can account for, or fit, our considered judgments, that means that the conception and judgments are in reflective equilibrium. But according to Rawls, there are two types of reflective equilibrium.[67] Narrow reflective equilibrium obtains when we find a conception that best fits our judgments after adjusting one or the other (or both) to eliminate inconsistencies. Wide reflective equilibrium, by contrast, requires more than this. Ideally, it requires that we be presented with "all relevant philosophical arguments" for the conceptions that might fit our judgments to varying degrees.[68] Short of that, it requires an independent argument of some sort. In the domestic case, for instance, the argument for justice as fairness is not merely that it accounts for our considered judgments. That would only establish narrow reflective equilibrium. The argument also includes the hypothetical contract argument. Because justice as fairness both accounts for our considered judgments and emerges from a fair hypothetical contract, Rawls argues, its principles stand in wide reflective equilibrium with those judgments.

"Clearly," Rawls says, "it is the second kind of reflective equilibrium that one is concerned with in moral philosophy."[69] Wide, not narrow, reflective equilibrium is what counts. Narrow reflective equilibrium merely describes our sense of justice. Wide reflective equilibrium tests it. Yet if Rawls were to defend associationist conceptions by claiming that they can account for human rights, he would only be showing that they establish narrow reflective equilibrium. Besides, comprehensive and political liberalisms also account for human rights. What *independent* argument is there for favoring associationist conceptions over these? Only a sound independent argument for that conclusion can show that associationist conceptions stand in wide reflective equilibrium with our judgments.

It is tempting to argue that if we make possession of associationist conceptions our precondition, we can have the widest overlapping consensus compatible with protecting human rights—a desirable result. Since associationist conceptions are flexible enough to be collapsed into individualist ones (by counting individuals as associations with one member), liberal societies, both comprehensive and political, can meet it. But decent hierarchicals can meet it too. By contrast, only societies organized by comprehensive or political liberalisms can satisfy the individualist conception; and only societies organized by political liberalism can meet any precondition requiring submission to a domestic original position. Although there is no guarantee that a society which enters the international original position will join an overlapping consensus on its outcome (e.g., after the veil is lifted, it may reject the duty of nonintervention), it stands to reason that a society is more likely to endorse the outcome if it has a voice in shaping it—that is, if it meets the precondition.

As tempting as this independent argument is, we must reject it as premature. It ignores what Rawls refers to as the two stages of his presentation. Rawls speaks of his domestic principles, justice as fairness, as being presented in two stages.[70] The first stage involves the argument from the original position, where parties choose principles from behind a veil of ignorance without investigating whether they can be the focus of an overlapping consensus. The second stage involves testing the principles to see if they can be the focus of such a consensus. Presumably, the same sequence is to be followed for his international principles. But at this point we are still trying to determine "the most philosophically favored interpretation" of the international original position—we are still working out the first stage. After that, we can consider the likelihood of the outcome becoming the focus of an overlapping consensus. But such considerations are not to influence the setup of the original position yet.[71]

At this point it seems as if we should just admit that Rawls doesn't have an argument for his precondition and try to fashion one for him. However, maybe we have been wrong all along in assuming that an argument is even needed. Maybe this is one of those areas "where our present judgments are in doubt and given with hesitation," the kind where, once we see how all our other judgments fit together in one coherent scheme, a judgment will *emerge* in wide reflective equilibrium—one that offers "a resolution which we can affirm on reflection," that "extrapolate[s] to previously unsettled cases in a reasonable way."[72] On this view, as long as independent arguments support enough other features of the original position, and the outcome supports enough of our other judgments, the fact that the precondition accounts for human rights, reasonably extrapolates to other cases, and is something we can affirm on reflection is enough to accept it. No other argument is needed.[73]

I think, however, that Rawls would be too optimistic to assume that associationist conceptions would emerge in wide reflective equilibrium as the precondition we would affirm on reflection. I believe that the intuitions that may lead one to expect them to emerge are based more on one very common but mistaken objection to having liberalism be the universal standard of domestic justice than they are on anything favoring associationist conceptions. According to that objection, unless we adopt the associationist precondition, which both liberal and nonliberal societies can satisfy, we would be giving liberal societies license to attack, militarily, nonliberal societies in an attempt to rid the world of them.[74] Surely that is rather alarmist. From the fact that a person or society violates some requirement of justice, it does not follow that we can respond in any way we like. The response itself must be proportionate, just, and pragmatic. For example, use of diplomacy and trade, not military intervention, may be the proper way to convince decent hierarchicals to liberalize.

It is not clear what other possible rationales there are to consider. If our search for a plausible one has been thorough enough, then it seems that we are entitled to draw one of two conclusions: either the full Rawlsian reply cannot support the case for human rights (even the rather minimal set that Rawls defends), or the burden of proof should shift to those who think that it can. I will describe what I think are the wider implications of taking the first and stronger of these two conclusions.

2.10 CONCLUDING REMARKS

If the argument presented here is sound, Rawls's approach to defending human rights fails. It fails because he makes the protection of human rights a *precondition* for entering a contract whose outcome is supposed to justify their protection—a premise, essentially, with the same content as his conclusion (§ 2.5). If he eliminates the precondition, there would be no agreement limiting internal sovereignty at all (§ 2.6). When we try to defend an alternative precondition, we cannot find a plausible rationale (§§ 2.7, 2.9). Even if we were able to find such a rationale, finally, the contract itself would not establish the limits on internal sovereignty.

Those limits would issue instead from the precondition on entry. The contract itself would be idle (§ 2.6).

The source of the problem is Rawls's reluctance to impose liberal principles and values on societies that reject them. Were he to champion a comprehensive liberalism, its principles would apply to all societies and require the protection of human rights. Were he to champion liberal individualism—as Pogge and others recommend—by having the delegates to his international contract represent the interests of persons, they would require all societies to protect human rights.[75] But Rawls rejects the imposition of liberal principles in the first case and liberal values in the second by having the delegates represent the interests of peoples, and that, we have seen, requires him to defend a precondition if human rights are to be supported.

It seems, therefore, that we face the following dilemma. Either impose liberal principles and values on societies that reject them, or else admit that we lack grounds for demanding that such societies protect human rights. Rawls, it is interesting to note, once claimed that however far we may wish to push the limits of tolerance, protecting human rights belongs to "the bedrock beyond which we cannot go."[76] If we agree, we may just have to realize that genuine tolerance can be an imposing demand.

NOTES

1. Onora O'Neill, "Ethical Reasoning and Ideological Pluralism," *Ethics* 98 (1988): 705–22, p. 709.
2. Samuel Scheffler, "The Appeal of Political Liberalism," *Ethics* 105 (1994): 4–22, p. 21.
3. John Rawls, "Justice as Fairness: Political not Metaphysical," *Philosophy & Public Affairs* 14 (1985): 235–51, p. 229. As he had earlier explained, "we are not trying to find a conception of justice suitable for all societies regardless of their particular social or historical circumstances. We want to settle a fundamental disagreement over the just form of basic institutions within a democratic society under modem conditions. . . . How far the conclusions we reach are of interest in a wider context is a separate question." John Rawls, "Kantian Constructivism in Moral Theory," *Journal of Philosophy* 77 (1980): 515–72, pp. 517–18.
4. See Brian Barry, *Theories of Justice* (Berkeley: University of California Press, 1989), pp. 183–89; Charles Beitz, *Political Theory and International Relations* (Princeton, NJ: Princeton University Press, 1979), pp. 127–76; Thomas Pogge, *Realizing Rawls* (Ithaca, NY: Cornell University Press, 1989), pp. 246–73.
5. See John Rawls, *The Law of Peoples*, pp. 59–60.
6. Rawls, *The Law of Peoples*, p. 37.
7. Rawls, *The Law of Peoples*, pp. 68–69.
8. Rawls, *The Law of Peoples*, pp. 14, 32.
9. Rawls, *The Law of Peoples*, p. 64.
10. Rawls, *The Law of Peoples*, pp. 65, 74.
11. Thomas Pogge, "An Egalitarian Law of Peoples," *Philosophy & Public Affairs* 23 (1994): 195–224, p. 206. Although Pogge is here opposing Rawls's earlier, article version of the law of peoples, the argument he makes applies to the book as well.

12. Pogge, "An Egalitarian Law of Peoples," p. 208.
13. Pogge, "An Egalitarian Law of Peoples," p. 198.
14. Pogge, "An Egalitarian Law of Peoples," pp. 209–10.
15. Pogge, "An Egalitarian Law of Peoples," pp. 210–11. Pogge also argues that even if we grant Rawls's assumptions that (1) each people only has an interest in maintaining the justice of their domestic institutions, and (2) peoples rather than persons count as the ultimate units of moral concern, we can still justify a liberal egalitarian principle of international "redistribution." The reason, according to Pogge, is that Rawls mistakenly views such a principle as redistributive, since he seems to assume that a laissez-faire distribution among societies is a natural benchmark deviations from which require justification. But for the same reason that Rawls charges Nozick with being mistaken in this assumption, Pogge charges that Rawls too is mistaken: there is no natural benchmark of justifiable distribution independent of a theory of just distribution (pp. 211–13).
16. Pogge, "An Egalitarian Law of Peoples," p. 215.
17. Pogge, "An Egalitarian Law of Peoples," p. 215. Also see Darrel Moellendorf, "Constructing the Law of Peoples," *Pacific Philosophical Quarterly* 77, no. 2 (June 1996): 132–54, pp. 137–39.
18. Ibid., pp. 215–16, quoting Rawls, "The Law of Peoples," p. 530. Similar language appears at Rawls, *The Law of Peoples*, 59.
19. Ibid., p. 217.
20. John Rawls, *Political Liberalism* (New York: Columbia University Press), p. 24.
21. Rawls, *The Law of Peoples*, 90.
22. This claim receives more extensive treatment in chapter 4. For present purposes, the aim is to find the most plausible basis for having the parties represent groups rather than individuals, in order to see where the argument then leads.
23. I take it that the principle enabling them to ratify and requiring them to observe mutually advantageous treaties in some sense follows from the principles guaranteeing their freedom and independence as a people. I also take it that the principles allowing them the right to wage war in self-defense and to place limits on the conduct of wars in some sense follow from the principle imposing a duty of nonintervention. That leaves only the principle that human rights are to be protected in need of explanation (the text goes on to show how).
24. John Rawls, *A Theory of Justice* (Cambridge, MA: Harvard University Press, 1971), p. 20 (my emphasis). See also, Rawls, *The Law of Peoples*, p. 27 for the suggestion that the law of peoples should "fit" the judgment that human rights ought to be protected.
25. For the description of human rights as "not politically parochial," see Rawls, *The Law of Peoples*, p. 65. For Rawls's characterization of considered moral judgments, see Rawls, *A Theory of Justice*, pp. 19–20.
26. Rawls, *A Theory of Justice*, p. 19.
27. Rawls, *The Law of Peoples*, p. 65.
28. Rawls, *A Theory of Justice*, p. 20.
29. Rawls, *A Theory of Justice*, p. 20.
30. This will be wide, not narrow, reflective equilibrium. See Rawls, *Political Liberalism*, p. 8 n. 8, for the distinction.
31. Rawls, *The Law of Peoples*, pp. 59, 64, 67.
32. Plus, when he first introduces them, he has yet to derive the law of peoples common to liberal and hierarchical societies, which again implies that they are additional requirements of some sort.
33. Rawls, *The Law of Peoples*, pp. 64–66, 71.
34. To take an analogy, suppose Rawls were to insist that, as a precondition for entering the domestic original position, the parties had to agree to his first principle of justice. It would hardly be surprising, in that case, if they chose that principle once they were in the original position. The one thing that is different in the international case is that, unlike the first principle of justice as fairness, a principle requiring the

protection of human rights is itself a considered moral judgment. Rawls allows that we can have considered moral judgments at all levels of generality, "from those about particular situations and institutions up through broad standards and first principles to formal and abstract conditions on moral conceptions." (See John Rawls, "The Independence of Moral Theory," *Proceedings and Addresses of the American Philosophical Association* XLVIII [1974–1975]: 5–22, p. 8.) In *A Theory of Justice* he usually cites the injustice of slavery and religious intolerance as examples of considered moral judgments—examples of "particular situations and institutions" that any plausible conception of justice ideally should fit. In *The Law of Peoples,* by contrast, it is a "first principle" that any plausible conception ideally should *include*. But while the principle that human rights ought to be protected is itself a considered moral judgment, this is not reason enough to justify making agreement on it a precondition for entering the contract. To be sure, some considered moral judgments will qualify as "formal and abstract conditions on moral conceptions," and thus serve as justifiable preconditions on the contract. In the domestic case, for instance, only those who possess the moral powers are permitted to enter, and this reflects a considered judgment that a moral conception meant for liberal citizens must respect their capacities for a conception of the good and a sense of justice. But the judgments which serve as preconditions must not be the same as those which are principles—otherwise we have the most vicious of circles. And that is exactly what we would have if we made the protection of human rights a precondition for entering a contract from which we hoped to derive a principle mandating their protection. If we want to exclude nonexpansionist outlaw regimes, we need a different precondition.

35. Rawls, *The Law of Peoples,* p. 65 (emphasis added).

36. As I will show in the next section, this eliminates the circularity of the contract argument for human rights but still makes the contract superfluous to their justification. The justification for them issues from the precondition, not the contract, which merely reaffirms and ratifies what the precondition requires.

37. Rawls, *The Law of Peoples,* pp. 71–78.

38. Rawls, *The Law of Peoples,* pp. 65–66 (emphasis added).

39. Rawls, *The Law of Peoples,* p. 67.

40. See Rawls, *A Theory of Justice,* p. 24, for this description of teleological theories.

41. In fact, Rawls himself rejects this interpretation. See *The Law of Peoples,* p. 71.

42. Rawls, *The Law of Peoples,* pp. 64, 71, 72–73.

43. Rawls, *The Law of Peoples,* p. 65, n. 3.

44. Rawls, *A Theory of Justice,* p. 18.

45. "[T]he conditions embodied in the description of the original position are ones that we do in fact accept. Or if we do not, then perhaps we can be persuaded to do so by philosophical reflection. Each aspect of the contractual situation can be given supporting grounds." (See Rawls, *A Theory of Justice,* p. 21.) Also see Rawls, *Political Liberalism,* pp. 22–28. I will be referring to these supporting grounds as a rationale or argument.

46. "Liberty in adopting a conception of the good is limited only by principles that are deduced from a [contract] doctrine which imposes no prior constraints on these conceptions." Rawls, *A Theory of Justice,* p. 254.

47. They presumably know that societies with such conceptions protect human rights anyway, since they possess full knowledge of general facts and social theory (as the parties in Rawls's domestic original position do).

48. Feminists have claimed that Rawls's domestic contract is similarly unable to restrict the internal sovereignty of male heads of households over families if the parties in the original position are heads of families (as Rawls repeatedly describes them in *A Theory of Justice*) rather than individuals. Just as the international contract imposes no new internal restrictions on societies not already accounted for by preconditions on entry, so too, these feminists claim, does the domestic contract impose no new internal restrictions on families not already accounted for by preconditions. Since Rawls offers no preconditions restricting the internal affairs of families, there are none. According-

ly, if the parties in the original position are heads of families rather than individuals, then Rawls "makes the family opaque to claims of justice." (See Jane English, "Justice Between Generations," *Philosophical Studies* 31 (1977): 91–104, p. 95.) If only heads of families must reach agreement on principles of justice, then "[it] is impossible to see how the viewpoint of their less advantaged members ever gets to be heard." (See Susan Moller Okin, *Justice, Gender, and the Family* (New York: Basic Books, 1989), p. 94.) Rawls has since clarified that the parties to his domestic contract are individuals rather than family heads, which should accommodate most of the feminist concerns. (For those that remain, see Okin, "Political Liberalism, Justice, and Gender," *Ethics* 105 (1994): 23–43, pp. 29–32, 35–37; and John Exdell, "Feminism, Fundamentalism and Liberal Legitimacy," *Canadian Journal of Philosophy* 24 (1994): 441–63.) But the basic point remains intact. The contract is capable of imposing internal limits on groups only if the agents in either original position represent individuals, and as we saw in § 2.4, the delegates must represent peoples, not persons—groups, not individuals. As long as the delegates represent peoples, the only way to set limits on the internal sovereignty of societies is to rely on preconditions to entering the contract.

49. For example, if the agents represent heterosexual male family heads, the principles are silent on what goes on in the family (e.g., wife beating). If the agents represent heads of religions, the principles are silent on what goes on in each religion (e.g., burning heretics). By contrast, if the agents represent individuals, they will figure that it is worse to be beaten than to be denied the right to beat, worse to be burned at the stake than to be angered by heresy, and so maximin reasoning will require protecting wives and heretics instead of leaving that to the discretion of group heads.

50. Rawls, *The Law of Peoples*, p. 37.

51. Nor should Rawls want to defend this principle on such an empirically contingent basis; he rejects utilitarian defenses of basic rights for that reason. Furthermore, it would ground human rights in the interests of countries not to be flooded by refugees instead of the wrongness of human rights abuses to the victims, something which seems to get the right result for the wrong reason.

52. Rawls, *A Theory of Justice*, p. 249.

53. Rawls, *A Theory of Justice*, p. 250.

54. Even if we could, we would get the right result for the wrong reason: that it is irrational for the rulers, not a wrong to the ruled, to violate human rights.

55. Rawls, *The Law of Peoples*, p. 26.

56. Nor can one be the outcome of a separate contract among individuals. Since the worst-off individuals in societies organized around political liberalism are better off there than in any other kind of society, the precondition individuals would adopt would result in the exclusion of all societies except those organized around political liberalism. But Rawls only needs to exclude nonexpansionist outlaws, not hierarchical and comprehensive liberal societies besides.

57. I say that he *seems* inclined to offer a procedural defense because the text is unclear on this point. In any case, it is worth attempting to reconstruct such an argument because otherwise he is left with a bare assertion. See Rawls, *The Law of Peoples*, pp. 71–78, where he seems to suggest this argument.

58. Rawls, *A Theory of Justice*, p. 20.

59. For the distinction between pure, perfect, and imperfect procedural justice, see ibid., p. 85.

60. As argued earlier in the chapter, decent hierarchical societies can meet the precondition by furthering the good of their internal associations. Liberal societies can meet it by counting individuals as associations with one member, effectively collapsing the distinction between individualist and associationist conceptions.

61. Perhaps egalitarian liberal societies will consider less egalitarian liberal societies to be minimally decent (and vice versa); and perhaps decent hierarchical societies will consider some liberal societies to be minimally decent (such those where the religion that is the state religion in the decent hierarchical society is a weak minority religion in the liberal society, a situation in which equal religious freedom seems like a net benefit

to, rather than a net hindrance on, that religion). Still, if there is a significant rift between liberal societies as a group and decent hierarchical ones as a group, the point in the text stands.

62. Rawls, *The Law of Peoples*, p. 74.

63. They will not be entitled to do so, however, in the latter case. Also, I say that Rawls *seems* to imply that liberalism is the universal standard because I suppose someone might object that the right in question could just be an effective right to emigrate to a nonliberal society where the inequalities in religious freedom aren't as great. To this objection I have two replies. First, it would still be the case that Rawls winds up defending a universal theory of justice (contrary to his announced aim of allowing for a range of "reasonable" conceptions of domestic justice). The standard would just be different. Everyone would be entitled to live in some (say) moderately hierarchical society, although individuals would be permitted to voluntarily sacrifice some of their (lesser) liberty for other ends. They would be permitted to join liberal societies, and societies where their religion is the state religion, too, should any exist, although they would not be entitled to do so. Second, why else would he say "in view of the possible *inequality* of religious freedom . . . it is essential that a hierarchical society allow . . . for the right of emigration" (Rawls, *The Law of Peoples*, p. 74; my emphasis) if not to suggest that this must be a right to emigrate to a country where there is *equality* of religious freedom?

64. David Hume, "Of the Original Contract," in Knud Haakonssen (ed.), *Hume: Political Essays* (New York: Cambridge University Press, 1994), p. 193.

65. Rawls, *Political Liberalism*, pp. 135–36. He goes on to say: "Political society is closed: we come to be within it and we do not, indeed cannot, enter or leave it voluntarily." He then adds a footnote explaining that "the right of emigration does not make the acceptance of political authority voluntary in the way that freedom of thought and liberty of conscience make the acceptance of ecclesiastical authority voluntary."

66. See Rawls, *The Law of Peoples*, p. 68.

67. See Rawls, *Political Liberalism*, p. 8 n. 8.

68. Rawls, *A Theory of Justice*, p. 49.

69. Rawls, *A Theory of Justice*, p. 49.

70. Rawls, *Political Liberalism*, p. 140 n. 7.

71. See also Darrel Moellendorf, "Constructing the Law of Peoples," p. 145. Even if we should discover (at the second stage) that the outcome was not likely to be the focus of an overlapping consensus—a discovery that might force us to reevaluate (at the first stage) our original precondition—we would still need to provide a rationale for the substitute precondition that was independent of the fact that it was needed to forge an overlapping consensus. We would need to do that because the first stage must be completed before proceeding to the second. See Rawls, *Political Liberalism*, pp. 140–41.

72. Rawls, *A Theory of Justice*, pp. 19, 332.

73. This may explain Rawls's remark that his account of decency is "developed by setting out various criteria and explaining their meaning," after which "[t]he reader has to judge whether a decent people . . . is to be tolerated as a member in good standing of the Society of Peoples." This looks more like an appeal to intuition, or "due reflection," than a positive argument in support of the criteria that comprise the precondition. Rawls, *The Law of Peoples*, p. 67.

74. Rawls sometimes writes as if he believes that failure to adopt this precondition *would* license such military action. See Rawls, "The Law of Peoples," p. 563 and Rawls, *The Law of Peoples*, p. 83.

75. See Pogge, "An Egalitarian Law of Peoples," p. 197.

76. Rawls, "The Law of Peoples," p. 562.

THREE

The Law of Peoples

Act II

3.1 THREE OBJECTIONS

In the last chapter we saw that Rawls's argument encounters two main objections. The *idle-contract* objection claims that Rawls's international contract does no work at all in establishing limits on internal sovereignty (and hence no work in establishing this crucial limit on international tolerance) (§ 2.6). The *two-stages* objection claims that even if Rawls's list of basic human rights holds the best prospect for being the focus of an overlapping consensus in a world that contains nonliberal societies, this fact alone is insufficient to justify them, since for Rawls a principle guaranteeing their protection must first be chosen in the international contract (we cannot, in other words, skip the first stage of his two-stage presentation and go straight to the second) (§ 2.9).[1]

Now I wish to add a third objection, which is best brought out by considering Rawls's argument chronologically, as he himself developed it, beginning with his 1993 article, "The Law of Peoples," and highlighting changes made to his argument in his 1999 book, *The Law of Peoples*. Call this the *almost-liberal* objection. The almost-liberal objection claims that, despite Rawls's reluctance to impose liberal values on nonliberal societies, the limits on international tolerance that he ultimately endorses are almost-liberal ones anyway. Since these limits are almost-liberal, one might naturally ask whether there is another way of accounting for them. I discuss this possibility toward the end of the chapter.

3.2 THE OLD LAW OF PEOPLES

Whether we consider the newer, book version of the law of peoples, or the older, article version of it, both versions incorporate a precondition on entering the international contract that requires a society to possess an associationist (common good) conception of domestic justice. Accepting this stipulation for the sake of argument, let's examine what happens when we try to apply it.

As we saw in the last chapter, associationist conceptions of domestic justice require protecting the full array of basic human rights (§ 2.5). Therefore, since nonexpansionist (as well as expansionist) outlaw societies fail to do that, they may not enter the contract. But are these the *only* societies that get excluded?

Recall that, for Rawls, a society possesses an associationist conception just in case it *furthers the good of each of its associations* (§ 2.5). While furthering the good of each association requires protecting the full array of basic human rights, including a right to religious freedom, in Rawls's view it does not mandate making religious freedom equal for all citizens. That raises the following question: how unequal can religious freedom be and still further the good of each association?

This question is especially important since Rawls seems to be of two minds when he initially characterizes hierarchical societies in his article.[2] On the one hand, he claims that a hierarchical regime takes the interests of all its citizens into account and citizens there do have the right to express dissent, so that such a regime's legal system at least respects basic human rights. Further, "no religions are persecuted, or denied civic and social conditions that permit their practice in peace," and citizens are permitted to emigrate if they choose.[3] All of this makes life in a hierarchical regime sound rather satisfactory. On the other hand, he claims that, "a state religion may . . . control government policy on certain important matters" so that members of that religion enjoy "certain privileges."[4] While Rawls does not say in any detail what such privileges might be, he does mention that "liberty of conscience and freedom of thought . . . are not in general equal for all members of society" and that "individuals do not have the right of free speech as in a liberal society," suggesting that members of the state religion possess greater rights and freedoms to pursue their faith than nonmembers do.[5] Depending on how unequal these freedoms are, and depending on what the state religion mandates, life in a hierarchical regime could be rather limiting and perhaps even barely tolerable for nonmembers of the state religion even if the government treats them with formal equality, respects their basic human rights, and protects them from persecution.

In the article, Rawls seems to think that as long as society guarantees "a measure" of such freedom, it furthers the good of each of its associations.[6] But surely it requires more than that. Otherwise, a government could place any number of restrictions on members of minority doctrines as long as it respected their human rights and permitted the most meager liberty—say, praying in groups of no more than three. As long as those members did not invite sanctions with massive public disobedience, and as long as the government did not adopt intrusive measures trying to detect private violations, enforcing these policies would not rise to the level of persecution. Indeed, the members might even derive some pride and inspiration as their religion survived in spite of the limitations. Yet this does not seem like furthering their good. From the fact that a government does not persecute an association, it does not follow that it promotes that association's good.

Nor does it seem plausible to claim that as long as members of that association choose not to emigrate, the state must be furthering that association's good. If that holds at all, it only holds where emigration is an effective option (§ 2.8). But emigration is not an effective option when the formal right to emigrate is only combined with an economic right to having one's basic needs met, which is all that Rawls's law of peoples requires. Even if we ignore the social and psychological costs, emigration for many people will not be financially feasible with that kind of economic minimum.

So in order for a society to possess an associationist conception, it cannot have too much inequality in religious freedom, or else it will fail to further the good of each of its associations. Since Rawls's characterization of hierarchical societies is compatible with significant inequalities in such freedom, though, it seems that some hierarchical societies, not just nonexpansionist outlaw ones, must be excluded by the precondition too.

Call the societies that are excluded—the ones with significant inequalities in religious freedom—*extreme* hierarchical societies. Call those with less significant inequalities *moderate* hierarchical societies. In moderate hierarchical societies, nonmembers of the state religion will enjoy conditions more favorable to the pursuit of their doctrines. Presumably, they will be guaranteed a higher economic minimum that makes emigration more feasible (financially) and gives them greater opportunity to advance their doctrine (they can establish more outposts for charitable relief, say), since that seems necessary in order to further the good of each association. Now notice this about moderate hierarchicals: their economic minimum could very well be the same as that found in the less egalitarian liberal societies. And while their religious freedoms are still unequal, they are not *too* unequal. Moderate hierarchical societies are almost liberal.

3.3 THE NEW LAW OF PEOPLES

Of the most significant changes to Rawls's argument, some are merely cosmetic. Hierarchical societies, for instance, are now called *decent* (or *decent hierarchical*) ones. Also, the duty to assist peoples burdened by unfavorable conditions—defended by Rawls in the article but not officially listed there in his statement of principles—is now added to his list of principles.[7] Similarly, Rawls introduces another type of society, *benevolent absolutisms*—peaceful societies that respect basic human rights but deny meaningful political participation—only to contrast them with decent societies, whose consultation hierarchies allow members meaningful (enough) participation, and which therefore (unlike benevolent absolutisms) deserve to be tolerated internationally.[8]

Other changes, however, are substantive. Most significantly, Rawls now strengthens what an associationist (common good) conception of justice requires. For example, whereas in the article Rawls held that such a conception must admit "a *measure* of liberty of conscience and freedom of thought, even if these freedoms are not in general equal for all members of society as they are in liberal regimes"[9]—a characterization compatible with widely unequal religious freedoms—in the book he holds that it must admit "a *sufficient* measure of liberty of conscience and freedom of religion and thought," even if they are unequal.[10] Sufficient, we might ask, for what? Elsewhere in the book he phrases it even more strongly, requiring that such a conception must admit "a sufficient measure of liberty of conscience to *ensure* freedom of religion and thought."[11] And when he describes a society that has such a conception of justice—the fictitious Kazanistan—he expressly limits religious inequalities to the holding of higher political and judicial offices: "Islam is the favored religion, and only Muslims can hold the upper positions of political authority and influence the government's main decisions and policies. . . . Yet other religions are tolerated and may be practiced without fear or loss of most civic rights, except the right to hold the higher political or judicial offices."[12] Indeed, Rawls insists that "they are not subjected to arbitrary discrimination, or treated as inferior by Muslims in public or social relations," which suggests that they are otherwise treated equally.[13]

These remarks suggest two different requirements for a conception of justice to qualify as a common good conception: one limits religious inequalities to the higher political and judicial offices (if we take the Kazanistan discussion to define that requirement), while the other allows wider inequalities (if we take it merely to illustrate it)—though not as wide as the article permits. Since Rawls introduces Kazanistan as an example of a society whose conception of justice is admissible, I will interpret his remarks as permitting wider inequalities, although I will also consider the alternative interpretation at the end of this section.

There is another respect in which Rawls strengthens what a common good conception of justice requires. Given the historic connections between religion and gender discrimination, it is compatible with Rawls's initial characterization of a hierarchical society for it to permit significant inequalities in rights between men and women (even in moderate hierarchical societies). But now, in the book, Rawls limits the permissible range of gender inequalities, just as he does religious ones. There must be "equal justice for women," he claims, for two reasons.[14] First, the inequality and subjection of women are among the leading causes of population pressures that burden a society relative to what its economy can sustain. Thus, removing the inequality and subjection of women and giving them equal justice is a good strategic reason for enabling a society to meet its members' subsistence needs, as required by the basic human right to life. (Rawls cites the Indian state of Kerala, which gave women rights to receive education, to own property, and to hold wealth, as one of several places where this strategy significantly reduced birth rates.[15]) Second, and more directly connected with the interests of women, the subjection of women simply violates their basic human rights.[16]

Now I don't think that either of these reasons adequately supports Rawls's view that there must be equal justice for women. That giving women equal justice is a good strategy for reducing birth rates, which is in turn a good strategy for enabling a society to meet its members' subsistence needs, is an empirically *contingent* reason for guaranteeing basic rights—the sort Rawls elsewhere rejects as too insecure.[17] At best, it supports the position that equal justice for women is required in burdened societies that are unable to meet their members' subsistence needs, but not elsewhere. The second reason, that the subjection of women violates their basic human rights, argues for upholding their basic human rights but no more. It does *not* argue for any right of nondiscrimination—a right conspicuously missing from Rawls's list of basic human rights—as the phrase "equal justice for women" seems to require. Perhaps Rawls means to suggest, through his example of the Indian state of Kerala, that women must have *some* rights to education, wealth and property, though not rights *equal* to men. (I am assuming that there can be some gender inequalities that intuitively seem to constitute discrimination, but do not rise to the level of subjection.) But this would be a nonstandard use of the phrase "equal justice for women." Rather than attribute this nonstandard usage to Rawls, I will interpret his claim that there must be equal justice for women as requiring a right to nondiscrimination on the basis of gender in spite of the apparent inability of his reasons to support that view.

On this interpretation of the new law of peoples, then, Rawls is claiming that societies may be may be represented in the international contract if and only if their conception of domestic justice allows a *sufficient* measure of religious freedom for all of their members, even if their freedoms are unequal, and it guarantees *equal* justice for women. This is the new precondition on entering the international contract. I'd like to raise three questions about this claim.

First, why does Rawls seem to permit religious discrimination while barring gender discrimination? By allowing unequal—though not too unequal—religious freedoms, Rawls seems to permit some form of what we would intuitively consider to be religious discrimination. In contrast, by insisting on equal justice for women, Rawls seems to require a right to nondiscrimination on the basis of gender. What justifies the difference?

The difference seems to involve an inconsistency in principle of the sort that Ronald Dworkin calls "checkerboard" law:[18] one that makes arbitrary distinctions in matters of principle, for example, a law making abortion illegal for women born in even years but not odd ones.[19] By contrast, a law making abortion illegal except in cases of rape, incest, or when the life or health of the mother is at stake, is not. Whether we think that the exceptions should be broader, narrower, or nonexistent, we at least recognize that this distinction is a principled one. But in Rawls's case, if official discrimination is a wrong that should be prohibited as a matter of justice, then it seems arbitrary to exempt religious discrimination from the scope of that principle. If so, then any conception of justice that permits such discrimination as a matter of law would seem to allow checkerboard law. But intuitively, this seems wrong. Instead, we should treat religious and gender discrimination the same.

Now one might want to reply on Rawls's behalf as follows. For Rawls, political philosophy should be practical: it should produce an outcome that can be supported by adherents of diverse comprehensive worldviews, whether they are views of the good, or of justice. Thus, Rawls may be perfectly justified in allowing religion—his paradigm case of a comprehensive worldview—to be used as a basis for making political distinctions, but barring gender from being used.

But notice what this reply assumes: it assumes that in trying to satisfy this practical aim, in trying to gain the support of diverse comprehensive worldviews, it is nonetheless permissible to impinge upon them to some extent. Gender discrimination, even if based on religion, is impermissible. (Presumably, it would be easier to achieve the practical aim if no impingements at all were permitted.) So the practical aim is not overriding. But once we accept some compromise in the practical aim, other impingements seem equally motivated. For instance, we might claim that racial and ethnic discrimination, like gender discrimination, should be impermissible, even if they are based on religion. And now religious discrimination, itself based on religion, begins to look like an isolated case. Why does the practical aim allow only this kind of discrimination, but not others? We seem to face the problem of checkerboard law all over again, even after taking Rawls's interest in the practical aim of political philosophy into account.

Even if one remains unpersuaded by these considerations, however, there is a more fundamental problem with the reply: as we saw earlier, it ignores what Rawls refers to as the two stages of his presentation (§ 2.9). At this point, we are still working out the first stage. After that, we can consider the likelihood of the outcome becoming the focus of an overlapping consensus.

Second, suppose that we do treat religious and gender discrimination the same, not by barring them both but by allowing both kinds of inequality (although everyone has "a sufficient measure" of religious freedom, and women have some rights to education, wealth and property). This avoids the problem of allowing checkerboard law. Does it make the precondition too weak, however?

It is tempting here to appeal to Rawls's notion of a consultation hierarchy. According to Rawls, a common good conception of justice may be satisfied with a consultation hierarchy: "a family of representative bodies whose role in the hierarchy is to take part in an established procedure of consultation and to look after what the people's common good idea of justice regards as the important interests of all members of the people."[20] In a consultation hierarchy, members of society are not regarded as "separate individuals deserving equal representation . . . according to the maxim: one citizen, one vote," as they would in liberal societies.[21] Rather, "persons belong first to estates, corporations, and associations—that is, groups."[22] Thus, "[e]ach person belongs to a group represented by a body in the consultation hierarchy."[23] And "as members of associations, corporations, and estates," persons "have the right at some point in the procedure of consultation . . . to express political dissent, and the government has an obligation to take a group's dissent seriously and to give a conscientious reply."[24] Hence, in response to the charge that the precondition is too weak, Rawls might reply that any inequalities on the basis of gender or religion that issue from a consultation hierarchy are reasonable since the interests of women and religious minorities were considered in that process.

This *would* be an effective reply, perhaps, if we were to assume that women and religious minorities accepted discrimination willingly and reflectively—as opposed to, say, simply acquiescing in it, or accepting it on the basis of adaptive preferences. But unless Rawls is going to allow acquiescence or adaptive preferences a role in determining what counts as reasonable inequalities—and give up the attempt to find an Archimedean point for assessing them—his reply must rest on their being accepted in some more robust sense. And then it is hard to see why women and religious minorities would not insist that discrimination against them neglects their fundamental interests—interests which the consultation process is supposed to uphold.

Third, suppose that we treat religion and gender the same, not by "leveling down" the status of women to that of religion, as we just did, but by "leveling up" the status of religion to that of women. On this view, societies may be represented in the international contract if and only if their conception of domestic justice guarantees equal justice for women *and* for minority religious groups by requiring a right to nondiscrimination on the basis of gender or religion. There is one exception, though: the higher political and judicial offices may still be reserved for members of the favored religion. Now in this case, where inequalities in rights and freedoms are indeed very limited, we may be inclined to agree that this is an appropriate price of admission to the original position. But it's important to notice that this brings them even closer to the family of liberal conceptions of justice than they were before—the main differences being that they permit some religious restrictions on the higher political and judicial offices, and that they allow rights of political participation that are collective (the consultation hierarchy) rather than individual. Since these nonliberal societies are now even closer to being liberal than they were in the article version of the law of peoples, we might ask whether there is some other way of accounting for the intuition that they may be represented.

3.4 THE INTUITION

Given the intuitive implausibility of allowing inequalities in rights and freedoms to be too wide (as his article seemed to allow), it is only natural that Rawls sought to strengthen (in the book) his view of what a common good conception of justice requires as the precondition on entering the international contract. But, as I have suggested, the most plausible way of interpreting that view is as requiring such conceptions to be almost liberal. This is about as strong as Rawls can make his view and still be consistent with his claim that liberalism requires the toleration of other, nonliberal, ways of organizing society.

Is there another way of accommodating this result? We *could* claim that only liberal conceptions of domestic justice are justifiable, but for practical rather than moral reasons concerning tolerance, we should exempt societies that follow nonliberal, but almost liberal, conceptions from even the mildest forms of intervention (like political and economic pressure) aimed at reforming them in a liberal direction. Instead, societies that follow liberal conceptions should simply lead by example.

As Michael Blake reminds us, we shouldn't underestimate the force of these practical reasons.[25] Often, governments will do just the opposite of what a coercing party demands—just to show their independence. Their citizens will resent the coercion (even more so if they are from a weak state and they are being coerced by a powerful one). Democracy, furthermore, is difficult to establish coercively. It requires citizens to accept majority decisions that they sometimes oppose. Such acceptance is "exceptionally difficult to inculcate from the outside."[26] Interventions frequently have unpredictable consequences, too. They set bad precedents for illiberal states to intervene in the affairs of others—especially, as often happens, when the basis for the precedent itself rests on "self-serving interpretations of facts"[27]—to say nothing of the epistemic limitations and bias involved in ascertaining facts (think of the claim, used to justify the Second Gulf War, that Iraq possessed weapons of mass destruction). Blake claims that these reasons "are exceptionally powerful, and ought to be recognized as such."[28] Accordingly, he suggests exempting societies that follow nonliberal, but almost liberal, conceptions from even the mildest forms of intervention.

This is not Rawls's view, of course, since for him the exemption is grounded in moral reasons concerning tolerance. Indeed, it is one he officially rejects. Yet there are times when he seems sympathetic to it. "All societies undergo gradual changes," he claims, "and this is no less true of decent societies than of others. Liberal peoples should not suppose that decent societies are unable to reform themselves in their own way. By recognizing these societies as *bona fide* members of the Society of Peoples, liberal people encourage this change."[29] This emphasizes a practical rationale for exempting decent societies from any outside pressures to liberalize in favor of letting them reform themselves. Second, he claims that, "in view of the possible inequality of religious freedom, if for no other reason, it is essential that a hierarchical society allow and provide assistance for the right of emigration."[30] The suggestion here (as we saw in § 2.8) seems to be that members of a religious minority should have an effective right of exit so that, if they wish to, they may seek entry into a society that guarantees equal rights of religious freedom, as in a liberal society. If so, then it almost seems as though Rawls thinks they ought to have, as a fallback position, the freedom to enter a liberal society—which comes very close to suggesting that all persons *everywhere* are entitled to liberal rights and freedoms *somewhere*.[31]

Just within Rawls's reach, then, is a view that Blake describes as "an alternative Rawlsian vision," one that he believes is "more attractive than the vision Rawls himself defended"—a vision in which we are "committed to the universality of liberalism, while convinced that we ought to be quite careful in our practical efforts to create liberal societies—and aware that we may not have the only respectable vision of what a liberal political society should look like."[32] Ultimately, though, Rawls declines to endorse it.

The upshot is that we have two ways of accounting for the intuition that societies that are almost liberal should be exempt from even milder forms of political and economic pressure aimed at reforming them in a liberal direction. One way is grounded in moral reasons concerning tolerance; the other is grounded in practical concerns about the efficacy of exerting such pressure on societies that are already almost liberal. The advantage, it seems to me, belongs with the latter view, since Rawls's version of the former appears to rest on nothing more than an intuition: an intuition about where the limits of tolerance are to be drawn. "The reader has to judge whether a decent people . . . is to be tolerated and accepted as a member in good standing of the Society of Peoples. It is my conjecture that most reasonable citizens of a liberal society will find [such] peoples . . . acceptable as peoples in good standing."[33] By contrast, the latter provides an *explanation* of those limits: a deflationary one.

3.5 CONCLUDING REMARKS

Although the changes that Rawls makes in his book strengthen his conception of basic human rights (primarily by requiring greater gender equality in societies whose traditions and culture reject it), they still do not go far enough or else produce tensions of their own. The remedy, once again, I maintain, is that we must reject Rawls's reluctance to impose liberal values more widely if we are to justify basic human rights.

If sound, the upshot of my argument in this and the preceding chapter is this. Many (if not most) critiques of Rawls's view seem to fall into one of two camps. On the one hand, there are those who challenge his abstention from liberal individualism and subsequent embrace of the independent moral significance of peoples.[34] On the other hand, there are those who accept (sometimes *arguendo*) his embrace of the independent moral significance of peoples, yet maintain that, nonetheless, more recognizably liberal principles can still be justified (particularly in the area of global economic distribution).[35] These chapters, however, add an arguably stronger critique, for they hold not that stronger liberal principles can be justified even if we accept the independent moral significance of peoples, but that *weaker* principles (ones guaranteeing basic human rights) would *fail* to be justified.

Accordingly, if our best attempts to justify basic human rights ultimately show that appeals to liberal values are unavoidable, then we should regard such appeals as no more of an imposition than the expectation that all societies must protect basic human rights. Even more significantly, if such appeals justify liberal freedoms that go beyond basic human rights, then arguments in support of basic human rights would also justify international efforts to advance further liberal reforms within nonliberal societies.

NOTES

1. Rawls, *Political Liberalism*, pp. 140–41.
2. Rawls substituted the term *decent hierarchical society* in the book for *hierarchical society*, the term he used in the article.

3. Rawls, "The Law of Peoples," p. 547, repeated nearly verbatim in Rawls, *The Law of Peoples*, p. 74.

4. Rawls, "The Law of Peoples," p. 547, repeated nearly verbatim in Rawls, *The Law of Peoples*, p. 74.

5. Rawls, "The Law of Peoples," pp. 546–47. The first phrase is repeated nearly verbatim in Rawls, *The Law of Peoples*, p. 74, while the second remains implicit in what he says on p. 72, where he claims that such rights belong to groups, not individuals.

6. Rawls, "The Law of Peoples," p. 547. As we will see in the next section, this standard gets materially changed in *The Law of Peoples*.

7. See Rawls, "The Law of Peoples," pp. 558–59, where he defends and elaborates on the principle, but does not list it on p. 540. He does list it, however, in *The Law of Peoples*, p. 37, as the eighth principle.

8. Rawls, *The Law of Peoples*, p. 4. Technically, this would seem to imply that there is a minimal right to political participation, but since this only clarifies what Rawls apparently took to be present in the original article, I classify it here as nonsubstantive.

9. Rawls, "The Law of Peoples," p. 547, emphasis added.

10. Rawls, *The Law of Peoples*, p. 74, emphasis added.

11. Rawls, *The Law of Peoples*, p. 64, emphasis added.

12. Rawls, *The Law of Peoples*, pp. 75–76.

13. Rawls, *The Law of Peoples*, p. 76.

14. Rawls, *The Law of Peoples*, pp. 9, 110.

15. Rawls, *The Law of Peoples*, p. 110.

16. Rawls, *The Law of Peoples*, p. 111.

17. The worry is similar to Rawls's worry in *A Theory of Justice* that utilitarianism provides an unacceptably contingent basis for securing basic rights and liberties.

18. Ronald Dworkin, *Law's Empire* (Cambridge, MA: Harvard University Press, 1986), pp. 178–84.

19. Dworkin, *Law's Empire*, p. 178.

20. Rawls, *The Law of Peoples*, p. 71.

21. Rawls, *The Law of Peoples*, p. 71.

22. Rawls, *The Law of Peoples*, p. 72.

23. Rawls, *The Law of Peoples*, pp. 71–72.

24. Rawls, *The Law of Peoples*, p. 72.

25. Michael Blake, *Justice & Foreign Policy* (New York: Oxford University Press, 2013), pp. 52–59.

26. Blake, *Justice & Foreign Policy*, p. 55.

27. Blake, *Justice & Foreign Policy*, p. 57.

28. Blake, *Justice & Foreign Policy*, p. 58.

29. Rawls, *The Law of Peoples*, p. 61, emphasis in original.

30. Rawls, *The Law of Peoples*, p. 74.

31. I say "almost" because having the freedom—or liberty right—to enter a liberal society does not strictly entail having an entitlement—or claim right—to such entry. But since the liberty would be of no value without the claim, one might plausibly interpret Rawls (or, alternatively, the best Rawlsian view) as being committed to the latter.

32. Blake, *Justice & Foreign Policy*, pp. 4, 6.

33. Rawls, *The Law of Peoples*, p. 67.

34. See, for instance, Charles Beitz, "Rawls's Law of Peoples," *Ethics* 110, no. 4 (July 2000), pp. 66–96; Simon Caney, "Cosmopolitanism and the Law of Peoples," *Journal of Political Philosophy* 10, no. 1 (2002): 95–123; Darrel Moellendorf, "Constructing the Law of Peoples," p. 143; and Thomas Pogge, "Rawls on International Justice," *Philosophical Quarterly* 51, no. 203 (April 2001): 246–53.

35. See, for instance, Buchanan, "Rawls's Law of Peoples: Rules for a Vanished Westphalian World," pp. 697–721; and Pogge, "Rawls on International Justice," pp. 246–53.

FOUR

The Communitarian Concession

Why did Rawls use collective agents in his international contract when he could have defended basic human rights without these problems by using individuals instead? If we can identify his underlying motivation, perhaps we can find a better way of accommodating it—one that avoids the idle-contract objection. The answer, I will argue, lies in a concession he makes to his communitarian critics.[1]

Starting in the late 1970s, liberalism in general, and Rawls's version of it in particular, faced criticisms that came to be known, collectively, as the *communitarian critique of liberalism*. Charging that Rawls (and liberalism more generally) misconceives the relation between individuals and their communal attachments, the chief proponents of this critique—Charles Taylor, Alasdair MacIntyre, Michael Sandel, and Michael Walzer—allege that Rawls's defense of liberalism fails as a result.

4.1 THE CRITIQUE OPPOSED

Perhaps their best-known criticism is that, by making justice depend on the choice of agents who know nothing about their particular attachments or ends, Rawls implausibly relies on a conception of the self that is prior to them all. Our ends, Rawls seems to imply (implausibly in their view), are instead all freely chosen—including the communities to which we belong—even our political society. Atomism, as Taylor calls this conception of the self at the heart of liberal political theory, asserts that "society [is] constituted by individuals for the fulfillment of ends which [are] primarily individual."[2] Whatever ends we have are ours by individual choice; whatever communities we belong to are ours through individual consent. As individual rights to choose are primary, there is no corresponding obligation to belong to or sustain society. Belonging to society, then, is optional: it exists solely as an instrument for fulfilling our chosen ends, and we can decline to join if we decide that we can do better without it. Atomism, therefore, Taylor concludes, "affirms the self-sufficiency of man alone."[3] Since the parties to Rawls's social contract have no ends, communal or otherwise, that they must have, and gain what ends they do have, after the veil is lifted, through their individual choice and consent, Rawls—Taylor seems to suggest—presupposes this atomistic conception of the self and the self-sufficient individual.

However, this atomistic conception of the self, Taylor argues, is incoherent. In asserting rights to choose our ends, he claims, we must presuppose "the worth of certain capacities without which [the assertion] would not make sense"—in particular, the capacity to make meaningful choices.[4] According to atomism, then, it cannot be a matter of indifference whether these capacities get developed or waste away. Therefore, if we can show "that men [are] not self-sufficient," meaning "that they [cannot] develop their characteristically human potentialities"—like the capacity to make meaningful choices—"outside of society or certain kinds of society," then, Taylor argues, atomism can be undermined.[5] Since that capacity requires for its fullest development not merely the family but an entire civilization with its achievements in art, science, philosophy, theology, politics, and other fields, atomism is undermined.[6]

Just as Taylor rejects this atomistic conception of the self, so too does MacIntyre reject the conception of the self as freely chosen. Like Taylor, MacIntyre claims that, for Rawls, "I am what I myself choose to be. I can always, if I wish to, put in question what are taken to be the merely contingent social features of my existence."[7] As a result, "[i]ndividuals are . . . primary and society secondary, and the identification of individual interests is prior to, and independent of, the construction of any moral or social bonds between them," just as Taylor too objects.[8] Rather than regard the self as freely chosen, however, it would be more plausible, he argues, to hold a conception of the self as "a narrative which links birth to life to death as narrative beginning to middle to end," for making sense of any action requires placing it in an ongoing narrative.[9] Even a simple action like gardening, he explains, depends for its explanation on the narrative to which it belongs. Did the agent garden for exercise, to please his spouse, or to save money on vegetables? The construction of that narrative, though, is not up to the agent alone, because we live our lives in relationships with others. Therefore, "we are never more (and sometimes less) than the co-authors of our own narratives" and as a result "we are always under certain constraints. We enter upon a stage which we did not design and we find ourselves part of an action that was not of our making."[10]

Not only does Rawls's conception of the self seems to deny this fact, claims MacIntyre. It compounds that fault by identifying individuals' interests prior to and independently of their given social and communal bonds. "I am a citizen of this or that city . . . I belong to this clan, that tribe, this nation. Hence," MacIntyre argues, "what is good for me has to be the good for one who inhabits these roles. . . . These constitute the given of my life, my moral starting point."[11] By placing conceptions of the good behind the veil of ignorance, though, Rawls implausibly denies this starting point.

Like Taylor and MacIntyre, Sandel objects to Rawls's conception of the self. Whereas Taylor emphasizes its lack of self-sufficiency, and MacIntyre its lack of narrative unity, Sandel stresses its shallowness—its lack of moral depth. Rawls's placement of conceptions of the good behind the veil of ignorance, Sandel argues, commits him to the priority of the self over its ends: "To identify any set of characteristics as *my* aims, ambitions, desires, and so on, is always to imply some subject 'me' standing behind them, and the shape of this 'me' must be given prior to any of the ends or attributes I bear."[12] But this conception of the self is implausible, he maintains, because under it, "No commitment could grip me so deeply that I could not understand myself without it. . . . No project could be so essential that turning away from it would call into question the person I am."[13] As a result, "It rules out the possibility of any attachment (or obsession) able to reach beyond our values and sentiments to engage our identity itself."[14] In particular, it rules out *un*chosen communal attachments that reach our identity—as members of a family, a people, or a republic, for example—loyalties and convictions without which many of us cannot even begin to understand ourselves. "The good of community," he insists, "cannot reach *that* far" on the Rawlsian conception of the self.[15] "To imagine a person incapable of constitutive attachments such as these," however, Sandel argues, "is not to conceive an ideally free and rational agent, but to imagine a person wholly without character, without moral depth."[16]

In each case, the objection is the same: whether it lacks self-sufficiency, narrative unity, or moral depth, Rawls's conception of the self fails to accurately represent our motivation as moral agents. In making justice depend on the choice of such agents, therefore, their choice cannot be binding on agents like us.

Denying that his domestic contract presupposes a metaphysical view of the self, Rawls rejects the criticism. Placing the ends and attributes of the parties behind the veil of ignorance, he claims, is not meant to represent a metaphysical view of the self. Rather, it is meant to model "what we regard . . . as fair conditions" under which we, using the parties as our representatives, "are to specify the terms of social cooperation."[17] In *A Theory of Justice*, he characterizes these conditions as restrictions on the reasons available to the parties, such as the restriction that no one should be able to tailor principles to his or her own advantage, or that no one should be disadvantaged by natural fortune or social circumstances.[18] In *Political Liberalism*, he makes explicit that these restrictions also preclude the parties from using "the fact that we affirm a particular . . . conception of the good" as "a reason . . . to propose, or to expect others to accept, a conception of justice that favors those of that persuasion."[19] Modeling these convictions, he argues, requires depriving the parties in the original position of knowledge of their natural assets, social position, and ends or conception of the good. It need not presuppose a metaphysical view of the self, or conception of human nature. To emphasize this fact, Rawls claims that the conception of the person represented by the parties to his domestic contract is "political not metaphysical"—that their interests, motivations, knowledge, and attributes are determined only by our theoretical needs in addressing questions of political justice.

If Rawls concedes nothing to this first communitarian criticism, he concedes nothing significant to the inferences drawn from it, considered independently, either. If our individual lives are best seen as quests for narrative unity, as MacIntyre suggests, for example, then we must have a purpose or telos, since a quest cannot even begin without one.[20] An individual's good, then, consists in part in fulfilling that purpose. By extension, a shared commitment to a purpose or telos, and the virtues that help sustain it, create a different kind of good, the good of community, and an individual's good consists in part in fulfilling that shared purpose. Without this shared commitment, by contrast, we have an impoverished community—one where our moral disagreements become unresolvable[21] and our social tradition fragments.[22] Justice, MacIntyre implies, consists in pursuing and fulfilling this shared telos and the virtues that comprise it.

Considered independently, the claim that justice requires sharing a telos and the virtues that comprise it seems to assume that the two must combine—an assumption Rawls denies. We can share virtues that are instrumentally valuable for sustaining a just society, Rawls agrees—virtues like tolerance, civility, fairness, and reasonableness.[23] Sharing such virtues, however, Rawls argues, does not require sharing a telos. It only requires sharing principles of justice, which we can defend without appealing to a shared telos as a premise.

Calling such a telos a *comprehensive doctrine*—a scheme of values, virtues, and ideals of character that apply to personal and political relations[24]—and defining *freestanding* principles as ones that are developed independently of such doctrines[25] and neutral in aim between them,[26] Rawls insists that, in a society regulated by such freestanding principles, individuals can still enjoy the good of political community.[27] "While it is true that they do not affirm the same comprehensive doctrine," he maintains, "they do affirm the same political conception of justice; and this means that they share one very basic political end . . . the end of supporting just institutions and of giving one another justice." A political society regulated by freestanding principles, therefore, he suggests, need not be an impoverished community.

In contrast with MacIntyre, who infers the need to base justice on a shared telos from his denial of Rawls's conception of the self, Taylor infers an obligation to belong to society.[28] Considered independently of that inference, however, the claim that we have an obligation to belong to society is never one Rawls denies. Stipulating that society is "a closed system isolated from other societies"[29] for the purpose of bracketing problems of international justice and focusing on domestic justice alone, Rawls takes this to imply that we already *do* belong. So the question whether *to* belong does not even arise. Rawls's principles are principles for *citizens*: those who already are members. Similarly, Rawls concurs that we have an obligation to sustain society as well: we have a natural duty of justice to support and further just institutions (including our own).[30] If Rawls concedes nothing significant to Taylor, then, it is because there is nothing for him to concede.

So Rawls concedes nothing of significance to Taylor, MacIntyre, and Sandel. He denies the conception of the self that they attribute to him. He denies that justice requires sharing a telos. He already allows that we have an obligation to belong to society. He already concurs that we have a duty to sustain it. While he acknowledges that we can share virtues that are instrumental for achieving justice, he denies that their justification depends on our sharing a telos or comprehensive doctrine. Rawls's communitarian concession is not to Taylor, MacIntyre, or Sandel. His concession is to Walzer.

4.2 THE CRITIQUE ACCEPTED

Like Taylor, MacIntyre, and Sandel, Walzer claims that Rawls misconceives the relationship between individuals and their communal attachments or ends. Rather than locating this misconception in some feature of the self, however, Walzer places it in the relationship between individuals and their communal norms: their principles, their social meanings, their shared understandings.

In a series of arresting images, Walzer likens the pursuit of traditional moral philosophy to either an *owl at dusk*, who, following the path of discovery, seeks a moral truth that exists independently of us, or to an *eagle at daybreak*, who, denying that there is any such truth to discover, follows the path of invention in creating morality to fill that void.[31] The owl at dusk brings back God's word or describes the law of nature. The eagle at daybreak, by contrast, "invent[s] the moral world that would have existed if a moral world had existed without [his or her] inventing it."[32] Since Rawls's principles issue from an exercise of pure procedural justice, Rawls, Walzer suggests, is one of our eagles.

However the path of invention, like the path of discovery, Walzer claims, rarely produces anything novel. "[T]he moralities we discover and invent always turn out, and always will turn out, remarkably similar to the morality we already have."[33] Our discoveries are "familiar and well-thumbed by now"—they are "there because they are really here, features of ordinary life."[34] Our inventions, similarly, build upon a morality whose value we acknowledge and already share.[35] Whatever morality we discover or invent, moreover, requires interpretation: it "gives rise immediately to arguments about the meaning of what has been accepted."[36] Like a lawyer or judge, then, who "struggles to find meaning in a morass of conflicting laws and precedents," the philosopher must ultimately seek meaning from a morass of moral principles—ones already in the community's common possession.[37] Since "discovery and invention . . . are disguised interpretations," and since what we discover or invent requires interpretation, "there is really only one path in moral philosophy," Walzer concludes: the path of interpretation.[38]

Taking the path of interpretation requires something to interpret, though, and in the case of justice we interpret *social meanings*—our shared understandings of the goods to be distributed and their value—goods like membership, security, welfare, money, office, free time, education, and the like. "A given society is just," Walzer asserts, "if its substantive life is lived . . . in a way faithful to the shared understandings of the members."[39] Since different societies may possess different shared understandings, they may likewise possess different principles. "Justice," he acknowledges, "is relative to social meanings,"[40] and "[e]very substantive account of distributive justice is a local account."[41] Even within each locality, there may be shifts in understandings over time: "The social world will one day look different from the way it does today, and distributive justice will take on a different character" as a result.[42]

Aware that such talk invites the charge of relativism, Walzer defends himself against the most common objection to that view: that it lacks the resources for criticizing social meanings that seem intuitively unjust or oppressive. Acknowledging that "[s]ocial meanings need not be harmonious,"[43] Walzer, citing Marx and Gramsci, observes that "every ruling class is compelled to present itself as a universal class," which enables radical critics to exploit tensions in the dominant ideology.[44] Challenging the relative weights of its principles, radical critics can subvert that ideology by reversing them, making primary what was previously secondary. In societies that pay lip service to an ideal of equality (as a nod by the ruling class to lower-class aspirations), for example, "The critic exploits the larger meanings of equality, which are more mocked than mirrored in everyday experience."[45]

The detachment promised by discovery or invention, therefore, is not necessary for radical criticism, according to Walzer. Rather than employing terms incomprehensible to the natives (as, say, a missionary might do in challenging local customs),[46] our critics ought to be *connected* critics—members of the society, who consult its own moral understandings, while filtering them for advantage. "Criticism," Walzer claims, "does not require us to step back from society as a whole but only to step away from certain sorts of power relationships within society. It is not connection but authority and domination from which we must distance ourselves."[47] At its best, then, criticism is just like revolution: an inside job.[48]

However we regard Walzer's views, Rawls appears persuaded by them. Disavowing the impression that he was following the path of invention, Rawls repositions himself as a connected critic interested in interpreting the fundamental ideas and principles of his own society.

Rawls surely invites the impression that he was following the path of invention. In *A Theory of Justice,* he claims that "[t]he idea of the original position is to set up a fair procedure so that any principles agreed to will be just. The aim is to use the notion of pure procedural justice as a basis of theory."[49] In later writings, he claims that "[t]he parties in the original position do not agree on what the moral facts are, as if there already were such facts. . . . Rather (for constructivism), there is no such order . . . the facts are identified by the principles that result."[50] Finally, in *Political Liberalism,* even he admits that *A Theory of Justice* "regards justice as fairness as [a] comprehensive doctrine,"[51] which, he then suggests, makes it seem like it contains "a transcendent element not admitting of compromise,"[52] as so many other comprehensive doctrines do, in virtue of their claims to universal truth.[53] If the aspiration for universal truth marks the abandonment of local interpretation, then Rawls cannot claim the mantle of connected critic. Given the other options (invention and discovery), one would naturally settle on reading him as attempting to invent justice anew.

In response, Rawls defends a new reading of justice as fairness. In order to justify the features of the original position, he appeals to "certain fundamental ideas . . . implicit in the public political culture" *of his own society*—essentially denying the link between pure procedural justice and invention, and implying its compatibility with connected criticism.[54]

Accordingly, Rawls concedes that "justice as fairness is framed to apply [only] to . . . a modern constitutional [liberal] democracy," and therefore whether it "can be extended to . . . different kinds of societies existing under different historical and social conditions" is an "altogether separate" question.[55] He accepts, in other words, Walzer's contention that "[e]very substantive account of distributive justice is a local account."[56] Since it applies only to liberal democracies, moreover, "it tries to draw solely upon basic intuitive ideas that are embedded in the political institutions of a constitutional democratic regime and the public traditions of their interpretation."[57] By "looking to the public culture itself as the shared fund of implicitly recognized basic ideas and principles"[58] and "start[ing] within the tradition of democratic thought,"[59] Rawls also appears to accept Walzer's contention that the philosopher's role is to interpret the shared understandings of the society to which those principles apply. "Since justification is addressed to others," he reflects, in a moment that seems to capture Walzer's underlying motivation, "it proceeds from what is, or can be, held in *common*" (my emphasis).[60]

If Rawls positions himself as a connected critic responsible for interpreting his society's shared understandings, he also inherits the burden of showing that they hold the resources for serious self-criticism. For Rawls, the fact that liberal societies contain a "deep disagreement . . . as to how the values of liberty and equality are best realized in the basic structure of society" provides just that occasion.[61] Libertarian liberalism, he argues, fails because it misconstrues equality of opportunity as merely formal rather than fair—a claim that recalls Walzer's insistence that critics should expose where "the larger meanings of equality . . . are more mocked than mirrored in everyday experience."[62] Utilitarianism, by contrast, misconstrues the basis of liberty. Far from supporting individual liberty, its aggregative methodology, he argues, gives it an insecure foundation. The sovereignty of the individual over his own body and mind, so cherished by Mill, gets threatened as it conflates all persons into one. "Utilitarianism does not take seriously the distinction between persons."[63] Where libertarianism upholds liberty at the expense of equality, utilitarianism, he seems to suggest, upholds equality ("each to count for one and no one for more than one") at the expense of liberty. We should read *A Theory of Justice*, then, Rawls seems to imply, as aiming to subvert both forms of liberalism from within, utilizing the very values (liberty and equality) shared by members of liberal societies themselves.

By far Rawls's biggest inside job, though, occurs in his later writings, when he applies liberalism's own principle of toleration to philosophy itself.[64] Not only should toleration apply to adherents of different faiths under liberal institutions, he argues. It should apply to the way in which we justify those institutions, too. So instead of promoting autonomy as an ideal that should govern all of life, and defending liberal institutions as what it requires politically, Rawls insists that liberal institutions ought to be compatible with a more capacious range of ideals—even ones that reject autonomy. As a result, he seeks to defend such institutions without relying on autonomy or any other ideal or comprehensive doctrine. As a connected critic, then, Rawls does try to exploit the larger meanings of equality, liberty, and toleration so as to demonstrate their critical potential—just as Walzer recommends.

Whether or not Rawls succeeds (or goes far enough for Walzer as a "liberal revolutionary"), Rawls does appear to accept Walzer's view that the justification for each society's principles of justice ultimately rests on the shared understandings of that particular political community. This apparent concession to Walzer immediately raises two questions of relevance for any attempt to develop a law of peoples. First, if political communities without liberal traditions might legitimately have different principles of justice—ones faithful to their own traditions—what principles might they legitimately have? Second, if we want to justify principles of international justice, what are the shared understandings from which they must derive?

For Rawls, the answer to the first question depends on the answer to the second. The range of eligible principles for nonliberal societies depends on what the principles of international justice allow. To find what they allow, though, will first require us to identify our shared international understandings—then derive the principles.

4.3 THE DOMESTIC PRECEDENT AND ITS INTERNATIONAL IMPLICATIONS

Reformulating the communitarian criticisms, Will Kymlicka and David Miller, each using a different strategy, identify a value that liberal and nonliberal political communities alike can share: the ethical significance of *nationality*.

When they suggest that some ties seem so inescapable to us that we cannot imagine ourselves without them, communitarians, Kymlicka argues, overstate their point. First, they do not seem to maintain that view consistently. MacIntyre admits that our participation in communal roles "does not entail that the self has to accept the moral *limitations* of the particularity of those forms of community."[65] Similarly, Sandel insists that "the subject is empowered to participate in the constitution of its identity."[66] Even they seem to admit, in other words, that we can stand back from and reassess our communal ends—and that we ought to at times. Second, given this, communitarians would be committed to the liberal freedoms needed for the reassessment.[67]

Although they often overstate the strength of the connection between our selves and our communal ends or attachments, communitarians nonetheless contribute an important insight, he claims, that liberalism should accept. It is not the alleged fixity of some of our ends that liberalism mistakenly fails to acknowledge. Rather, it is the importance of having a stable cultural community for the ability to exercise meaningful choices and to evaluate our ends—activities whose worth liberalism must presuppose.

Liberalism must presuppose the worth of these activities, Kymlicka argues, because otherwise, some central liberal freedoms—freedom of speech, liberty of conscience, and so on—would make no sense. These are precisely the rights that enable us to examine various ways of life and then to choose that which seems to us best.[68] Rawls in particular must presuppose their worth. "Rawls believes that the freedom to form and revise our beliefs about value," Kymlicka claims, "is a crucial precondition for pursuing our essential interest in leading a good life."[69] Our current beliefs might be mistaken, of course, and because they "underlie the most important decisions we make in life . . . we care whether these beliefs are true or false."[70] Yet despite the fact that they could be mistaken, it does not follow that others should decide them for us. We must lead our lives, as Kymlicka says, "from the inside" in order to live a life that is good in fact.[71] For these reasons, Rawls embraces "guarantees of personal independence (secured by the liberties of citizenship) needed to make such decisions freely."[72]

However, while liberalism in general and Rawls in particular presuppose the worth of these activities, Kymlicka argues, they both tend to ignore the importance of having a stable cultural community in order to engage in them. It is not as if we start *de novo* in deciding how to lead our lives, Kymlicka insists. Rather, as Rawls observes, we examine "definite ideals and forms of life that have been developed and tested by innumerable individuals, sometimes for generations."[73] Because *this* range of options cannot be chosen, our decisions, Kymlicka claims, are "always a matter of selecting what we believe to be most valuable from the various options available, selecting from a context of choice which provides us with different ways of life."[74] This context of choice is provided by our cultural heritage.[75]

In the stories we hear, we learn about potential role models. As we grow up, we learn about the forms of life (familial, religious, sexual, educational) in which we participate. We also encounter alternative forms of life that we may come later to endorse. "We decide how to lead our lives by situating ourselves in these cultural narratives, by adopting roles that have struck us as worthwhile ones," claims Kymlicka.[76] Only through a secure cultural structure can people "become aware, in a vivid way, of the options available to them, and intelligently examine their value."[77] A stable cultural community, therefore, he concludes, "is a good in its capacity of providing meaningful options for us, and aiding our ability to judge for ourselves the value of our life-plans."[78]

Recognizing that the term *culture* can describe any group from street gangs to a global civilization, Kymlicka claims that the kind of group whose stability counts is a *societal* culture, which he defines as a culture that "provides its members with meaningful ways of life across the full range of human activities, including social, educational, religious, recreational, and economic life, encompassing both public and private spheres."[79] It tends "to be territorially concentrated, and based on a shared language.[80] It also tends to be institutionally embodied, particularly in the schools and government. Given these characteristics, a societal culture, he claims, is roughly synonymous with what we call a *nation* or a *peoples*.[81]

Given the conditions of the modern world, with its pressures toward linguistic conformity and ability to break open native lands for settlement, a nation can find itself a dwindling minority in its own traditional land, its language and history increasingly marginalized, displaced by the majority's in the schools and government, eroding its ability to transmit them to the next generation, until its assimilation is finally complete.[82] Rather than succumbing to these assimilationist pressures, though, and their perceived reduced opportunities, members of minority nations, desiring to preserve their culture and institutions, often resist them.[83] Since nations are the entities with the "capacity and motivation to form and maintain such a distinct culture" in the face of these pressures, it is the stability of these cultures, these societal cultures, that liberalism requires if the exercise of some central liberal freedoms is to be meaningful.[84]

Whatever we think of the merits of this argument, Kymlicka's goal is clear: to defend the ethical significance of nationality within a broadly liberal individualist framework. He seeks to vindicate the importance to *individual* freedom of belonging to a secure societal culture or *nation*. Of all the communitarians, Taylor comes closest to this idea when he suggests that our capacity to make meaningful choices requires us to belong to or to sustain a certain kind of society. Unlike the communitarians, though, Kymlicka denies that having a stable national culture requires sharing a telos or comprehensive doctrine and asserts that it is compatible with revising our ends.

Like Kymlicka, Miller defends the ethical significance of nationality, but whereas Kymlicka defends its instrumental value for promoting individual freedom, Miller defends its value *as such*. For Miller, the value of nationality is neither derivative nor instrumental: its value is fundamental.

Echoing Sandel's claim that Rawlsian liberalism rests on an implausible view of the self as prior to its ends, Miller rejects considering the moral subject "as an abstract individual, possessed of the general powers and capacities of human beings . . . but not fundamentally committed to any particular persons, groups, practices, institutions, and so forth."[85] Instead he regards the subject "as partly defined by its relationships," so that, "[t]o divest oneself of such commitments would be, in one important sense, to change one's identity"[86]—a claim that recalls Sandel's insistence that some of our attachments are "able to reach beyond our values and sentiments to engage our identity itself."[87] If so, then it becomes possible, Miller argues, for us "to regard as a constituent of personal identity [even] our unchosen membership [in] an historical community"—like a nation.[88]

Not only is it possible for us to regard these unchosen ties as constituents of our identity, he argues, it is rationally defensible for us to do so too. Unlike *ethical universalism*, which claims that all ethical principles are universal in form—so that particular attachments, like attachments to one's colleague or country, are justifiable only derivatively, through acts of voluntary choice, for instance, or perhaps as useful conventions for fulfilling natural duties[89]—*ethical particularism* holds that "agents are already encumbered with [particular] ties and may *begin* their ethical reasoning from such commitments" (my emphasis).[90] Whereas particular "facts like 'he is my brother' cannot count at the basic level for determining my duties to him" under ethical universalism, they can under ethical particularism.[91] The same holds for national attachments. If ethical particularism is plausible, therefore, then our attachments to our conationals and our nation will be justifiable—and the value of nationality vindicated—without needing to derive their value from liberal individualism or any other universal ethical principle or value.

Compared with universalism, though, particularism, Miller argues, gives a more plausible account of moral agency and motivation. Consider agency. According to universalism, "we discover what our duties are by abstract reflection on the human condition . . . for instance, having decided that the basis of ethics is the general happiness, we resolve to act according to those rules of conduct that are best calculated to promote that objective."[92] However, this seems to imply that "[n]o considerations about who I am, where I have come from, or which communities I see myself as attached to are to be allowed to influence my ethical reasoning"—essentially "driving a wedge between ethical duty and personal identity."[93] Under particularism, by contrast, such considerations are allowed to influence our ethical reasoning. Summing up the problem that he sees with universalism, Miller asks (rhetorically): "If the theory embodies a view of the subject which is far removed from people's actual experience of agency, what claims can it make on them? Why should they accept its interpretation of rationality?"[94]

Just as particularism offers a more plausible account of moral agency, so too, he contends, does it provide a more plausible account of moral motivation. Under universalism, "I am supposed to act simply out of a rational conviction that I am doing what morality requires of me."[95] However, "it seems unlikely that rational conviction can carry the weight required of it" for most ordinary individuals.[96] Under particularism, by contrast, we can accommodate natural sentiments toward the objects of our attachments, enabling us to rely on a richer, more diverse, more realistic combination of motives to obtain compliance with what morality requires.[97]

Far from insulating our unchosen identities from rational scrutiny, moreover, particularism does enable us to reflect on and revise them. Without appealing to universal principles, we can consider them on their own terms, deciding how to integrate them with others that we bear.[98] "If one is born a Jew," Miller illustrates, "there is a sense in which one has no option but to be the bearer of a Jewish identity in one form or another."[99] But the form that this identity takes—whether to be practicing or nonpracticing, orthodox or liberal, how to integrate it with our other chosen and unchosen commitments, and whether to make it central or peripheral to our overall identity—can be worked out by us even if there is no single answer at which we must all arrive.

Since particularism offers more plausible accounts of moral agency and motivation, and since, contrary to what universalists allege, particularism does enable us to reflect on our unchosen identities, Miller concludes that it is more plausible overall. Given this, our particular attachments, including our attachments to our conationals and our nation, will hold ethical significance even if they are unchosen—and their significance will be fundamental rather than derivative or instrumental.

Having reformulated the communitarian criticisms, Kymlicka and Miller provide Rawls with a candidate capable of linking liberal and nonliberal political communities together—an area of commonality between them—an understanding (as Walzer might say) that they share. What they share is an agreement on the value of national groups, a collective agent. For Kymlicka, that value is grounded in liberal individualism. For Miller, by contrast, it is consistent with its rejection and compatible with the view that the group, the collective agent, possesses value as such. Regardless of which strategy for defending the value of national groups is stronger, members of liberal and nonliberal political communities alike can affirm their value—just as Rawls believes that adherents of different comprehensive doctrines can affirm the features of his domestic contract. Accordingly, Rawls's concession to Walzer in *Political Liberalism* creates a precedent for *The Law of Peoples* that finds expression in Rawls's use of collective agents. Call this reliance on collective agents *the communitarian concession*.

4.4 THE CONCESSION AND ITS AFTERMATH

So the communitarian concession offers a plausible explanation for Rawls's reliance on collective agents. Rawls was hardly unaware of these intellectual cross-currents, plus they give him a suitable candidate for his argumentative needs. While we are not necessarily bound to it in developing the best Rawlsian view, we should endorse it nonetheless, for its significance endures. If Kymlicka and Miller, writing before and during the composition of *The Law of Peoples*, can be credited with influencing Rawls's views, then the recent work of Alan Patten and Michael Walzer, writing afterward, demonstrate the continuing significance of nationality as a plausible candidate linking liberal and nonliberal political communities.

Like Kymlicka, Patten defends the ethical significance of nationality within a broadly liberal individualist framework. But whereas Kymlicka limits minority rights to groups that have viable societal cultures, Patten argues that they should apply more widely.[100] Patten also challenges Kymlicka on two further fronts. First, where Kymlicka rests his position on the claim that a stable context of choice provides us with meaningful options, Patten denies that this claim, even if true, supports minority rights.[101] Second, where Kymlicka insists that no state can be completely neutral when it comes to culture, Patten counters that this claim rests on an implausible conception of neutrality.[102] Confronted by what he regards as liabilities in Kymlicka's view, Patten tries to rehabilitate the liberal case for minority cultural rights—which the equal treatment of minority cultures, he argues, requires.

Even if a stable context of choice provides us with meaningful options, Patten claims, it does not follow that the loss of one's culture is an injustice. Only if its loss leaves one with less access to an adequate range of options, or if the options one has access to are inadequate, he maintains, would its loss constitute an injustice. However, it does not necessarily follow from the loss of one's culture that one will have less access to an adequate range of options. Assuming that the dominant culture provides an adequate range of options, one could still integrate into the dominant culture. Given this possibility, the loss of one's culture is "insufficient to show why the state ought to extend cultural rights to vulnerable cultures rather than more fully integrating [their members] into the dominant culture."[103] Even if one were to regard the dominant culture's options as inadequate, Patten claims, their subjective inadequacy for minority group members does not necessarily give rise to an injustice either. Instead, "it may well be the case that the danger of cultural loss arises because of others exercising their rights, or because others use the resources to which they are legitimately entitled in certain ways."[104] Accordingly, Patten concludes that, "[r]ather than try to ground the case for cultural rights directly in some account of the badness of cultural loss, [we should] develop an account of the fair treatment of cultures."[105]

What makes a culture valuable, he argues, is not the options that it provides, but rather its strong connection with *individual self-determination*. Individual self-determination is valuable because, "[a]s a general matter, valuable goods and activities do not make a person's life go better unless those goods and activities figure in some positive way in the person's conception of the good"—that is, from the agent's own perspective.[106] Individual self-determination (roughly, autonomy) is also often regarded as valuable for its own sake.[107] Finally, certain special commitments in a person's conception of the good render self-determination valuable toward those commitments—these are commitments that play a pivotal role in a person's system of ends, or that have a nonnegotiable character in the agent's eyes, or whose acknowledgement and recognition by others possesses great social salience (Patten mentions marriage as an example).[108] "When a preference occupies a pivotal role in a person's conception of the good, or when it has a nonnegotiable character, or when it is salient to the individual's enjoyment of the recognition and respect of others," he explains, "then there is reason to think that the individual has a particularly strong interest in being able to fulfill that aspect of her conception of the good."[109] While religious convictions, for example, often fill this role, it is not limited to them. Since the cultural aspects of a person's conception of the good often possess these features, he concludes, culture itself is valuable for this reason. While "[a] culture is not a conception of the good . . . [and while] cultures are not defined by shared conceptions of the good, their disappearance matters because of the impact on members who have particular conceptions of the good."[110]

Similarly, even if no state can be completely neutral when it comes to culture—its official language, boundaries, school curriculum, public holidays and symbols inevitably favor some particular cultures over others—this kind of neutrality violation, he argues, does not constitute injustice. This kind of neutrality violation assumes that neutrality requires neutrality of *effects*: that the policies that the state adopts must leave different ways of life more or less equally successful, judged by their popularity or the ease with which citizens can pursue them.[111] However, this conception of neutrality is implausible, he insists, for *all* policies have nonneutral effects. "Policies that seek to establish a fair distribution of material resources"—to take one example—"make it relatively harder for people with expensive tastes to realize the ways of life they value."[112] Rather than conferring greater resources upon those with expensive tastes so that they can be as successful in their pursuits as those with cheaper tastes are in theirs, justice instead regards those with expensive tastes as responsible for adjusting their own conceptions of the good in light of fair background conditions.[113]

If the case for cultural rights must be justified, not by the loss of options when a culture dies, but by the fair treatment of cultures, and the fair treatment of cultures requires a form of liberal neutrality other than neutrality of effects, then the form that liberal neutrality should take, Patten argues, is that of neutral *treatment*. "If the basic idea of neutrality of effects is to equalize across outputs of the policy process," he claims, "the idea of neutrality of treatment is to equalize across the state's inputs." More precisely, "The state violates this requirement when, relative to an appropriate baseline, its policies are more accommodating of some conceptions of the good than they are of others."[114] *Accommodations* are "customized . . . to fit specific features" of a conception of the good that are "identity-related"—that express a group identification that the agent values—and play a pivotal role in a person's system of ends, have a nonnegotiable character in the agent's eyes, or whose acknowledgement and recognition by others possesses great social salience.[115] Given the importance of one's culture for pursuing one's conception of the good, it follows, he argues, that when the state accommodates the majority culture alone (recognizes its language alone officially, tailors public holidays and the school curriculum to it alone, etc.), it violates neutral treatment. And since public institutions *must* operate in a particular cultural format (they must choose an official language, have an official calendar, etc.), accommodating *no* culture at all is not feasible. Neutral treatment, he concludes, therefore requires *equal* accommodation—or as Patten puts it, equal recognition—of minority cultures.[116] Although equal recognition does not imply that "groups [validly] claiming equal recognition [must] possess their own viable societal culture or national community" (since, for example, minority language rights may be validly claimed even in the absence of one), he insists that it is "compatible with an inclusive, 'multinational' form of belonging, which shares some characteristics with nationalism."[117] Nonetheless, neutral treatment does not guarantee cultural survival—and hence does not rest on neutrality of effects—for a given culture might still die through the choices of its members even when fair background conditions are present.[118]

Within a broadly liberal individualist framework, then, Patten, like Kymlicka, defends the ethical significance of nationality. Citizens' fundamental interests, on Patten's view, are their interests in *individual* self-determination—in the success of their conception of the good. Yet liberal neutrality requires the state to remain neutral among competing conceptions of the good. Since no state can remain neutral toward certain central aspects of citizens' conceptions of the good, liberal neutrality requires equal treatment of those aspects. Since those aspects include a citizen's culture, liberal neutrality requires equal treatment, or equal recognition, of minority cultures—and where viable societal cultures exist, of minority nations. Equal treatment requires customized, identity-related accommodations of them—whether through language rights, special rights of self-government, or recognition of their symbols, customs, or holidays. While such accommodations provide no guarantee that they will survive, they at least give them a fair chance.

Like Patten, Walzer defends the ethical significance of nationality, but whereas Patten defends its value for individual self-determination, Walzer defends its value for individuals and groups alike—and does it without treating the interests of groups as reducible to those of individuals.

Walzer examines the *paradox of liberation* and offers a solution to it. The paradox goes as follows. On the one hand, in order to liberate a peoples long oppressed by foreign rule, their nationalist liberators must first get them to cast off their old habits, especially their habits of deference and accommodation. On the other hand, the people often cherish their old ways. This is the paradox. As a result of it, when nationalist liberation movements occur that seek to create secular democratic states (as Walzer believes occurred in Algeria, Israel, and India), the revolutions tend not to stick—eventually, traditionalists, and especially religious traditionalists, stage a religious counterrevolution. Instead of repudiating the old ways, Walzer suggests, the nationalist liberation movements would have been more successful if they had engaged the traditionalist worldviews and negotiated terms that were more familiar to them.[119] If national liberation requires "some kind of religious reform," he claims, it also requires "the reform of liberation."[120]

Now we find in this brief sketch a combination of causal and normative claims. Walzer suggests that lack of engagement by militant liberators, who held secular, democratic ideals, with more traditional religious worldviews held by those whom they were seeking to liberate, contributed to social instability. He implies that, had they engaged with them, they would have been more likely to establish a more stable society (though he admits the counterrevolutions might not have been averted).[121] In addition, he seems to accept social stability as a value. Social stability, for Walzer, exerts some normative pull, even if the pull that it exerts is indeterminate between stability achieved through an overlapping consensus and stability achieved through a modus vivendi. Finally, Walzer appears to *recommend* the terms negotiated (or that would have been negotiated) between liberators and traditionalists, even if the terms vary from place to place.

In offering different visions for their nation, the liberators and traditionalists, I would like to suggest, propose competing conceptions of that nation—and in so doing, both accept the ethical significance of nationality even though they disagree. The liberators offer an individualist vision, the traditionalists offer a collective one, and the terms they negotiate strike a synthesis of the two.

For example, in characterizing the nationalist liberators, Walzer writes:

> All three of these national liberation movements claimed [however imperfectly they lived up to their claims] that they were going to create a democratic state and a just legal order. And in all three of them, democracy and justice were generally understood in standard, that is, European ways. . . . They imitated the values of the European Enlightenment, which are expressed in universal terms and which certainly set the militants against their own people's parochialism. They were nationalists who wanted their nations to measure up to principles established elsewhere.[122]

We see in this passage several familiar themes—the contrast between universalism and relativism ("parochialism"), the distinction between the morality of invention ("principles established elsewhere") and the morality of interpretation—with Walzer endorsing the second in each pair. Less readily apparent, perhaps, though just as important, is this. If we take "the values of the European Enlightenment" to include liberal democracy and individual human rights, then the suggestion that the nationalist liberators were advocating those values seems to imply that they were championing a liberal individualist conception of their nation.

By contrast, in characterizing the practices of the religious traditionalists, he notes that "[t]he old ways were sustained in temples, synagogues, and mosques, but also, and perhaps more importantly, in interpersonal relations, in families and in life-cycle celebrations."[123] These were places "where the sustaining behaviors were hardly visible to secular militants busily at work on the big project of modernization." They were practices that "connect[ed] the liberated people to their own past [and provided] a sense of belonging and stability in a rapidly changing world"[124]—in contrast with the "radical break with family and friends and with all forms of established authority" often urged by their nationalist liberators.[125] "The culture of liberation was apparently too thin to sustain these people," writes Walzer, "the newness was too artificial."[126] As a result, "after a couple of generations," after "uprooting" themselves in the liberationist struggle, they begin "willingly rerooting" themselves in their familiar, traditional groups. Ultimately,

> After a time, when national liberation has receded in memory, these traditionalists stage a counterrevolution: thus the rise of Islamic radicalism in Algeria (and in Palestine), of Hindutva in India, and of Jewish zealotry in Israel. The religious resurgence is a shock to the national liberation elites, who had grown complacent about the victory of newness.[127]

These religious traditionalists offer a competing vision. Unlike that of their religious counterparts in postrevolutionary America, theirs does not rest on an individualist, "Protestant sociology." "Radical individualism," Walzer notes, "made for separations, splits, and breakaways, and the eventual consequence of continual fissure was the denominational pluralism that distinguishes religion in America from the traditional orthodoxies of India, Israel, and Algeria."[128] Instead, Walzer implies, the religious traditionalists propose a competing conception of their nation in which the value of nationality rests on the value of their collective religious life.

Just as Kymlicka and Miller, then, provide Rawls with a candidate capable of linking liberal and nonliberal political communities together, so too do Patten and Walzer. For Patten, the value of national groups is grounded in liberal individualism, whereas for Walzer, it is consistent with liberal individualism, consistent with its rejection, and consistent with a synthesis of collective and individualist views. Regardless of which strategy for defending the value of national groups is best, members of liberal and nonliberal political communities alike can affirm their value.[129] If Kymlicka and Miller initially provide Rawls with the candidate, Patten and Walzer demonstrate its continuing vitality as the basis for Rawls's communitarian concession.

4.5 THE CONCESSION MODELED

From this concession, it does not follow that these collective agents ought to be parties to the international contract, as there may be other ways of modeling the ethical significance of nationality. However, the more obvious alternatives seem less attractive. For instance, were he to place knowledge of one's nationality behind the veil of ignorance, he would be misconstruing its value according to Kymlicka and Miller, for, despite their differences, they agree that nationality is not an object of choice but either its precondition (Kymlicka) or an unchosen constituent of identity (Miller). Alternatively, were he to allow the parties to know their nationality, it would raise the question of whether there are other, group-based, unchosen constituents of identity (to family, tribe, religion, etc.) that they ought to know as well. If so, it would quickly convert Rawls's communitarian concession into a full-scale capitulation instead. More importantly, on either horn of this dilemma, the parties to the international contract would be individuals. The principles chosen would then be justified according to how well they serve their interests. The justification for the principles, in that case, would seem to rest on liberal individualism—violating the view that it should derive from shared international understandings.

By representing these collective agents as parties to the international contract, then, Rawls avoids these problems. Yet he seems uncertain about the exact collectivity that they represent. Although he explicitly rejects the view that they represent states with traditional powers of sovereignty, it is unclear whether the national groups they represent must be organized as political societies.

Unlike states as traditionally conceived, which possess rights to wage war in pursuit of their interests and to unrestricted "autonomy . . . in dealing with [their] own people,"[130] the collective agents in Rawls's international contract possess weaker powers of sovereignty that "deny . . . rights to war and to unrestricted internal autonomy."[131] This is meant to reflect the dramatic shift in international law since World War II, he says, which "tends to limit a state's right to wage war to instances of self-defense" and "to restrict a state's right to internal sovereignty" to cases where it protects human rights.[132] Unlike states, then, the collective agents in Rawls's international contract have a "moral character," meaning that "[t]hey are not moved solely by their prudent or rational pursuit interests" and are prepared to "limit their basic interests" to conform to principles of international justice.[133]

Aside from the fact that they do not represent states with traditional powers of sovereignty, it is unclear whether Rawls intends them to represent *peoples* or *societies* (where the latter requires some form of political organization). Were we simply to take the title of the book, the statement of the principles themselves,[134] the fact that he uses the term *peoples* on virtually every page, and the fact that *nations* and *peoples* are roughly synonymous terms,[135] we would have abundant evidence for claiming that these collective (national) agents represent *peoples*. If they do represent peoples, though, that would seem to imply that all peoples everywhere possess the rights, powers, and duties that Rawls defends—even if they lack the institutional structures associated with politically organized societies.[136] As Allen Buchanan suggests, this would be a "radical" theory, since it "ascribes many of the powers of sovereignty, including that of self-determination, to hundreds, if not thousands, of groups that exist within state boundaries but which do not have states of their own."[137] Alternatively, since Rawls does seem to use the terms *peoples* and *societies* interchangeably, and since many of the powers and duties that he defends only make sense when exercised through political institutions, we also have strong evidence for claiming that they represent *societies*—in fact, *states* (with more limited powers than states as traditionally conceived).[138] If they represent societies, though, that would seem to imply that *only* peoples with political institutions (that is, with societies) have the rights, powers, and duties that Rawls defends.[139] As Buchanan likewise suggests, this would be a conservative theory, granting these powers to national groups who currently control state institutions but denying them to minority nations residing in their territories that aspire to those very same powers.[140]

Either way, Rawls appears caught in a dilemma between idealizing away the problems posed by minority nations (the radical view) and ignoring them (the conservative view)—dodging the very problems that motivate Kymlicka's and Miller's work. In developing the best Rawls*ian* view, therefore, we will seek a way of navigating the horns of this dilemma.

Ironically, Rawls himself is hardly unaware of the challenges posed by minority nations. "Historical conquests and immigration," he realizes, "have caused the intermingling of groups with different cultures and historical memories who now reside within the territory of most contemporary democratic governments."[141] Surely he realizes that the same point holds for nonliberal societies without democratic governments too. Nonetheless, Rawls believes that we can establish principles that "satisfy the reasonable cultural interests and needs of groups with diverse ethnic and national backgrounds."[142] Yet despite this suggestive promissory note, Rawls's international theory lacks principles that deal with the challenges that minority nations pose, such as rights to independence, regional autonomy, or special group representation, which philosophers like Kymlicka and Miller have been concerned about defending.[143]

However, if we construe the collective agents as representing societies without knowing whether, or to what extent, they contain minority nations—as surely Rawls must have allowed—then we can at least acquit Rawls of having failed to address the challenges they pose. By recasting

Rawls's view in this way, moreover, we can capture the force of reasons that Rawls himself accepts elsewhere. In his domestic theory, for instance, Rawls himself accepts that, for theoretical purposes, domestic society should be considered closed, as one "we enter only by birth and exit only by death," since, as individuals, "we come to be within it and we do not, and indeed cannot, enter or leave it voluntarily."[144] Even possessing a right of emigration, he argues, does not suffice to make individuals' membership in society voluntary. Leaving it is such a "grave step"—we abandon "the society and culture in which we have been raised . . . whose language and culture we use in speech and thought to express and understand ourselves, our aims, goals," values, history, customs, conventions, and so on.[145] Like individuals, though, minority nations simply find themselves "born into" domestic society regardless of their voluntary choices. Similarly, given the costs and gravity of secession, the possibility of seceding makes remaining in it no more voluntary for minority nations than the possibility of emigrating makes it voluntary for individuals. So we have a further reason for construing the collective agents as representing societies without knowing whether, or to what extent, they contain minority nations. If, for theoretical purposes, we should regard societies as closed in order to justify principles of justice that are appropriate given the general infeasibility of emigration, then we should also regard them as closed in order to justify principles of justice that are appropriate given the general infeasibility of secession.

At the beginning of this chapter, we asked, what was Rawls's underlying motivation for using collective agents in his international contract, and is there a better way of accommodating it? We now have some answers. Accepting Walzer's claim that justification should proceed from shared understandings, Rawls needed to identify the content of our shared international understandings. Since we share an agreement on the value of national groups, Rawls modeled this conviction by making the parties to his international contract collective agents who represent such groups—ones he referred to (ambiguously) as peoples or societies. However, the manner in which Rawls did so appeared either to idealize away the problems of minority nations or to ignore them. The current proposal aims to split the horns of this dilemma. It does so by insisting that these agents represent societies without knowing whether, or to what extent, they contain minority nations. We can now face the question that initially prompted our inquiry. Can this proposal avoid the idle-contract objection?

NOTES

1. Rawls of course denies making changes in response to his communitarian critics. He says: "The changes in the later essays are sometimes said to be replies to criticisms raised by communitarians and others. I don't believe there is a basis for

saying this. Of course, whether I am correct in this belief depends on whether the changes can be satisfactorily explained by an analytic view of how they fit into the revised account of stability. It is certainly not settled by my say so." We can think of this chapter, then, as one where we take Rawls up on his invitation to explain the apparent changes to his theory by offering "an analytic view of how they fit into" his later works. See Rawls, *Political Liberalism*, p. xvii, for the reference.

2. Charles Taylor, *Philosophy and the Human Sciences: Philosophical Papers, Vol. 2* (New York: Cambridge University Press, 1985), p. 187.
3. Taylor, *Philosophy and the Human Sciences*, p. 189.
4. Taylor, *Philosophy and the Human Sciences*, p. 195.
5. Taylor, *Philosophy and the Human Sciences*, p. 197.
6. Taylor, *Philosophy and the Human Sciences*, pp. 204-6.
7. Alasdair MacIntyre, *After Virtue: A Study in Moral Theory* (Notre Dame, IN: University of Notre Dame Press, 1981), p. 220.
8. MacIntyre, *After Virtue*, p. 250.
9. MacIntyre, *After Virtue*, p. 205.
10. MacIntyre, *After Virtue*, p. 213.
11. MacIntyre, *After Virtue*, p. 220.
12. Michael Sandel, *Liberalism and the Limits of Justice* (New York: Cambridge University Press, 1982), p. 19.
13. Michael Sandel, *Liberalism and the Limits of Justice*, p. 62.
14. Michael Sandel, *Liberalism and the Limits of Justice*, p. 62.
15. Michael Sandel, *Liberalism and the Limits of Justice*, p. 149.
16. Michael Sandel, *Liberalism and the Limits of Justice*, p. 179.
17. Rawls, *Political Liberalism*, p. 25.
18. Rawls, *A Theory of Justice*, p. 18.
19. Rawls, *Political Liberalism*, p. 24.
20. MacIntyre, *After Virtue*, p. 219.
21. MacIntyre, *After Virtue*, p. 248–50.
22. MacIntyre, *After Virtue*, pp. 222–23.
23. Rawls, *Political Liberalism*, p. 194.
24. Rawls, *Political Liberalism*, p. 13.
25. Rawls, *Political Liberalism*, p. 12.
26. Rawls, *Political Liberalism*, p. 194.
27. Rawls, *Political Liberalism*, pp. 201-6.
28. Taylor, *Philosophy and the Human Sciences*, p. 206.
29. Rawls, *A Theory of Justice*, p. 8.
30. Rawls, *A Theory of Justice*, p. 334.
31. Michael Walzer, *Interpretation and Social Criticism* (Cambridge, MA: Harvard University Press, 1987), ch. 1.
32. Walzer, *Interpretation and Social Criticism*, p. 12.
33. Walzer, *Interpretation and Social Criticism*, pp. 20–21.
34. Walzer, *Interpretation and Social Criticism*, p. 6.
35. Walzer, *Interpretation and Social Criticism*, p. 17.
36. Walzer, *Interpretation and Social Criticism*, p. 26.
37. Walzer, *Interpretation and Social Criticism*, p. 20.
38. Walzer, *Interpretation and Social Criticism*, p. 21.
39. Walzer, *Spheres of Justice*, p. 313.
40. Walzer, *Spheres of Justice*, p. 312.
41. Walzer, *Spheres of Justice*, p. 314.
42. Walzer, *Spheres of Justice*, p. 319.
43. Walzer, *Spheres of Justice*, p. 314.
44. Walzer, *Interpretation and Social Criticism*, pp. 40–42.
45. Walzer, *Interpretation and Social Criticism*, p. 43.
46. Walzer, *Interpretation and Social Criticism*, p. 44.
47. Walzer, *Interpretation and Social Criticism*, p. 60.

48. Walzer, *Interpretation and Social Criticism*, p. 45.
49. Rawls, *A Theory of Justice*, p. 136.
50. See John Rawls, "Kantian Constructivism in Moral Theory," *Journal of Philosophy* 77 (September 1980): 515–72, reprinted in Freeman (ed.), *John Rawls: Collected Papers*, 303–58. The quotation appears on p. 354.
51. Rawls, *Political Liberalism*, p. xvi.
52. Rawls, *Political Liberalism*, p. xxvi.
53. Rawls, *Political Liberalism*, p. xx.
54. Rawls, *Political Liberalism*, p. 13. See also Rawls's remarks on political constructivism in lecture III of *Political Liberalism*, especially his claim that "[A] constructivist political conception . . . develops the principles of justice from public and shared ideas of society as a fair system of cooperation and of citizens as free and equal" (p. 90). If constructivism is (normally) equated with invention and with the denial of realism and discovery, then we can read such remarks as an attempt by him to reconcile his constructivism with interpretation and connected criticism.
55. See John Rawls, "Justice as Fairness: Political not Metaphysical," *Philosophy & Public Affairs* 14 (1985): 223–52, reprinted in Freeman (ed.), *John Rawls: Collected Papers*, 388–414. The quotations appear on pp. 389–390.
56. Walzer, *Spheres of Justice*, p. 314.
57. Rawls, "Justice as Fairness: Political not Metaphysical," reprinted in Freeman (ed.), *John Rawls: Collected Papers*, p. 390.
58. Rawls, *Political Liberalism*, p. 8.
59. Rawls, *Political Liberalism*, p. 18.
60. Rawls, *Political Liberalism*, p. 100.
61. Rawls, "Justice as Fairness: Political not Metaphysical," reprinted in Freeman (ed.), *John Rawls: Collected Papers*, p. 391.
62. Walzer, *Interpretation and Social Criticism*, p. 43.
63. Rawls, *A Theory of Justice*, p. 27.
64. Rawls, "Justice as Fairness: Political not Metaphysical," reprinted in Freeman (ed.), *John Rawls: Collected Papers*, p. 388.
65. Kymlicka, *Liberalism, Community, and Culture*, p. 56, quoting MacIntyre, *After Virtue*, p. 205.
66. Kymlicka, *Liberalism, Community, and Culture*, p. 55, quoting Sandel, *Liberalism and the Limits of Justice*, p. 152.
67. Kymlicka, *Liberalism, Community, and Culture*, pp. 55–57.
68. Kymlicka, *Liberalism, Community, and Culture*, p. 11.
69. Kymlicka, *Liberalism, Community, and Culture*, p. 163.
70. Kymlicka, *Liberalism, Community, and Culture*, p. 163–64.
71. Kymlicka, *Liberalism, Community, and Culture*, p. 12.
72. Kymlicka, *Liberalism, Community, and Culture*, p. 164.
73. Kymlicka, *Liberalism, Community, and Culture*, p. 164, quoting Rawls, *A Theory of Justice*, pp. 563–64.
74. Kymlicka, *Liberalism, Community, and Culture*, p. 164.
75. Kymlicka, *Liberalism, Community, and Culture*, p. 165.
76. Kymlicka, *Liberalism, Community, and Culture*, p. 165.
77. Kymlicka, *Liberalism, Community, and Culture*, p. 165.
78. Kymlicka, *Liberalism, Community, and Culture*, p. 166.
79. Kymlicka, *Multicultural Citizenship*, p. 76.
80. Kymlicka, *Multicultural Citizenship*, p. 76.
81. Kymlicka, *Multicultural Citizenship*, pp. 11, 76.
82. Kymlicka, *Multicultural Citizenship*, pp. 76–80.
83. Kymlicka, *Multicultural Citizenship*, p. 84–89.
84. Kymlicka, *Multicultural Citizenship*, p. 80.
85. David Miller, "The Ethical Significance of Nationality," *Ethics* 98, no. 4 (July 1988), p. 649.

86. David Miller, "The Ethical Significance of Nationality," *Ethics* 98, no. 4 (July 1988), p. 650.
87. Michael Sandel, *Liberalism and the Limits of Justice*, p. 62.
88. David Miller, *On Nationality*, p. 42.
89. David Miller, *On Nationality*, pp. 51–53.
90. David Miller, *On Nationality*, p. 50.
91. David Miller, *On Nationality*, p. 50.
92. David Miller, *On Nationality*, p. 57.
93. David Miller, *On Nationality*, p. 57.
94. David Miller, "The Ethical Significance of Nationality," *Ethics* 98, no. 4 (July 1988), p. 651.
95. David Miller, *On Nationality*, p. 57.
96. David Miller, *On Nationality*, pp. 57–58.
97. David Miller, *On Nationality*, p. 58.
98. David Miller, *On Nationality*, pp. 43–44.
99. David Miller, *On Nationality*, p. 43.
100. Alan Patten, *Equal Recognition: The Moral Foundations of Minority Rights* (Princeton, NJ: Princeton University Press, 2014), p. 177.
101. Alan Patten, *Equal Recognition: The Moral Foundations of Minority Rights*, ch. 3.
102. Alan Patten, *Equal Recognition: The Moral Foundations of Minority Rights*, pp. 7–8, 104–5, 113–14.
103. Alan Patten, *Equal Recognition: The Moral Foundations of Minority Rights*, p. 72.
104. Alan Patten, *Equal Recognition: The Moral Foundations of Minority Rights*, pp. 101–2.
105. Alan Patten, *Equal Recognition: The Moral Foundations of Minority Rights*, p. 72.
106. Alan Patten, *Equal Recognition: The Moral Foundations of Minority Rights*, p. 131.
107. Alan Patten, *Equal Recognition: The Moral Foundations of Minority Rights*, p. 132.
108. Alan Patten, *Equal Recognition: The Moral Foundations of Minority Rights*, pp. 133–36.
109. Alan Patten, *Equal Recognition: The Moral Foundations of Minority Rights*, p. 29.
110. Alan Patten, *Equal Recognition: The Moral Foundations of Minority Rights*, p. 159.
111. Alan Patten, *Equal Recognition: The Moral Foundations of Minority Rights*, pp. 113–14.
112. Alan Patten, *Equal Recognition: The Moral Foundations of Minority Rights*, p. 114.
113. Alan Patten, *Equal Recognition: The Moral Foundations of Minority Rights*, p. 139.
114. Alan Patten, *Equal Recognition: The Moral Foundations of Minority Rights*, p. 115.
115. Alan Patten, *Equal Recognition: The Moral Foundations of Minority Rights*, pp. 157–58.
116. Alan Patten, *Equal Recognition: The Moral Foundations of Minority Rights*, pp. 161–71.
117. Alan Patten, *Equal Recognition: The Moral Foundations of Minority Rights*, p. 177.
118. Alan Patten, *Equal Recognition: The Moral Foundations of Minority Rights*, p. 31.
119. Michael Walzer, *The Paradox of Liberation: Secular Revolutions and Religious Counterrevolutions* (New Haven, CT: Yale University Press, 2015), ch. 1.
120. Michael Walzer, *The Paradox of Liberation*, p. 125.
121. Michael Walzer, *The Paradox of Liberation*, p. 132.
122. Michael Walzer, *The Paradox of Liberation*, p. 93.
123. Michael Walzer, *The Paradox of Liberation*, p. 26.
124. Michael Walzer, *The Paradox of Liberation*, p. 28.
125. Michael Walzer, *The Paradox of Liberation*, p. 19.
126. Michael Walzer, *The Paradox of Liberation*, p. 29.
127. Michael Walzer, *The Paradox of Liberation*, p. 56.
128. Michael Walzer, *The Paradox of Liberation*, p. 138.
129. For Walzer, this extends to their subcommunities as well—an important observation, as political communities are neither completely liberal nor completely nonliberal.

130. Rawls, *The Law of Peoples*, pp. 25–26.
131. Rawls, *The Law of Peoples*, p. 27.
132. Rawls, *The Law of Peoples*, p. 27.
133. Rawls, *The Law of Peoples*, pp. 27, 29.
134. Rawls, *The Law of Peoples*, p. 37.
135. See, for example, Kymlicka, *Multicultural Citizenship*, p. 11.
136. This is how Kok-Chor Tan reads him. See Kok-Chor Tan, "The Problem of Decent Peoples," in Rex Martin and David Reidy (eds.), *Rawls's Law of Peoples: A Realistic Utopia?* (Malden, MA: Blackwell Publishing, 2006): 76–94.
137. Buchanan, "Rawls's Law of Peoples: Rules for a Vanished Westphalian World," p. 699.
138. This is how Allen Buchanan reads him. See Allen Buchanan, "Rawls's Law of Peoples: Rules for a Vanished Westphalian World," *Ethics* 110, no. 4 (July 2000): 698, 697–721.
139. Buchanan, "Rawls's Law of Peoples: Rules for a Vanished Westphalian World," p. 699.
140. Buchanan, "Rawls's Law of Peoples: Rules for a Vanished Westphalian World," pp. 716–20.
141. Rawls, *The Law of Peoples*, p. 24.
142. Rawls, *The Law of Peoples*, p. 25.
143. Buchanan, "Rawls's Law of Peoples: Rules for a Vanished Westphalian World," p. 716.
144. Rawls, *Political Liberalism*, pp. 135–36.
145. Rawls, *Political Liberalism*, p. 222.

FIVE

From Justice to Recognition

5.1 THREE STRATEGIES

Conceding that justification should proceed from shared understandings, acknowledging the shared value of national groups, and representing them with collective agents, Rawls encounters our three objections. However, by modifying his international contract, we can begin to answer them all—in particular, the formidable idle-contract objection.

Although a full answer must await the final chapter, the first step to answering it is to recast slightly the question that Rawls seeks to answer. As Rawls frames it, the question is, *which nonliberal societies should liberal societies tolerate?*[1] Leaving aside momentarily the one-sided focus of this question, we can rephrase it in terms recommended by the analysis of the preceding chapter, terms not much different from his own, terms implicit in the original. Considering the ethical significance of nationality, the value of national belonging, and the importance of minority nations, we can ask, *which societies (liberal or nonliberal) with minority nations should we tolerate?* In other words, we can distinguish the questions:

1. Which nonliberal societies should liberal societies tolerate?
2. Which societies (liberal or nonliberal) with minority nations should we tolerate?

construe Rawls as interested in asking the second rather than the first, and position him to answer it by having the collective agents in the international contract represent societies without knowing whether, or to what extent, they contain minority nations. The next step in answering the idle-contract objection is to notice that Rawls will occasionally add the phrase "as a *member* in good standing of the Society of Peoples," suggesting that his concern is with tolerating domestic societies as members of international society.[2] As we will see, this focus on membership provides the key to our answer.

Clearly, much more needs to be said in order to show how this response enables Rawls to avoid the idle-contract objection, and in fact, the full explanation will occupy the rest of this book. However, in the rest of this chapter, I will defend the claim that this is the most promising strategy for handling the difficulties that Rawls encounters in *The Law of Peoples*.

Recall that Rawls's argument possesses three main features (§ 1.2):

1. A social contract
2. Collective agents
3. Principles of international justice

In response to the difficulties Rawls encounters, many defenders of Rawls sacrifice the second of these features by substituting individuals for collective agents as the parties in the original position. Retaining the social contract, they then generate principles of international justice that are recognizably liberal.[3] This cosmopolitan strategy has much to recommend it. It offers a straightforward way of overcoming the idle-contract objection and a secure justification for basic human rights (and more). Although it assumes that liberal individualism is defensible, this should be no problem if that assumption is correct. While it dispenses with the effort to find a political conception of international justice, this may be the best course for a defender of Rawls under the circumstances (assuming that his own effort to find a political conception of international justice fails to provide adequate justification for basic human rights).

Nothing I say here is meant to contradict the cosmopolitan strategy for defending principles of international justice—in fact, the view that I defend is meant to be compatible with it. However, I will soon call into question its assumption that Rawls's aim is to defend principles of international justice, the third feature above.

In contrast with the cosmopolitan strategy, the political liberal strategy sacrifices the first feature, giving the social contract no role in justifying restrictions on internal sovereignty. Retaining the collective agents, it relies instead on ideas from political liberalism—like reasonableness, public reason, or an overlapping consensus—to establish them.

Rawls connects these three ideas in *Political Liberalism* as follows. Because citizens in liberal democracies no longer generally share a comprehensive view,[4] social unity and stability, he argues, require an overlapping consensus on principles of justice—a consensus among adherents of diverse and conflicting comprehensive views.[5] In order to achieve such a consensus, though, we cannot simply base our principles on what we believe to be the true comprehensive view, even if it should turn out that that view is true. To do that would be "exclusive, even sectarian, and so likely to foster political division."[6] Instead, we should aim to establish, not the truth of our principles, but their reasonableness. "The advantage of staying within the reasonable," he claims, "is that there can be but one true comprehensive doctrine, though . . . many reasonable ones."[7] While the term *reasonable* is a technical term for Rawls that has a variety of uses, one of its central uses (and the one used by advocates of the political liberal strategy) employs the notion of a "reasonable person."[8] Given that citizens in liberal democracies no longer generally share a comprehensive doctrine, reasonable persons will refrain from basing state power on their own comprehensive view.[9] Instead, they stand "ready to propose principles and standards as fair terms of cooperation and to abide by them willingly, given the assurance that others will likewise do so."[10] These are principles that "they view as reasonable for everyone to accept and therefore as justifiable to them."[11] Reasonable persons, this seems to imply, honor *reciprocity* in their mutual relations.

Public reason, then, just involves using these principles rather than one's own comprehensive view when publicly debating constitutional essentials and matters of basic justice.[12] It also involves utilizing guidelines of inquiry, principles of reasoning, and rules of evidence that are likewise publicly acceptable to reasonable citizens and not controversial.[13] While not meant to be a legal requirement, the use of public reason forms part of an ideal of liberal citizenship that covers how we attempt to justify our claims to one another.[14]

Now this of course is only a brief sketch (I will say much more in § 5.2 about an overlapping consensus). For our purposes, the crucial point is the following. This combination of ideas from political liberalism still leaves open the *content* of the principles—which the first stage of Rawls's presentation (the social contract) determines. For Rawls, therefore, their emergence from a social contract still forms an *essential* part of their justification. The family of ideas from political liberalism only comes into play *later*, at the second stage, which *tests* whether the principles that emerge from the first stage can be the focus of an overlapping consensus. Under the political liberal strategy, however, these ideas play a far stronger role.

We find versions of this strategy in Avila, Reidy, and Bernstein. Avila essentially concedes that the international contract plays no role in establishing any internal restrictions for liberal societies—deferring to the first, domestic, contract to fill that gap. Normative requirements for a liberal people, he claims, "are carried forward from our domestic theorizing."[15] These "determine its internal affairs," and "it is only here . . . that any substantive criteria are included in a Law of Peoples that address the internal affairs of a people."[16] Since this strategy is unavailable for decent societies (since they have no domestic contract analogue),[17] their restrictions would seem to have to come from the international contract. But then, Avila argues, *decent societies ought to be excluded from it*, on the grounds that, being organized around comprehensive doctrines, they are by definition politically unreasonable: whereas liberal societies are reasonable "insofar as they offer fair terms of cooperation to other citizens that do not rely upon any particular comprehensive doctrine,"[18] decent societies "do not regard it as a valid requirement that they set aside their comprehensive doctrine when it comes to matters of political legitimacy, whether domestic or international."[19] Because "the criteria of reasonableness are ones that by definition appeal only to liberal peoples," he claims that a liberal people "has only to answer to its own standards of reasonableness."[20] As a result, a decent peoples is "not going to recognize the normative force of the original position to begin with and so including or excluding them is of no consequence."[21] Applying a liberal peoples' own standards of reasonableness, Avila maintains that a liberal peoples will give due allowance to the distinguishing characteristics of decent societies ("their unique relationship to their comprehensive doctrines"[22]), and as a result will embrace roughly the set of basic human rights as Rawls conceives them rather than the full set of liberal rights that issue from his domestic contract.[23]

Like Avila, Reidy also excludes decent societies from the international contract. The argument for basic human rights, he claims, "depends in no way on invoking the second international original position, within which agents represent only decent peoples."[24] Instead, "[t]here is only the inquiry by liberal democratic peoples into the moral basis of their own claims to self-determination and nonintervention within the international order."[25] The possibility that decent peoples might also affirm this same law of peoples, he maintains, "ensures that liberal democratic peoples honor their own moral commitment to reciprocity and . . . locates the law of peoples within an existing or reasonably possible overlapping consensus within international public reason."[26] Drawing on this notion of reciprocity, Reidy then argues that this liberal self-inquiry reveals that, only in societies that embrace a common good conception of justice, is there sufficient reciprocity, domestically, to accord them tolerance internationally.[27] Having identified a common good conception of justice as the outcome of this inquiry, though, there is no need to use the contract to determine limits on internal sovereignty. As with Avila, what does all the normative work for Reidy is this appeal to the notion of reciprocity (which for him is equivalent to Rawls's notion of reasonableness).[28] The contract gets left aside.[29]

Whereas Avila and Reidy rely on reasonableness to derive restrictions on internal sovereignty, Bernstein relies on public reason. "[W]hich rights are to count as . . . basic human rights," Bernstein claims, "should meet the requirements of public reason."[30] However, a basic human right to democratic government, she argues, does not meet the requirements of international public reason. International public reason does not support the claim that *only* democratic governments show or require respect for the *other* basic human rights, which *do* meet the requirements of international public reason.[31] Only if we can prove that Rawls's example of Kazanistan—which does respect those other human rights despite being undemocratic—is an empirical impossibility, she argues, can we support that claim consistently with international public reason. Since we cannot prove that a society like Kazanistan is an empirical impossibility, though, we ought to reject that claim. Therefore, she concludes, there are no grounds consistent with international public reason for including a right to democratic government among the rights that count as basic human rights. As with Avila's and Reidy's arguments, Bernstein's bypasses the international contract and relies instead on ideas from *Political Liberalism*, in this case public reason, to determine limits on internal sovereignty.

Unlike the cosmopolitan strategy, though, the political liberal strategy has much less to recommend it. While it dispenses with the need to defend liberal individualism and continues to seek a political conception of international justice, it offers a far less straightforward way of overcoming the idle-contract objection: it abandons the contract entirely. Were our only choices for handling the difficulties Rawls encounters the cosmopolitan strategy and the political liberal one, this fact alone would be sufficient for rejecting the second in favor of the first. In short, the political liberal strategy simply fails to take Rawls seriously as a social contract theorist. Yet even if we were willing to jettison the contract, regarding it as an unnecessary liability, the political liberal strategy would suffer from a more fundamental problem still: it assumes that the justification for principles of justice should depend on their ability to be the focus of an overlapping consensus. We ought to reject that assumption.

5.2 THE BARRY BOMB

Public reason, a political conception, the burdens of judgment, reasonableness—these ideas (and more) are arguably all instrumental toward achieving what is central to political liberalism, an overlapping consensus. So if we can undermine the claim that we need to achieve one, then we can justify principles without acquiring or even seeking one.

In his review of *Political Liberalism*, Brian Barry offers a compelling, fundamental challenge to that work that any defender of it must confront.[32] Since I accept his argument, my aim in this section will be to defend and develop it—recasting it where necessary in order to strengthen its fundamental insights, extending it in ways that demonstrate its force. While his argument is more wide-ranging than what I focus on, and while I elaborate it in ways that he might not accept, I take his central claim to be that the inability of principles to be the focus of an overlapping consensus should not be sufficient reason for rejecting them.

Like Meno, who famously suggests that we cannot seek that which we have already obtained,[33] Barry insists that we need not seek an overlapping consensus if the existence of one is already guaranteed. In two ways, however, Rawls seems to guarantee the existence of one, Barry argues.

First, in *A Theory of Justice*, as a solution to the problem of congruence—the problem of showing that the "disposition to take up and to be guided by the standpoint of justice accords with the individual's good"[34]—Rawls proposes a "Kantian interpretation" of his theory. According to this interpretation, "acting justly is something we want to do as free and equal rational beings."[35] The desire to act justly "is a desire to conduct oneself in a certain way above all else, a striving that contains within itself its own priority."[36] Seizing on this claim, Barry counters that "[t]he problem of decisiveness is then solved definitively, since we can express our nature as free and equal rational beings only to the extent that we commit ourselves unconditionally to give our sense of justice precedence over our other interests."[37] The Kantian interpretation, in other words, dissolves any tensions that might exist between Rawls's principles and individuals' comprehensive conceptions of the good—guaranteeing not only that the principles of justice are honored, but that they are honored for the *sake* of justice. In that case, an overlapping consensus obtains necessarily.

If we are reluctant to embrace this "Kantian ace in the hole,"[38] as Barry puts it—either because it motivates "only . . . those who believe in it"[39] or because often people give no such precedence to justice when it conflicts with their comprehensive views[40]—then we need an alternative approach. For these very reasons—plus Rawls's realization that resting his theory on the Kantian interpretation would be incompatible with "the fact of reasonable pluralism"—Barry notes that Rawls grew dissatisfied with it and decided on "taking another shot" in *Political Liberalism*.[41] But then Rawls raises the stakes considerably by linking an overlapping consensus to the exercise of legitimate political authority. Only if justice as fairness "can win its support by addressing each citizen's reason"[42]—by being the focus of an overlapping consensus—Rawls says, "is it an account of the legitimacy of political authority."[43] Therefore, claims Barry, "it would [now] be a catastrophe if there were people with "reasonable comprehensive views" that could not accommodate the demands of justice, since that would undermine the legitimacy of Rawlsian institutions."[44]

Although the evidence is mixed, Barry argues, Rawls, in an apparent effort to avoid such a catastrophe, occasionally seems to *define* reasonable comprehensive views as ones that are compatible his principles—in which case an overlapping consensus would obtain necessarily, since there could be no conceivable conflict between his principles and reasonable comprehensive views.[45] This is to give "a content-based criterion for a reasonable doctrine" and is the second way in which Rawls seems to guarantee the existence of an overlapping consensus.[46]

At other places, however, he appears to reject this content-based criterion in favor of a content-free criterion, defining reasonable comprehensive doctrines as ones involving the exercise of theoretical and practical reason and belonging to a tradition of thought.[47] This content-free criterion, Barry notes, leaves open the possibility that a reasonable doctrine might not be compatible with justice as fairness. Coming down squarely on the side of this view, Barry argues, "Rawls lists a number of 'reasonable comprehensive views' and then proceeds to make a case for the compatibility of each with 'justice as fairness.' This whole exercise would be otiose if it were conceptually impossible for a reasonable view to fail to be compatible with Rawlsian justice."[48]

To make any sense of the need to argue for an overlapping consensus, therefore, we must allow for the possibility that some comprehensive doctrines that qualify as reasonable do *not* conform with Rawls's principles. But then, using Rawls's own examples of reasonable comprehensive views, Barry goes on to argue that many of them would in fact fail to endorse Rawls's principles.[49] The best that we can hope for, he maintains, is that they would endorse his first principle of justice (but not the second).[50] Then we come to a crucial juncture. Either we must reject Rawls's principles on the grounds that they would fail to be the focus of an overlapping consensus, or else we must reject the claim that failing to be the focus of an overlapping consensus is sufficient reason for rejecting them. Barry's wholesale repudiation of *Political Liberalism*, combined with his enthusiasm for *A Theory of Justice*, commits him to rejecting the need for an overlapping consensus.

This brief summary, no doubt, fails to do justice to the full range and subtlety of Barry's view. Nonetheless, it should enable us to proceed. Now we must grant, I think, that no definition of "reasonable comprehensive views" should preclude the possibility of one failing to be compatible with Rawls's principles, for otherwise, it would make no sense at all for Rawls to have to *argue* that his principles could be the focus of an overlapping consensus. So what I want to focus on is the next step in Barry's argument, where he contends that many of Rawls's own examples of reasonable comprehensive views would fail to endorse his principles. While some Kantian views would clearly be compatible with Rawls's theory, for example, others, Barry notes, contest its redistributive elements as violations of the prohibition on treating others as mere means.[51] Similarly, while some comprehensive religious views would endorse Rawls's theory due to their account of free faith, others would not. If "the three major monotheistic religions are to count as reasonable," as Barry believes Rawls intends[52] (reading him as accepting the content-free criterion), then it is easy "to read the books on which they are based as rejecting the 'account of free faith'" required by Rawls's first principle.[53] "The Gods of Moses, Mahomet, and Saint Paul (Jesus is perhaps an exception)," he claims, "do not sound like liberals."[54] They likewise "embrace a similar spread of views," egalitarian and inegalitarian, on economic matters, rendering some, but not others, compatible with Rawls's second principle.[55] Using a similar strategy, Barry also attempts to show that, on some interpretations, Rawls's other examples of comprehensive views would endorse his principles, while on other interpretations, they would reject one or both of them.

Given Rawls's introduction of these examples, he admittedly invites the kind of examination that Barry provides. We need to be cautious, however, in view of Rawls's admonitions against being "political in the wrong way,"[56] which can occur, he says, if we allow the content of principles to be affected by "the particular comprehensive doctrines that may exist in society."[57] Barry's examination, though, appears to recommend precisely this by implying that, if we accept the need for an overlapping consensus, we must alter the content of the political conception (sacrificing Rawls's second principle), based on the particular comprehensive doctrines that Barry examines. Since Rawls's reasonable doctrines are intended by him merely as illustrations of a more general point about the ways in which comprehensive doctrines and a political conception may be related, the examination needs to be conducted at that more general level.

For Rawls, comprehensive doctrines may be related to the political conception in three main ways. In some cases, the principles that comprise the political conception may be derived from the comprehensive doctrine.[58] The principles, he claims, can be deduced from it, or are continuous with it. They are, we might say, positively supported by it. Call these doctrines the *derivatives*.[59] In other cases, the principles cannot be derived from the comprehensive doctrine, but neither do they contradict it. We can think of such doctrines as possessing separate domains of value, with Rawls's principles occupying one domain and nonpolitical values occupying another—the two domains fitting together.[60] Call these doctrines the *compatibles*.[61] Then there are doctrines that contradict the political conception (either in whole or in part). Call them the *incompatibles*.[62] While these three relations do not exhaust the logical possibilities, they provide the main ones relevant for our analysis.[63]

Clearly the derivatives and compatibles pose no problem for an overlapping consensus, since they can endorse Rawls's principles without compromising their values. Only the incompatibles pose a problem. As we have seen, some of these must qualify as reasonable. Now Rawls seems to acknowledge that these reasonable incompatibles can be incompatible with justice as fairness to varying degrees. For instance, he considers the possibility that some of them might endorse it "provided it [does] not conflict too sharply with their comprehensive views,"[64] as well as the possibility that "under reasonably favorable conditions that make democracy possible," they would allow that "political values normally outweigh whatever nonpolitical values conflict with them."[65] Those that fall into this category, he suggests, might do so because they recognize that political values "govern the basic framework of social life—the very groundwork of our existence" and are therefore "very great values . . . not easily overridden."[66] "[T]he values that conflict with the political conception," he claims, "may be normally outweighed because they come into conflict with the very conditions that make fair social cooperation possible on a footing of mutual respect."[67] As a result, such doctrines might endorse justice as fairness all-things-considered (or at least not oppose it "as a whole"[68]) despite occasional conflicts with its requirements. Call this subset of incompatibles the *moderate incompatibles*. These too pose no problem for an overlapping consensus.

Call the remaining incompatibles the *significant incompatibles*. By hypothesis, some of these must qualify as reasonable. The question then becomes whether they could be recruited to an overlapping consensus in the same manner as the moderate incompatibles—that is, not by employing "workable sanctions," but through winning their support "by addressing each citizen's reason."[69] Bracketing the content of the doctrines he examines, Barry's argument essentially denies that some of these doctrines would join an overlapping consensus on Rawls's principles.

This, of course, does not contradict Rawls's claim that they *could* join such a consensus.[70] We find powerful historical evidence for this claim, he argues, from the Reformation, in the principle of toleration. Just as adherents of various religions at first reluctantly accepted that principle as a mere modus vivendi but came gradually to affirm it for its own sake once they experienced the favorable social conditions that it helped create, so too, Rawls conjectures, could adherents of reasonable comprehensive doctrines accept justice as fairness initially as a modus vivendi (as the basis, say, for a constitution) but later come to affirm its principles for their own sake once they appreciate the social conditions that it tends to generate.[71] Distinguishing between "the initial . . . appreciation of the political conception and the later adjustment or revision of comprehensive doctrines . . . when inconsistencies [with it] arise," Rawls suggests that these "adjustments or revisions . . . [may] take place slowly over time as the political conception shapes comprehensive views to cohere with it."[72] So even if Barry is correct in denying that some significant incompatibles would join an overlapping consensus, it does not follow that they could not do so, given enough time for their doctrines to adjust and evolve. If the principle of toleration can start out as modus vivendi yet come to be honored for its own sake, why not the same for Rawls's principles?

However, even if Rawls's causal story is correct, and even if, as a result, all reasonable doctrines could join an overlapping consensus on Rawls's principles, we can still ask, hypothetically, what if those principles *were* unable to persuade adherents of some significant incompatibles to adjust their views sufficiently so as to affirm the political conception in the same manner as the moderate incompatibles? (What if they were to "stick to their guns" until time immemorial? What if, hypothetically, they *couldn't* join an overlapping consensus?) Should we say, so much the worse for Rawls's principles—or should we say instead, so much the worse for those comprehensive doctrines? Call these doctrines the *holdouts*. Barry's most fundamental point is that, if we are inclined to say, so much the worse for the holdouts, then the inability of principles to be the focus of an overlapping consensus should not be sufficient reason for rejecting them.[73]

Are we inclined to say, so much the worse for the holdouts? His argument does seem to assume that we share this intuition with him—but on this point, he seems absolutely right.

Rather than rely on intuition, though, we can advance various theoretical considerations in favor of it. In the first stage of his exposition, for example, Rawls already argues that, "the fact that we affirm a particular religious, philosophical, or moral comprehensive doctrine with is associated conception of the good is not a reason for us to propose, or to expect others to accept, a conception of justice that favors those of that persuasion."[74] As a result, he constructs his domestic contract so as not to favor or disfavor adherents of any particular doctrine in the choice of principles—one that aims to treat them equally and fairly. Then, he derives the principles. Assuming that his argument is successful, what further accommodations must we make for holdouts?

Rawls's own instincts on this question are instructive. "What if it turns out that the principles of justice cannot gain the support of reasonable doctrines?" he asks.[75] He answers: "[I]t is not a satisfactory political conception of justice," in that case, "and it must be in some way revised."[76] As we saw earlier, though, revising it requires us to alter the contractual circumstances in an effort to derive different principles, since we cannot simply make direct changes to the principles themselves (§ 2.5). But then, presumably, we would still need to represent the parties fairly and equally: no one would receive an unfair advantage in the choice of principles, no one would be treated unequally. Otherwise, our effort to accommodate the holdouts would seem to be "political in the wrong way." So a reconstructed contract would still honor commitments to fairness and equality. It would just issue in a different conception of how they best combine.

Notice, though, that we can raise the very same challenge to this different liberal political conception. Even if all reasonable doctrines could join an overlapping consensus on it, we can still ask, hypothetically, what if there were holdouts? In fact, we can put the challenge even more strongly: what if they were the same holdouts as before? Should we reject the principles, in that case, or should we reject instead the need for an overlapping consensus? Rather than countering the challenge, this proposal postpones it.

We can even raise this challenge against a possibility that Rawls considers as his ultimate fallback position: the possibility that, if an overlapping consensus could not exist on justice as fairness or any other liberal political conception taken singly, one could exist on "a class of liberal conceptions" taken jointly.[77] Again, what if there were holdouts to this entire class—indeed, the same holdouts as before? If we are to accommodate the holdouts in this case, we have (by hypothesis) no other recourse than to embrace a comprehensive doctrine, which Rawls stipulates could *not* be the focus of an overlapping consensus. We would have other holdouts.

If we have confidence in the ideal that Rawls initially proposes, if we find attractive its commitments to fairness and equality, if we find appealing how it models these convictions, if we find persuasive the argument from the original position, and if we find convincing its outcome upon due reflection, then we should find judicious its attempt to navigate between the Scylla and Charybdis of rival comprehensive views, capacious the forms of life that it encourages, and no need to resort to instituting any further accommodations for holdouts. It is one of Barry's many important insights that the existence of actual or possible holdouts impugns not the principles that they reject but the doctrines they hold.[78] Like those who pursue unreasonable doctrines in violation of the principles of justice, who Rawls acknowledges may be legitimately coerced, those who contravene those principles by following holdout doctrines, Barry suggests, may be legitimately "contained," as Rawls puts it, "so that they do not undermine the unity and justice of society."[79] If we agree, as I believe we should, then the inability of principles to be the focus of an overlapping consensus should not be sufficient reason for rejecting them. Rawls's principles should not be held hostage to the possibility that some doctrines would be unable to affirm them.

5.3 CHALLENGES TO THE BOMB

Suitably extended and developed, Barry's argument, I have shown, is both illuminating and defensible. As a result, we ought to reject the assumption that the justification for principles of justice should depend on their ability to be the focus of an overlapping consensus. Moreover, this result reinforces our earlier claim that we ought to reject the political liberal strategy. We ought to reject the political liberal strategy because it fails to take Rawls seriously as a social contract theorist (§ 5.1), and because it requires an overlapping consensus for its principles to be justified (§ 5.2).

In their efforts to defuse Barry's argument, however, Samuel Freeman, Paul Weithman, and Jonathan Quong develop counterarguments of their own. These counterarguments, I now hope to show, nonetheless fail to undermine what I take to be Barry's central claim.

Barry seems to have two aims, one explanatory, one normative. The explanatory aim is to show why Rawls apparently changed his view from *A Theory of Justice* to *Political Liberalism*. He rejects Rawls's own explanation, and offers what he regards as a more plausible one on Rawls's behalf. The normative aim is to argue that an overlapping consensus is not necessary for Rawls's principles to be justified, and to show that they would not be the focus of an overlapping consensus in any case. I take the normative aim to be more central, despite the fact that he devotes most of his attention to the explanatory aim. It's as if to say, *whatever* the reason is that motivated Rawls to change his view, he should not have changed his view by requiring an overlapping consensus. Rawls's first stage argument (the argument from the original position) is sufficient. The second stage (overlapping consensus) is not necessary. I've focused mainly on what I am calling Barry's normative aim, although his argument is more wide-ranging than this since it also includes his explanatory aim.

Why does Barry reject Rawls's own explanation of why he needed to require an overlapping consensus? He gives four main reasons:

1. Contrary to Rawls's belief, *A Theory of Justice* did not offer a comprehensive doctrine. It was limited in scope and excluded conceptions of value (or ends). Rawls believed that his theory would not be stable because it was a comprehensive doctrine. Barry rejects the premise that it was a comprehensive doctrine. So he concludes that there was no need to revise his view.[80]
2. Rawls thinks he needs to show the possibility of an overlapping consensus because he believes that it is irrational for people to do their duty out of a sense of duty (the "doctrine of the pure conscientious act"). Thus he believes he needs to show congruence between justice and one's comprehensive view. But he mistakenly believes that it is irrational for people to do their duty out of a sense of duty (a standing, regulative, desire to do the right thing). So there was no need to revise his view.[81]
3. Once one accepts the need to show congruence, though, only the Kantian interpretation guarantees the decisiveness of the motive to be just. However, not everyone accepts a Kantian comprehensive view. This could explain why he felt he needed to require an overlapping consensus. But then why not say that those for whom justice is not decisive may be legitimately coerced, as he allows in *A Theory of Justice*? So there was no need to revise his view.[82]
4. We don't need the second stage (an overlapping consensus) provided that people seeking agreement have Scanlonian motivation—

> that they are reasonable *persons*. Thus, the first stage suffices, since this is the motivation that they are stipulated to have (holding this motivation commits them to the first stage procedure and its result). Assuming that stability requires gaining free assent among reasonable people to the same principles, it does not follow that this requires an overlapping consensus. It only requires the willingness to submit to the results of the first stage.[83]

Since these reasons all fail, in Barry's view, he proposes what he regards as a more plausible explanation on Rawls's behalf. Rawls, he suggests, may have regarded recognition of "the fact of [reasonable] pluralism"—"understood not as a brute fact about the actual existence of disagreement but as a claim about the irreducible variety of reasonable views under conditions in which freedom of thought is established"—as too controversial for a political conception to rest on.[84] If so, then some significant incompatibles (which reject the fact of reasonable pluralism) must qualify as reasonable, too, which he believed had to be recruited to an overlapping consensus in order to secure stability.

Now, while Freeman challenges some of Barry's explanatory claims, he does not challenge his normative claim. For example, he charges Barry with misconstruing Rawls's rejection of the doctrine of the conscientious act. Freeman claims that Rawls was only concerned to reject Ross' view that what motivates us to act is grasping a simple, unanalyzable, nonnatural moral property, and that grasping such a property is sufficient to motivate us to do what is right. So Rawls can accept that people may be motivated to do their duty out of a sense of duty after all, in which case Barry's charge misses its target.[85] Otherwise, Freeman agrees with Barry that the Kantian interpretation guarantees the decisiveness of the motive to be just,[86] and *concedes* that, once one rejects it, "in a well-ordered society it seems there is no assurance after all that justice will occupy a supremely regulative position in each person's conception of the good."[87] These persons, moreover, are not necessarily unreasonable, or holders of unreasonable comprehensive doctrines, in his view. Although Freeman suggests that adherence to Rawlsian principles may causally influence many of their reasonable comprehensive views, so that they do not remain significantly incompatible with Rawls's principles, in the end he admits that "[i]t may be that many [such] people cannot be expected to subordinate their nonpolitical ends to justice."[88] In short, Freeman seems to acknowledge that an overlapping consensus is not guaranteed, and says nothing to challenge the view that an overlapping consensus is unneeded for principles of justice to be justified.

Like Freeman, Weithman primarily attempts to explain "why Rawls became dissatisfied with [*A Theory of Justice*'s] arguments for stability and why he recast justice as fairness as a political liberalism."[89] However, he also denies one of Barry's normative claims, charging that Barry fallaciously infers that, just because justice as fairness would not be the focus of an overlapping consensus in our non-well-ordered society, it follows that it would not be the focus of an overlapping consensus in a well-ordered one (where everyone starts out accepting Rawls's principles, knows that everyone else does too, and knows that society satisfies those principles). Referring to Barry, he claims:

> Once Rawls's treatment of stability is before us, we can also see that one objection commonly raised against it is based upon misunderstanding. Critics sometimes suppose that to show an overlapping consensus is possible, Rawls must show that religions in their current state endorse or are likely to endorse the starting premises of justice as fairness, or endorse or are likely to endorse its principles. If it is then asserted that they don't or can't, the argument for the possibility of such a consensus is taken to fail. It should now be clear how badly this objection misses the mark. . . . The world in which we live is, however, a world from which the just institutions [and formative effects] of a [well-ordered society] are notably absent. Arguments drawn from the injustice of our world cannot, therefore, tell against the possibility of an overlapping consensus or against the conclusion that justice as fairness would be stable for the right reasons.[90]

But while Barry's argument, as initially presented, may have been vulnerable to this criticism, it is not vulnerable to it as reformulated and elaborated in the last section. Instead, we recast his argument so that it did not rest on his claim that the various reasonable comprehensive doctrines that he canvasses (as they currently exist in our admittedly non-well-ordered society) would not join an overlapping consensus on Rawls's principles. For the sake of discussion, we even supposed that Rawls's causal story was correct (that, given sufficient time, reasonable comprehensive doctrines would adjust themselves to the political conception), and that, as a result, all reasonable comprehensive doctrines in a well-ordered society could form an overlapping consensus on Rawls's principles. We assumed, in other words, that there were no holdouts in a well-ordered society. However, we then supposed for the sake of discussion that there *were* such holdouts in a well-ordered society, and investigated whether that should impugn Rawls's principles, or the doctrines that reject them. We argued that the possibility of holdouts does not give us sufficient reason for rejecting Rawls's principles, and therefore concluded that the inability of principles to be the focus of an overlapping consensus should not be sufficient reason for rejecting them.

Nothing Weithman says contradicts this fundamental normative claim of Barry's. Although Weithman insists that "stability for the right reasons is important," being important or valuable is not the same as being necessary: not the same as requiring an overlapping consensus for principles of justice to be justified.[91] Stability for the right reasons is important if we are to reduce reliance on what Weithman calls *imposed* stability—reliance on penal sanctions and other state enforcement efforts to solve the mutual assurance problem. While true, such reliance will exist regardless of whether those who reject Rawls's principles hold reasonable or unreasonable doctrines—in which case, Barry suggests, if the latter may be legitimately coerced, then so may the former. In short, we can acknowledge the value in reducing reliance on penal sanctions—we can acknowledge that it would be good to have an overlapping consensus—without committing ourselves to the much stronger normative claim that the justification of principles of justice requires their ability to be the focus of an overlapping consensus.

Unlike Freeman and Weithman, Quong tackles Barry's normative claim directly. Barry, he says, puts his objection in the form of a dilemma:

> (a) either the overlapping consensus is superfluous within political liberalism, since reasonable people will by definition endorse the (correct) political conception of justice, or (b) the overlapping consensus is not superfluous, and people could (in the second justificatory stage) reject the political conception without being unreasonable. But if we embrace the second horn of this dilemma, this leads right back to the initial worry that people could veto the liberal conception of justice by claiming that it is not congruent with their illiberal comprehensive views.[92]

In response to this dilemma, Barry insists that "the overlapping consensus *is* superfluous, and so should be jettisoned from the justificatory structure of political liberalism."[93]

Quong's response to the dilemma preserves the need for an overlapping consensus, but changes the subject of that consensus. Instead of the subject of that consensus being principles of justice, Quong proposes that:

> The subject of the overlapping consensus is all, and only those, political values or ideals which all citizens in a well-ordered liberal society would endorse, and which thus form the foundation for any freestanding argument for public reason. Each reasonable citizen will find, from within their own comprehensive doctrine, reasons to embrace these political values and to give those values deliberative priority over comprehensive or non-public values.[94]

These political values, he claims, are the fundamental ideas of society as a fair system of social cooperation, and of citizens as free and equal. Because these fundamental ideas guide the setup of the original position, Quong maintains that "political liberalism is better understood as *beginning* with the overlapping consensus,"[95] and thus that the overlapping consensus belongs to "the *first* stage of political liberalism's justificatory structure"[96] (the setup of the original position and the argument from it to principles of justice). The overlapping consensus is on the inputs to the original position, in other words, not its outputs. We can therefore escape Barry's dilemma, he argues, while preserving the need for an overlapping consensus, once we recognize that the dilemma "is premised on the assumption that the overlapping consensus represents a second stage or test necessary to secure the full or public justification of justice. But once we dispense with this assumption, the dilemma disappears."[97]

The benefit to interpreting Rawls this way, Quong argues, is that it facilitates public reason.[98] If we have an overlapping consensus on these fundamental ideas, we have a common stock of concepts and values that we can rely on when we deliberate about how we should interpret or apply the principles of justice in cases where we disagree over how to interpret or apply them. By contrast, if we do not rely on this common stock of concepts and values as grounds for our principles—as informing our interpretations and applications of them—we invite reliance on our comprehensive doctrines as grounds for our principles instead. But this will undermine the practice of using public reason, since citizens in liberal societies hold different comprehensive views.

Whatever the merits of this last argument, what's worth noting about it is that Quong acknowledges that, on his, alternative proposal "there is no need to achieve consensus on our conclusions about justice: we only need to have a consensus on the fundamental ideas from which we begin our reasoning about justice."[99] He admits that, on this proposal, "the free standing [first stage] argument requires no further justificatory support."[100] He *concurs* with Barry's normative claim, then, that the inability of principles of justice to be the focus of an overlapping consensus should not be sufficient reason to reject them. Quong answers Barry's objection by conceding it. Neither Freeman, Weithman, nor Quong defuse the objection.

5.4 IMPLICATIONS OF THE BOMB

Given the arguable lack of need for an overlapping consensus, the weight of Rawls's argument properly belongs on the first stage: the original position and the derivation of principles from it. By jettisoning the international contract, then, and by relying solely on ideas drawn from political liberalism to handle the difficulties Rawls encounters in his law of peoples, defenders of the political liberal strategy err doubly. As an interpretive matter, they do not take Rawls seriously as a social contract theorist. As a substantive matter, they assume that the justification for principles of justice should depend on their ability to be the focus of an overlapping consensus. Therefore, we can safely reject the political liberal strategy, and concentrate instead on the cosmopolitan one.

Before turning to the cosmopolitan strategy, I want to draw one further implication from Barry's argument. As Barry shows, even if we accept the claim that the ability to be the focus of an overlapping consensus is necessary for justifying principles of justice, we must still assume that it is possible for some reasonable doctrines to be incompatible with Rawls's principles—at least initially. Otherwise, we do not get a problem in the first place that an overlapping consensus is designed to solve, in which case there is no need to argue that Rawls's principles could be the focus of one. In Rawls's international theory, this would imply that, in order to get a problem in the first place, we must assume that it is possible for some reasonable conceptions of domestic justice to be incompatible—at least initially—with Rawls's principles. The hypothesis would then be that they could be persuaded, freely, over time, to affirm them, and thus become members of an overlapping consensus, ones that *could* join one.

However, as Rawls characterizes them, liberal and decent, nonliberal societies can already endorse, without compromise, the principles of his law of peoples. They are the international analogues, respectively, of our derivatives and compatibles. On the other hand, outlaw societies, as Rawls characterizes them, are the international analogues of those who hold unreasonable (perhaps even irrational or mad) doctrines. As he treats them, they do not need to be recruited to an overlapping consensus. They only need to be contained. So then, for Rawls, which kinds of societies, initially incompatible with the law of peoples, are to be persuaded, freely, over time, to affirm it? They can't be the burdened societies. The question they present, for Rawls, is how to assist them. Nor can they be the benevolent absolutisms. Rawls's references to them are too sparse and fleeting.[101] As with burdened societies, there is no discussion of how their conceptions of domestic justice might adjust and evolve over time so as to affirm the law of peoples, freely, all things considered. Since neither burdened societies nor benevolent absolutisms qualify as well-ordered ones, for Rawls, the only question that concerns them is what kinds of interventions or sanctions would help them improve, not whether they can be freely persuaded to endorse the law of peoples without such efforts. While we could describe a kind of society *for* Rawls that serves as an example of a reasonable incompatible, the fact that Rawls himself does not do so, I want to suggest, is very telling.

According to the almost-liberal objection, Rawls, despite his reluctance to impose liberal values on nonliberal societies, winds up defending limits on international tolerance that are almost-liberal ones anyway. When the chips are down, Rawls's core instincts push him in the direction of a universal liberalism—only for him to hesitate and pull back from it in the end. We saw this manifested in several ways. In the article version of his argument, for example, we noticed that only moderate hierarchical societies—which are already almost liberal—could meet the precondition on entry to the contract, which then ratified and reaffirmed the limits on internal sovereignty that they already accepted (§ 3.2). Then, in the book version of his argument, we observed that the societies that met this precondition on entry grew increasingly liberal (§ 3.3). We also maintained that Rawls's inclusion of a right to emigrate seems to commit him to the proposition that all individuals everywhere are entitled to liberal rights and freedoms somewhere (§ 2.8 and § 3.4). Finally, we also called attention to Rawls's practical rationale for letting decent societies reform themselves in a liberal direction rather than pressuring them to do so, a rationale that seems to imply a universal liberalism as the standard at which we should aim (§ 3.4).

We now have further evidence of this tendency. On the one hand, we have the absence of any discussion of how a society with a reasonable conception of domestic justice, though one incompatible with the law of peoples, might adjust its conception of domestic justice over time so as to evolve into a well-ordered society that freely affirms that law. This is attributable to the fact that Rawls himself does not provide an example of such a society. On the other hand, Rawls does discuss how, by affording decent, nonliberal societies respect and toleration, they may evolve, freely, on their own terms, in a liberal direction. The absence of the one discussion and the presence of the other should strike us as a curious combination. If Rawls were concerned to show that his law of peoples could be the focus of an overlapping consensus, we would expect a discussion of the first sort. What we get instead is a discussion of the second sort. One explanation for this fact is that Rawls is simply being inattentive to what his argument needs. Another explanation is that, without realizing it, he treats decent, nonliberal societies as if *they* are the reasonable incompatibles that, over time, could come freely to affirm liberalism, which seems to imply that the law of peoples requires liberal domestic institutions of all societies. The almost-liberal objection continues to haunt Rawls.

5.5 FOREIGN POLICY, MEMBERSHIP, AND RECOGNITION

In contrast with the cosmopolitan strategy, which retains the international contract but substitutes individuals for collective agents, the strategy that I will defend retains both the international contract and collective agents but denies that Rawls's ambition was to generate principles of international justice (the third feature we identified). It differs from the cosmopolitan strategy, then, on interpretive grounds, but is compatible with it substantively: that is, it can accept (but does not require accepting) the view that an international social contract among individuals is the best strategy for defending principles of international justice.

"By the 'Law of Peoples,'" Rawls writes, in his book's opening sentence, "I mean a particular conception of right and *justice* that applies to the principles and norms of international law and practice" (my emphasis).[102] This clearly makes it sound as if Rawls wants to defend a theory of international justice. Then, throughout the book, he repeatedly refers to his principles as principles of justice.[103] "A Society of Peoples is reasonably just," he claims, "in that its members follow the reasonably just Law of Peoples in their mutual relations."[104] Such a society is realistically utopian, he adds, because "it depicts an achievable social world that combines political right and justice for all liberal and decent peoples in a Society of Peoples."[105] When he first introduces his principles, he calls them "basic principles of political justice" that "constitute the basic charter of the Law of Peoples."[106] If we were simply to count the number of references involved, it would be fair to say that this represents his dominant way of describing his principles.

At other times, however, Rawls seems to suggest that he is seeking something far more modest: a liberal *foreign policy* (my emphasis). In describing the outcome of the first session of the international contract, for example, he says that "we work out the ideals and principles of the *foreign policy* of a reasonably just *liberal* people" (Rawls's emphases).[107] The outcome of the second session, he argues, shows that "liberal principles of foreign policy are also reasonable from a decent nonliberal point of view."[108] In combination, the two sessions establish that "the guiding principle of liberal foreign policy" should not be "to shape all not yet liberal societies in a liberal direction, until eventually . . . all societies are liberal."[109] In each case, he refers to the principles *themselves* as principles of foreign policy and not, as we might expect, as principles of justice that are to be used as standards for appraising foreign policy. While this way of describing his principles is not featured as prominently as the first way, it still occurs quite frequently.[110]

When we consider Rawls's concern with membership, though, this latter way of characterizing his aim makes much more sense. One foundational aspect of foreign policy and international relations is determining who counts as a member of the international community of states. Members of the international community of states possess rights to nonintervention. So if we take Rawls's concern to be with determining the class of entities that possess a right to nonintervention, then we can construe him as aiming to establish criteria for determining which entities belong to that class. Entities belonging to that class will constitute member states of the international community.

Like his references to foreign policy, Rawls's references to membership occur quite frequently.[111] Rawls claims that he is interested in determining which kinds of society are "worthy of membership in a Society of Peoples."[112] Such societies, he says, are "acceptable as members in good standing in a reasonable Society of Peoples."[113] Not only will they include "a reasonably just constitutional democracy . . . as a member of a reasonably just Society of Peoples."[114] They will also include some decent "nonliberal societies as equal participating members in good standing of the Society of Peoples."[115]

Only liberal and decent nonliberal societies, according to Rawls, are members of the society of peoples.[116] Only they, according to Rawls, are to be tolerated. To tolerate, he explains, requires us "to refrain from exercising political sanctions—military, economic, or diplomatic—to make a people change its ways."[117] By honoring human rights, allowing some form of meaningful political participation, and behaving peacefully, such societies, Rawls suggests, fulfill conditions "sufficient to exclude justified and forceful intervention by other peoples . . . by diplomatic and economic sanctions, or in grave cases by military force."[118] In fulfilling these conditions, he seems to imply, they become entitled to rights to nonintervention.[119] Since those who are members, and those who possess rights to nonintervention, are the same class of entities for Rawls, we may construe him as attempting to defend, on normative grounds, criteria for determining which entities should be regarded as members, with rights to nonintervention. Since their rights to nonintervention depend on meeting these criteria, we may refer to these members as member *states*, without implying that they possess "traditional rights to war and to unrestricted internal autonomy."[120] These members will be member states of the international community.

Under international law, the criteria for determining which entities count as member states, with the rights, powers, and immunities of statehood, are referred to as the criteria for *recognizing* states. Accordingly, we may construe Rawls as aiming to defend, on normative grounds, such criteria. In *The Law of Peoples*, Rawls's aim is not to defend principles of international justice, but a theory of international recognition.[121]

Despite some resemblances between them, a theory of international recognition should not be confused with a theory of secession. Theories of secession will defend conditions under which a political entity has the right to secede from its parent state. By implication, they specify the conditions under which it ought to be recognized as a member state of the international community, too. Taking as their starting point the current array of internationally recognized states, they are theories for recognizing *new* members of the international community. Like theories of secession, theories of international recognition take as their starting point the current array of internationally recognized states. However, unlike theories of secession, theories of international recognition concern themselves not only with which entities to add, as newly recognized states, to the international community, but also with which ones to subtract—that is, with which currently recognized states to derecognize.

Just as we can ask whether this or that future political entity ought to be recognized as a state, so too can we ask whether this or that current political entity ought to have been recognized as a state—that is to say, we can ask whether its standing, as a recognized member of the international community, ought to be *revoked*. For two reasons, we need a theory that enables us to answer such a question. First, theoretical consistency demands that the same standards that apply prospectively also apply retrospectively. In other words, unless we can give a justification for treating them differently, the standards that we apply to new claimants for recognized statehood should also apply (and be met by) those entities that we continue to recognize as member states of the international community. Second, moral consistency requires this as well. When we deny state recognition to political entities, we owe their representatives a credible explanation—one that shows that we are treating like cases alike. Continuing to recognize member states that fail to meet the criteria used to deny recognition in these cases undercuts the credibility of that explanation. A theory of international recognition strives to meet both requirements of theoretical and moral consistency.

Reading Rawls as defending a theory of international recognition is our next step in answering the idle-contract objection.

NOTES

1. See Rawls, *The Law of Peoples*, pp. 59–60.
2. My emphasis. Rawls, *The Law of Peoples*, p 67. See also the references in § 5.5.
3. See, e.g., Brian Barry, *Theories of Justice*; Beitz, *Political Theory and International Relations*; Moellendorf, "Constructing the Law of Peoples"; Pogge, *Realizing Rawls*; and David A. J. Richards, "International Distributive Justice," in J. Roland Pennock and John W. Chapman (eds.), *Ethics, Economics, and the Law: Nomos XXIV* (New York: New York University Press, 1982), pp. 275–99. In fairness to most of these authors, however, it should be mentioned that they wrote well before *The Law of Peoples* was on the scene.
4. Rawls, *Political Liberalism*, p. xvi.
5. Rawls, *Political Liberalism*, pp. 133–34.
6. Rawls, *Political Liberalism*, p. 129.
7. Rawls, *Political Liberalism*, p. 129.
8. See Leif Wenar, "Political Liberalism: An Internal Critique," *Ethics* 106, no. 1 (October 1995): 32–62, p. 36.
9. Rawls, *Political Liberalism*, pp. 60–61.
10. Rawls, *Political Liberalism*, p. 49.
11. Rawls, *Political Liberalism*, p. 49.
12. Rawls, *Political Liberalism*, p. 214, 223.
13. Rawls, *Political Liberalism*, pp. 223–24.
14. Rawls, *Political Liberalism*, p. 213.
15. Avila, "Defending a Law of Peoples: Political Liberalism and Decent Peoples," p. 100.
16. Avila, "Defending a Law of Peoples: Political Liberalism and Decent Peoples," p. 100.
17. See Rawls, *The Law of Peoples*, p. 70, which Avila quotes from and cites at p. 100, n. 38 of "Defending a Law of Peoples: Political Liberalism and Decent Peoples."
18. Avila, "Defending a Law of Peoples: Political Liberalism and Decent Peoples," p. 94.
19. Avila, "Defending a Law of Peoples: Political Liberalism and Decent Peoples," p. 104. See generally, pp. 104–7.
20. Avila, "Defending a Law of Peoples: Political Liberalism and Decent Peoples," p. 107.
21. Avila, "Defending a Law of Peoples: Political Liberalism and Decent Peoples," p. 106.
22. Avila, "Defending a Law of Peoples: Political Liberalism and Decent Peoples," p. 113. This unique relationship is due to the fact that "*decent* peoples . . . do share, on the whole, comprehensive doctrines and do rely on their particular comprehensive doctrine as a basis for state authority" (p. 96).

23. Avila also hints that we may be able to derive an even more robust set of such rights. See Avila, "Defending a Law of Peoples: Political Liberalism and Decent Peoples," p. 116, n. 60. Avila's reliance on reasonableness (and his bypassing of the international contract) to determine restrictions on internal sovereignty may also be found in Mitchell Avila, "Human Rights and Toleration in Rawls," *Human Rights Review* 12, no. 1 (March 2011): 1–14, pp. 8, 11–12.

24. Reidy, "Political Authority and Human Rights," p. 184.

25. Reidy, "Political Authority and Human Rights," p. 185.

26. Reidy, "Political Authority and Human Rights," p. 185.

27. Reidy, "Political Authority and Human Rights," pp. 182–84. Reidy's reliance on this liberal self-inquiry (and his bypassing of the international contract) to determine restrictions on internal sovereignty may also be found in David Reidy, "A Just Global Economy: In Defense of Rawls," *The Journal of Ethics* 11, no. 2 (June 2007): 193–236, pp. 207–17, esp. 217; and his "Human Rights: Institutions and Agendas," *Public Affairs Quarterly* 22, no. 4 (October 2008): 381–404, esp. 394–97.

28. See Rawls, *Political Liberalism*, pp. 16, 49–50 for his equating of reciprocity and reasonableness. See also Alyssa Bernstein's nice discussion of this equivalence in "A Human Right to Democracy? Legitimacy and Intervention," pp. 283–84.

29. In fact, when Reidy elsewhere offers a contractarian argument on Rawls's behalf, it's clear that the contract itself does no work in establishing restrictions on internal sovereignty. Peoples, he argues, are a type of agent that is both *corporate* and *moral*. In order to qualify as a corporate *moral* agent, though, it must meet certain conditions. In particular, a peoples must possess a common good conception of justice (with the restrictions on internal sovereignty that that entails, such as respect for basic human rights). Placed in a hypothetical contract, such corporate moral agents would agree not to restrict their autonomy internationally by introducing any new limits on their internal sovereignty beyond those required to maintain their status as corporate moral agents. Hence, the contract merely ratifies and reaffirms limits on internal sovereignty (possession of a common good conception of justice) that were established independently by appeal to reciprocity (or reasonableness). See David Reidy, "Rawls on International Justice: A Defense," *Political Theory* 32, no. 3 (June 2004): 291–319, esp. pp. 303–5.

30. Bernstein, "A Human Right to Democracy? Legitimacy and Intervention," p. 282. Bernstein's reliance on public reason (and her bypassing of the international contract) may also be found in Alyssa Bernstein, "Justifying Universal Human Rights via Rawlsian Public Reason," *Human Rights and Ethics/Derechos Humanos y Ètica: Proceedings of the 22nd IVR World Congress* (Granada, Spain, 2005), Volume III: 90–103, pp. 102–3; and Alyssa Bernstein, "Human Rights, Global Justice, and Disaggregated States: John Rawls, Onora O'Neill, and Anne-Marie Slaughter," *American Journal of Economics and Sociology* 66, no. 1 (January 2007): 87–112, pp. 93–97.

31. Bernstein, "A Human Right to Democracy? Legitimacy and Intervention," pp. 285–86.

32. Barry, "John Rawls and the Search for Stability," pp. 874–915.

33. Referring to our knowledge of virtue, Socrates, paraphrasing Meno, explains, "[A] man . . . cannot search for what he knows—since he knows it, there is no need to search" (*Meno*, 80e).

34. Rawls, *A Theory of Justice*, p. 567.

35. Rawls, *A Theory of Justice*, p. 572, quoted at Barry, "John Rawls and the Search for Stability," p. 886.

36. Rawls, *A Theory of Justice*, p. 574.

37. Barry, "John Rawls and the Search for Stability," p. 886.

38. Barry, "John Rawls and the Search for Stability," p. 908.

39. Barry, "John Rawls and the Search for Stability," pp. 887–88.

40. Barry, "John Rawls and the Search for Stability," pp. 884–85, 887.

41. Barry, "John Rawls and the Search for Stability," pp. 888.

42. Rawls, *Political Liberalism*, p. 143, quoted at Barry, "John Rawls and the Search for Stability," p. 890.

43. Rawls, *Political Liberalism*, p. 143. This addition is not quoted by Barry.

44. Barry, "John Rawls and the Search for Stability," p. 890.

45. See Barry, "John Rawls and the Search for Stability," p. 896, quoting Rawls, *Political Liberalism*, pp. 226, 244, n. 32. Statements by Rawls elsewhere in *Political Liberalism* also seem to suggest this criterion. See esp. pp. 61 (reasonable persons, who by stipulation affirm only reasonable doctrines, therefore "endorse some form of liberty of conscience and freedom of thought"), 64 n. 19 (unreasonable doctrines reject one or more democratic freedoms), and 65 (contrasting reasonable doctrines with those "that would suppress altogether the basic rights and liberties").

46. Barry, "John Rawls and the Search for Stability," p. 896.

47. See Barry, "John Rawls and the Search for Stability," p. 897, quoting Rawls, *Political Liberalism*, pp. 59–60.

48. Barry, "John Rawls and the Search for Stability," p. 898.

49. Barry, "John Rawls and the Search for Stability," pp. 905–10.

50. Barry, "John Rawls and the Search for Stability," pp. 910–13.

51. Barry, "John Rawls and the Search for Stability," p. 907.

52. See Rawls, *Political Liberalism*, p. 170.

53. Barry, "John Rawls and the Search for Stability," p. 909.

54. Barry, "John Rawls and the Search for Stability," p. 909.

55. Barry, "John Rawls and the Search for Stability," p. 911.

56. Rawls, *Political Liberalism*, p. 142.

57. Rawls, *Political Liberalism*, p. 141.

58. Rawls, *Political Liberalism*, p. 169.

59. Kant's moral philosophy with its ideal of autonomy, he says, is an example. See Rawls, *Political Liberalism*, pp. 160, 169.

60. Rawls, *Political Liberalism*, p. 170.

61. A "comprehensive pluralist view," he says, is an example. See Rawls, *Political Liberalism*, pp. 155, 159–60, 170. I also place utilitarian views—which, Rawls claims, might regard justice as fairness as a "workable approximation" to them—in this category (p. 170).

62. Rawls, *Political Liberalism*, p. 160.

63. For example, we can imagine mixed categories, such as the partially derivative and partially compatible. Rawls's example of "religious doctrines with an account of free faith" might fall into this category. See Rawls, *Political Liberalism*, p. 170. Partially derivative and partially incompatible doctrines, and partially compatible and partially incompatible ones, would fall into the category of incompatibles, as defined above.

64. Rawls, *Political Liberalism*, p. 40. See also p. 134, where Rawls considers the possibility that doctrines might affirm justice as fairness provided that it is "not too much in conflict with citizens' essential interests as formed and encouraged by their social arrangements."

65. Rawls, *Political Liberalism*, p. 146.

66. Rawls, *Political Liberalism*, p. 139.

67. Rawls, *Political Liberalism*, p. 157.

68. Rawls, *Political Liberalism*, p. 155.

69. Rawls, *Political Liberalism*, p. 143.

70. Rawls seems to prefer the indicative mood ("can" rather than "could"). See, e.g., *Political Liberalism*, pp. 65, 143.

71. Rawls, *Political Liberalism*, p. 159. See generally, pp. 158–72.

72. Rawls, *Political Liberalism*, p. 160, n. 25. Joshua Cohen's provides a nice account of how this process might work in practice in his "A More Democratic Liberalism," *Michigan Law Review* 92, no. 6 (May 1994): 1503–46, pp. 1530–36.

73. Weithman claims that Barry "badly . . . misses the mark" with his objection to the possibility of an overlapping consensus, arguing that Barry assumes, fallaciously, that because there would be holdouts currently, in our non-well-ordered society, there

would also be holdouts in a well-ordered society. This seems to me to underestimate the force of Barry's objection, since it can be recast in the form presented above (that if there *were* holdouts in a well-ordered society, we still confront the Barry dilemma). I address this more fully in the next section of this chapter. See Paul Weithman, *Why Political Liberalism? On John Rawls's Political Turn* (New York: Oxford University Press, 2010), p. 346.

74. Rawls, *Political Liberalism*, p. 24.

75. Rawls, *Political Liberalism*, p. 65.

76. Rawls, *Political Liberalism*, p. 141.

77. Rawls, *Political Liberalism*, p. 164.

78. Barry calls these doctrines *reasonable dogmatisms*: reasonable in virtue of their being exercises of theoretical and practical reason within a tradition of thought, dogmatic in virtue of holding that no reasonable person could reject them. See Barry, "John Rawls and the Search for Stability," pp. 901–3.

79. Rawls, *Political Liberalism*, p. xix. See Barry, "John Rawls and the Search for Stability," pp. 888-89 and 914 for the suggestion.

80. Barry, "John Rawls and the Search for Stability," pp. 876–80.

81. Barry, "John Rawls and the Search for Stability," pp. 883–85.

82. Barry, "John Rawls and the Search for Stability," pp. 887–90.

83. Barry, "John Rawls and the Search for Stability," pp. 890–96, 898–901.

84. See Barry, "John Rawls and the Search for Stability," p. 901, and pp. 901–3 generally.

85. Samuel Freeman, "Congruence and the Good of Justice," in Samuel Freeman, ed., *The Cambridge Companion to Rawls* (New York: Cambridge University Press, 2003), ch. 7, pp. 281–82.

86. Freeman, "Congruence and the Good of Justice," pp. 297–99.

87. Freeman, "Congruence and the Good of Justice," p. 308.

88. Samuel Freeman, "Political Liberalism and the Possibility of a Just Democratic Constitution," *Chicago-Kent Law* Review 69 (1994): 619–68, pp. 641–43. The quote appears at p. 641.

89. Weithman, *Why Political Liberalism? On John Rawls's Political Turn*, p. 344.

90. Weithman, *Why Political Liberalism? On John Rawls's Political Turn*, p. 346.

91. Weithman, *Why Political Liberalism? On John Rawls's Political Turn*, p. 344.

92. Jonathan Quong, *Liberalism without Perfection* (New York: Oxford University Press, 2011), p. 167.

93. Quong, *Liberalism without Perfection*, p. 169.

94. Quong, *Liberalism without Perfection*, p. 185.

95. Quong, *Liberalism without Perfection*, p. 180.

96. Quong, *Liberalism without Perfection*, p. 182.

97. Quong, *Liberalism without Perfection*, p. 190.

98. Quong, *Liberalism without Perfection*, pp. 170–80.

99. Quong, *Liberalism without Perfection*, p. 186.

100. Quong, *Liberalism without Perfection*, p. 186.

101. See Rawls, *The Law of Peoples*, pp. 4, 63, 92.

102. Rawls, *The Law of Peoples*, p. 3.

103. See Rawls, *The Law of Peoples*, pp. 5, 6, 7, 9, 11, 17, 18, 19, 22, 25, 37, 38, 42, 44, 45, 60, 70, 78, 82, 86, 87, 91, 113–20, 124, 125, and 128.

104. Rawls, *The Law of Peoples*, p. 5.

105. Rawls, *The Law of Peoples*, p. 6.

106. See Rawls, *The Law of Peoples*, p. 37.

107. Rawls, *The Law of Peoples*, p. 10. Similar phrasing occurs on p. 55.

108. Rawls, *The Law of Peoples*, p. 58.

109. Rawls, *The Law of Peoples*, p. 60.

110. See Rawls, *The Law of Peoples*, pp. 8, 10, 48, 55, 56, 58, 60, 63, 65, 82, 83, 85, 93, and 128.

111. See Rawls, *The Law of Peoples*, pp. 4, 5, 6, 11, 52, 59, 63, 64, 67, 68, 80, 84, 93, 111, 113, 114, 118, 120, 124, 126, 127, and 128.

112. Rawls, *The Law of Peoples*, p. 4.

113. Rawls, *The Law of Peoples*, p. 5.

114. Rawls, *The Law of Peoples*, p. 11.

115. Rawls, *The Law of Peoples*, p. 59.

116. "I shall use the term 'Society of Peoples' to mean all those peoples who follow the ideals and principles of the Law of Peoples in their mutual relations." Rawls, *The Law of Peoples*, p. 3.

117. Rawls, *The Law of Peoples*, p. 59.

118. Rawls, *The Law of Peoples*, p. 80.

119. For further evidence that Rawls seeks to determine a normative threshold for justifiable intervention, see Rawls, *The Law of Peoples*, pp. 59, 60, 61, 79, 80, 81, 83, 84, 90, 93–94 (n. 6), and 110.

120. Rawls, *The Law of Peoples*, p. 27.

121. The claim is not that Rawls consciously had in mind the aim of establishing a theory of recognition. The claim is that, however vaguely and inchoately, Rawls may have had this aim in mind, and more importantly, the best Rawlsian position is to attribute this aim to him.

Part II

Solution

Constructing a Theory of International Recognition

SIX

The Justice-Based and Pragmatic Theories

6.1 RAWLS'S THEORY OF INTERNATIONAL RECOGNITION

Reinterpreting Rawls's claims about international justice as claims about international recognition, we get a view like the following. Let's say that *minimal justice* requires respect for basic human rights and peaceful foreign relations. Meeting these minimum requirements of internal and external justice is both necessary and sufficient for recognizing a political entity as a state. Therefore, political entities ought to be recognized as states if and only if they meet minimum requirements of internal and external justice. Call this the *justice-based* theory of international recognition.[1]

In this chapter, I will argue that we should reject *any* justice-based theory of recognition: not only one that incorporates the particular minimum that Rawls defends, but ones that incorporate any other minimum as well. In rejecting the justice-based theory, therefore, we will have our first departure from Rawls's own theory of international recognition. Also in this chapter, I introduce an alternative, which I call the *pragmatic* theory, and defend it against various objections. Then, in chapters 7 through 9, I elaborate the pragmatic theory and derive its principles from an international contract with collective agents who reason from behind a veil of ignorance. Having rejected Rawls's own theory, we will develop a *Rawlsian* view that is sounder.

6.2 THE STAKES

When the international community recognizes political entities as states, it confers upon them the rights and powers of statehood.[2] These include the right to territorial integrity, the right to noninterference in their internal affairs, the power to make treaties, and the right (subject to certain restrictions) to enforce legal rules on those within their territory.[3] According to the *justice-based* theory of recognition, political entities ought to be recognized as states if and only if they satisfy minimal requirements of internal and external justice. According to the *pragmatic* theory, they ought to be recognized as states if and only if cooperating with them and giving them international support would advance peace and justice among and within them—that is, international peace and justice—whether or not they themselves currently satisfy minimal requirements of internal and external justice.[4]

My aim is to show that, despite the intuitive appeal of the justice-based theory, we should embrace the pragmatic theory instead. Before doing that, though, I want to explain what is at stake in the disagreement between them. The political stakes involve securing long-term international peace and justice and maintaining the credibility of the international community when its officials speak in a public forum. If we embrace the justice-based theory, I hope to show, the international community would be forced to choose between endangering international peace and justice and compromising its credibility. This problem is inherent in any justice-based view that (rightly) concedes a role to pragmatic considerations. But the stakes are philosophical as well. Any theory of recognition must concede a role to pragmatic considerations if it is to be taken seriously. By conceding this, though, they risk compromising our standards of justice. To avoid this, we should keep our standards for recognition separate from our standards for justice, as the pragmatic theory recommends. Admittedly, this does involve a compromise: we may have to grant recognition to some unjust entities as a result. But it is a compromise in the right place. It is a political compromise, not a philosophical one. Our theories of justice need to be taken seriously too.

By rejecting the justice-based theory, I realize that I will be laboring against a view that holds considerable intuitive appeal. The justice-based theory seems to have the best of both worlds: normative force *and* real-world applicability. It has normative force, because it apparently makes the most reasonable of moral demands in requiring entities seeking state-recognition to be minimally just. It also has real-world applicability, because it acknowledges a rightful role for pragmatic considerations. By contrast, the pragmatic theory seems to sacrifice its normative force because it does not even place *minimal* moral demands on entities seeking state recognition. In the interest of letting the international community reach decisions about recognition without requiring minimal justice from the entities that seek it, the pragmatic theory seems overly concerned with real-world applicability, at the cost of being soft on injustice. In addition to defending the pragmatic theory, therefore, I will try to show why these respectable and understandable sentiments about being soft on injustice are misplaced.

While my primary concern in this chapter is with the recognition of states, I will also argue that the justice-based view is not plausible as a theory for recognizing governments either, and that the pragmatic view is superior in this area as well.[5] But in order to see why, we must first decide what criteria we should have for recognizing states, for two reasons. First, under international law, decisions about whether to recognize a government as the legitimate agent of a state *presuppose* recognition of that state. So we need criteria for state recognition before we can even consider whether to recognize the government of a state. Second, the reason why the justice-based view fails as a theory for recognizing governments is strikingly similar to the reason why it fails as a theory for recognizing states. Once we appreciate why the justice-based view fails as a theory for recognizing states, therefore, we will be better positioned to see why it fails as a theory for recognizing governments, too.

To defend these claims, I will begin by explaining the concept of minimal justice, and then, drawing on this discussion, present the central argument against the justice-based theory of state-recognition and for the pragmatic one. Next, I consider amendments to the justice-based theory—including recasting it as a theory for recognizing governments—and argue that they fail. With this done, I show that the main objection to the pragmatic theory—that it makes the international community an accomplice in injustice by allowing some unjust entities to be recognized—rests on mistaken assumptions about what it must claim. Finally, I consider the wider implications of these results. The weaknesses of the justice-based account, I suggest, are symptomatic of a deeper mistake about the role that practical considerations should play in our theorizing about international recognition and justice, and unless we correct it, we risk compromising the credibility of the normative advice that we want our public officials to follow.

6.3 MINIMAL JUSTICE

When we judge that a political entity satisfies minimal requirements of justice, what we mean is that it is minimally just, in the sense of being *good enough* or *acceptable*. What we mean by this, though, is ambiguous. In many contexts, what we mean by "good enough" (or "acceptable") is relative to a particular role or purpose. In other contexts, what we mean is not relative to any particular role or purpose but is rather an overall assessment of some sort.[6] In order to clarify this distinction, and to determine what we mean when we judge an entity to be minimally just, let us consider some situations where we make one or the other of these judgments.

Suppose that we want to hire a philosopher. After reading the candidates' files, conducting interviews, and bringing several candidates to campus, we meet with our colleagues to rank the finalists. For the sake of simplicity, we can assume that the members of our department all agree on what qualities the ideal candidate should possess and the extent to which each finalist has or lacks them (although this is not necessary). As a result, we all agree in our rankings. Now comes the crucial decision. Should we make an offer to the leading candidate? It depends. If the leading candidate is unimpressive, we may well decide to reopen the search or postpone it until the following year. Suppose, though, that we judge that she is good enough to merit an offer, but she declines. The second-ranked candidate then comes under consideration, but we judge that he is not good enough to merit an offer. As a result, we reopen the search.

Notice the following about this situation. First, the judgments that we make are relative to a particular role or purpose. For the purpose of being a new member of the department, only the top-ranked candidate is good enough—only she exceeds the minimal standards for teaching, research, and collegiality that the department expects. Second, while these standards need not be the product of a formal or explicit decision, our sense for where they lie involves a substantive determination, not an arbitrary choice. If two members of the department disagreed over what the minimum should be, we would recognize them as having a substantive disagreement, not an arbitrary one (like one over the minimum hair someone can have without being bald). Third, we reach these judgments by comparison with a certain standard or ideal. We decide what qualities the ideal candidate should possess, then evaluate candidates by comparing them with that standard. In principle, we could even list these qualities, give them a lexical ordering, then rank the candidates by deciding which of them possess the ones most important for the position. Yet once we have this information, we must still decide whether a candidate meets our minimal standards. Again, we make a comparison. How far from the ideal can a candidate's qualities be and still be good enough or acceptable—that is, still meet minimal standards?[7] We must exercise judgment, no doubt, in making this decision, and in some sense we must draw a line. But as we have just seen, the decision is still a substantive one, which explains why we take it seriously.

However, these judgments, while clearly evaluative, do not seem to be *moral* ones, as they would be if we were giving an overall assessment of a candidate's personal character. One's talent as a philosopher may be related to one's excellence or virtue as a person, but it is not what we typically regard as the whole of it. Suppose we learn many terrible things about the top-ranked candidate. She is routinely insensitive, cruel, even criminal in her dealings with everyone except her students and colleagues (which the search process failed to uncover). The second-ranked candidate, by contrast, volunteers significant amounts of time each week at the soup kitchen and devotes large portions of his income to famine relief. In this situation, we would be inclined to say that the first candidate, despite her redeeming qualities as a philosopher, is not even a minimally decent person, while the second candidate, despite his shortcomings as a philosopher, is truly an excellent one. The first candidate fails to meet the minimal standards for being a decent person. The second candidate does meet them.

Although these latter judgments are not relative to any particular role or purpose, the way we reach them is the same. We judge a person's character by comparing it with a certain standard or ideal. Were we to make the standard explicit, it would specify certain qualities possession of which makes a person fully good, and lack of which makes a person fully bad (or evil), depending on the degree to which a person has or lacks them. In principle, we could even give them a lexical ordering and rank individuals as better or worse depending on how closely they approximate the ideal. Yet once we have this information, we can still intelligibly ask for an overall assessment of their character. We can ask whether they are minimally decent persons, despite their imperfections. So we make another comparison. How far from the ideal can someone's character be and still be good enough or acceptable—that is, still meet minimal standards? Again, the decision requires judgment, and in some sense draws a line, but is still substantive. If two people disagreed over what the minimum should be—over the standard which, if unmet, labels a person beyond the pale, someone we don't want to deal with unless we have to—we would recognize them as having a substantive disagreement, not one over the arbitrary application of a term.[8]

Sometimes, we combine these two types of judgment. We sometimes *embed* a judgment that makes an overall assessment within one made relative to a particular role or purpose. A member of the clergy, for example, is usually expected to have an exemplary personal character in addition to certain administrative, counseling, public speaking, and community relations skills. In many cases, however, the expectations are lower, and implicit. When we make an offer to the top-ranked candidate, for instance, we may only expect her to be a minimally decent person, not an exemplary one, even if our expectations of her teaching, research, and collegiality are higher. In principle, though, we can separate the overall assessment from the purpose-relative judgment and consider it independently of that purpose.

Which of these types of judgment are we making when we judge an entity to be minimally just? In some cases, we are making a purely moral judgment. We mean not that the entity is "good enough" or "acceptable" relative to a particular role or purpose, but that, as an overall assessment of some sort, it is "good enough" or "acceptable." In other cases, we are embedding this overall assessment within a purpose-relative judgment. If being minimally just is a condition for membership on certain international bodies, for example, then we mean that its favorable overall assessment enables it to meet one of the conditions for being declared "good enough" or "acceptable" for that purpose.

Either way, we are left with an intelligible notion of minimal justice. Like judgments of minimal decency, judgments of minimal justice make a comparison with a certain standard or ideal—in this case, with the best theory of justice—and the minimum is determined by its proximity to what that theory requires.[9] How far from the ideal can an entity's political institutions be and still be good enough or acceptable—that is, still meet minimal standards? Like the previous decisions, this decision also requires judgment, and in some sense draws a line, but is still substantive.

One feature of these judgments that will interest us is the extent to which pragmatic considerations may justifiably influence them. Again, consider the analogy with the faculty search. Suppose that for the fifth consecutive year, we fail to fill the position because none of the candidates has published his or her dissertation, which is one of our minimal standards. Meanwhile, our class sizes are increasing faster than we can handle with existing faculty (and the dean is growing *very* irritated). These kinds of pragmatic considerations might convince us that our minimal standards are too utopian, and we might justifiably adjust them downward as a result.

But while pragmatic considerations may influence our minimal standards to this extent, there are some important qualifications. If our minimal standards are not utopian to begin with, for instance, we might decide that the problem is not with the standards themselves, but with the way the world is. There are limits to how far we can adjust them without compromising them altogether. Suppose that the only way to fill the position is to hire someone who commits basic logical fallacies and teaches students that, according to Plato, there is no difference between knowledge and opinion. In that case, it would be more candid to admit that pragmatic considerations force us to hire someone who *fails* to meet minimal standards than to suggest that he meets minimal standards that pragmatic considerations have convinced us to adjust. A similar point holds for our overall assessment of his personal character. Pragmatic considerations *might* appropriately influence whether we decide to hire someone who is minimally decent rather than exemplary as a person. But they do not appropriately influence our judgment of what counts as minimal decency itself. If the only way to fill the position is to hire a known criminal and thug, for instance, then again, it would be more candid to admit that pragmatic considerations force us to hire someone who fails to meet minimal standards of decency than to suggest that he meets minimal standards of decency that pragmatic considerations have convinced us to adjust.

Similarly, pragmatic considerations might appropriately influence whether we decide to grant state recognition to entities that are minimally rather than fully just. But they do not appropriately influence our judgment of what counts as minimal justice itself. If the only way to achieve our pragmatic aims is to recognize some entities that are *international* thugs, for example, then it would be more candid to admit that they fail to be minimally just than to suggest that they satisfy minimal requirements of justice that pragmatic considerations have convinced us to lower.[10]

We can summarize these findings as follows. The notion of minimal justice carries independent weight. It is not an inherently flexible standard that can be adjusted to whatever level is necessary to achieve our pragmatic aims and needs, or whatever other ends we may have. It is not a mere consequence of decisions we make on pragmatic grounds. It is, in this sense, objective, because its level is not entirely up to us to determine. To emphasize this, I shall from this point forward refer to *the best theory of justice* as what determines or sets the minimum, or according to which the minimum is set, even though, of course, *we* must ultimately do the determining or setting. As we will see, the justice-based theory has difficulty accommodating this fact about minimal justice.

6.4 THE CENTRAL ARGUMENT

We are now ready to consider the central argument against the justice-based theory and for the pragmatic one. To begin, both theories of recognition assume that, for the foreseeable future, decisions about whether to recognize certain entities as states will remain on the international agenda. This is not to deny that other matters, related to state recognition, deserve international attention—whether to recognize certain peoples as having special rights of self-determination within a recognized state, for example, or as having the right to form a state even if they do not yet have a recognized territory. But given that states today are the primary international actors, and given the tremendous importance attached to state recognition (in some cases whether an entity survives as a state depends on it), there is a pressing practical need to develop a theory of state-recognition, which both theories try to fill. As Allen Buchanan writes, "The decision whether to recognize an entity as a state has important moral implications. . . . [Recognized states] are entitled to support for their territorial integrity and to noninterference in their domestic affairs, and ought to be allowed to participate in the basic processes of international law."[11]

In addition, both theories accept the following claims. First, international justice is an appropriate goal for the international legal system—it is neither unrealistic nor merely instrumental for achieving peace. Second, if international justice is to be a realistic goal, then the criteria for recognition must be realistic, too. At the very least, they should not be so utopian as to make the pursuit of international peace and justice self-defeating. Like the criteria for an adequate theory of any sort, but especially for a normative theory, the criteria for an adequate theory of recognition must not have (too many, significantly) implausible implications, either in actual circumstances or in hypothetical ones—and one way in which a theory can have implications that are implausible enough to reject it is by being self-defeating.[12] Third, in addition to conferring the rights and powers of statehood, recognition confers an entitlement to participate in the processes for formulating, adjudicating, and implementing international law—processes crucial to realizing long-term international peace and justice.[13]

In accepting these claims, however, the justice-based theory encounters a problem that the pragmatic theory avoids: it lets pragmatic considerations rather than the best theory of justice determine what counts as minimal justice. The reasoning goes like this. If the best theory of justice sets a standard of minimal justice that is high enough, then on the justice-based theory, where minimal justice is required for recognition, only a few entities may qualify for recognition as states. If only a few entities qualify for recognition as states, though, then only a few entities will be entitled to participate in the processes for formulating, adjudicating, and implementing international law. But if only a few entities are entitled to participate in these processes, that may make the pursuit of international peace and justice inefficacious. If so, then the requirement that our criteria for recognition be realistic dictates lowering our standard of minimal justice so that enough entities qualify for recognition as states to make the realization of peace and justice a genuine possibility. That suggests that pragmatic considerations—not the best theory of justice—drive the level of the minimum. Alternatively, even if enough entities do qualify under the higher standard to make the pursuit of peace and justice efficacious, the requirement that our criteria for recognition be realistic still implies that, hypothetically, if too few did qualify, we would have to lower the minimum. That again suggests that pragmatic considerations drive the minimum. Since the justice-based theory allows its minimum to be adjusted to whatever level is necessary for enough entities to qualify—since its standard for state recognition must be adjusted to satisfy that pragmatic need—it seems like the justice-based account is really a pragmatic theory in disguise.

The pragmatic theory is more straightforward: it candidly admits that pragmatic considerations determine which entities we should recognize as states. Moreover, by severing the connection between the recognition of an entity and minimal justice, it prevents the exigencies of international politics—the need to bring enough entities into the processes for formulating, adjudicating, and implementing international law—from influencing our judgment of what constitutes minimal justice.

We can see the central problem with the justice-based view, then, in the following example. Suppose for the sake of argument that the best theory of justice is a liberalism that requires neutrality toward the good, respect for equal liberal rights (democratic political rights and rights against discrimination), and a guarantee of the fair value of the political liberties. Political entities that satisfy these requirements are *fully just*. Also suppose that, according to this theory, entities that do not respect basic human rights—defined as rights to life (to personal security and means of subsistence), to liberty (to freedom from slavery, serfdom, forced labor), and against religious persecution—are *severely unjust*. Between these two points lies a continuum. Assume that: (1) Entities that fail to guarantee the fair value of the political liberties but otherwise respect the equal liberal rights and observe neutrality toward the good are the next closest to being fully just. (2) Entities that fail to guarantee the fair value of the political liberties but do respect the equal liberal rights—yet are not neutral toward the good—come next. (3) Then come entities that do not respect the equal liberal rights—that are nondemocratic, permit discrimination, or both—but do respect basic human rights.

How should we establish where minimal justice falls on this continuum? The answer, we have seen, is: by comparison with the best theory of justice. Suppose, then, that according to the best theory of justice, official discrimination involves such a deep affront to human dignity that even minimal justice must forbid it. The equal liberal rights forbid such discrimination—whether it is based on race, gender, religion, or any other morally irrelevant feature of persons. By contrast, basic human rights do not, since they permit unequal religious liberties and thus some degree of religious discrimination (provided it does not rise to the level of persecution). However, according to the best theory of justice, entities that do not guarantee the fair value of the political liberties or observe neutrality toward the good (that use state funds to promote art and culture, say)—though they depart from full justice—do not commit a deep affront to human dignity the way that entities that officially discriminate do. Therefore, according to the best theory of justice, minimal justice demands that entities respect the equal liberal rights, even if they do not guarantee the fair value of the political liberties or observe neutrality toward the good; minimal justice requires (2). No doubt the reasoning here is largely intuitive. But the exact reasoning is unimportant. What is important is that minimal justice is determined by the best theory of justice—as it intuitively seems it should be—not by pragmatic considerations.[14]

But the justice-based theory cannot accept this as long as the possibility of conflict exists between what the best theory of justice requires for minimal justice, and what the realities of international politics require for recognition if we are to bring enough entities into the processes for formulating, adjudicating, and implementing international law.[15] Because it accepts the claim that our criteria for recognition should not be so utopian as to make the pursuit of peace and justice inefficacious, it must resolve this conflict by lowering its standard for recognition beneath what the best theory of justice requires for minimal justice, while insisting, misleadingly, that this standard identifies what minimal justice is.[16]

6.5 THE REAL WORLD

Although the force of this argument rests solely on the possibility of conflict between what the best theory of justice requires for minimal justice and what the realities of international politics require for recognition, I shall now argue that this conflict *actually* exists with the standards that any plausible theory of justice would deem minimally just. As a result, the justice-based theory would require lowering them even further—exactly as the objection charges.

Consider two different standards for minimal justice. Both require entities to respect basic human rights, but one is stronger than the other. According to the *weak* standard, the basic human rights are rights to life (to personal security and means of subsistence), to liberty (to freedom from slavery, serfdom, forced labor), and against religious persecution. The weak standard intends to capture the idea that an entity could enjoy basically peaceful and benevolent rule even if it is not democratic and allows some inequalities based on gender, race, ethnicity, nationality, or religion. According to the *strong* standard, the basic human rights also include rights against discrimination based on gender, race, ethnicity, nationality, and religion; and rights to democratic governance in the minimal sense of requiring representative bodies, accountable officials, and some free speech and assembly (to be sensitive to the different ways that democracy can be realized in different culturally specific settings).[17]

In what follows, I will mostly focus on whether entities meet these standards in their internal relations, even though, with the weak standard, we can ask whether they meet it in their external relations as well. This is mainly due to the availability of evidence. In any case, if too few entities qualify for state recognition when we consider internal relations alone, even fewer will qualify if we consider both internal and external ones.

The Strong Standard

Is the strong standard feasible? Will enough entities qualify for recognition as states under it to make the pursuit of peace and justice—the moral goals of the international legal system—efficacious? That depends on whether it brings enough entities into the processes for formulating, adjudicating, and implementing international law to achieve them. Rather than focusing on whether it brings enough entities into these processes from the entire world, however, let us focus on a few strategic regions and ask whether it brings in enough entities from those regions to make the pursuit of peace and justice *there* efficacious. This will be a more manageable task, and if we can show that the pursuit of peace and justice in those regions would be inefficacious, then we will have established a presumption against the strong standard (at least if the regions are large enough or important enough strategically for the purpose of establishing international peace and justice).

The best recent evidence available suggests that no country in the strategically important Middle East (which includes parts of northern Africa) meets the strong standard.[18] Even under the most charitable interpretation of their political practices, Algeria, Bahrain, Israel, Kuwait, Oman, Qatar, and United Arab Emirates all fail to meet the strong standard, in most cases because they legally discriminate on the basis of gender, race, nationality, or religion.[19] The rest of the countries in the region—Egypt, Iran, Iraq, Jordan, Lebanon, Libya, Morocco (including Western Sahara, which Morocco administers), Saudi Arabia, Syria, Tunisia, and Yemen—all fail to meet the strong standard because they do not even meet the weak one, in most cases because their security forces arbitrarily arrest or detain people, commonly use torture or abuse, or commit extrajudicial killings to such an extent that it constitutes a violation of personal security guaranteed by the right to life.[20]

If the international community recognized no country in the Middle East—if, among other things, UN membership from the region dropped from eighteen to zero—how would that have affect prospects for peace and justice there? The answer seems obvious. Peace and justice do not happen on their own. They have to be worked at. They require the collective efforts of many countries—enough to form a critical mass willing to work under difficult circumstances to overcome decades (or centuries) of suspicions that have ossified into hatreds. But if every single country in the Middle East is barred from the processes for formulating, adjudicating, and implementing international law in that region—as the strong standard seems to imply—that isn't likely to happen. The prospects for peace and justice look bleak.[21]

The Strong Standard Reconsidered

Rather than take this a priori shortcut to that conclusion, however, let us establish it empirically. To do this, we will first need to get clearer about which kinds of relations are open to, or permitted with, unrecognized entities.

Recall that recognition confers certain advantages. Recognized states possess the moral power to form agreements, treaties, and alliances with other states, a power that nonstate entities generally do not possess. Further, recognized states possess rights to preserve their territorial integrity and direct their own internal affairs, rights that the international community has a duty to support. Since unrecognized entities lack those rights, they cannot justifiably claim that other states act wrongly in providing aid to rebels or secessionists or in taking their territory. Finally, recognition is what entitles states to participate in the processes for formulating, adjudicating, and implementing international law.

However, this seems too restrictive. Surely unrecognized entities should be permitted to form certain bilateral (or multilateral) agreements—like ones to reduce their militaries, say, or pull back from disputed borders—and have the international legal system recognize them as binding. To the extent, therefore, that such agreements would be recognized as legally binding, unrecognized entities would have some role in formulating international law.

Perhaps, then, unrecognized entities should be permitted to have some role, but a secondary one in comparison with recognized states. But then, we might ask, what other relations should they be permitted to have? Since we don't want to act toward them in ways that will threaten world peace and justice, it is very tempting to answer prudentially. When we refuse to recognize entities, for instance, surely we should not be required to refuse to negotiate with them, or to engage in hostile actions toward them that are likely to result in war. Instead, it seems, we should be allowed to exercise prudence in exerting pressure—both individually and collectively, through regional or international institutions—to encourage peaceful and just behavior. Therefore, although unrecognized entities earn no entitlements to participate in any particular way (as recognized states do), they should still be permitted to form whatever relations best promote peace and justice (like bilateral agreements to reduce their militaries) as a matter of simple prudence.

The more general point is this: from the fact that unrecognized entities lack rights or entitlements to do certain things, nothing follows about what they ought to be permitted to do, or what recognized states ought to be permitted to do with respect to them. Nothing follows, that is, about what relations should be open to them and to recognized states in dealing with them. So the justice-based theory needs to provide some account of what those relations are. The proposal under consideration is that unrecognized entities should be permitted to form whatever relations best promote peace and justice.

But however reasonable this proposal may seem, the justice-based theory cannot accept it without failing once again to distinguish itself from the pragmatic theory. The reason is as follows. When the justice-based theory argues against recognizing an entity, the pragmatic theory will either agree or disagree with that judgment. Now suppose the two theories agree. In that case, the justice-based theory will hold that the entity should be permitted nonetheless to form whatever relations best promote peace and justice. But so will the pragmatic theory. Alternatively, suppose they disagree. In that case, the pragmatic theory will hold that it should be recognized as a state with the rights and powers of statehood, and an entitlement to participate in the processes for formulating, adjudicating, and implementing international law. The justice-based theory will claim instead that it should not be recognized and that it should only be permitted to form whatever relations best promote peace and justice. However, by hypothesis, the relations that best promote peace and justice are the ones that it would have if it were recognized as a state with the rights and powers of statehood and an entitlement to participate in the processes for formulating, adjudicating, and implementing international law—that, after all, is why the pragmatic theory recognizes it. It follows, then, that the justice-based theory is also committed to recognizing it as a state, with the rights, powers, and entitlements of statehood—for the exact same reason that the pragmatic view does—that it best promotes peace and justice. Therefore, if the justice-based theory holds that unrecognized entities should be permitted to form whatever relations best promote peace and justice, the two theories will wind up being equivalent once again, with the same ground for recognizing entities as states, and the same criteria for how we ought to treat unrecognized entities.

So the justice-based theory must provide some other account of what relations are open to unrecognized entities. I would like to suggest that we should distinguish the secondary processes that unrecognized entities are permitted to engage in from the primary ones they aren't on the basis of their military, economic, and political significance, since this can be done in a way that generally accords with the justice-based view. The idea is this. The justice-based view seeks a principled connection between the relations that entities are permitted to have and the moral appraisal that they receive. Entities that meet minimal standards of justice get to be full participants in the processes for formulating, adjudicating, and implementing international law. Entities that fail to meet those standards get something less. They pay a moral penalty: they may only engage in less significant military, economic, and political processes.

For example, let us suppose that unrecognized entities may not receive military assistance from or form military alliances with recognized states, for if (as the justice-based theory contends) recognizing them would make the international community an accomplice in their injustices, providing military support would make it more so.[22] Nor may they establish formal trade relations with recognized states, since that would compel the legal systems in recognized states to acknowledge their right to put forth claims in trade disputes, which would essentially give them standing in an important process for adjudicating international law. Similarly, they may not obtain full membership in international trade mechanisms like the World Trade Organization, International Monetary Fund, or World Bank, since membership on these bodies would involve them in important processes for adjudicating and implementing international law. They may not hold positions of authority within international standards-setting bodies like the International Atomic Energy Agency, since that too would involve them in important processes for formulating international law. Finally, they may not have direct diplomatic ties with recognized states, since such ties are by definition an aspect of recognition. These all seem like relations reserved for primary participants in international law.

Secondary participants would seem to be eligible for processes with less significant economic or political consequences. For example, individuals in these territories may engage in informal trade with individuals in recognized states. Secondary participants may sign international conventions whose provisions they enforce internally, but recognized states would incur no obligation to provide them with related assistance. They may recognize the jurisdiction of the International Atomic Energy Agency or sign onto the Biodiversity Convention, for instance, but they may not enter NATO or the European Union. Finally, they may deal with recognized states only through covert or informal meetings, or negotiate with them through intermediaries.

Given these prohibitions and permissions on their relations, what would the consequences be for world peace and justice if the international community recognized no country in Middle East? We can only speculate, of course, but the following seem like reasonable conjectures.

First, it is very likely that the Iraq-Kuwait conflict would have escalated. The direct military intervention by the allied coalition, recall, was legally justified by recognizing the territorial integrity of Kuwait.[23] But if Kuwait had no right to its territorial integrity, as the strong standard implies, then it could not validly claim that Iraq acted wrongly in taking its territory. And if Kuwait could not validly assert that claim, then the allied coalition could not legally justify its intervention by claiming that it was righting that wrong.[24] In fact, if the allied coalition did intervene to defend the Kuwaiti regime, then—on the justice-based view—it would become an accomplice in Kuwait's injustices.[25]

However troubling the allied invasion was for other reasons, no one denied that Iraq acted wrongly in taking Kuwaiti territory.[26] The strong standard, therefore, would have barred the allied coalition from acting for that reason (even if further conditions should have been met to justify the allied invasion morally). Intuitively, this seems too broad of a restriction. I will say more momentarily about other bases for acting.

If the allied coalition had simply let Iraq annex Kuwait, the consequences for peace and justice on the Arabian Peninsula would have been severe indeed. Iraq, a clearly aggressive power, would have controlled the northern Persian Gulf area, home to over 20 percent of the world's known oil reserves at the time.[27] Most likely, it would have used its increased oil revenues to strengthen its military capability.[28] With a strengthened military, Iraq most likely would have set its sights on settling territorial disputes with Iran and Saudi Arabia.[29] Even if that did not occur, Iran and Saudi Arabia might have been tempted to annex or otherwise dominate Qatar, Bahrain, and the United Arab Emirates (none of which has a right to territorial integrity on the strong standard), since the power imbalances between the former and the latter were comparable to that between Iraq and Kuwait.[30] The consequences of a major war in this region, which contained over 65 percent of the world's known oil reserves at the time, would have had a ripple effect throughout the economies of many nations, exacerbating injustices already present there.[31]

Second, it is very likely that the Arab-Israeli conflict would have escalated. In the thirty-one years prior to the signing of the Camp David Accords in 1979, there were four major wars between Israel and its neighbors, creating a Palestinian refugee crisis that destabilized Jordan, Syria, and Lebanon. In the twenty-five years that followed the accords, there was just one—the Israeli invasion of Lebanon—caused in part by the issue of the final status of Palestinian refugees. This stands in contrast to the period since then, which follows the failure of the Oslo Accords and Roadmap for Peace to fulfill their promises of a final-status settlement by 1998 and 2005, respectively—fueling frustrations contributing to three wars. The Camp David Accords thus had a significant impact on the Arab-Israeli conflict.[32]

But under the strong standard, the Camp David Accords (or something similar) most likely would not have been negotiated.[33] The Accords committed the United States to providing billions of dollars in military assistance to Israel and Egypt.[34] But military assistance is not permitted to states not recognized by the international community. Further, the United States would have been barred from conducting direct negotiations with both governments, as well as subsequent negotiations with Jordan, Syria, and the Palestinians, which have proven instrumental for other peace talks.[35] As a consequence, the resolution of one of the causes of the 1973 war—the occupation of the Sinai Peninsula by Israel—which was brought about in part at Camp David by United States negotiators, would have been much less likely to occur.[36] Thus, Egypt, which at the time desired to tie itself more closely to the United States and distance itself from the Soviet Union, would have most likely calculated that its interests did not lie with the United States, and would have continued hostilities.[37] In that case, it is likely that Israel would still be fighting wars on several fronts instead of local conflicts in Lebanon and the occupied territories.

Now in order to avoid these consequences of following the strong standard, it is very tempting to invoke a generic duty of justice to authorize action by the international community. A defender of the justice-based account might then claim that, although Kuwait lacked a right to territorial integrity that the international community had a duty to support, the international community still had a duty of justice to remedy the injustices that accompanied the taking of Kuwait's "territory" (like the violence done to the civilian population) even if they did not consist in taking that territory. Similarly, although Egypt and Israel both lacked a right to territorial integrity that the international community had a duty to support, the international community still had a duty of justice to prevent injustices that would accompany any future aggression between the two countries, a duty it judged it could best fulfill by providing military and diplomatic support. Thus, a defender of the justice-based account might claim that, when a country lacks a right to territorial integrity, it is not as if a moral vacuum exists. The duty of justice fills the gap.

But if we invoke the duty of justice like this whenever unjust aggression threatens to place global peace and justice in severe danger, then the crucial normative work is being done by this general duty and not the success of our policy in recognizing enough entities as states. To see this quite clearly, suppose that we make full, not minimal, justice our standard for recognition and that no entities in the entire world meet it. According to this view, there is, strictly speaking, no international community of recognized states. Yet suppose that a group of unrecognized entities bands together and, acting on this general duty of justice, successfully resists all threats to global peace and justice. (We can even imagine them forming their own international institutions, although not, of course, with full justice as the criterion for membership.) Now clearly, if the efforts of this "international community" did make the pursuit of peace and justice efficacious, that would be in *spite* of, not *because* of, our policy of recognizing only entities that meet full standards of justice, for by hypothesis no entities at all meet it. It would be more accurate to say that our pursuit of peace and justice was efficacious because the duty of justice, operating in the background, provides blanket authority to all unrecognized entities to form whatever relations promote peace and justice (or at least avoid endangering these goals). As a result of that blanket authority, we were able to salvage efforts to achieve peace and justice that would otherwise fail. But since this blanket authority exists regardless of what our standard for recognition is and how many (or few) entities meet it, we can generalize this argument. Therefore, if we invoke a general duty of justice to authorize action that our policy of recognition fails to authorize, and, as a result, we salvage efforts to achieve peace and justice that would otherwise be doomed, then it is this general duty that is doing the crucial normative work and saving our policy of recognition from the consequences of its failure.

To prevent this subterfuge, we must evaluate standards for recognition without appealing to a general duty of justice. And according to the strong standard, unrecognized states like Kuwait, Egypt, and Israel may not receive military and diplomatic support even if that is critical to achieving peace and justice in the region.

So if we adopt the strong standard for minimal justice, our efforts to achieve peace and justice in the Middle East—an area of intense hostility in the last half century and the focus of much international attention—would be inefficacious. And whatever benefits there are to following this standard elsewhere in the world, they could not cancel out the threat to peace and justice that it would cause here.

The Weak Standard

Perhaps one might want to object that this does not undermine all justice-based accounts, just ones that use the strong standard for minimal justice. What if we *lower* our standard and adopt the weak one instead?

But in Africa (excluding Morocco, Algeria, Tunisia, Libya, and Egypt, which were counted in the Middle East), less than one-third of the countries would qualify for recognition under that standard. Under the most charitable interpretation of their political practices, only fifteen countries—Benin, Botswana, Burkina Faso, Cabo Verde, Comoros, Gabon, Lesotho, Namibia, Niger, Sao Tome and Principe, Senegal, Seychelles, Sierra Leone, Tanzania, and Togo—would qualify (and four of them are located in the Atlantic or Indian Oceans).[38] The other thirty-four countries—including Angola, Chad, Rwanda, Sudan, Uganda, and Zimbabwe, among others—all fail to meet that standard, in most cases because of arbitrary arrests, torture, abuse, or extrajudicial killings committed by their security forces.[39] Africa's UN membership would therefore drop from forty-nine to fifteen.

Again, we can only speculate about the impact that refusing to recognize this many countries would have on prospects for peace and justice in Africa. But the following seem like reasonable conjectures.

First, UN peacekeeping operations in Africa and elsewhere in the world would be significantly affected. Currently, nearly one-half of all UN peacekeepers come from Africa.[40] Yet over two-thirds of them would be ineligible to participate, since they come from countries that fail to meet the weak standard, which would render them ineligible to implement international law. In Africa, this would be particularly troublesome. Peacekeeping missions conducted there would be greatly complicated by barring so many soldiers, police, and observers from the region who possess the experience, cultural acuity, and language skills that are crucial for successful peacekeeping. In addition, the demographic makeup of troops eligible to participate would be much less likely to reflect that of Africa—something that would not only open the UN to charges of racial bias, but would also place these troops in greater danger, given the region's hostility and sensitivity to colonial domination. This in turn would alter the calculation in support of each specific mission.

Second, even if these limits on contributing troops could be overcome, the weak standard still implies that over two-thirds of Africa's countries had no rights of territorial integrity or noninterference, and thus cannot validly claim that other entities act wrongly in taking their territory or interfering in their affairs. But if they cannot validly assert these claims, then the international community cannot justify corrective action by claiming that it is trying to right such wrongs. In Africa, where twenty-six countries experienced interstate war, internal conflict, major political or religious violence, or wars of independence during 2015 alone, this would clearly be troublesome.[41] Of course, we could always invoke a general duty of justice to authorize action that our policy of recognition fails to authorize. But then, as we saw earlier, even if this succeeds in containing the threats to peace and justice, it would be this duty, not our policy of recognition, that does the crucial normative work.

Under either standard, therefore, it seems that the pursuit of peace and justice would be inefficacious in some strategically significant regions. I take this to create a strong presumption against the feasibility of either standard worldwide. Ideally, to establish this stronger conclusion, we would have to consider how each standard fares in all parts of the globe. Nonetheless, in these regions, the costs to peace and justice are sunk. They do not disappear. The threats to peace and justice that they pose will continue to exist no matter what benefits there are to following each standard elsewhere. Matters can only get worse.

If these findings are sound, then the justice-based account would must respond by lowering its standard even further, since it accepts the claim that our criteria for recognition should not be so utopian as to make the pursuit of global peace and justice inefficacious. But this would compromise the international community's credibility, since countries that systematically violate the weak standard surely are *not* minimally just. If international officials ever were to claim that even (some) systematic violators of the weak standard should be recognized because they are minimally just, it would be widely (and rightly) perceived as a mere pragmatic attempt to bring more entities into the processes for formulating, adjudicating, and implementing international law—not as a stand having anything to do with justice. I take this to be sufficient reason for rejecting the justice-based account in the form in which we've considered it so far.[42]

6.6 AMENDMENTS

If the justice-based theory fails, it fails because it insists that minimal justice should be necessary for state recognition. I now want to consider amendments to it that weaken that claim. All of the amendments share one thing in common: they concede that minimal justice should not be strictly necessary for recognition, but they insist that facts about injustice still ought to play a role in decisions about it. They differ from one another in how those facts matter.

For example, the justice-based theory might claim that failing to meet minimal standards of justice is still a consideration against recognition, though one that can be outweighed. This seems plausible enough. Who would deny it? Unfortunately, this is precisely the problem with it: the pragmatic theory does not deny it either. To see why, recall that, according to the pragmatic theory, political entities ought to be recognized as states if and only if cooperating with them and giving them international support would advance international peace and justice. International justice, though, is composed of just relations among states (just external relations), and just relations within them (just internal relations). It follows that political entities that fail to meet minimal standards of justice will fail to be a part of that composite. So, according to the pragmatic account, failing to meet minimal standards of justice will also be a consideration against recognition—though one that can be outweighed if it can be shown that recognizing some such entities as states advances international peace and justice in the long run.

If the justice-based theory is to be distinguishable from the pragmatic one, then, facts about injustice must carry more weight than merely being a consideration against recognition. For example, the justice-based theory might claim that failing to meet minimal standards of justice creates a strong presumption against recognition that can only be overridden by a compelling argument about international peace and justice. In contrast, the pragmatic theory accepts a weaker presumption that is more easily overridden. Since the pragmatic theory implies that this presumption is overridden whenever cooperation and international support would advance international peace and justice, the justice-based theory must insist on imposing an additional burden of some sort. What might this additional burden be?

The most logical candidate (for a justice-based view) would be to claim that we must not recognize political entities that are *too unjust* even if recognizing them would advance international peace and justice. The justice-based view would then set a standard for identifying which entities are too unjust, and therefore ineligible for recognition.[43]

However, this version of the justice-based view encounters the same problem that the unamended version did. Too few entities may qualify for state recognition under this standard to make the pursuit of international peace and justice efficacious. If so, then the requirement that our criteria for recognition be realistic dictates lowering our standard so that enough entities qualify. That suggests that pragmatic considerations drive the level of the standard. Alternatively, even if enough entities do qualify under this standard, the requirement that our criteria for recognition be realistic still implies that, hypothetically, if too few did qualify, we would have to lower it. That again suggests that pragmatic considerations drive the level of the standard. Since the justice-based view allows this standard to be adjusted to whatever level is necessary for enough entities to qualify—since its standard for recognition must be adjusted to satisfy that pragmatic need—we find once again that the justice-based view is a pragmatic theory in disguise.[44]

At this point, a defender of the justice-based view might try a different strategy: lowering not the standard needed to qualify for recognition but the penalty for failing to meet it. For example, suppose that a defender of the justice-based view were to claim that entities that fail to meet minimal standards of justice should not be denied the rights and powers of statehood, but only membership in international organizations like the UN. Would that make it defensible? For two reasons, the answer has to be no. First, this move basically concedes that the justice-based account fails as a theory for recognizing states, for on this view all entities, regardless of their moral quality, are to be recognized as states and granted the rights and powers of statehood—they get these rights and powers, morally, for free. Second, even if we reinterpret the justice-based account as a theory for determining which recognized states ought to be members of international organizations, it would still be implausible, because too few African states would qualify to make the pursuit of peace and justice there efficacious. Several recent United Nations reports contrast the extreme economic vulnerability and dependency that exists in developing countries with the amount of influence they possess in international organizations like the International Monetary Fund, World Bank, and World Trade Organization. The 2015 *Human Development Report*, for instance, states that, of the 188 countries ranked by their human development index (a weighted function of life expectancy, education, and income, among other factors), twenty-seven of the bottom thirty were all African.[45] Despite some gains beginning this century (following losses in the 1990s), these countries—especially the ones at the bottom—were nonetheless among the most vulnerable casualties of the global economic recession that started in 2008. "Developing countries, and especially the poor in these countries, are among the hardest hit victims of a crisis they had no role in making," states the *Report of the Commission of Experts of the President of the United Nations General Assembly on Reforms of the International Monetary and Financial System*.[46] To protect their interests, as well as to prevent future global financial crises, the report makes several recommendations, among them:

1. "There is a need to provide more effective voice and representation for developing countries, which now represent a much larger proportion of world economic activity than in 1944, when the World Bank and the IMF were created. Developing countries, as a group, also have a direct interest in a more equitable global governance system. Above all, it is imperative that reform of the existing institutions should re-establish their credibility as truly international institutions contributing to growth with equity and stability for all countries."[47]
2. "The inconsistency between the economic and financial weight of developing countries in the world economy and their role as recipients of IMF and World Bank funds, on the one hand, and their representation in these institutions, on the other, is one of the factors behind the loss of legitimacy and relevance of those organizations in addressing systemic issues. Better voice and representation of developing countries in [International Financial Institutions] must therefore be high on the agenda. Governance reform must strengthen, in particular, the weight of low-income countries."[48]

But of course, by denying membership in international organizations to so many African countries, a defender of (this version of) the justice-based view would be recommending the exact *opposite* course of action. The result can only be to make efforts to achieve peace and justice in this region even more inefficacious than they have been.

What if we lower the penalty further? What if we claim, instead, that entities that fail to meet minimal standards of justice should be denied neither the rights and powers of statehood, nor membership in international organizations, but that their *governments* should not be recognized, with the right to exercise the rights and powers of statehood for these states? Would that make it defensible?

Once again, the answer has to be no, for two reasons. First, by suggesting that all entities, regardless of their moral quality, are to be recognized as states, granted the rights and powers of statehood, and admitted as members to international organizations, this move basically concedes that the justice-based account fails both as a theory for recognizing states and as a theory for determining which recognized states ought to be members of international organizations. On this view, all entities get these rights, powers, and membership, morally, for free. Second, even if we reinterpret the justice-based account as a theory for recognizing governments, it is still implausible, because too few governments in the Middle East and Africa would qualify to make the pursuit of peace and justice there efficacious. Under the weak standard, it would require us to deny recognition to forty-five of the region's sixty-seven governments—two-thirds of the governments in one-third of the globe. So it's not as if the justice-based view would require us to isolate a few, select, rogue regimes—the very worst of the worst—like the regimes of Saddam Hussein and Robert Mugabe. It would require the wholesale isolation of most of an entire continent and beyond. Given that normal international relations are part of what government recognition involves, and given that economic relations are a part of that, it would follow that there could be no legitimate economic relations with those who control the political and economic institutions in wide swaths of the globe (much of it destitute). It is hard to see how such a blanket prohibition is compatible with the pursuit of peace and justice.

Suppose we lower the penalty even further. For instance, suppose we claim that entities that fail to meet minimal requirements of justice should be denied neither the rights and powers of statehood, nor membership in international organizations, and that those who control the political and economic institutions of those entities should have the right to exercise certain state powers (like the power to make treaties), regardless of the moral quality of those institutions, but that only recognized governments (those that do meet minimal requirements of justice) should be granted the right to exercise the other rights and powers of states. Now it seems clear that pragmatic considerations are simply driving the level of the penalty. The penalty itself carries no independent weight. It has become an inherently flexible standard that can be adjusted to whatever level is necessary to achieve our pragmatic aims and needs—a mere consequence of decisions made on pragmatic grounds.

We can put that point another way. As a matter of justice, we should expect the moral penalty to be proportional to the moral crime. Thus, entities that systematically violate basic human rights, it would seem, should pay a moral penalty proportional to that moral crime. But instead, what we find, with this version of the justice-based view, is that the penalty will be raised or lowered to whatever level is necessary to make the pursuit of peace and justice efficacious. There is no concern with proportionality.

There is one final amendment to consider. A defender of the justice-based view might insist that we can maintain both our standard of minimal justice and an appropriate moral penalty for failing to meet it if we simply claim that we will treat (some of the) entities that fail to meet that standard *as if* they are entitled to recognition (upholding their rights to territorial integrity, admitting them into international institutions, and so on), even though in fact they are not entitled. According to this view, *as-if recognition* differs from regular recognition in that the latter expresses, while the former does not, moral approval of the entity. The idea that motivates this suggestion is that the regular act of recognition ought to be construed as a symbolic expression of moral approval. Thus, international officials should tailor their statements and organize their ceremonies so that the act is understood as an expression of moral approval, the withholding of recognition as disapproval—and as-if recognition as something in between.

Now obviously we could have one type of practice—call it legal recognition—which confers the rights and powers of statehood, but another type of practice—call it symbolic recognition—which expresses moral approval. The main problem with this suggestion is that it basically concedes what we have been arguing all along, which is that the justice-based view fails as a theory of legal recognition: what grounds the conferral of the rights and powers of statehood in that case is no longer the fact that the entity satisfies minimal standards of justice. Nothing prevents us, of course, from having a practice of symbolic recognition that runs simultaneously with a practice of legal recognition. But that would not obviate the pressing practical need for a theory of legal recognition.

In order to avoid conceding that the justice-based view fails as a theory of legal recognition, then, its defender must insist that it guide both our practice of conferring rights and powers under international law, and a practice of expressing moral approval—that it guide both legal and symbolic recognition. Its defender might then claim that, in addition to conferring certain rights and powers, there ought to be an important symbolic element to recognition, which only a justice-based view can justify. But as I have argued, if we embrace the justice-based view as a theory of legal recognition, it would endanger international peace and justice (thereby rendering the view self-defeating). So unless a defender of the justice-based view is prepared to deny that claim, the present proposal amounts to the view that, for symbolic reasons, we should uphold certain standards for recognition even if it endangers international peace and justice. But that view hardly seems plausible. However important morally symbolic behavior may be, surely it must yield if it endangers international peace and justice.

I conclude that all of the amendments to the justice-based theory fail, either because they fail to distinguish the justice-based theory from the pragmatic one, or because they force the international community once again to choose between jeopardizing international peace and justice and compromising its credibility. We may therefore justifiably reject the justice-based view in all of its forms, and turn our attention to the pragmatic one.

6.7 THE MAIN OBJECTIONS TO THE PRAGMATIC THEORY

The pragmatic theory, by contrast, candidly admits that, unfortunate as things are in the world, we must sometimes recognize unjust entities if we wish to make moral progress. If the pragmatic theory is superior, then, it is only because it candidly admits what its rival obscures: that pragmatic considerations, not justice or minimal justice, determine which entities we should recognize.

Let's look more closely at what the pragmatic theory claims. According to the pragmatic theory, entities (taken now to include both states and governments) ought to be recognized if and only if doing so would advance international peace and justice. This formulation, notice, is formal in two respects. First, it does not indicate the specific criteria for recognition that would advance international peace and justice. Second, it does not indicate the content of international justice. These facts have enormous importance for properly understanding the pragmatic theory of recognition.

For instance, the pragmatic theory does not deny that normative criteria may be among the specific criteria for recognition that would best promote international peace and justice. All the pragmatic theory claims is that such criteria are driven by our pragmatic need to recognize enough entities to make the pursuit of peace and justice efficacious; they can be raised or lowered to whatever level is necessary for satisfying that pragmatic need; and that this level is not necessarily identical with any plausible standard of minimal justice. The criteria, in short, lack independent weight, are inherently flexible, and are a mere consequence of decisions made on pragmatic grounds. They are not, in the sense specified earlier, objective.

Given that the pragmatic theory may employ normative criteria for recognition, it would be a mistake to confuse it with the view that all entities, regardless of their moral quality, should be granted recognition automatically (automatic recognition), or with the view that states, in their foreign policy decisions, including decisions to grant recognition, should consult only their own interests (realpolitik). Nor is it likely that the pragmatic theory would entail the rejection of normative criteria altogether. In order for that to be the case, it would have to be true that, by completely excluding normative criteria from our criteria for recognition, we would advance international peace and justice—a claim that on its face seems highly problematic. Of course, the pragmatic theory would reject making minimal justice our standard for recognition, if that would make our pursuit of international peace and justice inefficacious. But that does not preclude it from accepting a lower standard if that would advance international peace and justice. From the fact that the pragmatic theory may require us to recognize some unjust entities, it does not follow that it necessarily requires us to recognize all such entities.

The upshot is that the pragmatic theory does not commit us to recognizing all entities regardless of their moral quality, including the very worst of the worst—like, say, the governments of Saddam Hussein and Robert Mugabe.[49] If anyone were to suggest that the pragmatic theory does commit us to doing that, we would rightly demand proof. There would have to be evidence—compelling evidence—that the governments of Saddam Hussein and Robert Mugabe satisfy criteria for recognition that would advance international peace and justice. It is not knowable a priori.

Just as the pragmatic theory does not indicate the specific criteria for recognition that would advance international peace and justice, neither does it indicate the content of international justice. The pragmatic theory leaves that matter entirely open—to be determined by the best ideal theory of international justice. It does *not* assume that consequentialism is the best ideal theory of international justice—despite the consequentialist sound to its claim that entities ought to be recognized if and only if that *advances* international peace and justice. In fact, it is consistent with many deontological views, including the (strongest) version, which holds that there are some types of acts that it would be wrong to perform no matter what the consequences. It would only deny that the act of granting recognition to an unjust entity is one of those acts.[50] I will say more about this in a moment. The upshot is that, in order to reject the pragmatic theory, it will not suffice to "expose" it as being based on consequentialism—and then run the standard anticonsequentialist arguments up the flagpole. One can consistently accept the pragmatic theory of recognition with a deontological view of international justice.

Now that we have looked more closely at the pragmatic theory, let us consider the most serious objections to it. According to one objection, if we grant recognition to internally unjust entities, as the pragmatic theory allows, then the international community would become an accomplice in injustice. This is because, when we grant recognition to such entities, we confer upon them the right to noninterference in their internal affairs, and thus support their ability to continue wielding unjust coercive power within their territories.[51]

However, if recognizing unjust entities necessarily makes us accomplices in their injustices, then this is equally an objection to the justice-based theory. Clearly, this is the case with the amended versions, which explicitly do not make minimal justice a necessary condition for recognition. They too allow us to grant recognition to internally unjust entities. But ironically, it is also the case with the unamended version, which does make "minimal justice" a necessary condition for recognition. The reason is this. As long as the possibility exists of a conflict between what the best theory of justice requires for minimal justice, and what the realities of international politics require for recognition, then as we saw ealier, the unamended justice-based view must lower its standard of "minimal justice" beneath what the best theory of justice requires for that. Even the unamended justice-based view, then, licenses granting recognition to some unjust entities, despite calling them minimally just—a label that obscures that fact. So if recognizing unjust entities necessarily makes us accomplices in their injustices, then the justice-based and pragmatic theories are partners in guilt.

Does recognizing unjust entities make us accomplices in their injustices, though? To become an accomplice in injustice, it seems, the international community would have to be doing something blameworthy. However, it is far from obvious that the international community would be doing something blameworthy if it acted on those rules (or criteria) which experience has shown promote peace and justice, relied on its best information in determining whether those rules were met, used its best efforts and resources in gathering that information, and exercised its best judgment in applying them—all of which the pragmatic theory demands.[52] This is a case where, by hypothesis, the international community is doing the best it can: self-deception, negligence, or malice is not involved. This is also a case where, by hypothesis, the alternative—demanding minimal justice according to the best theory of justice—would result in too few entities being recognized to make the pursuit of international peace and justice efficacious (in which case the injustices we want to remedy would remain). Although it may be a paradox, therefore, it does seem true: we do not become accomplices in injustice by granting recognition to some unjust entities.

Perhaps someone might protest that, even if we promote international justice between states by recognizing some unjust entities, we are still accomplices in the injustices that occur within the ones we recognize. But this claim rests on a false assumption. It assumes that the goal of international justice—a goal that the pragmatic theory embraces—refers solely to justice between states. There is no reason to construe international justice so narrowly, however. Surely international justice involves more than that: it involves justice within states as well as between them.[53] Thus, when the international community acts on those rules which experience has shown promote peace and justice, it is aiming to promote justice within states as well as between them. So long as it relies on its best information, uses its best efforts to gather that information, and exercises its best judgment in applying these rules—as long as it does the best it can, as the pragmatic account requires—then it does not appear to be doing anything blameworthy, in which case it is not an accomplice in injustice.[54]

Furthermore, a theory of recognition is concerned (strictly speaking) with just one type of political act: the act of granting or withholding recognition. Political acts taken pursuant to granting recognition—the type and level of force used to help a country repel insurgents, for instance—are a separate matter, and involve different sorts of strategic and moral considerations. For example, assuming that the pragmatic account requires us to recognize both the state and government of, say, Yemen (which may or may not be the case), it follows that the government may enforce that state's right to noninterference, a right that the international community has a duty to support. It does not follow, however, that actions taken by the Yemeni government in enforcing this right, or ones taken by members of the international community in fulfilling this duty, are exempt from moral considerations. In particular, it does not follow that the international community, or any individual members, must provide equipment, intelligence, and training to its military when it is with good reason believed that the aid will be used against domestic protesters, fall into enemy hands, or (as with drone strikes) inflict death and suffering disproportionately on innocent civilians.[55] All that follows is that the Yemeni government has a right under international law to resist the Houthi rebels who are battling it, and that it is not ineligible to receive international assistance in its efforts. Of course, once we grant recognition, questions about what actions (if any) to take pursuant to that open up which would otherwise be foreclosed, so the two are related. But they are in principle distinguishable, and it is the morality of granting recognition to unjust entities that is at issue here.

Similarly, recognition does not require commercial engagement either. Whether, how much, and under what circumstances to engage commercially with unjust entities are separate matters, and likewise involve different strategic and moral considerations. Despite recognizing Sudan, for example, the United States has maintained various economic sanctions upon it for decades. As Leif Wenar explains:

> The United States has used these sanctions to shape commercial relations with Sudan in exquisite detail . . . under the sanctions American persons may not legally purchase Sudanese oil from anyone. . . . Yet the sanctions also, for example, explicitly license US persons to buy Sudanese gum arabic. . . . With these sanctions, the United States decides exactly the way it wishes (not) to engage commercially with the Sudanese. Still, throughout all the years of sanctions, the United States has recognized Sudan as an independent, sovereign state.[56]

Following the Arab Spring uprisings, similarly, the United States, despite continuing to recognize the state and government of Libya, issued an executive order that "froze all property of the Government of Libya (Gaddafi's regime), with the effect that no U.S. corporation could gain legal title to any of Libya's oil."[57] Again, we can distinguish the considerations that bear on whether to recognize a state or a government from those that bear on the question of which actions, if any, to take pursuant to it—and focus here on the former.

Nonetheless, one might accept these points yet press the following objection. Granted, the international community does not do anything blameworthy when it recognizes unjust entities. Its desire to do justice, its commitment to using proven rules for promoting that, and its determination to exercise its best judgment in applying them are all admirable. These are dispositions that deserve praise. It would be wrong to blame the international community and its officials for having them. But from the fact that the act of blaming international officials would be wrong, it does not follow that the act of granting recognition to unjust entities itself is not wrong or unjust, for this may be a case of blameless wrongdoing. So while it may be too strong to claim that the international community is an accomplice in injustice (which suggests malevolent or criminal motivation), it still commits an injustice by recognizing unjust entities, even if its dispositions and motives deserve to be praised.

This objection seems to assume that it is always unjust to recognize unjust entities. Of course, if this assumption were analytically true, then it would be not just false but self-contradictory to deny it. But it would also beg the question against the pragmatic theory, which does deny it. Here is an all-too-common counterexample. Suppose that an entity's practices fall below the threshold of what the best theory of justice regards as minimal justice (perhaps marginally so). Yet it justifiably feels besieged by rebels funded by a foreign power and based just across its border. As a result, it overreacts by taking, or tolerating, domestic security measures that violate basic human rights. Nonetheless, the international community judges that peace and justice in the region would likely improve if the threat would subside. It bases this judgment on extensive experience and its acquaintance with both the regime in power and the rebels. Its experience is summarized in the form of a rule. Its acquaintance with both the regime in power and the rebels justifiably leads international officials to believe that the situation falls under the rule. So the international community grants recognition to the entity, which opens up questions about what actions to take pursuant to that, questions that would otherwise be foreclosed. For example, it can now consider whether it ought to provide peacekeepers or other kinds of support in the justified expectation that the regime will make progress toward minimal justice as it becomes more secure from the outside threat. In addition, it now becomes eligible to participate in certain international processes, and this may contribute to trust building. Does granting recognition in this type of case seem obviously unjust? I doubt it.[58] If anything, this type of case strongly suggests that the burden of proof should shift to the defender of the justice-based theory to explain why it is always unjust to recognize unjust entities.

Perhaps the objection to granting recognition to unjust entities instead lies in this fact: unjust entities are usually or always *illegitimate*. But only legitimate entities properly possess the powers, rights, and immunities of statehood.

Before we attempt to answer this objection, let us try to understand it better first. When we speak of a state as being legitimate, we sometimes mean only that it is a good or *just* state. Sometimes, however, we mean something different. We mean that there is a special moral relationship between that particular state and each particular citizen through which the state acquires the exclusive right to enforce legal rules on that citizen and that citizen acquires a political obligation *to that state* to obey them.[59]

This relationship is created through some morally significant interaction between them, like a citizen's consenting to that state's authority or her acceptance or receipt of its benefits. Exactly which kind of interaction carries this moral significance depends on what the best theory of political obligation is. It is this kind of interaction, though, that is claimed to legitimate the state's authority over that citizen. If a state has had this kind of morally significant interaction with a large enough segment of the population living in its territory, then we may speak of it as being minimally legitimate or legitimate "on balance," whereas if it has done so with every individual in its territory, then we may speak of it as being completely or fully legitimate.

The objection that unjust entities are (usually or always) illegitimate clearly does not use the term *legitimate* in the first sense, where it is equivalent in meaning to *just*. If it did, it would merely assert the tautology that unjust entities are unjust. The objection expresses a different idea: the fact that an entity is unjust *explains* why it is illegitimate. But in order to express that idea (rather than a bare tautology), the objection must assume, as the second sense of *legitimate* assumes, that the concepts of justice and legitimacy are distinct. So let us understand the objection as claiming that unjust entities are usually or always illegitimate in this second sense: they fail to have the appropriate kind of morally significant interaction with enough of their population.

This might be the case for a number of reasons. It might be the case because justice is *necessary* for this special moral relationship to exist between an entity and an individual, as it is on (what has been described as) Lockean accounts of political obligation.[60] On this view, one cannot bind oneself morally to obey an unjust entity any more than one can bind oneself morally to commit an unjust deed like murder. An unjust entity thus becomes morally disabled from having the kind of interaction through which it acquires the right to enforce legal rules on, and thus legitimate authority over, any individual. Alternatively, it might be the case because justice is *necessary and sufficient* for this special moral relationship to exist, as it is on (what has been described as) Kantian accounts of political obligation.[61] Unlike the Lockean view, this view insists that if an entity is just, the special moral relationship obtains in virtue of that fact, but like the Lockean view, it holds that an unjust entity is morally disabled from establishing this relationship with any individual. On both the Lockean and Kantian views, unjust entities are always illegitimate, since justice is necessary for legitimacy.

It might still be the case, however, if justice is *neither necessary nor sufficient* for the special moral relationship to exist.[62] Like the Lockean view, this view agrees that the justice of an entity is not alone sufficient to establish this relationship, but unlike the Lockean view, it holds that one can bind oneself morally to obey an unjust entity. This is because an entity's bad character, as it were, does not prevent one from binding oneself morally to obey it any more than a person's bad character prevents one from binding oneself morally to perform some deed for him. Even if justice is neither necessary nor sufficient for the relationship, though, we might suppose, perhaps, that an entity's justice is a useful proxy for determining whether it has a special moral relationship with enough of its population to be on balance legitimate.[63] If it is just, that is likely to be the case; if it is unjust, that is not. On this view, then, unjust entities are usually illegitimate.

I do not want to dispute the claim that unjust entities are usually or always illegitimate. What I want to point out, though, is that the source or *ground* of the objection, in this case, is not that the pragmatic theory grants to some unjust entities all of the powers, rights, and immunities of statehood but that it grants these to some illegitimate ones. So let us focus on that objection instead. According to that objection, it is implausible to grant all of the powers, rights, and immunities of statehood to entities which have not had the kind of morally significant interaction with enough of their population to be on balance legitimate.

Now in one sense, of course, this claim is correct, if only because it is trivially true. According to theories of political obligation, a legitimate state just is a state that has acquired, through the appropriate kind of morally significant interaction, the exclusive right to enforce legal rules on a large enough segment of the population living in its territory. Because it acquires this right exclusively, it possesses the right to noninterference and territorial integrity.[64] And the rules it has the right to enforce presumably permit it to make treaties and wage just war as necessary to enhance and protect its citizens' welfare (respectively). Hence a legitimate state just is a state that has acquired this bundle of rights. It follows trivially that an illegitimate state is one that lacks these rights.

Nonetheless, we can still ask whether it would be worth having an international practice of *conferring* such rights on certain entities even if those rights are not *acquired* in accordance with the best theory of political obligation. We can still ask, that is, whether it would be worth granting recognition to some entities that are illegitimate according to the best theory of political obligation.

For two reasons, I think the answer clearly has to be yes. First, suppose that according to the best theory of political obligation, a state is fully legitimate if and only if it is just and every individual member of its population has consented to its authority in a way that is morally binding. Also suppose that it is minimally legitimate (legitimate "on balance") if and only if it is just and at least half of these individuals have consented to its authority in a morally binding way. Finally, suppose that too few entities qualify for recognition under this minimal legitimacy standard to make the pursuit of peace and justice—the moral goals of the international system—efficacious. What should we do in this situation? We could lower our standard for minimal legitimacy—or change our theory of political obligation—so that enough entities do qualify. But in that case we would be letting pragmatic considerations dictate what counts as minimal legitimacy. This would be the case even if enough entities did qualify under the higher standard provided that, hypothetically, if too few did we would be prepared to lower the standard—which seems true given the stakes (more on this in a moment). Alternatively, instead of letting pragmatic considerations dictate what counts as minimal legitimacy, we could simply be more candid and sever the connection between the recognition of an entity and its legitimacy as theories of political obligation use that term. That would permit us to grant recognition to entities that are illegitimate according to the best theory of political obligation (entities which may, after all, be just). This is what the pragmatic theory recommends.

Second, the stakes are simply too high. International peace and justice do not happen on their own—they have to be worked at. Working at them requires bringing (enough) entities into the processes for formulating, adjudicating, and implementing international law, processes which are admittedly crucial (if not indispensable) to the realization of long-term international peace and justice. So it seems worth having an international practice of conferring the rights of statehood on certain entities even if those rights are not acquired in accordance with the best theory of political obligation—especially if those entities are just.

The pragmatic theory, then, offers numerous advantages. It lets the best theory of justice rather than pragmatic considerations determine what counts as minimal justice. It lets the best theory of political obligation rather than pragmatic considerations determine what counts as minimal legitimacy. It enables the international community to avoid endangering international peace and justice, on the one hand, without compromising its credibility, on the other. It offers all of these advantages, moreover, without implicating the international community in injustice. For all of these reasons, therefore, we should prefer the pragmatic theory to the justice-based one.

I expect that many will want to resist this disappointing conclusion. After all, doesn't it seem morally outrageous for the international community to grant recognition to unjust countries, especially ones that systematically violate human rights? It is understandable that we want to condemn such countries in the strongest terms. Denying them recognition seems like an appropriate way to express our moral outrage—a way to make it count. If we recognize them, by contrast, it seems like we are being soft on injustice. But it is important here to remember that we don't need to invoke the concept of recognition to express our moral outrage. The concept of justice has room enough. We can continue to condemn systematic violators of human rights as strongly as anyone else can by invoking the concept of justice. Countries that commit systematic violations of human rights are *unjust*. The more serious their violations are, and the worse their abuse is, the more gravely unjust they are and the more strongly we, as philosophers, should condemn them. Nor are we being soft on injustice if we are doing our best to remedy it (as the pragmatic theory demands). If anything, we are standing up for justice by insisting that its most basic and minimal commands not be altered to make them more palatable politically. If as philosophers we do not take up arms in the quest for justice, then the least we should do is stick to our guns.

NOTES

1. Incorporating Rawls's arguments for basic human rights as the standard of minimal justice, Allen Buchanan defends a justice-based theory of international recognition in "Recognitional Legitimacy and the State System," *Philosophy & Public Affairs* 28, no. 1 (Winter 1999): 46–78; "Rule-governed Institutions versus Act-Consequentialism: A Rejoinder to Naticchia," *Philosophy & Public Affairs* 28, no. 3 (Summer 1999): 258–70; and *Justice, Legitimacy, and Self-Determination: Moral Foundations for International Law* (New York: Oxford University Press, 2004). Although I discuss Buchanan's view in passing, my concern in this chapter is much broader: with any view that embraces minimal justice as a requirement for recognition, whatever its level. Buchanan's view itself seems to have evolved between his earlier and later work on the topic. See notes 17 and 42.

2. International law distinguishes the *existence* of states from their *recognition*. As one international legal text puts it:

> A state comes into existence when the community involved acquires the basic characteristics associated with the concept of a state: a defined territory, an operating and effective government, and independence from outside control. . . . [However, a] state may exist for a long time, functioning as an operative political community, without being a "state" in the legal sense. Transformation into the legal personality known as a state comes about only through the admission of the entity in question as a recognized member of the community of nations. Numerous communities possessing territory, citizens, a government, and all other appurtenances commonly associated with the concept of a state were not "persons" in international law until admitted to the community.

Thus, in one sense, a state just is an entity that possesses certain political characteristics—like territory, a government, and independence—which make it eligible to receive recognition. But it does not become a state in the legal sense unless the international community decides to recognize it as a fellow member, with certain rights and powers under international law. Following international law texts, I will call the former *political entities* (or simply, *entities*), to distinguish them from recognized states. (See Gerhard von Glahn, *Law Among Nations: An Introduction to Public International Law*, 6th ed. [New York: Macmillan, 1992], pp. 87, 54.)

The role of a normative theory of recognition is to offer criteria for determining which political entities the international community *ought* to recognize as states. For example, a theory might claim that all political entities, regardless of their moral quality, should be granted recognition automatically, or that they should be granted recognition if and only if they meet minimal requirements of justice, or that they should be granted recognition if and only if doing so would be the best means of achieving global peace and justice. Other positions are available as well, but my concern here is with the latter two.

3. Gerhard von Glahn, *Law Among Nations: An Introduction to Public International Law*, 6th ed. (New York: Macmillan, 1992), p. 125. Unfortunately, the term *recognition* seems to suggest that to recognize a political entity as a state is merely to acknowledge that it possesses the characteristics of statehood. But in fact, to recognize an entity as a state involves much more than that: it confers legal personality upon that entity, with certain rights and powers under international law. It is "a political act with legal consequences"—indeed, highly significant ones, like conferring (or acquiring) the right to territorial integrity, the right to noninterference in their internal affairs, the power to make treaties, and the right (subject to certain restrictions) to enforce legal rules on those within their territory (von Glahn, *Law Among Nations*, p. 85). A decision to grant or withhold recognition is therefore a highly important *moral* decision.

4. Technically, the granting of recognition is performed by individual states, not by the international community as a whole. (von Glahn, *Law Among Nations*, p. 89.) But here I will speak of the international community as the agent that grants (or ought to grant) recognition, since a normative theory of recognition is a theory of the conditions under which any state (and hence all states) should recognize another entity as a fellow member of the international community, with certain rights and powers under international law. Similarly, the granting of recognition by any state, or even by all states, technically does not commit any international body (like the United Nations) to admit the recognized state into its membership (ibid.). But here I will assume that, if the international community should recognize another entity as a fellow member, with the rights and powers of statehood, then it should also be a member state in international organizations like the UN. (Later, in § 6.6, I relax this assumption to see how it affects the argument.)

5. Besides distinguishing the existence of states from their recognition, international law also distinguishes the recognition of *states* from the recognition of *governments*:

> Recognition of a government is a political act differing from the recognition of a state only in the nature of the entity being recognized. . . . What is involved is the authority of a new group or a new person to act as the governing agency of a state and to represent it (to act as its agent) in its international relations.

By recognizing a state's government, then, members of the international community confer upon it the right to exercise the rights and powers of statehood for that state. They also indicate that they will enter into normal international relations with it, exchange diplomats, and hold it accountable for that state's international obligations. (von Glahn, *Law Among Nations*, pp. 94, 99.)

6. The distinction I have in mind in the examples below is roughly analogous to the one Aristotle draws at 1097b25-1098a20 of the *Nicomachean Ethics*, where he distinguishes the good or virtue of someone who performs a particular function (like that of a carpenter, leatherworker, or harpist) from the good or virtue of a human being. The main difference is that I am concerned with one's *minimal* goodness (or virtue) at a particular function, or as a human being.

7. Notice that even if we hold different ideals and decide to set the minimum where they overlap, our individual judgments will still be reached by comparison with some ideal or other—just different ones. Each one of us will have decided to draw the line (so to speak) where the overlapping consensus exists. Since the minimum is still determined by its distance from an ideal—which is the basic point—it will simplify the exposition if we continue our discussion under the assumption that we share the same ideal, but keep this qualification in mind.

8. They would be disagreeing, that is, over whether possession of certain qualities (in certain degrees) is *morally sufficient* for being minimally decent, which is a substantive moral disagreement.

9. See note 7.

10. Ronald Dworkin makes a similar point in a different context. If security concerns require us to treat legal immigrants unfairly, Dworkin argues, then we should at

least be candid about that and admit that our treatment of them is unfair (yet required for security reasons) instead of insisting that such treatment meets lower standards of fairness. See Ronald Dworkin, "The Threat to Patriotism," *New York Review of Books* 28 (February 2002), pp. 44–49. In the next section, I will have more to say about the content of the pragmatic aims mentioned.

11. Buchanan, "Recognitional Legitimacy and the State System," p. 51.

12. To be self-defeating is to have the theory's point or purpose undermined or thwarted by satisfying the theory's criteria. Assuming that the point or purpose of a theory of international recognition is to make moral progress toward international peace and justice, then any criteria that would thwart progress toward that goal must be rejected.

13. As we shall see, there are two different versions of the justice-based account that accept these claims. There are strong versions, according to which failing to meet minimal requirements of justice automatically defeats a claim to state recognition. (See, for example, Buchanan, "Recognitional Legitimacy and the State System," pp. 46–78.) There are also weaker versions, according to which failing to meet minimal requirements of justice merely creates a presumption against state recognition that can be defeated. My focus here is on both kinds of justice-based theory, and in arguing that we should reject them in favor of the pragmatic account, I shall be embracing these same three claims.

14. This substantially develops and extends the reasoning first sketched in Naticchia, "Recognition and Legitimacy: A Reply to Buchanan," pp. 242–57.

15. Notice that this argument is perfectly general. It does not rest on the assumption (used for purposes of illustration) that the best theory of justice is a variety of liberalism. It can also be easily extended to cover Rawlsian "overlapping consensus"-type defenses of minimal justice. If an overlapping consensus among *reasonable* conceptions of justice establishes x as minimal justice, but standard y (lower than x) is needed to bring enough entities into the processes for formulating, adjudicating, and implementing international law, we reach the same result.

16. Another way of putting this is that its notion of minimal justice carries no independent weight. It can be lowered to whatever level is necessary to bring enough entities into the processes for formulating, adjudicating, and implementing international law. Its level, in other words, is merely a consequence of a decision we make on pragmatic grounds. Surely, though, it would be more straightforward simply to admit this fact, as the pragmatic account does.

17. Depending on how broadly we construe it, then, minimal democracy could include, say, an Afghan-style *loya jirga*. The strong standard for state recognition is defended by Allen Buchanan in "Recognitional Legitimacy and the State System," p. 53; and "Justice, Legitimacy, and Human Rights," in *The Idea of a Political Liberalism: Essays on Rawls*, ed. Victoria Davion and Clark Wolf (Lanham, MD: Rowman & Littlefield, 2000), pp. 73–89. As I explain in note 42, however, Buchanan seems to lower his standard for state recognition in *Justice, Legitimacy, and Self-Determination*.

18. Here I rely primarily on the US State Department (DOS) Country Reports on Human Rights Practices, which, while having certain limitations, are not as limiting as United Nations pronouncements or Nongovernmental Organization (NGO) reports, the main alternatives. UN pronouncements are limiting because the UN only reviews the human rights practices of a few countries each year, whereas the DOS reports cover all countries annually. In addition, the UN is notoriously reticent to condemn countries for human rights violations and its language is painstakingly meek. When it does condemn them in Security Council (S/RES), General Assembly (A/RES), or Commission on Human Rights (UNCHR) resolutions, we may rely on these official pronouncements, but we should understand that there will probably be other countries that violate the strong (or weak) standard as well. NGO reports are a bit better, but because the DOS reports rely on multiple sources (such as domestic and international reports as well as reports from individuals, academics, and embassy employees), they are more likely to be complete than a report drafted by an independent organization

using its own sources and contacts. Further, the State Department has access to intelligence information, which gives it an independent way of verifying accusations that a country violates human rights (accusations often raised by NGOs themselves). The main drawback to relying on the DOS reports, of course, is that they do not address whether human rights are adequately honored in the United States. Consider this statement from the UN Human Rights Committee, Subcommittee on the International Covenant on Civil and Political Rights (ICCPR). "The Committee . . . regrets the easy availability of firearms to the public and the fact that federal and state legislation is not stringent enough in that connection to secure the protection and enjoyment of the right to life and security of the individual guaranteed under the Covenant" (Concluding Observations of the Human Rights Committee: United States of America. 03/10/95. CCPR/C/79/Add. 50; A/50/40, para. 282). (Although this statement was issued in 1995, I doubt that circumstances have changed enough since then to render it inapplicable.) Using this statement as authority, we would have to conclude that the US violates the *weak* standard—something the DOS reports could hardly acknowledge. Still, for the purpose of assessing the justice-based account, I shall stipulate that the United States would now receive recognition under the strong standard, since that is the interpretation most favorable to establishing the feasibility of the strong standard elsewhere and worldwide (and hence the interpretation most favorable to the justice-based account).

19. See appendix 1.

20. See appendix 2.

21. In response to this argument, someone perhaps might want to press the distinction between recognizing *states* and recognizing *governments*. That is to say, one might reply that my objections are to a too stringent standard for recognizing governments, not states. I will examine this reply in detail in § 6.6.

22. The basic idea, according to the justice-based account, is that if we recognize internally unjust entities, we confer upon them the right to noninterference in their internal affairs and thus support their ability to continue wielding unjust coercive power within their territories—and this, claims the justice-based account, makes us an accomplice in injustice. I will examine this claim in detail in § 6.7. For now, we need only note that, for the purposes of this section, we are attempting to characterize a "best version" of the justice-based account that respects this commitment. So, for present purposes, references to conduct that makes us an accomplice in injustice should be understood as referring to *what the justice-based account claims or implies*.

23. S/RES/661 (1990).

24. In addition, allied coalition members Egypt, Saudi Arabia, and Syria, which fail the strong standard, would have been ineligible to implement S/RES/661.

25. "Voting was restricted to male citizens over 21—about 3.5 percent of the population" prior to the war, so Kuwait failed the strong standard back then too. See *Middle East Report* (Nov/Dec 1990), p. 14.

26. One may consistently accept the points made in this paragraph whatever one's positions are regarding (i) whether sanctions should have been given more time to work before the war began; (ii) whether the postwar sanctions were justified; (iii) whether the particular way the war was conducted (like the "turkey shoot" on the "highway of death" at war's end) was justified; (iv) whether members of the allied coalition overconsume oil.

27. *Middle East Report* (Nov/Dec 1990), p. 13.

28. "Invading Iraqis Seize Kuwait and Its Oil; U.S. Condemns Attack, Urges United Action," *The New York Times*, August 3, 1990, p. A1 (citing government analyst).

29. Anthony Cordesman, "Symposium on Dual Containment: U.S. Policy Toward Iran and Iraq," *Middle East Policy* (Fall 1994): 11–13.

30. Hassan Hamdan al-Alkim, "The Gulf Subregion in the Twenty-First Century: U.S. Involvement and Sources of Instability," *American Studies International* (February 2000): 72–95.

31. *Middle East Report* (Nov/Dec 1990), p. 13.

32. Shlomo Gazit, "Israel and the Palestinians: 50 Years of War and Turning Points," *Annals of the American Academy of Political & Social Science* (January 1998): 82–97.

33. Egypt failed the strong standard in 1978–1979 due to a state of emergency that had been in force since 1967, which curtailed rights to liberty. Israel also failed it in 1978 and 1979 due to discriminatory laws against Arabs. See report by UN Human Rights Committee, Subcommittee on the International Covenant on Civil and Political Rights, Concluding Observations of the Human Rights Committee: Israel. 18/08/98. CCPR/C/79/Add. 93 (covering the period 1978–1998).

34. Stephen Zunes, "The Strategic Functions of U.S. Aid to Israel," *Middle East Policy* (October 1996): 90–91.

35. Stephen Zunes, "The Israeli-Jordanian Agreement: Peace or *Pax Americana*?" *Middle East Policy* (April 1995): 57.

36. Shibley Telhami, "From Camp David to Wye: Changing Assumptions in Arab-Israeli Negotiations," *Middle East Journal* (Summer 1999): 380–82.

37. See ibid; also see: A. Safty, "Sadat's Negotiations with the United States and Israel: Camp David and Blair House," *American Journal of Economics & Sociology* (October 1991): 473–85.

38. See appendix 3.

39. See appendix 4.

40. The UN Peacekeeping Operations Reports by the Secretary General, February 2016, state that there were 105,314 total UN peacekeepers, of which 47,745 were African. Of the contributing African countries, only Benin, Burkina Faso, Gabon, Namibia, Niger, Senegal, Sierra Leone, Tanzania, and Togo pass the weak standard. Together, they supply 14,992 peacekeepers, roughly 31 percent of African peacekeepers and 14 percent of the total.

41. See the Heidelberg Conflict Barometer for 2015 at http://hiik.de/de/konfliktbarometer/pdf/ConflictBarometer_2015.pdf.

42. It might be objected that the theory is only *meant* to apply to future cases of recognition, not to past cases. But it is important to see that this position is incompatible with anything that deserves to be considered *justice*-based, since it allows scores of countries which have rarely, perhaps never, met its minimum standards—many of them massively unjust—to enjoy the rights and powers of statehood, and an entitlement to participate in the processes for formulating, adjudicating, and implementing international law, while denying those same rights and entitlements to entities which may actually be morally better. Similarly, it is important to see how the argument of this section actually *predicts* (see note 1 above) the way in which Buchanan's argument evolves in his latest work on this topic, *Justice, Legitimacy, and Self-Determination*. In four critical respects, he lowers his standard for state recognition from the strong standard, which he embraced in his earlier work (see note 17 above). First, he claims repeatedly that, in order to merit recognition, states need only make *credible efforts* to satisfy minimal standards of justice (pp. 70, 187, 234, 247, 257, 260, 331, 336, 375, 434). But making credible efforts to satisfy minimal standards of justice falls short of *actually satisfying* those standards. Second, he permits states to be recognized even if they fail to be minimally democratic—which he regards as a minimum standard of justice—and even if minimally democratic institutions are not feasible in the short run, provided that such institutions could be developed in the long run with the benefits of recognition (pp. 235, 254, 257, 259). Third, he permits states to be recognized even if their agent, the government, violates minimal standards of justice, provided that their constitution guarantees these standards (pp. 354–55). But despite the fact that we often speak of constitutional "guarantees," the constitution itself does not guarantee that these standards are satisfied. The constitution is just a piece of paper. It would be more accurate to say that the constitution *promises* to satisfy these standards. But promising to satisfy minimal standards of justice falls short of *actually satisfying* them. Fourth, and most dramatically, he insists that his theory is only meant to apply to future cases of recognition, not to past cases (pp. 273–78), since it would result in withdrawing

recognition from too many existing states. But this is problematic for reasons explained in the paragraph above. All of these moves appear to be motivated by the need to bring enough entities into the processes for formulating, adjudicating, and implementing international law. The result is not a plausible standard of minimal justice but rather an acknowledgment that, if we are to make moral progress, we must (unfortunately) recognize many entities that fail to satisfy minimal standards of justice (p. 277)—exactly as the pragmatic account admits.

43. By *too unjust*, I mean a standard that falls farther *below* the standard for minimal justice.

44. Notice that this argument applies no matter *how* we identify what counts as being too unjust. Whether we identify it with a failure to protect certain rights and liberties, or with a failure to garner a certain level of popular support (however we might determine that in the absence of democracy), if too few entities qualify under that standard, we must lower it further.

45. United Nations Development Program, *Human Development Report 2015*: 210–11.

46. See p. 12. The UN General Assembly Report, issued in 2009, is available at http://www.un.org/ga/econcrisissummit/docs/FinalReport_CoE.pdf.

47. Ibid., p. 87.

48. Ibid., p. 93.

49. Where to draw the line is itself a strategic decision resting on a balance of two considerations: (1) the extent to which conferring any benefits of recognition at all on unjust entities weakens incentives for moral progress (since an entity may be satisfied with those benefits and interested in no more); and (2) the extent to which conferring further benefits of recognition strengthens those incentives. I assume that the more unjust an entity is, the less interested it is in acquiring further benefits, and so at some point granting recognition to entities that are too unjust does not advance but hinders the pursuit of global peace and justice. For further discussion of how to balance these incentives, see Naticchia, "Recognition and Legitimacy: A Reply to Buchanan," pp. 252–53.

50. There are other kinds of deontological view with which the pragmatic account is consistent. For instance, it is consistent with deontological views that require us to protect basic interests without requiring us to maximize value (a policy of recognizing some unjust entities may best protect basic interests even if it doesn't maximize value). Depending on how we are to frame and universalize maxims in (extremely) nonideal circumstances, it may even be consistent with deontological views that reach moral judgments by testing maxims. The only type of theory it is inconsistent with is the (in my view, oversimplified) deontological type that claims that some acts are wrong no matter what the consequences—and then only on the question-begging assumption that recognizing an unjust entity is one of those acts. Of course, *which* of these views (if any) the pragmatic account should accept depends on which of them is independently best justified. Nothing said here implies that the pragmatic account *must* accept the strongest (oversimplified) deontological view if indeed it is implausible.

51. See, for example, Buchanan, "Rule-governed Institutions versus Act-Consequentialism: A Rejoinder to Naticchia," pp. 264–67.

52. I am assuming that the pragmatic account need not use a case-by-case approach to granting recognition, and that it can and should use rules for that purpose if there are good pragmatic grounds for doing so (such as that decisions granting recognition would likely be more predictable, impartial, and easily reached).

53. Again, see the first paragraph of § 6.2 for this characterization of international justice.

54. It would be mistaken to infer from this that the pragmatic account admits no moral constraints at all on the pursuit of peace and justice. Despite the fact that it regards peace and justice as *goals* to be pursued, it does not follow that any means whatsoever may be used to pursue them—that "the ends justify the means." Suppose, for instance, that the best theory of justice includes nonconsequentialist restrictions (or even rule-consequentialist ones) on the pursuit of the ends it takes to be valuable. In

that case, there are such moral constraints—though they would apply to acts other than acts of granting recognition.

55. See "Pentagon loses track of $500 million in weapons, equipment given to Yemen," *The Washington Post,* March 17, 2015, at https://www.washingtonpost.com/world/national-security/pentagon-loses-sight-of-500-million-in-counterterrorism-aid-given-to-yemen/2015/03/17/f4ca25ce-cbf9-11e4-8a46-b1dc9be5a8ff_story.html.

56. Leif Wenar, *Blood Oil: Tyrants, Violence, and the Rules that Run the World* (New York: Oxford University Press, 2016), p. 111.

57. Leif Wenar, *Blood Oil,* p. 113.

58. This is clearest in the case of consequentialist theories. But it is also consistent with many types of deontological view, for reasons explained earlier (see note 50).

59. Here and in the rest of the paragraph I follow A. John Simmons, "Justification and Legitimacy," *Ethics* 109 (1999): 739–71, pp. 746, 752. See also his *Moral Principles and Political Obligations* (Princeton, NJ: Princeton University Press, 1979), especially chapter 2.

60. For this reading of Locke, see A. John Simmons, *On the Edge of Anarchy: Locke, Consent, and the Limits of Society* (Princeton: Princeton University Press, 1993), chapter 5; and Simmons, "Justification and Legitimacy," p. 746 n. 18, p. 752.

61. See Simmons, "Justification and Legitimacy," pp. 755–60, for this interpretation of Kant.

62. This is Simmons' own view. See Simmons, *Moral Principles and Political Obligations,* p. 78.

63. This, however, is *not* Simmons' view. I intend here only to illustrate how one view of the connection between justice and legitimacy might be used to support the claim that unjust entities are usually illegitimate.

64. This is compatible with acknowledging that there may be some philosophical difficulties involved in showing that the territory a particular state has a right to is the same as the territory intuitively associated with it. For a description of some of these difficulties, see David Copp, "The Idea of a Legitimate State," *Philosophy & Public Affairs* 28, no. 1 (Winter 1999): 15.

SEVEN

The Critical Mass Principle

7.1 TWO DEPARTURES FROM RAWLS

By enabling us to stick to our guns, the pragmatic theory of recognition *frees* us. It frees us to imagine and defend the best theories of legitimacy and justice that we can devise for an ideal world, while leaving the messiness of the nonideal world for theories of recognition. It lets us set high standards for members of the international community to meet, while acknowledging the very real strategic difficulties involved in getting states to meet them. This is a *liberating* consequence, and additional reason to prefer it.

My argument, then, should be construed as a plea to keep our concepts straight. Justice and legitimacy belong to ideal theory. They—along with peace—provide goals that states should work toward. Recognition belongs to nonideal theory. It informs us how to achieve those goals in a world where states are imperfectly just, legitimate, and peaceful.

In a world where states are imperfectly just, legitimate, and peaceful, a theory of recognition tells us which acts of recognition (or derecognition) are permissible, required, or forbidden as we transition to a more just, legitimate, and peaceful world. Starting with the status quo, adding entities as recognized states, and derecognizing some currently recognized states, a theory of recognition guides that transition by making adjustments to the current array of internationally recognized states. These adjustments constitute steps toward the targeted state of affairs. A theory of recognition, therefore, is inherently *transitional*.

In Rawls's terms, this targeted state of affairs is the *ideal*, it is the outcome of ideal theory, it is established through ideal theorizing, and it is expressed in terms of *justice*—in this case, international justice. As he characterizes it in *A Theory of Justice*, the aim of ideal theory is "to guide the course of social reform."[1] Through "transition cases," we approach it.[2] Later, in *The Law of Peoples*, he elaborates this idea. "[U]ntil the ideal is identified, at least in outline," he claims, "nonideal theory lacks an objective, an aim, by reference to which its queries can be answered."[3]

Posing "questions of transition," nonideal theory asks "how this long-term goal," international justice, "might be achieved, or worked toward, usually in gradual steps."[4] Addressing noncompliance with what the ideal requires, as well as unfavorable conditions that pose barriers to meeting its requirements, it seeks "policies and courses of action that are morally permissible and politically possible as well as likely to be effective."[5] For Rawls, then, ideal theory gives us principles satisfaction of which establishes the target at which we should aim, while nonideal theory gives us principles for guiding the transition to it when that ideal is unsatisfied.

If defending a pragmatic rather than justice-based theory of recognition was our first departure from Rawls's view, then developing a nonideal rather than ideal theory represents our second, for Rawls himself regards his principles as belonging to ideal theory.

This chapter pursues two tasks. Its primary task is to defend and develop the pragmatic theory of recognition. As it stands, the pragmatic theory combines a denial of the justice-based theory (defended in chapter 6) with the positive assertion that political entities ought to be recognized as states if and only if cooperating with them and giving them international support would advance peace and justice among and within them. Up until this point, however, the defense of that positive assertion has consisted entirely of replies to objections to it (§ 6.7). So it still requires a positive defense. In addition, we need to make its formulation more precise. In particular, what counts as *advancing* the cause of peace and justice among and within them? It would be one thing if nonideal theory were limited to insisting that we pursue that target directly. But there is no conceptual necessity that this must be so. As John Simmons has put it, if we need to, we can take one step back in order to take two steps forward.[6] For instance, we should not be required to take steps "that might at once make our institutions more closely approximate those of an ideally just society, but that would be likely to precipitate a conservative backlash that would leave us stranded forever or for a much longer period of time in a deeply unjust society."[7] For that reason, he argues, nonideal theory "may dictate the pursuit of 'third-' or 'fourth-best' options instead, which may constitute less direct, less dramatic, less rapid progress toward the ideal, if this is what is necessary if we are ever in the future to actually reach the ideal."[8] In any case, I take it to be a legitimate and interesting question, the answer to which is not obvious, what nonideal theory requires of us in advancing toward the ideal, and I propose to use a social contract among collective agents, who reason from behind a veil of ignorance, both to defend the pragmatic theory's positive assertion and to make its formulation more precise.

A secondary, if preliminary, task of this chapter is to answer a question left open by our recasting of Rawls's theory as a theory of recognition. Once we have recast it as a theory of recognition, notice, we've vacated its claims about what international justice, our ultimate target or ideal, consists in. As the above remarks suggest, though, Rawls believes that we do need to identify what international justice consists in if we are to develop a nonideal theory—we need an ideal to guide our transitional, or nonideal, principles. However, if, as I have argued, a social contract among collective agents cannot plausibly establish principles of international justice, how are we to establish them, and what is their content?

7.2 SEN'S CHALLENGE

There is of course an alternative view, defended by Sen, who argues that identifying the "perfectly just social arrangement"—the ideal, in Rawls's terms—is neither necessary nor sufficient for ranking alternatives as more or less just.[9] If he is right about that, then it seems that we don't need to determine what international justice consists in before we develop a nonideal theory. We can proceed directly to that task instead.

"The characterization of spotless justice," writes Sen, referring to a perfectly just social arrangement, "would not entail any delineation whatever of how diverse departures from spotlessness would be compared and ranked."[10] He offers an analogy: "the fact that a person regards the *Mona Lisa* as the best picture in the world does not reveal how she would rank a Picasso against a Van Gogh."[11] There are simply too many dimensions to be assessed, and they are incommensurable.[12] A similar point holds for justice. If we compare two breaches of liberty covered by Rawls's first principle, for example, his first principle provides us with no guidance as to which one is worse. Hence, identifying the ideal is not sufficient for ranking alternatives as more or less just.

Just as identifying the ideal is not sufficient for such a ranking, Sen argues, neither is it necessary. "In arguing for a Van Gogh over a Picasso," he claims, returning to his analogy, "we do not need to get steamed up about identifying the most perfect picture in the world, which would beat the Van Goghs and the Picassos and all other paintings in the world."[13] Again, a similar point, he maintains, holds for justice. "When Condorcet and Smith argued that the abolition of slavery would make the world far less unjust, they were asserting the possibility of ranking the world with and without slavery. . . . Slavery as an institution can be assessed without evaluating—with the same definitiveness—all the other institutional choices the world faces."[14]

What drives the perceived need for an ideal, Sen suggests, is the belief that incommensurability threatens to undermine the judgments we make. Unless we find some way of rendering all of our alternatives commensurable so that we can rank them on a single scale, we risk being embarrassed by contradictory results. Yet this belief is false, or at least overstated, Sen suggests.

> For example, to show that slavery severely reduces the freedom of the slaves, or that the absence of any guarantee of medical attention curtails our substantive opportunities of living, or that severe undernourishment of children, which causes immediate agony as well as underdevelopment of cognitive capabilities, including reduction of the ability to reason, is detrimental to justice, we do not need a unique set of weights on the different dimensions involved in such judgements. A broad range of not fully congruent weights could yield rather similar principal guidelines.[15]

As long as we have a convergence of (enough, relevant) different partial rankings, in other words, we can remain confident in (at least some of) the particular judgments we reach. Therefore, we do not need commensurability across a single scale or an ideal to inform it.

Now my purpose here is not to undertake a refutation of Sen's view, but merely to show that it poses no bar to developing a nonideal theory in the way we propose. Either Sen is correct, and we can rank alternatives as more or less just without referring to an ideal, or he is incorrect. Let's explore both possibilities.

Suppose that he is correct. In that case, his view still would not undermine the nonideal theory of recognition that we will develop—the pragmatic theory—for two reasons. First, its first two principles only require consistency with making moral progress—comparing the status quo to other states of affairs that we are in position to bring about. True, if we can make this comparison without referring to an ideal, then we can skip trying to determine what (specifically) international justice consists in. But this does not undercut the pragmatic theory itself. Second, while the pragmatic theory's third principle does refer to a specific ideal—a generic liberalism—Sen himself does not appear opposed to operating with a rough ideal, only to requiring a "fully-articulated" ideal before we can rank alternatives.[16] He acknowledges that we often make moral judgments by using incomplete ideals—ones that don't rank all alternatives on a single scale—and he accepts as legitimate appeals to theories that provide partial rankings (especially if a number of different theories converge on the same partial ranking). Operating with an incomplete ideal, in other words, does not imply operating without even a rough ideal. So if we accept Sen's admonition not to get "steamed up" about articulating a full ideal that provides a complete ranking of all alternatives, and we accept, as good enough for this purpose, that liberalism of some form or other provides a rough account of the ideal, then Sen's argument does not undermine the case for the pragmatic theory's third principle either.

In short, even if Sen is correct, and we can rank alternatives as more or less just without referring to an ideal (fully articulated), it will not undermine the case for the pragmatic theory of recognition, even though it will imply that, technically, we could have skipped the task of establishing what (specifically) international justice consists in before developing it.

Alternatively, suppose that Sen is incorrect. Then of course we must defend an ideal before developing a nonideal theory. But there are other reasons for doing this as well. First, since we are *also* trying to develop the best *Rawlsian* view, it seems appropriate to accept Rawls's claim about the relation of ideal to nonideal theory unless it is obviously wrong. Second, it can't hurt either: even if it is not strictly necessary to the task, we will have a more systematic and robust view with than without it. Finally, even if we can rank alternatives as more or less just without referring to an ideal, we are not merely ranking alternatives as more or less just. We are also deciding whether it's permissible to seek a more just alternative over a less just alternative when a less direct route to international justice may be better in the long term (and the conditions under which we may do so).[17] That *permissibility* judgment differs from a *ranking*, and may require referring to an ideal even if a ranking does not.

So whether Sen is correct or incorrect in his claim that we can rank alternatives as more or less just without referring to an ideal, it will not undermine the case for the pragmatic theory of recognition.

7.3 STAGE ONE

In *A Theory of Justice*, Rawls uses his domestic contract not only to select principles of justice, but also to adopt a constitution, enact legislation, and establish administrative and judicial rules.[18] He calls this process the *four-stage sequence*, with each stage constraining the options available at later stages and revealing gradually more information to the parties. At the first stage, for instance, behind a full veil of ignorance, the parties choose his principles of domestic justice. At the second (constitutional) stage, with slightly more information, they adopt a constitution optimally designed, given knowledge of the circumstances of their particular society (but not their particular place in it), to protect the rights and liberties guaranteed by the first principle of justice and to lead to legislation consistent with it. At the third (legislative) stage, knowing both the circumstances of their particular society and the details of their constitution, they enact legislation optimally designed to satisfy the difference principle. Finally, at the fourth stage, with the veil completely lifted, they establish administrative and judicial rules.

In developing a theory of international recognition, I will follow a similar sequence, where each stage constrains the options available at later stages—except that I will use a *full* veil at each stage *subsequent to the first*. The first stage, then, establishes what international justice, our target or ideal, consists in (more on this in a moment), and constrains what the subsequent (second, third, and fourth) stages can generate as nonideal principles regulating the transition to that ideal. Those three later stages will determine in more precise terms the content of the pragmatic theory of recognition.

Now clearly this leaves wide open a rather huge question, which is, what is the outcome of this first stage? Rather than engage that question directly, though—which would merit a book in its own right—I will simply make an assumption in the alternative. Seeing that Rawls repeatedly encounters the almost-liberal objection (in chapter 3 and § 5.4), I will assume, as the cleanest and most straightforward solution to that problem, that the outcome is a *universal liberalism* and take no position as to how it gets established. For example, it can be a liberal comprehensive doctrine (not established by a social contract). It can be justice as fairness applied to each and every society. It can even be the outcome of a global original position with individuals as parties to the contract, as cosmopolitans argue. Whatever its content, however it gets established, liberalism (considered in general) will be regarded by Rawlsians as defensible, and those who are inclined to push Rawls in a more universal direction (like myself) can then construe the pragmatic theory of recognition as an attempt to detail a Rawlsian account of international relations under that assumption. As Michael Blake observes in defending his own account of justice and foreign policy (itself based on a universal liberalism), "Rawls's work is rich enough that an entirely distinct theoretical structure might usefully have been derived from it."[19]

Alternatively, for those who are not inclined to push Rawls in a universal direction, we can replace the assumption of a universal liberalism with an ideal broad enough to count some nonliberal societies as just. In that case, I will argue, the outcomes of the second and third stages will still be the same—only the fourth stage will be affected.

Either way, we get a contractarian defense of a theory of recognition, a result that will interest philosophers, legal academics, and international relations scholars alike.

7.4 THE REGULATIVE PRINCIPLE

Distinguish three propositions. The first is our initial statement of the pragmatic theory of recognition:

1. Political entities ought to be recognized as states if and only if cooperating with them and giving them international support would advance peace and justice among and within them.

As we saw in chapter 6, the argument for this proposition has consisted, so far, primarily in a denial of its rival, the justice-based theory, which conditions recognition on meeting minimal requirements of internal and external justice. Simply put, insisting on meeting such requirements would prevent us from making moral progress toward the ideal, either in actual or hypothetical circumstances. Whether such requirements are in fact consistent with making moral progress toward the ideal will depend on contingent empirical circumstances: namely, whether enough entities happen to satisfy them.

In *A Theory of Justice*, Rawls argues against leaving the protection of our basic rights and liberties to contingent empirical circumstances—in particular, to how the balance of utilities happens to tally up.[20] For that reason (among others), he maintains that we should reject utilitarianism, and embed a commitment to protecting those rights and liberties directly in his first principle of justice. In this case, similarly, we should make the parallel arguments. Just as we should not leave the protection of our basic rights and liberties to contingent empirical circumstances, neither should we leave to contingent empirical circumstances our ability to make moral progress toward the ideal. Therefore, just as we should embed a commitment to protecting our basic rights and liberties in the first principle of justice, so too should we embed, in our first principle of recognition, a commitment to recognizing enough entities as states to make moral progress toward the ideal.

Call the number that constitutes enough political entities a *critical mass*. If we are to have any hope of making moral progress at all, we need a critical mass of entities working together as recognized members of the international community, participating in the processes for formulating, adjudicating, and implementing international law, under the most extraordinarily difficult of circumstances. Therefore, we may formulate the first principle of our theory of recognition as follows:

2. Political entities ought to be recognized as states if and only if they belong to the critical mass of entities which, working together, is necessary for making at least some moral progress toward the ideal.

This is the proposition that I will defend in this chapter, as one way of specifying what counts as *advancing* the cause of peace and justice among and within them. In chapters eight and nine, I will defend further specifications of that term. I will say more about the nature and composition of this critical mass in § 7.7.

Call this second proposition the *critical mass principle*. As I will explain momentarily, my defense of the critical mass principle will rest on a view that I call *the necessity of moral progress*, which holds that:

3. Necessarily, in matters moral, we are permitted to make moral progress toward the ideal.

This view calls for comment. The necessity of moral progress denies that some acts are prohibited no matter what the circumstances, and no matter what the consequences. It denies, in other words, moral absolutism: the view that there are justifiable absolutist prohibitions. It does not follow from this that, according to this principle, "the ends always justify the means." It merely denies that the ends never justify the means. The ends sometimes justify the means.[21] At a minimum, they justify the means as a last resort, not as a first (or second, or third) one. At the least, they justify the means on grounds of necessity.

The necessity of moral progress is so fundamental to nonideal theorizing that we may call it the *regulative principle* of nonideal theory, since nonideal theory simply cannot get off the ground without it. Nonideal theory presupposes that we are permitted to make moral progress toward the ideal, and its principles indicate how. A theory of recognition, as a nonideal theory, indicates how we may transition to an ideal that fully manifests international justice. The pragmatic theory, in particular, permits us to recognize some unjust political entities as states as we transition to that ideal, if that is necessary in order to make progress toward it.

A blanket prohibition on recognizing unjust entities as states, however, even if their inclusion as member states of the international community is the only route to making moral progress toward the ideal, appears to deny this regulative principle. Such a prohibition seems to be an instance of an absolutist prohibition, if not even grounds of necessity would justify relaxing it.

Earlier, I denied that the act of recognizing an unjust state makes us accomplices in their injustices (§ 6.7). For the sake of argument, I now want us to assume the opposite. If there is an absolutist prohibition against being complicit in injustice, then (under that assumption) the critical mass principle is false, since the critical mass principle would allow us to recognize unjust entities. By contrast, if the necessity of moral progress is defensible, then there are no justifiable absolutist prohibitions. So if the necessity of moral progress is defensible, then this argument for the falsity of the critical mass principle is undercut.

In addition to undercutting this argument for the falsity of the critical mass principle, the necessity of moral progress would help establish its truth. Stated positively, the argument would proceed like this. If we are necessarily permitted to make moral progress toward the ideal, and making moral progress toward the ideal requires recognizing a critical mass of entities as states, then, even if some of them are unjust, and even if recognizing the unjust ones makes the international community complicit in their injustices, we are nonetheless permitted, under the special circumstances of necessity, to recognize them—overriding what under more ordinary circumstances would be a general (but not absolute) prohibition against being complicit in injustice. We can then strengthen that permission into a requirement or imperative [to capture the force of the "ought" in (2)] by appealing to the urgency of the occasion, and the international community's unique (and sole) position to remedy it.[22] In short, if we can show that the necessity of moral progress is defensible, then by implication we will show the critical mass principle to be true.

The challenge, then, is to argue systematically for the necessity of moral progress. By "systematically," I mean arguing in a way that avoids dead-end appeals to contrasting intuitions.[23] For example, were someone to insist that, no matter what the consequences, no matter what the circumstances, surely we are prohibited from torturing innocent children, but someone else were to insist (just as strongly) that it would be permissible to torture one such child in order to prevent an evil demon from torturing a billion such children (before forever destroying all sentient creation), we would need to adjudicate that dispute in a way that reaches beyond the appeals to these intuitions themselves. Nor will "tightening" the example settle the issue. To claim that torturing innocent children *for fun* falls under an absolutist prohibition, for instance, smuggles in the stipulation that the circumstances under which the act is contemplated are frivolous, and therefore begs the question against those who claim that there are some circumstances grave enough to justify the act of torturing innocent children. In order for the claim that some acts are wrong or prohibited no matter what the circumstances even to make sense, we cannot build into the description of the act either a full description of the circumstances or a partial, but loaded or question-begging, description of them. Instead, we must allow them to vary.

Is there a systematic way of arguing for the necessity of moral progress? Stage two of the four-stage sequence maintains that there is.

7.5 STAGE TWO

In setting up his domestic contract, the original position, Rawls defends a number of decisions.[24] Casting the nature of the parties as continuing persons or genetic lines,[25] identifying the subject of justice as the basic structure, presenting the alternative principles in the form of a short list, enabling the parties to enter the contract at any time, characterizing the circumstances of justice in terms of Hume's moderate scarcity, mandating that the principles they choose satisfy various formal conditions (generality, universality, publicity, ordering, finality), placing them behind a veil of ignorance, stipulating that the parties are mutually disinterested and rational, requiring that their agreement be unanimous and held in perpetuity, assuming that their agreement is strictly complied with, and indicating that general egoism would be the outcome of nonagreement, Rawls maintains that a contract with these features represents "the most philosophically favored" interpretation of the original position.

In setting up our international contract, we confront a similar set of decisions. Roughly speaking, we can group these decisions as follows. We must specify the target of the negotiations, the rules under which the parties are to conduct them, and the characteristics of the parties—in particular, what their interests are and how much knowledge they possess.[26] The target of the negotiations, clearly, is a set of principles for determining which political entities ought to be recognized as states, with the rights, powers, and immunities of statehood, including a right to nonintervention. Such principles, however, should not be interpreted as entailing the criteria that international law and practice should actually use, as if one should simply "read off" the criteria that are to be codified or institutionalized on their basis. Rather, the principles supply the grounds for deciding what the institutionalized criteria ought to be. Combining them with expert knowledge from outside philosophy—from fields like law, political science, and international relations—we attempt to identify the best-justified criteria. Still, the principles themselves must satisfy what Rawls calls the "finality" condition: they are the final court of appeal in our practical reasoning about recognition, there being no higher standards to which we (or they) must answer. Similarly, they must be principles that we can all publicly acknowledge, rather than be esoteric principles, ones known only to a privileged few, there being no theoretical basis for determining who among us are to be the privileged knowers. Likewise, they should be able to order claims to recognition, distinguishing the recognized from the unrecognized and the derecognized, and enabling us to prioritize claims to recognition (particularly among secessionist entities desiring independent statehood) as appropriate. Finally, there seems no reason to allow proper names or rigged definite descriptions into the formulation of principles, or to exempt any parties (still to be characterized) from their scope—the principles must possess generality and universality, in other words. In short, all of the formal conditions that Rawls insists principles of domestic justice must satisfy appear to be reasonable as conditions that we should expect transitional principles of recognition to satisfy too.

As with Rawls's domestic contract (under rules for negotiation), our international contract will require unanimity in order to secure an agreement, which the parties must acknowledge to hold in perpetuity, too. The unanimity condition ensures that every party's interests are looked out for, and the perpetuity condition forces a sober assessment of the risks: once the veil of ignorance is lifted, the parties must endure the conditions they face knowing that relief depends entirely on the transitional principles they select. As with Rawls's domestic contract, our international contract also holds that the nonagreement point is general egoism—or what we have been calling *realpolitik*—the view that societies, in their foreign policy decisions, including decisions to grant recognition, should consult only their own interests (§ 6.7). This too will inevitably affect the parties' assessment of the risks of nonagreement.

In order to model the value of nationality, the parties are collective agents: delegates who represent societies without knowing whether, or to what extent, they contain minority nations (chapter four). Their veil of ignorance deprives them of this bit of knowledge, in addition to the knowledge that Rawls denies them—knowledge of the size, population, military strength, natural resources, and economic development of their society (§ 2.2). More generally, they know no particular facts about their own societies. They do not know their conceptions of domestic justice, nor can they infer whether their particular society's conception falls within a certain range of views. They cannot infer that they represent either a liberal or decent nonliberal society. For all they know, they could represent a society whose conception of domestic justice falls outside that range. However, they do know many general facts. They know that the circumstances of justice obtain. They know that the objective circumstances obtain: no one can dominate the rest, all are vulnerable to attack, conditions of moderate scarcity exist. They know that the subjective circumstances obtain too: they make conflicting claims on resources, they have different ends, their knowledge is imperfect, self-interest often distorts their judgments.

Besides these features, the parties know that they are mutually disinterested and rational. They take no interest in one another's interests, and they are rational in the pursuit of their interests (still to be specified). They try to advance those interests as far as possible, given the constraints of the international contract and the invitation to reach agreement with the other parties. Since they know that the target of their negotiations is to select transitional principles of recognition, they know that their global order fails to manifest full international justice, from which they (being rational) will infer that there is mere partial compliance with the outcome of the first stage. Nonetheless, their choice of transitional principles presupposes that they are generally complied with, knowledge of which enables them to negotiate without the fear that, should they reach agreement, it will have been in vain. They can trust one another to keep their agreement, should they reach one.

Any collective agent, representing any society under such a veil of ignorance, can enter this hypothetical international contract at any time. We preserve, in other words, the present time of entry interpretation. However, we must add one crucial stipulation: an international practice of recognition exists, and there is no escaping one for the foreseeable future (§ 6.4). Although there may be other types of entities under international law that have standing and thus certain legal powers, the major actors for now and for the foreseeable future are recognized states. Recognized states are the major participants in formulating, adjudicating, and implementing international law, and their participation in these processes is crucial to achieving long-term international justice (§ 6.4). No practicable route to a world that manifests full international justice exists that bypasses this international practice of accepting members into the international community of states through international recognition.[27] No other types of act can bring us full international justice. In order to realize full international justice, we *must* confront the task of deciding what our criteria for recognition ought to be.

Even if the setup of this international contract differs markedly from both Rawls's domestic and international ones, its underlying rationale should be the same: to prevent factors arbitrary from a moral point of view from influencing the outcome of the contract, and to treat all of the parties fairly, as equals. While stipulating that the parties are rational reproduces the context in which questions of justice arise (since the rational pursuit of their ends puts them in conflict), placing them behind the veil of ignorance forces them to adjudicate their disputes through the selection of principles that they can all regard as fair. No delegate can tailor these principles to her society's advantage, and no society is advantaged by chance or natural fortune in the negotiations. The main difference is that they are selecting principles of transitional justice, rather than principles of justice.

To complete the setup, two tasks remain. The first is to specify the interests of the parties, the second to give a list of the alternatives they consider. After that, we ascertain their reasoning.

Specifying the parties' interests is the harder of the two tasks. In order to simplify it, I will specify their interests gradually, in increasing detail, in each of the three stages subsequent to the first stage. This should not be construed as gradually increasing the amount of information available to the parties, and hence as a gradual lifting of the veil of ignorance (as in Rawls's actual four-stage sequence). Rather, it is meant as a means of avoiding distracting details irrelevant to the argument at that stage of the social contract. The full veil still applies throughout.

At this stage, the second stage of the four-stage sequence, I will give a very thin description of their interests, simply because I believe that a thicker description serves no theoretical purpose. In fact, I believe that, at this stage, it will suffice to rely on our ability to imagine what the circumstances would be like under each alternative they consider. If we wish to, we can try to describe the interests at stake, but this will clearly be an after-the-fact exercise that in no way affects the outcome. Further, and relatedly, I believe that, at this stage, the distinction between collective and individual agents does not matter. Either way, the conclusion will be the same. Nonetheless, I will rely on the weaker stipulation, which is that the parties are collective agents. Relying on the stronger stipulation and obtaining the same conclusion only reinforces the result of relying on the weaker one. What this shows us, I believe, is that the argument to come is perfectly general, and of interest beyond the specific context of recognition. It is a contractarian argument against absolutist prohibitions, a finding of interest not just to political philosophy, but to moral theory more generally.

Reasoning from behind their veil of ignorance, our collective agents, representing societies without knowing whether, or to what extent, they contain minority nations, consider a list that includes two alternatives, one that asserts the necessity of moral progress, and another that denies it by asserting moral absolutism, the view that there are justifiable absolutist moral prohibitions. As we saw earlier, if they select the necessity of moral progress over its denial, then by implication we establish the critical mass principle (§ 7.4).

7.6 THE REASONING

Directing us to adopt the best-worst outcome from among the alternatives, the maximin rule, Rawls argues in *A Theory of Justice*, is particularly apt when a choice situation possesses three features.[28] First, "there must be some reason for sharply discounting estimates of [the] probabilities" of various circumstances obtaining—that is, "the situation is one in which a knowledge of likelihoods is impossible, or at best extremely insecure." Second, "the person choosing . . . cares very little, if anything, for what he might gain above the minimum stipend that he can, in fact, be sure of by following the maximin rule." Third, "the rejected alternatives have outcomes that one can hardly accept"—the situation "involves great risks." While all three features need not be completely present in order for the maximin rule to be rational, Rawls stresses that "these features work most effectively in combination" and that the "paradigm situation" for using it "is when all three features are realized to the highest degree."[29] Short of that, Rawls later suggests, the maximin rule may be rational when the third feature alone fully obtains, provided that the others partially obtain: that the best-worst outcome, if not completely satisfactory, is nonetheless reasonably satisfactory (second feature); and that even if the parties possess some evidence for estimating probabilities, the evidence does not consist of well-established facts or the estimate involves considerable speculation (first feature).[30]

Given the thickness of the veil of ignorance, the parties have no basis for estimating the likelihoods of the different circumstances that their society may encounter in a world in which the regulative principle operates, or in which its denial operates. As in Rawls's domestic contract, "the course of history is closed to them; they have no information about how often society has taken this or that form, or which kinds of societies presently exist."[31] Therefore, they have no information that enables them to play the odds. The first feature, therefore, seems to obtain in full.

To determine the extent to which the second and third features obtain, though, we need to describe the worst outcomes under the two alternatives. Notwithstanding my earlier claim that we can rely on our imaginations to do so, I think that this exercise will require no great literary skill from us. Whether we are collective or individual agents, representing societies or individual persons, the worst outcome seems pretty much the same under the regulative principle, and pretty much the same under its denial.

Consider its denial first. This is a world in which there are some justifiable absolutist prohibitions. In this world, the worst outcome would be to be stuck, forever, in injustice, perhaps deep injustice, without any prospect for relief, because of our observance of an absolutist prohibition that prevents us from remedying it. As individuals, we might be victims of oppression at the hands of the state: tortured, imprisoned without charge, denied access to lawyers, beaten at will by the police or vigilantes, segregated, discriminated against, and so on, with no end in sight. As a peoples or a nation in a multinational society, we might be oppressed and marginalized by the larger, majority nation: facing the same sorts of injustices just described, but in addition, forcible relocation, the breaking up of our lands for settlement and development, the erasing our histories in the schools, the suppression of our languages in public life. As societies, we might be invaded, conquered, subdued, annexed—or we might simply see our economies strangled and our people starved by neighbors who arbitrarily determine what can enter or leave our borders. Every day, at every checkpoint, we might be victims of their raw power. In each case, as individuals, nations, or societies, the worst outcome is essentially the same. We must lead our individual and collective lives under such conditions with no end in sight—ever.

Under the regulative principle, by contrast, the worst outcome would be to be the victim of an act that violates what would otherwise be (under the regulative principle's denial) an absolutist prohibition—but which the regulative principle permits under exceptional circumstances. As individuals, for instance, we might be innocent victims of an intentional, violent act designed to prevent greater numbers of innocent victims from being killed. As a peoples or a nation in a multinational society, we might be victims of an oppressive government whose authority over us is reinforced through its acceptance by other countries—all so that its diplomats might be used to persuade governments elsewhere to relax their constraints on similar groups. As societies, we might find our annexation legitimated in an effort to bring the resulting state into international processes designed to reduce illegitimate annexations. Here, too, then, in each case, as individuals, nations, or societies, the worst outcome is essentially the same. We risk being victims of the violation of an "absolutist prohibition"—victims of an act designed to help others who would otherwise be similar victims, or victims of acts equally grave, or situations equally serious, or attempts to break free from remaining mired in injustice.

According to the second feature, when an agent can ensure a satisfactory outcome under maximin, and cares little for what she can obtain beyond that outcome by using another decision rule that involves greater risk, then maximin becomes more rational to use. In this choice situation, however, it seems that *neither* worst outcome is satisfactory at all. Remaining perpetually mired in injustice is hardly a satisfactory outcome. Even having some chance at breaking free from it (at risk of being a victim of a "violation") is hardly satisfactory either. Since the veil of ignorance prevents us from knowing how far from the ideal we are, for all we know our options leave us with two quite unsatisfactory outcomes. So even a "violation" that brings us closer to the ideal may leave us stranded far from it. It seems, therefore, that we *do* strongly care for what we can obtain beyond the best-worst outcome under either alternative. The second feature, therefore, seems not to hold, even partially.

As these remarks also suggest, however, the worst outcome under the denial of the regulative principle *does* seem to be one that we can hardly accept, and one that involves grave risks, whereas the worst outcome under the regulative principle itself, which offers us both the prospect and a hope of breaking free from that unacceptable plight, may or may not leave us with an acceptable outcome, depending on how near or far we are from the ideal. Since even one unacceptable, hardly acceptable, or grave outcome shows that the third feature holds, it seems that the choice situation does possess the third feature in full.

Judged against Rawls's own assessment of how these features must combine in order for maximin to be rational, though, it seems that the parties should not use that decision rule, since, even though the first and third features fully obtain, the second feature does not obtain, even partially. If that's the case, then Rawls mentions two other decision rules that could possibly be rational in their choice situation.[32] They could engage in probabilistic utilitarian reasoning—they could play the odds. However, this doesn't seem rational under the circumstances, since they have no basis for calculating their chance of facing perpetual injustice (on the one hand), or of being victimized by someone violating what would otherwise be an absolutist prohibition (on the other). Alternatively, given this lack of information, they could rely on the principle of insufficient reason, and simply assign equal probabilities to being mired in perpetual injustice or being victimized by someone violating what would otherwise be an absolutist prohibition. But this should strike us as rather strained—to risk everything in a choice this grave, on a 50-50 assignment of probabilities to these two outcomes, as if there were no other salient outcomes as well. Yet specifying what the other salient outcomes would be, and nonarbitrarily deciding upon their number (which will greatly affect the assignment of probabilities under the principle of insufficient reason), seems like a tall order indeed. In short, the choice situation, with its veil of ignorance, deprives us of the very information needed to make this a meaningful exercise.

In light of these difficulties, I suggest, we should revive the case for using maximin. Notice first that Rawls himself suggests that it is a *sufficient* condition for maximin to be rational that the third feature alone fully obtain, provided that the other features partially obtain.[33] This leaves open the possibility that having the second feature obtain, even partially, is not a *necessary* condition. In motivating this second feature, moreover, Rawls himself stresses the importance of the contractual parties acting as responsible trustees—refusing to gamble for higher indexes of primary goods when they can ensure a decent outcome for those whom they represent and can avoid risking grave outcomes. However, this rationale is silent in circumstances like this, where the parties cannot ensure a decent outcome no matter what and must risk grave outcomes no matter what. What does acting as a responsible trustee require in these circumstances? In deciding how to handle dire circumstances where we must either follow or violate an absolutist prohibition, parties who are neither guessing nor gambling must *inevitably* establish a safety net.[34] Since avoiding the very worst outcomes seems, intuitively, to be a rational way of setting it—even if it does not prevent all bad outcomes—the maximin rule seems rational even when the second feature does not obtain, provided that the first and third features fully obtain, as is the case here.

If that is correct, then the remaining question is the critical one: what *does* maximin require in our choice situation? Does it require affirming, or denying, the regulative principle? As the above remarks suggest, we may put the question as follows:

> Is it worse to be stuck, forever, in injustice, perhaps deep injustice (the worst outcome if we honor absolutist prohibitions when violating them is the only way to break free from such a plight), or is it worse instead to risk being the victim of someone's violating what would otherwise be an absolutist prohibition that could break us free from that plight (the worst outcome if we honor the regulative principle)?

The maximin rule forces us to imagine being in the shoes of the worst-off agent (collective or individual). But it is difficult if not impossible to imagine outcomes worse than being stuck, forever, in deep injustice—with no end in sight. The former outcome seems to be not just worse, but *much* worse. In fact, worse outcomes seem *unimaginable*. Basically, the choice situation asks the parties to compare a severely intolerable outcome with no hope of escaping it, to an outcome that offers some hope of escaping it albeit at risk of being victimized by the action or policy designed to remedy it—a choice between a policy of letting such losses simply lie where they fall, and a policy of attempting to do something about it—even violating, as a last resort, what would otherwise be an absolutist prohibition. Rational agents in a suitably constructed international contract would neither acquiesce nor succumb to such a realistic dystopia: they would select the regulative principle over its denial.

In selecting the regulative principle over its denial, the parties establish, by implication, the critical mass principle—the first principle of the pragmatic theory of recognition. Although a social contract among collective agents cannot establish limits on internal sovereignty—and so cannot justify a theory of international justice—one can establish a theory of international recognition. *The contract is idle no more.*

7.7 THE CRITICAL MASS

According to the critical mass principle, political entities ought to be recognized as states if, and only if, they belong to the critical mass of entities which, working together, is necessary for making at least some moral progress toward the ideal. In this section, I want to show that this principle accounts for some of the judgments that, upon reflection, we are prepared to make (with relative confidence) about recognition—in particular, judgments concerning the nature and composition of the critical mass.

Whereas the critical mass principle itself commits us to recognizing enough entities to make moral progress rather than having such progress depend on contingent empirical circumstances, the derivative judgments that the principle accounts for *will* depend on contingent empirical circumstances—unavoidably so. In determining what *any* principle implies in practice, in considering any derivative judgment, we must rely on (actual but) contingent empirical circumstances—no less so in this case. However, I will also consider alternative circumstances, since we may legitimately test principles by considering their implications in hypothetical as well as actual (contingent empirical) circumstances.

For instance, while the critical mass principle, as formulated, is consistent with recognizing only a single superpower or group of great powers, in practice it is likely to be capacious, requiring us to recognize not just one critical mass for the entire globe, but a series of critical masses for various regions of the globe—ones whose efforts overlap with others outside each region and combine to improve the world as a whole. The argument for this claim will be largely empirical, asserting that efforts to advance international justice are usually best accomplished by those who have the strongest knowledge of, and greatest stake in, the culture, history, language, environment, politics, and circumstances of the region, and who are positioned, often in virtue of their sheer geographical proximity, to make the strongest contributions to regional peace and prosperity. Clearly, this is a generalization, not an exceptionless maxim, so allowance should be made for the fact that sometimes entities outside a region will be better contributors to moral progress there, or at least be positioned to influence events there (sometimes significantly). Nonetheless, if that generalization is true, it shows that the critical mass principle accounts for the judgment that we should not rely on the efforts of a few superpowers but should instead concentrate on recognizing enough entities in each particular region of the globe to constitute the critical mass of entities needed *there* to make moral progress.

Similarly, while the critical mass principle, as formulated, is consistent with recognizing some entities whose moral quality (whose degree of internal and external justice) is lower than others whose recognition it rejects, in practice it is likely to endorse an overall general practice of recognizing states whose moral quality is highest. Again, the argument for this claim will be largely empirical, asserting that the entities that are able to make the strongest contributions to advancing international justice are usually those whose moral quality is highest (an insight that the justice-based theory tries to capture by mistakenly setting the bar too high for recognition). Again, this is a generalization, not an exceptionless maxim, so allowance should be made for the fact that some entities will be recognized while other entities will remain unrecognized despite having a higher moral quality. Nonetheless, if that generalization is true, it shows that the critical mass principle accounts for the judgment that, all else equal, entities whose moral quality is higher are more worthy of international recognition than those whose moral quality is lower.

Moreover, while the critical mass principle, as formulated, is consistent with recognizing peoples who lack states, or states-in-waiting (such as secessionist entities), in practice it is likely to give preference to recognizing de facto states—entities that possess a permanent population, a defined territory, a government, and the capacity to enter into relations with other states—features that have come to define statehood.[35] Once again, the argument for this claim will be largely empirical, asserting that the ability to evaluate an entity's moral quality (and hence the likely strength of its contribution to advancing international justice) presupposes a track record, and generally it will be the institutional features of de facto states that supply the track record upon which to base such evaluations. This is not to say that no nonstate entities have institutional features that supply a track record. It may be, for example, that the Palestinian Authority has institutional features that supply a track record capable of being evaluated despite its arguably lacking the (independent) capacity to enter into relations with other states (and hence arguably not qualifying as a state). Nor is it to say that we should only recognize de facto states. As we will see in the next chapter, there is room within the pragmatic theory for recognizing independence movements that have yet to acquire the institutional features of states, or for claiming that entities such as nations without states ought to be recognized as states and assisted in forming states, as was the case with recognition decisions made in the midst of decolonization in Africa in the 1960s. The essential point is that the claim that typically only de facto states have a track record capable of being evaluated is a generalization, not an exceptionless maxim. Nonetheless, if that generalization is true, it shows that the critical mass principle accounts for the judgment that, in conferring recognition, we should generally give preference to de facto states ahead of other political entities, such as states-in-waiting or peoples without states.

With the critical mass principle, then, the emphasis will be on existing states, whether recognized or unrecognized. An entity that satisfies the international law definition of a state, but which is currently unrecognized internationally—like Taiwan—might well qualify for recognition according to this first principle. In contrast, a currently recognized state whose inclusion is not necessary for progress toward the ideal (and whose inclusion may well be a positive impediment) might qualify for derecognition. Far from being counterintuitive, though, this is exactly what we should expect from a theory of recognition, for, as a normative theory—even as a nonideal theory—it will not simply bless the status quo, but contain a critical edge.

However well the critical mass principle accounts in actual circumstances for judgments concerning the nature and composition of the critical mass, then, it admittedly performs less well in hypothetical ones. It is consistent with limiting recognition to a single superpower, or small group of great powers. It is consistent with recognizing entities as states whose moral quality is lower than other entities whose recognition it rejects. It is consistent with recognizing entities as states that lack the features of statehood. What do these implications tell us? In particular, do they tell us that we should reject the pragmatic theory of recognition? Of course, we might decide to revise or reject our intuitions about these matters. Supposing that we continue to affirm them, though, what then? Here I think Rawls has things exactly right when he says: "Objections by way of counterexamples are to be made with care, since these may tell us only what we know already, namely that our theory is wrong somewhere. . . . All theories are presumably mistaken in places. The real question . . . is . . . which [one] is the best approximation overall" to our judgments considered as a whole.[36] The challenge, in that case, is to defend an alternative to *both* the pragmatic and justice-based theories that does an even better job of accounting for our judgments considered as a whole—a task that presupposes that we have finished presenting the pragmatic theory. The critical mass principle, however, is not the pragmatic theory's only principle. As the next two chapters show, it also includes the justifiable secession and economic development principles.

NOTES

1. Rawls, *A Theory of Justice*, p. 245.
2. Rawls, *A Theory of Justice*, p. 248.
3. Rawls, *The Law of Peoples*, p. 90. See also Rawls, *Political Liberalism*, p. 285 for a similar claim.
4. Rawls, *The Law of Peoples*, pp. 89–90.
5. Rawls, *The Law of Peoples*, p. 89–90.
6. Simmons, "Ideal and Nonideal Theory," p. 23.
7. Simmons, "Ideal and Nonideal Theory," p. 21.
8. Simmons, "Ideal and Nonideal Theory," p. 25.
9. Amartya Sen, *The Idea of Justice* (Cambridge, MA: Harvard University Press, 2009): 98–102.
10. Amartya Sen, *The Idea of Justice*, p. 99.
11. Amartya Sen, *The Idea of Justice*, p. 101.
12. Amartya Sen, *The Idea of Justice*, p. 99.
13. Amartya Sen, *The Idea of Justice*, p. 101.
14. Amartya Sen, *The Idea of Justice*, p. 398.
15. Amartya Sen, *The Idea of Justice*, p. 243.
16. Amartya Sen, *The Idea of Justice*, pp. 103–5. Also see Simmons, "Ideal and Nonideal Theory," pp. 34–36.
17. Again, see Simmons, "Ideal and Nonideal Theory," p. 25, for this idea.
18. Rawls, *A Theory of Justice*, pp. 195–201.
19. Blake, *Justice & Foreign Policy*, p. 41.
20. Rawls, *A Theory of Justice*, section 26.
21. For instructive remarks on these matters, see Michael Phillips, "Reflections on the Transition from Ideal to Non-Ideal Theory," *Nous* 19, no. 4 (1985): 551–70, pp. 560–61.
22. The idea here is meant to be similar to Christine Korsgaard's suggestion that the urgency of a matter may convert an imperfect duty of mutual aid (which allows for discretion in fulfilling it) into an imperative, particularly when you are the only one in position to deliver its fulfillment, as is the case with the person who can protect an intended victim from the murderer at the door, who demands to know his whereabouts, by telling a lie. See Christine Korsgaard, *Creating the Kingdom of Ends* (New York: Cambridge University Press, 1996), p. 145.
23. For an outstanding example of such a systematic argument, see Samuel Scheffler, *The Rejection of Consequentialism* (New York: Oxford University Press, 1982), especially chapter 4. Although my argumentative strategy differs from his, we concur that absolutist prohibitions (what Scheffler calls "agent-centered restrictions") are intuitions "in search of a foundation"—an unsuccessful search (p. 112).
24. Rawls, *A Theory of Justice*, pp. 146–47.
25. He later modified this feature and accepted that the parties were individuals. See § 1.2 above, citing Rawls, *Political Liberalism*, p. 274, and Rawls, *Justice as Fairness: A Restatement*, p. 160.
26. Here I follow Gregory Kavka's helpful exposition in his *Hobbesian Moral and Political Theory* (Princeton, NJ: Princeton University Press, 1986), pp. 188–89ff.
27. As-if recognition, which we rejected in § 6.6, counts as one such attempt to bypass that practice.
28. Rawls, *A Theory of Justice*, p. 154.
29. Rawls, *A Theory of Justice*, pp. 154–55. See also Rawls, *Justice as Fairness: A Restatement*, p. 99.

30. Rawls, *Justice as Fairness: A Restatement*, pp. 99–104.
31. Rawls, *A Theory of Justice*, p. 200.
32. Rawls, *A Theory of Justice*, pp. 164–65.
33. Rawls, *Justice as Fairness: A Restatement*, p. 99.
34. As Scheffler puts it, one that "accomplishes a redistribution"—or as I would put it, a "distribution"—"of moral protection." See Scheffler, *The Rejection of Consequentialism*, p. 113.
35. See the Montevideo Convention on the Rights and Duties of States of 26 December 1933.
36. Rawls, *A Theory of Justice*, p. 52.

EIGHT

The Justifiable Secession Principle

8.1 JUSTIFIABLE SECESSION

Whereas our first principle, the critical mass principle, focuses on existing states, our second principle, the justifiable secession principle, focuses on entities (like minority nations) that often do not satisfy the international law definition of a state—*aspiring* states. Under what circumstances, if any, is secession justifiable? If there is a right to secede, does it imply a right to recognition? To answer these questions, and to show how the answers derive from the contract, we must specify the parties' interests more fully.

We must also relax an assumption. Previously, we claimed that, for theoretical purposes, we should assume that societies are closed to secession (just as Rawls proposes, in his domestic theory, that they are closed to emigration) (§ 4.5). For two reasons, we must now relax that assumption. First, in order to be plausible, a theory of recognition *must* address secession. After all, secessionist entities aspire to recognized statehood. In order to be plausible, therefore, our theory must identify the circumstances (if any) in which their aspirations will be vindicated. Second, the ground for that previous assumption was the general infeasibility of secession (§ 4.5). Were we developing an ideal theory of justice, that assumption would make sense: it would force us to consider the perspective of minority nations without being influenced by the possibility that they could secede (which might lead us to accept a weaker set of protections for their interests). Developing a nonideal theory, however, alters that situation. A nonideal theory must take into account the messiness of the nonideal world (§ 7.1). This includes the general infeasibility of secession. By taking into account the factors that make it infeasible, we can develop a theory that is appropriately sensitive to them.

8.2 THE PARTIES' INTERESTS

In our reconstruction of the international contract, the parties represent societies without knowing whether, or to what extent, they contain minority nations (§ 4.5). The question now concerns the interests that they represent, and how to represent them. To answer this question, I will consider in more detail the dilemma that confronts Rawls, examine how he appears to resolve that dilemma, then defend an alternative solution.

Confronting Rawls is the dilemma over how to characterize the exact collectivity that his collective agents represent (§ 4.5). They could represent peoples (nations), understood as groups with a shared history, culture, and language—regardless of whether they possess political institutions—or they could represent societies, understood as peoples (nations) that possess political institutions. Earlier, we argued that the best Rawlsian position was to split the horns of this dilemma by claiming that they represent societies, but, so as not to ignore the challenges posed by minority nations, they would not know whether, or to what extent, their own society contains minority nations. I now want to consider this dilemma in more depth.

Suppose that Rawls had adopted the first alternative: the collective agents represent peoples. In that case, Rawls would have had to confront the question of how to characterize their interests. However he had characterized their interests, though, one thing would have been certain about the outcome of this contract. Just as the parties to his domestic contract have no reason to accept anything less than the most extensive system of equal basic rights and liberties within the society in which they will later find themselves, so too would the parties to this international contract (peoples) have no reason to accept anything less than equal standing with other peoples in any multinational society in which they might find themselves. In other words, had Rawls's collective agents represented peoples, the outcome of this contract would surely have included the analogue, for peoples, of his first principle, or equal maximum liberty principle, for individuals. Not only would this principle of equal standing for peoples seem to preclude the kinds of basic inequalities that Rawls's law of peoples allows (or similar kinds applied to minority peoples rather than minority religions). It would also seem to require (under the principle's analogue of freedom of association) regional autonomy and even outright independence for peoples who desire it. All peoples everywhere, in that case, would be entitled to at least a consociational form of society and would never have to acquiesce in having minority status as a minority nation in a multinational state.[1] Clearly, this would have drawn the limits of tolerance much more narrowly than Rawls himself drew them, and would have restricted membership in the international community further than Rawls was prepared to accept, for it would have denied membership to any society that did not accord equal standing to all of its peoples.

Rather than grant to peoples such broad rights and freedoms to pursue their interests within a multinational state, Rawls did something strikingly different. Using either a liberal or common good conception of justice, he attempted to account for their interests under a *centralized* state. As he characterizes them, these liberal or common good conceptions of justice describe the interests of societies, not peoples. The interests of peoples are thus handled centrally and derivatively—through democratic procedures, or a consultation hierarchy—which aggregate and combine them with others. The collective agents then represent the aggregate interests of their societies in the international contract. Any conflicts of interest that may have existed between a peoples and the broader society are settled prior to the collective agents' entry into the international contract. Having already been settled, they disappear from consideration in the contractual choice.

Now obviously it is a false dilemma to suppose that, in the international contract, the collective agents must either represent peoples, and only their interests, or societies, and only theirs. Another option is that, in representing societies, without knowing whether, or to what extent, they contain minority nations, the collective agents can represent *both* the interests of the nations or peoples that their societies contain, and the interests of their society. In fact, if we want to model, theoretically, the tensions that exist when questions of secession arise, then we must represent both sets of conflicting interests within the model.[2] The challenge then becomes to individuate and specify them.

Let us suppose, then, that, in representing their society, the collective agents aim to advance the interests of the various nations or peoples that they contain, plus a *remainder*, composed of interests, attributable to the broader society, separate from, and independent of, the interests of their peoples. As this formulation implies, in representing their society, the interests that they aim to advance are not reducible to the interests of their various peoples alone. They are moved by both sets of interests—they are trustees of both.

In his domestic theory, Rawls stipulates that the parties to his domestic contract represent persons with three interests:

1. a highest-order interest in exercising their capacity for a sense of justice, which is their capacity to understand, apply, and act from principles of justice;
2. a highest-order interest in exercising their capacity for a conception of the good, which is their capacity to form, revise, and rationally pursue such a conception;
3. and a higher-order interest in advancing their determinate conception of the good, whatever it turns out to be, as best they can.[3]

Using this as a starting point, let us examine whether we may stipulate, for peoples, a parallel set of interests.

A parallel set of interests would assert, first, that, just as persons have an interest in exercising their capacity to understand, apply, and act from a conception of justice, so too do peoples have an interest in exercising, as a peoples, a similar capacity in evaluating the justice of their treatment by, and of, others in society. Second, it would assert that, just as persons have an interest in exercising their capacity to form, revise, and rationally pursue a conception of the good, so too do peoples have an interest in exercising, as a peoples, a similar capacity in developing a conception of themselves as a peoples. I will say more about this in a moment. Third, it would assert that, just as persons have an interest in advancing their determinate conception of the good, so too do peoples have an interest in advancing, as a peoples, a determinate conception of themselves as a peoples.

What is it for a peoples, then, to have a determinate conception of themselves as a peoples? Let us say that it involves their having a conception of their own history, culture, and language—authentically interpreted, by their own members, free from assimilationist pressures. Such a conception, let's say, provides the initial roles, models, and forms of life that their members sort through as they assess, shape, and modify them—and among which they ultimately decide how to situate themselves.[4] Woven together into their own historical narratives, rendered vivid in their own native language, evolved from their own authentic aspirations, they supply their members with meaningful ways of life from which to choose, across the full spectrum of human activities.[5] Taken together, they provide members with effortless, secure belonging within their cultural group, avenues of participation in common practices within it, relative freedom from the distorting influences of assimilationist pressure, and a source of mutual recognition and trust.[6] Although such a conception is the analogue, for peoples, of Rawls's conception of the good for individuals, the two are not identical, and should not be confused, for a peoples' having a conception of themselves as a peoples, of their own history, culture, and language, is compatible with their diverse members holding different conceptions of the good among them.[7]

In addition to representing the interests of the nations or peoples that their societies contain, the collective agents must also represent the remainder, composed of interests attributable to the broader society, that are separate from, and independent of, the interests of their various peoples. Let's say that this interest consists of the good of the composite whole continuing to exist together—a shared identity that derives, not from shared nationhood, but from something that ties the various nations or peoples in a multinational state together. It is a civic good, a source of civic pride, deriving perhaps from certain shared historical achievements and the construction of a shared historical narrative that celebrates them.

In its best form, it is a good that values and cherishes diversity.[8] However, just as a peoples' conception of themselves as a peoples does not imply that their members share a conception of the good, neither does a society's having an interest in the continuity of a shared identity of this sort imply that their members must share a conception of the good. This interest is more capacious than that. As we will now see, it is also the antisecessionist interest.

8.3 THE REASONING FOR THE GENERAL RIGHT

Situated symmetrically, reasoning from behind a veil of ignorance, blind to whether they contain minority nations, unaware of the extent to which their society is multinational if they do, and motivated by interests to advance their peoples' determinate conceptions of themselves as peoples—as well as to maintain the shared identity of their society as a good in itself—what principles governing secession would the collective agents in our international contract select? In the rest of this chapter, I will argue that, in this—the third stage of our four-stage sequence—they would indeed grant a right to secede, although they would attach certain conditions to it. This argument will proceed, analytically, in three steps:

1. In this section, I will argue that, in the third stage of our four-stage sequence, they would grant a general right to secede. By a *general* right, I mean that the parties would acknowledge some general circumstances in which the right holds, not that the right is unconditional.[9] For reasons explained momentarily, the argument in this section abstracts from the transaction costs involved in transitioning to the state of affairs implied by exercising the right.
2. Then, in the next section (§ 8.4), I will maintain that this right belongs to transitional justice—nonideal theory.
3. Finally, in the last section of this chapter (§ 8.5), I will attach conditions to the right and defend them—taking into account factors that contribute to the messiness of our nonideal world (in particular, the transaction costs just mentioned). Not only would our collective agents grant a right to secede when it occurs with the parent state's consent or when such consent is conditioned on the outcome of a plebiscite (the easy cases). They would also grant such a right as a remedy for grave, persistent, and pervasive violations of human rights at the hands of government forces (the intermediate cases)—and even, possibly, in some cases where a nation or peoples simply aspires to internationally recognized independent statehood without the blessing of their parent state and in spite of its resistance (the hard cases).

The idea is that, by isolating the transaction costs in the third step, then showing that they do not call for a *repeal* of the general right established at the first step, we secure the general right's justification. Then, by showing in the connecting step that the general right belongs to nonideal theory, we may conclude that the conditions we attach next are appropriately sensitive to the circumstances of our nonideal world. I turn now to executing this strategy.

In the second stage of our four-stage sequence, in considering the choice between the regulative principle (the necessity of moral progress) and its denial, we saw that it was rational for the collective agents to use maximin in those circumstances (§ 7.6). Behind the veil of ignorance, they had no objective basis for assigning probabilities to the various outcomes, and the worst outcomes were ones that they could hardly accept. This was sufficient to make it rational to use maximin.

Now in this, the third stage of our four-stage sequence, likewise, it seems that these same two features obtain in full. Just as it did in the second stage, the veil of ignorance deprives the parties of information that would give them an objective basis for assigning probabilities to various outcomes. Similarly, the very worst outcomes are ones that they can hardly accept—as we saw in vivid detail in the last chapter. To recall just one example, a peoples might face forcible relocation, the breaking-up of their lands for settlement and development, the erasing of their histories in the schools, the suppressing their languages in public life—to say nothing of more violent forms of oppression (§ 7.6). There are others.

Given that it's rational for them to continue to use maximin in their contractual circumstances, the question that our collective agents initially face in the international contract is the following:

> Is it worse to be a secessionist with no right to secede, or an antisecessionist living in a society in which others may exercise their right to secede?

Not only does it seem worse to be a secessionist with no right to secede. It seems *far* worse. Lest this claim seem to rely too heavily on intuition, though, or to rest too much on our imaginative abilities, there are, I believe, sound theoretical reasons that we can offer in defense of it.

In his domestic theory, Rawls describes the capacity for a sense of justice and the capacity for a conception of the good as "highest-order" interests in order to indicate that they trump lesser interests, including the "higher-order" interest in advancing a determinate conception of the good.[10] As highest-order interests trump higher-order ones, the primary goods used to advance the former (which are the basic rights and liberties) hold absolute priority over the ones used to pursue the latter (which are wealth, income, and opportunities). No tradeoffs are permitted between them; no sacrifices in the former are permitted in order to achieve a higher index of the latter. This gets manifested in the lexical priority of Rawls's first principle to his second principle.

Let's assume, then, that the only interest at stake for peoples when questions of secession arise is their interest in advancing a determinate conception of themselves as a peoples (the analogue, for peoples, of an individual's interest in advancing a conception of the good [§ 8.2]). According to the above characterization, this would be a high*er*-order interest instead of a high*est*-order one—a *weaker* interest. Admittedly, their other interests will likely be implicated as well, but for the sake of argument the following reasoning will rest on this weaker assumption.

Since a people's interest in advancing a determinate conception of themselves as a peoples is the analogue, for peoples, of an individual's interest in advancing a conception of the good (§ 8.2), then, just as the latter is a higher-order interest, so too is the former. As higher-order interests trump ordinary, first-order (lesser-order) interests, the question then becomes, what kind of interest is the antisecessionist interest, the interest in the remainder?

On a liberal view, the answer seems straightforward. Just as forced conformity is worse than tolerance on a liberal view (§§ 2.4, 2.6), so is forced integration worse than tolerating voluntary disassociation. As a result, the collective agents would distribute to the peoples whose interests they represent a general right to secede so that they may judge for themselves whether they can best advance their determinate conception of themselves as a peoples through independent statehood. That interest is a higher-order interest that trumps the remainder, which by implication is a lower-order interest.

On a nonliberal view, alternatively, while the reasoning would be different, the result reached would be the same. Even supposing that the interest in the remainder is a strong one, it still seems to be a lesser interest than the higher-order one, since the good of integration—maintaining the shared identity of their society as a good in itself—seems to *presuppose* the thriving of the *collective* parts that constitute that society. Without the thriving of those parts, their integration would hardly seem to constitute a good. Thriving peoples would therefore seem to be a prerequisite for, or necessary condition of, the good of integration, and for that reason the remainder would seem to be a lesser interest than the higher-order one. Maintaining the shared identity of their society as a good in itself, in other words, *is* a good in itself only on condition that the constituent parts of that society, including its collective constituent parts, that is, its peoples or nations, thrive—which is equivalent to holding that a peoples' interest in advancing a determinate conception of themselves as a peoples is a higher-order interest than the remainder. To reverse these, and to insist that integrating nations into a society constitutes a good so valuable that it trumps even their own judgments of the degree to which it is worth continuing to share that social identity (if ever it was shared), is not to offer us an appealing alternative to liberalism that champions collectivities over individuals, but to elevate the interests of collectivities who long for a vanishing, nostalgic past over collectivities who have little interest in preserving that fantasy for them.[11]

8.4 THE GENERAL RIGHT AS A NONIDEAL PRINCIPLE

Supported by sound theoretical reasons that reinforce clear intuitions (and our imaginative capacities), the general right to secede, held by peoples or nations, is not a blanket right to secede at will but a right that holds only under certain conditions. It is a conditional right to secede. In the next section, I will defend specific conditions that attach to the right—conditions that limit its exercise. In this section, I defend a claim prerequisite to that task: that because the general right to secede belongs to nonideal theory, the conditions that attach to it must be appropriately sensitive to the circumstances of our nonideal world.

One need not be a liberal to endorse the view that rule acquired by conquest or annexation is unjust. The question is whether this view rests on a deeper view that accounts for these injustices, yet extends beyond them to other types of unjust rule too.

Here is one plausible candidate: these types of rule are both instances of *alien rule*. The existence and injustice of alien rule can be easily explained by liberal consent theory. Conquest and annexation are perhaps the most glaring instances of rule that violates the consent of the governed. Colonialism, moreover, would be yet another instance, easily accounted for by liberal consent theory. Not only can liberal consent theory account for the injustice of conquest and annexation, therefore. It can also extend beyond them to account for the injustice of colonialism. But the injustice of conquest, annexation, and colonialism need not rely on liberal consent theory, with its tacit individualism. It can also be accounted for by views that regard the nation, for instance, as a collective agent, fundamentally rather than instrumentally valuable. On these views, conquest, annexation, and colonial subjugation are unjust because they all subvert national self-determination—where the unit of self-determination is taken to be the nation, not the individual. All three involve alien rule.

However we account for the injustice of alien rule, though, its existence manifests itself not only through conquest, annexation, or colonialism. "Decolonization," writes Mikulas Fabry in his masterful historical account of international recognition practice, "did not eliminate the problem of 'alien rule' even as it dismantled the institution of formal empire."[12] The problem is that, even after colonial powers withdraw from their former colonies, many ethno-national groups still regard themselves as being under alien rule, even if their new rulers are indigenous to the territory. This typically occurs when the boundaries of their political unit remain the same as the ones drawn by their colonial rulers, which may separate them from their fellow nationals and leave them ruled by members of rival nations. "[T]he really vexing issue," Fabry continues, "is how to treat the groups that clearly refuse to be part of those jurisdictions as they become independent, and particularly when these groups object to being separated from their ethno-national group."[13] Concluding on a pessimistic note, he observes, "The post-colonial experience has shown that the retention of historical and colonial boundaries, which fails to take account of the actual political loyalties on the ground, can lead to failed states or continuing civil conflicts."[14]

Moreover, just as alien rule can persist where colonialism recedes, so too can it appear where neither conquest, nor annexation, nor colonialism had ever existed.[15] Over time, as national loyalties develop, shift, or grow, or as relations between dominant and minority groups change, a feeling of estrangement may set in and intensify, leaving national groups feeling alienated from the larger society (and its official decisions) in a way that makes using the term *alien rule* apt. Alien rule is a phenomenon that can exist with or without colonists, aliens, or a previous history of either.

If alien rule is a type of injustice, a general right of secession, by itself, is not a remedy sufficient to reestablish the justice of ruling arrangements, for other injustices, institutional or otherwise, can remain or arise following its exercise. Yet as these remarks indicate, eliminating alien rule is a necessary condition for establishing the justice of ruling arrangements. Insofar as international justice consists of just internal and external relations (§ 6.2, § 6.6), therefore, a general right of secession contributes to it by enabling us to transition toward it. Inherently remedial and transitional, a general right of secession belongs to nonideal theory (§ 7.1).

As a right belonging to nonideal theory, it must take into account the circumstances of our nonideal world—in particular, the factors that contribute to the general infeasibility of secession—when we specify its content more fully. Before turning to that task, however, I want to contrast my defense of this right with two other views. First, although this right belongs to nonideal theory, the justification for it is independent of any considerations regarding its prospective codification or institutionalization. As we have seen, its justification rests on the claim that alien rule is an injustice, which the right to secede seeks to eliminate. When considering the question how best to make such a right part of international legal institutions, of course we must take into account the likely effects of its institutionalization—its publicity effects, incentives it creates, likely repercussions for international peace and justice, and so on. These are factors that influence the content of the right that gets codified. Here, however, I have been concerned with its grounding or justification, the logically prior task.[16] Second, despite the fact that its justification takes no notice of its prospective codification or institutionalization, it does not follow that this right should be included in any package of rights conferred under ideal theory either. Possessing this right is not part of any targeted state of affairs at which we should aim. On the contrary, the target should be one that *lacks* this right, for by hypothesis, that target is one in which alien rule is entirely absent, obviating the need to possess the right at all. At this phase in the argument, then, the right defended is nonideal and noninstitutional.[17]

8.5 THE REASONING FOR CONDITIONS ON THE GENERAL RIGHT

As we will see, current international law appears to hold that there is no unilateral right to secede, even as a remedy for persistent, widespread, and serious human rights violations at the hands of government forces (§ 10.3[F]). There is only a bilateral (or multilateral), consensual right to secede. Secession currently requires the agreement of the parent state (sometimes conditioned on the outcome of a plebiscite). So under current international law there appears to be only a conditional right to secede, and the conditions are very limiting.

Since the argument so far establishes only a general right to secede, it now remains to show what conditions the contracting parties would attach to that right. As I hope to show, the parties would attach less limiting conditions. In addition to allowing a right to secede by bilateral, mutual consent, they would also embrace a remedial right to secede as a response to persistent, widespread, and serious human rights violations at the hands of government forces. In some cases, they may even accept rights to secede without a parent state's consent and absent widespread human rights violations—provided solely that a peoples or nation desires internationally recognized independent statehood.

As with any argument that moves from moral assessment to institutional requirement, some care must be taken to consider incentive and publicity effects. Unavoidably, we must rely on empirical claims from the social sciences to supplement it. Nonetheless, I believe that we can sustain two important conclusions, one by hypothetical contractarian reasoning alone, and one by relying on relatively modest social scientific claims. The first of these conclusions is that we can rank secessionist claimants to recognition in order of their normative priority. Those that receive their parent state's consent (perhaps conditioned on the outcome of a plebiscite) should receive top priority, since their recognition involves little or no costs in terms of international resources (including, but not limited to, providing international peacekeepers or coalition military forces). It's when states resist secession that the hard cases arise, since they involve (transaction) costs in international resources. In these cases, claimants who suffer under unjust circumstances without being under any sort of alien rule should receive priority over ones who are under alien rule without suffering under (otherwise) unjust circumstances. In any case, this latter claim is the one that I will sustain by appealing to hypothetical contractarian reasoning. If correct, it implies that secessionist claimants who suffer persistent, widespread, and serious human rights abuses at the hands of government forces should receive priority in recognition decisions over those who suffer no such abuses but who feel themselves to be under alien rule (and arguably *are* under such rule, as in, for instance, cases of annexation) and seek to remove themselves from it by establishing an independent state of their own.

Clearly it's consistent with this ranking for international institutions to grant recognition only to the first group of secessionist claimants—those that receive their parent state's consent—as is apparently the case under current international law, or even to none at all (which would represent a repeal of the general right). According to the second conclusion, however, we can show that, by overcoming what Rawls calls the *assurance problem,* international institutions can and should honor more secessionist claims to recognition than current international law honors. I will say more about this problem momentarily, but for now we can say that the assurance problem involves assuring "cooperating parties that [their] common agreement is being carried out," since "[e]ach person's willingness to contribute [to upholding it] is contingent upon the contribution of the others."[18] Combined with some modest empirical assumptions about how taxing it would be on international resources to honor additional secessionist claims to recognition, we can support the case for institutionalizing a less limiting set of conditions on the right to secede. I now turn to defending these two conclusions.

Having already established the propriety of maximin reasoning in justifying the general right to secede, we can also use such reasoning to rank secessionist claimants to recognition when their parent states resist their independence. The question faced by our collective agents seems to be this:

> Is it worse to be a nation under alien rule but otherwise justly treated by the central government of one's society, or to be one denied the components of basic justice by that government but otherwise not suffer from alien rule under it?

The first alternative is meant to correspond to (some of) the kinds of situation that Kymlicka describes, situations involving forcibly incorporated national minorities who may be outvoted or outbid on resources by the broader society but who are otherwise treated consistently with basic requirements of justice, such as respect for basic human rights. Although they are under alien rule, they are not otherwise treated unjustly. The second alternative, by contrast, corresponds to the kinds of situation on which Buchanan focuses, situations involving national minorities who are brutally treated by their governments but who may not have been previously conquered, annexed, colonized, or alienated over time through state policies or measures not involving denials of basic justice. Although they are not under alien rule, they are otherwise treated unjustly.

Judged from the standpoint of our collective agents, the answer must be decided by reference to their peoples' higher-order interest in advancing a determinate conception of themselves as a peoples. Since it seems harder to advance that determinate conception when denied the components of basic justice than when one's nation or peoples is guaranteed those components, and protected by them, but otherwise outvoted or outbid, it seems like the second alternative is worse. It is worse, that is, to be denied the components of basic justice than to suffer alien rule.[19]

If this reasoning is correct, then we can rank secessionist claimants to recognition in order of their normative priority, giving highest priority to the claimants whose independence requires little or no international resources—those claimants who receive the consent of their parent state—and then, among those who do not receive such consent, giving priority to the claims of those who suffer under unjust conditions over those who do not but who wish to break free from what they regard as alien rule. This is equivalent to arguing that remedial rights of secession take priority over primary rights of secession, where primary rights are held by nations or peoples and may be exercised by them even in the absence of their being victims of widespread, grave, and persistent human rights violations at the hands of government forces.

The next question we face is, how far along this continuum (if at all) should we go in codifying and institutionalizing the right to secede? What conditions (if any) ought we to attach to it? As we will see, how we overcome the assurance problem affects the answer.

As Rawls describes it in relation to his domestic contract, the assurance problem is the problem of making sure that, once the parties reach an agreement, it does not unravel through growing defections from it, which is typically achieved by employing "some device for administering fines and penalties" in enforcing its rules.[20] The existence of an effective sovereign, he notes, and the belief in her efficacy, plays a "crucial role" in assuring the cooperating parties that their common agreement is being fulfilled, thereby reducing their tendency to defect. Since the contracting parties take the strains of commitment into account—the strains involved in keeping any agreement they make—and refrain from making agreements that they believe are likely to unravel under those strains, the content of their agreement is affected by their beliefs (supported by the general knowledge allowed to them through the veil) about how efficacious a sovereign is likely to be in enforcing their agreed-upon rules. Hence, their estimates of how strong the strains of commitment are under the terms that they are considering, coupled with their degree of confidence in a solution to the assurance problem, influences the content of their agreement.

Within our international contract, though, we have two main differences. First, the outcome of the international contract is a set of nonideal, transitional principles rather than, as in the domestic contract, a set of ideal principles. Despite this fact, however, the assurance problem is basically the same: just as agreement on ideal principles can unravel, so too can agreement on nonideal principles. Second, and more importantly, the contracting parties will face a world order without anything like a domestic sovereign. No doubt this affects their reasoning about the efficacy of enforcing rights to secession, and hence their judgments about the conditions that they should attach to those rights. Whatever conditions they agree to attach, they must be able to honor their agreement—not have it unravel under the strains of trying.

There is a public benefit to living in a world where each peoples has the right to secede: the benefit that your peoples will not live under alien rule. Any agreement to adopt such a right, though, comes with a corresponding burden: honoring the correlative duty, the duty of the parent state not to interfere with its exercise. In the easy cases, where the parent state consents (or does so conditioned on the outcome of a plebiscite), the parent state by hypothesis does not interfere with its exercise. The hard cases occur when parent states resist. Any agreement to allow secession without parent state consent threatens to unravel once those states that have assumed the burden of honoring the duty not to interfere with secessionist rights see other states not honoring it but getting away with it. This is precisely where a sovereign would enter—to assure compliance with the duty by issuing effective sanctions, actual or threatened.

In place of a domestic sovereign, the international community substitutes international collective action in the use of force. Now the defender of limiting secessionist rights to cases where parent states consent seems to assume that such collective action is effective only in these cases. But this seems unjustifiably narrow. Even if it cannot be effective enough to support the struggle for independence for all peoples seeking it, surely it can be effective for some—extending beyond cases of (mere) parent state consent, which do not require use of force at all. If the concern is that international resources (particularly military resources) will be stretched too thin, in other words, the response is not to refrain from using them at all. That would be to convert the sovereign substitute into a mere figurehead—entirely devoid of normative power—which is justifiable only on the unduly pessimistic assumption that she likewise altogether lacks physical power.

Instead the proper response is to be more selective in deciding which cases beyond ones involving parent state consent to support, and our ranking provides a principled basis for selection. At the very least, the international community can use its finite resources to support the struggle for independence of peoples or nations seeking to free themselves from widespread, grave, and persistent human rights abuses at the hands of their government's forces—remedial right cases. Limiting the right to secede to these cases seems like a more fitting response to concerns about overtaxing the international community's (military) resources, and overcoming the collective action problem involved in employing them, than not employing them at all. Instead of overcoming the assurance problem by positioning the international community so that it need not issue sanctions at all, in other words, this would position the international community so that there is at least an assurance problem to overcome—in fact, *the least* problem to overcome.

Generating an assurance problem in the first place, then, requires extending the right to secede beyond cases involving parent state consent to remedial cases. Only justified skepticism about the efficacy of international collective action in using force in these remedial cases would defeat the case for extending the right to secede to them. I have suggested that such skepticism is unduly pessimistic, and implied that rejecting it would be a modest empirical assumption. If this is correct, then agreeing to a less limiting set of conditions on the right to secede, a set that allows secession in remedial cases, would be part of an agreement that the contracting parties would be reasonably confident that they could keep, rather than one ruled out by the strains of commitment. I will now briefly consider three challenges to this conclusion.

First, it will come as no surprise that the contracting parties will foresee that there will be some remedial cases where we can justifiably doubt the efficacy of international collective action in using force—particularly where the parent state is both resistant and powerful. However, from the fact that we can envision some such cases, it does not follow that we should endorse skepticism across the board about its efficacy, since we can also affirm its efficacy in other remedial cases. There is a problem here, admittedly, but it is a problem in formulating the exact language of the condition, not with including a remediation condition itself. As I later suggest (§ 10.4), this may be an occasion that requires expert knowledge outside the discipline of philosophy—in fields like law, political science, and international relations. The challenge is to formulate a condition that avoids withdrawing remedial rights altogether, on the one hand, without jeopardizing the international community's credibility by promising more than it can deliver, on the other. For my part, I see no hindrance to stating what everyone already knows, which is that use of force to enforce remedial rights of secession is contingent on calculations of its efficacy, and that it is cause for regret when those calculations suggest that it should not be used—and not to worry about the incentive effects of such wording, as abusive governments the world over already know that they can insulate themselves from international intervention by acquiring enough physical power, and the marginal contribution of such wording to that realization is minimal. The final word on these matters, though, properly belongs to the experts previously mentioned.

Second, there will be concern that, no matter how narrowly formulated, any rights to secession will bring secessionists out of the woodwork, leading to problems with *infinite secession,* as secessionists within secessionist movements seek further secession once independence is achieved, eventually overtaxing the international community's resources. One would have hoped that limiting secessionist rights to those who are victims of widespread, grave, and persistent human rights abuses at the hands of the government's security forces would be sufficient to alleviate this concern, but skeptics will note that determined secessionists will be adept at provoking reprisals against themselves (and their peoples) so as to qualify for the remedial right. Again, I admit that there is a problem here, but it seems like a problem in formulating the exact language of the condition, not with including a remediation condition itself. As before, its formulation is probably best left for experts outside philosophy. For my part, I see no reason why international judicial bodies could not be empowered to engage in fact finding over such matters. This would give a "caveat emptor" to would-be secessionists bent on provoking reprisals against them and their peoples: if they lose the case, their efforts will be to no avail.[21]

Third, there will also be concern about the determination of the international community itself to rise to the occasion and to impose or threaten sanctions (or force) on reluctant duty-fulfillers, or to expend considerable international resources to support secessionists in their quest for independence—or whether instead it will waver in its commitment to recognizing new entities as states as they grasp for, and sometimes struggle to develop, the attributes of statehood. The strains of commitment, in other words, exist not only on societies required to fulfill their duty to respect secessionist rights, but also on the international community to enforce this duty when needed, and to underwrite the correlative right. While this is no doubt a serious concern, we should also note that the strains of commitment are a two-way street. Were we to deny remedial rights to secession, peoples who suffer under widespread, grave, and persistent human rights abuses at the hands of their government's security forces would be making a tremendous sacrifice just so that members of the international community of recognized states would not be required to act or to get their hands dirty. Not only does that seem intuitively wrong. The contract accounts for it. From behind the veil of ignorance, surely our collective agents would regard it as being far worse to be a peoples suffering under these remedial circumstances than a society required to contribute its share in a collective scheme to remedy them. Counting the strains of commitment, the parties would likely conclude that the more difficult agreement to fulfill would be the one that denies remedial rights, not the one that includes them.

These points aside, the question now becomes whether the parties would embrace an even less limiting set of conditions on the right to secede, a set that allows secession, not only in remedial cases, but in other cases as well. For instance, would they embrace a right to secede in cases where a nation or peoples simply aspires to internationally recognized independent statehood, and if so, which ones? As the above remarks suggest, the answer depends on how optimistic or pessimistic we should be toward overcoming the assurance problem. (I have also suggested that the matter is probably best deferred to experts in other fields.) True, the assurance problem is greater once we extend the right even further, for there will predictably be even more cases where states resist the exercise of secessionist rights, and hence a greater call for international resources to overcome that resistance and enforce compliance with this proposed duty. The international community would be called upon, for instance, to use its finite resources to support the struggle for independence of peoples or nations seeking to free themselves from (what they regard as) alien rule. Yet if the facts should show that we have reason to be less pessimistic about overcoming the assurance problem than I have assumed, we would have grounds for extending the right further.

Throughout this discussion, I have assumed that the right to *secede* implies a right to *recognition*, which now calls for comment. As mentioned before, with the justifiable secession principle, the emphasis turns from entities that meet the international law definition of statehood to ones that typically do not (§ 1.5, § 8.1). Secessionist entities, often minority nations, oppressed or seeking relief from alien rule, may not have the institutional structures that satisfy the international law definition of statehood: a permanent population, a defined territory, a government, and the capacity to enter into relations with other states.[22] Yet historically, many such entities have been eligible for and have received international recognition as a state, despite lacking the features of statehood at the time of their recognition (primarily during the period when many African nations acceded to recognized statehood following decolonization) (§ 10.3[E]). Although this historical precedent carries no normative weight for purposes of developing a theory of recognition, it does reveal that it is possible within such a theory to confer a right to secession without conferring a right to recognition—perhaps making the latter depend on further conditions (such as satisfying the international law definition of statehood).[23] As I have developed and defended the pragmatic theory in this chapter, though, there is one further condition that is *not* required (satisfying the international law definition of statehood), and one that is not stated but *assumed* as part of the right to secede. For these reasons, the right to secede, according to the pragmatic theory, does imply the right to recognition.

According to the pragmatic theory, an entity need not achieve de facto statehood at the time of recognition in order to be admitted as a recognized member of the international community of states. For this reason, a secessionist entity that qualifies for the remedial right to secede is also entitled to recognition as a state even if it does not yet possess the features that have come to define statehood under international law. The reason for this is straightforward: were achievement of de facto status required, such entities could be denied membership by the active resistance and hostility of the states from which they attempt to secede, the ones refusing to fulfill their duty correlative with the right that the secessionist entities possess by hypothesis. In fact, their recognition, and inclusion in the international processes for formulating, adjudicating, and implementing international law, combined with the international community's ongoing support, may enable them to consolidate, over time, enough control over their domestic institutions to establish the features of de facto statehood. Although international recognition is no guarantee that they will eventually achieve de facto statehood, nonrecognition leaves them much more vulnerable to never achieving it.[24]

While achievement of de facto statehood is not a requirement of recognition for entities possessing the right to secede, their recognition must nonetheless be consistent with continued progress toward the ideal established at the first stage of the four-stage sequence. Since each stage of the sequence constrains the options available at later stages (§ 1.5, § 7.3), the justifiable secession principle (established at the third stage) is constrained by the critical mass principle (established at the second stage), which in turn is constrained by the ideal established at the first stage. Since the critical mass principle forbids recognizing entities as states unless doing so enables us to make at least some moral progress toward the ideal, then whatever further entities we recognize as states must be compatible with our continuing to make such progress. This assumption is implicit in the four-stage sequence.

It will be logically possible, then, for a peoples to be victims of widespread, grave, persistent human rights abuses, yet lack a right to secede, and thus lack a right to recognition, when it is (correctly) judged that recognizing their secessionist entity as a state is incompatible with continued progress toward the ideal. Exactly what the circumstances are under which that logical possibility obtains we can only speculate. Holding good evidence that abuses and reprisals—ones committed by the security forces of the newly recognized state—would intensify and proliferate by granting recognition seems like one set of circumstances. But in that case, refusing recognition does not seem obviously objectionable. Would there be other circumstances, though, in which it would be objectionable? Supposing there would be, the challenge, in that case, is the same that we noted at the end of the last chapter: to defend an alternative to the pragmatic theory that does an even better job of accounting for our judgments considered as a whole. The critical mass and justifiable secession principles, however, are not the pragmatic theory's only principles. It also includes the economic development principle.

NOTES

1. For a useful description of the contrast, see Michael Walzer, *On Toleration* (New Haven, CT: Yale University Press, 1997), pp. 22–30.
2. See Rawls's parallel remarks about assuming that the parties to his domestic contract are rational and mutually disinterested in order to model the situation when questions of justice arise. See Rawls, *A Theory of Justice*, pp. 129–30.
3. See Rawls, "Kantian Constructivism in Moral Theory," in Samuel Freeman (ed.), *John Rawls: Collected Papers* (Cambridge, MA: Harvard University Press, 1999), pp. 312–13.
4. Such features are suggested by Kymlicka, *Liberalism, Community, and Culture*, p. 165.
5. These features are suggested by Kymlicka, *Liberalism, Community, and Culture*, p. 165; Kymlicka, *Multicultural Citizenship*, p. 76; and Miller, *On Nationality*, pp. 23–24.
6. See Kymlicka, *Multicultural Citizenship*, pp. 76, 105, and Miller, *On Nationality*, pp. 22–23, 80, 89 for these suggested features.
7. This accords with Kymlicka, *Liberalism, Community, and Culture*, pp. 167–68, 172, 191, 239; Kymlicka, *Multicultural Citizenship*, p. 105; and Miller, *On Nationality*, p. 26.
8. Such features are suggested by Kymlicka, *Multicultural Citizenship*, p. 189.
9. This stipulative definition is not meant to follow the taxonomy developed by H. L. A. Hart in his article, "Are There any Natural Rights?" *Philosophical Review* 64, no. 2 (April 1955): 175–91, pp. 183–88.
10. Rawls says that they are "supremely regulative" and "govern deliberation." Rawls, "Kantian Constructivism in Moral Theory," p. 312.
11. See also Miller, *On Nationality*, chapters 4 through 6, especially pp. 155–65, which concurs with the ordering defended in this section.
12. Fabry, *Recognizing States: International Society & the Establishment of New States Since 1776*, p. 163.
13. Fabry, *Recognizing States*, p. 204.
14. Fabry, *Recognizing States*, p. 204.
15. Fabry appears to hold that the former republics of the USSR (other than the Baltics) and the constituent ethnonations of former Yugoslavia (and Kosovo) fall into this category. See Fabry, *Recognizing States*, chapter 6.
16. It thus contrasts with the position defended by Allen Buchanan in *Justice, Legitimacy, and Self-Determination*.
17. It thus contrasts with the position defended by Christopher Heath Wellman in *A Theory of Secession: The Case for Political Self-Determination* (New York: Cambridge University Press, 2005). See especially chapter 7 and page 160.
18. Rawls, *A Theory of Justice*, p. 270.
19. This ranking accords with the emancipatory trajectory that Altman and Wellman suggest those fighting colonial domination typically follow. After fighting to end various series of discrete abuses and injustices, native peoples under colonial administration, previously unable to fathom self-rule, begin to fathom its possibility—suggesting that, however important eventual self-rule is for them, ending the abuses and injustices takes priority. See Andrew Altman and Christopher Heath Wellman, *A Liberal Theory of International Justice* (New York: Oxford University Press, 2009), pp. 12–13.
20. Rawls, *A Theory of Justice*, p. 270.
21. Buchanan suggests that the institutional structures already exist for monitoring compliance with human rights norms. See Buchanan, *Justice, Legitimacy, and Self-Determination*, p. 225.

22. See the Montevideo Convention on the Rights and Duties of States of 26 December 1933.

23. See Buchanan, *Justice, Legitimacy, and Self-Determination*, pp. 334–37, defending the view that secessionist entities must also make credible commitments to protect human rights, and seeming to imply that they must also establish de facto statehood (that is, come to satisfy the international law definition).

24. See Fabry, *Recognizing States*, p. 164.

NINE

The Economic Development Principle

9.1 BEYOND THE CRITICAL MASS

In the fourth stage of our four-stage sequence, the parties to our international contract add one further principle to the critical mass and justifiable secession principles of international recognition: the economic development principle. The reason for including it is as follows. Despite the fact that satisfying the critical mass principle enables us to make moral progress toward the ideal, we may justifiably wonder whether that principle is too narrow—requiring us to recognize too *few* entities, so that we *merely* progress toward the ideal. Might not the parties to our international contract have a further interest in *accelerating* such progress beyond what they can achieve using solely the critical mass? If they were to recognize further entities, and recognizing them would accelerate progress toward the ideal, shouldn't they be added as recognized states? If so, is the contract able to account for that result? This chapter considers these questions.

Drawing on Rawls's observations about a just savings principle, I will argue that, while the parties do have an interest in accelerating progress toward the ideal, they nonetheless do not have an interest in accelerating it as rapidly as possible. As a consequence, they would adopt a principle that claims that further political entities (beyond those recognized in accordance with the first two principles) are to be recognized as states if and only if recognizing them *hastens* the economic advance of the least well-off entities so that they come closer to the point at which they would no longer seriously countenance tradeoffs between economic goods and liberal freedoms—but that does not require accelerating this advance as much as possible. As this formulation of the principle suggests, this principle, unlike the other two, does presuppose liberalism as the target at which we should aim (that is, the result of the first stage, which establishes what international justice consists in), since it builds into the statement of the principle itself the aspiration of protecting liberal freedoms without sacrificing them for economic goods.

9.2 ACCELERATING THE TRANSITION

In the last two chapters, we characterized the parties' interests in our contract by gradually adding to, and thickening, their details (as suited to the nature of their choice). In chapter 7, for instance, in deciding whether to accept or reject the regulative assumption of nonideal theorizing (the necessity of moral progress), the parties' interests were described thinly, relying solely on our ability to imagine what the circumstances would be like under each alternative they consider (§ 7.5). Next, in chapter 8, in deciding whether to adopt a general right of secession (and if so, with what conditions), the parties' interests were described more thickly, adding interests in having a conception of themselves as a peoples, and an interest in the good of their broader society as a composite whole (the remainder) (§ 8.2). These two choice situations corresponded to the second and third stages, respectively, of the four-stage sequence.

Now, in the fourth stage, we add further detail, making a reasonably weak, and intuitively plausible, stipulation: that both peoples and the broader society have an additional interest in having a higher (rather than lower) economic standard of living. Since the parties, as collective agents, act as trustees for both of these groups, they represent both of their interests simultaneously, which now includes this stipulated interest.

Given that the first stage establishes what international justice requires, we may assume that it establishes what international economic *distributive* justice requires—for each individual, each society, or each subgroup or peoples within society, as the case may be. Call these requirements, for each individual or group specified, that individual's or group's *first-stage entitlement*. At the later stages, when we operate under nonideal theory, a gap exists between the status quo and these first-stage entitlements. The selected principles attempt to close it. At the second stage, for instance, under the critical mass principle, we are able—by recognizing as states only those political entities belonging to the critical mass—to make some degree of moral progress from the status quo toward those first-stage entitlements.

At the fourth stage, the question is whether the parties, acting as trustees of both their peoples and their broader societies, would adopt a principle allowing recognition of further entities as states if doing so would enable them to make more *rapid* progress toward their first-stage entitlements (and if so, under what conditions). Would they adopt a principle, in other words, that permits them to recognize as states entities outside the critical mass (including ones that are not minimally just), entities that, by definition, are not needed in order to make some moral progress toward their first-stage entitlement? To answer that question, I will appeal to the stipulated interest in their having a higher (rather than lower) economic standard of living.

Since we are operating under nonideal theory, we may assume that tradeoffs between economic goods and political freedoms are permitted. This would be the case, for example, even if we were we to assume that justice as fairness defines international justice (within each domestic society, across societies, or both), since, under what Rawls calls the *general conception* of justice as fairness, tradeoffs between the two principles are permitted. Under the *special conception*, by contrast, conditions are favorable enough so that the general conception no longer applies, in which case the two principles are lexically ordered, forbidding sacrifices in liberal freedoms for economic goods. At that point, in fact, we are operating under ideal theory, for we have achieved the targeted state of affairs.[1]

Using a universal liberalism as the outcome of the first-stage (justice as fairness being one possible version of it), I will show that the parties, with the interest stipulated, would adopt a principle requiring them to recognize further entities beyond the critical mass if that will hasten the economic advance of the least well-off entities so that they come closer to the point where they would no longer seriously countenance tradeoffs between economic goods and liberal freedoms. Essentially, this principle challenges us to specify *how* much haste is required in transitioning from the general to the special conception, and to interpret the economic development principle of our theory of recognition accordingly. For that purpose, Rawls's discussion of a just savings principle offers valuable guidance.

9.3 THE JUST SAVINGS PRINCIPLE

When he introduces the just savings principle in *A Theory of Justice*, Rawls claims that "it is not possible . . . to define precise limits on what the rate of savings should be"—although we can give a rough formulation of them that derives from the contract.[2] Rather than imagining the parties in the original position as representatives of all actual generations, though, Rawls insists that they are contemporaries.[3] This creates a problem, which Rawls recognizes. Since "[e]ither earlier generations have saved or they have not . . . there is nothing the parties can do to affect it," and therefore "there is no reason for them to agree to undertake any saving whatever."[4] To avoid this difficulty, Rawls alters the motivational assumption of mutual disinterestedness for the special case of determining a just savings principle.[5] Instead, the parties "care at least for their immediate successors,"[6] which enables them to balance what "they would be willing to save for their immediate descendants against what they would feel entitled to claim of their immediate predecessors."[7] Accordingly, "the persons in the original position are to ask themselves how much they would be willing to save at each stage of [society's] advance on the assumption that all other generations are to save at the same rates."[8] However they answer that question for themselves provides the content to the just savings principle.

Later, Rawls revises his initial account of how the parties arrive at the just savings principle. Whereas his initial account relaxes the motivational assumption of mutual disinterestedness, his later account preserves that assumption but requires the parties "to agree to a savings principle subject to the condition that they must want all previous generations to have followed it" without knowing their place (as contemporaries) among generations.[9] This adjustment enables Rawls to preserve both the present-time-of-entry interpretation of the original position and the motivational assumption of mutual disinterestedness, since he no longer assumes that the parties care for their descendants (enabling the contract to rest on weaker motivational assumptions).

Whichever way he defends it, Rawls's characterizations of it imply that it is a principle of *transitional* justice—which makes it, according to our previous analysis, a principle belonging to *nonideal* theory (§ 7.1). For example, in *A Theory of Justice*, he says that "[e]ventually once just institutions are firmly established, the net accumulation required [by the savings principle] falls to zero. At this point a society meets its duty of justice by maintaining just institutions and preserving their material base."[10] This statement makes it sound as though the principle's aim is transitional toward the ideal state of affairs where just institutions are established. Reinforcing this impression, he later claims that, "characteristic of the contract doctrine [is defining] a just state of society at which the entire course of accumulation aims"—a course that the just savings principle guides as it approaches that ideal.[11] Since reaching this ideal involves sharing the burdens and benefits of savings, the just savings principle strives to distribute them fairly across generations: "The just savings principle can be regarded as an understanding between generations to carry their fair share of the burden of realizing and preserving a just society."[12] Applied to generations, it is a principle of justice or fairness in transition to this fully just or ideal state of affairs. In the meantime, while society falls short of this fully just state of affairs, "the general conception of justice is likely to apply rather than the two principles in serial order."[13]

Despite the fact, then, that Rawls never officially labels the just savings principle in *A Theory of Justice* as a principle belonging to nonideal theory, his statements there commit him to this position. Lest there remain any doubt, however, Rawls's discussion of the principle in *The Law of Peoples* should remove it, for there he assimilates the principle to the duty of assistance—which for Rawls falls under nonideal theory—that well-ordered peoples have toward economically burdened societies.[14] Contending that "the aim [of the duty of assistance] is to realize and preserve just (or decent) institutions," he denies that it requires us "to increase, much less to maximize indefinitely, the average level of wealth, or the wealth of any society or any particular class in society."[15] So in this respect, he concludes, "the duty of assistance and the duty of just savings express the same underlying idea."[16] Like the duty of assistance, that is, the just savings principle has "a defined goal, aim, or cut-off point"—the realization of a just (ideal) state of affairs—and its purpose is to guide us in transitioning toward it.[17] Like the duty of assistance, then, the just savings principle is a requirement of transitional justice, and thus belongs to nonideal theory.[18]

Since the just savings principle belongs to nonideal theory, it is quite different from the difference principle, which forms part of the ideal of justice as fairness. In fact, it would make no sense to use the difference principle to determine what justice between generations requires in the context of savings. Presumably, the worst-off generation is the first one (or at least the earlier ones). Attempting to maximin with respect to them would require retroactive transfers from later to earlier generations—an impossibility. So whatever content the parties give to the just savings principle, it would not be identical to the difference principle.[19]

What content would they give to it then? While we cannot say with much precision, the following seem like plausible constraints. First, they would not choose to save nothing. Even though they cannot benefit from their own savings (which is meant for later generations), they can still benefit from previous generations' savings. From behind the veil of ignorance, therefore, they would be deciding between a risky course of action—saving nothing, which, if no generation before them saved anything, would guarantee that they would be no better off than the worst-off generation, which could be objectively very poorly off—and one that offers them at least the chance to improve their lot over that of the worst-off generation (despite the burden that it imposes on them to save for future generations). Second, they would not choose to save maximally (consistent with subsistence) either, for that would guarantee that every generation in the transition to just institutions would merely subsist—hardly a fair way of distributing the burdens of transition (as even subsequent generations, enjoying its fruits, would acknowledge). So rather than saving nothing at all or everything they have (except for what they need to subsist), they would choose to save something.

Can we be more precise, though? First, they must save at least enough to make some progress toward the ideal, where just institutions are established. Otherwise, assuming that no generations before them made any progress toward that ideal either, they would remain no better off than the worst-off generation, which could be objectively very poorly off—a course ruled out by our previous reasoning. Second, it would be rational for them to elect to save *more* than the minimum amount needed to make some progress toward the ideal, provided that their doing so would make the subsequent generation's economic standard of living, after subtracting its higher savings contribution, better than it would have been, after subtracting its lower savings contribution, had all previous generations saved only the minimum. Presumably, with the extensive general knowledge that they possess behind the veil, they can calculate whether that condition is met. If the condition is met, then they must save more than the minimum needed to make some progress toward the ideal (in an effort to hasten its attainment). If the condition is unmet, then, by saving the minimum—and continuing to make some progress—they are hastening things as best they can under the circumstances. Third, they must assess whether that condition is met, not from the standpoint of the statistically average person in each generation, but from the standpoint of the least advantaged person in each generation. As Rawls puts it, the just savings principle "is defined from the standpoint of the least advantaged in each generation" and thus "[s]aving is [to be] achieved by accepting as a political judgment those policies designed to improve the standard of life of later generations of the least advantaged."[20]

Given that circumstances can vary greatly, though, we need a more nuanced, qualified principle that is sensitive to the different burdens involved at each stage of society's advance—and in fact, despite his claim that we should not expect anything too precise, Rawls himself suggests the contours of just such a principle:

> The parties do not know to which generation they belong or, what comes to the same thing, the stage of civilization of their society. They have no way of telling whether it is poor or relatively wealthy, largely agricultural or already industrialized, and so on. The veil of ignorance is complete in these respects. . . . [T]hey are to consider their willingness to save at any given phase of civilization with the understanding that the rates they propose are to regulate the whole span of accumulation. In effect, then, they must choose a just savings principle that assigns an appropriate rate of accumulation to each level of advance. *Presumably this rate changes depending upon the state of society.* When people are poor and saving is difficult, a lower rate of saving should be required; whereas in a wealthier society greater savings may reasonably be expected since the real burden is less.[21]

As a principle belonging to nonideal theory, then, the just savings principles possesses two features relevant for our purposes. First, as Rawls suggests, the just savings principle does not require saving everything one has (consistent with subsistence), as if the goal is to reach conditions favorable to realizing the special conception as soon as possible, even if that means that we must require much greater sacrifices from some generations so that later generations may enjoy the benefits of maximal progress. Just as the just savings principle does not require continuous maximizing of average wealth, neither does it require us to maximize the rate of speed at which we approach the ideal. Second, as Rawls likewise suggests, the just savings principle does not require each generation to save merely the minimum necessary to make some progress toward the ideal either, since later generations may legitimately complain that this unfairly places them further from the ideal than they should have been had previous generations saved adequately. While nothing more precise than this can be reasonably expected in formulating the principle's specific requirements, these two features, in combination, indicate a happy medium that any specific formulation of that principle must satisfy. Although each generation is not required to save maximally, neither is each generation permitted to save minimally, for just as we are not required to reach the ideal as quickly as we possibly could, neither are we permitted to approach it as slowly as we possibly could, consistent with continuing in its direction. As we will see, these findings offer valuable guidance for defending the economic development principle.

9.4 ECONOMIC GOODS AND LIBERAL FREEDOMS

As in the second and third stages of the four-stage sequence, the fourth stage finds the parties symmetrically situated, deprived of knowledge by the veil of ignorance, and bound by the results of the previous stages. As in the third stage, they are motivated by interests to advance their peoples' determinate conceptions of themselves as peoples, as well as to maintain the shared identity of their society as a good in itself. As in all the prior stages, they represent their societies without knowing whether, and to what extent, they possess minority nations or peoples—and represent the interests of both. This time, however, they also have an additional interest in having a higher (rather than lower) economic standard of living, an interest possessed by their societies as a whole, as well as by the peoples that their societies contain (should they contain more than one). Acting as collective agents who are trustees of both sets of interests, which now includes the interest in having a higher economic standard of living, the question is, would they adopt a principle requiring the recognition of additional political entities as states—a principle supplementing the critical mass and justifiable secession principles—and if so, under what conditions? As I will argue, if they would adopt a just savings principle, they would also adopt the economic development principle.

Although the argument relies on the hypothetical choice of collective agents, its structure is essentially the same as the one that uses individuals. In the domestic contract, the parties, who represent individuals, have an interest in forming, revising, and rationally pursuing a conception of the good. In order to advance it, they distribute wealth and income (among other primary goods). Similarly, in confronting the question of how much to save for future generations, they must decide how much of these same primary goods to save and invest in order to bring their future society's level of economic advance closer to the ideal, where they would no longer seriously countenance tradeoffs between economic goods and liberal freedoms. As we have seen, they are deciding upon a principle of transitional justice (§ 9.3) by appealing to this interest and the primary goods needed to advance it.

Just like the parties in the domestic contract, though, the parties in the international contract, who are collective agents, have an interest that requires the primary goods of wealth and income to advance—except that in this case the interest is one in having a higher economic standard of living. Facing a question similar to their domestic counterparts, they too must decide how much of these primary goods to save and invest in order to bring their societies and nations closer to the (liberal) ideal, where they would no longer seriously countenance tradeoffs between economic goods and liberal freedoms. They too, in other words, are deciding upon a principle of transitional justice by appealing to the stipulated interest and the primary goods of wealth and income needed to advance it. Therefore, just as the individuals in Rawls's domestic contract would adopt a just savings principle as a principle of transitional justice, so too would the collective agents in this international contract. The structure of the argument is essentially the same, with the substitution of collective agents for individuals apparently making no difference to its outcome.

Like the parties in the domestic contract, the collective agents in this international contract also have good reason to use maximin, and therefore, they have good reason to take the standpoint of the least advantaged society or nation when considering the amount of savings required by them. Like the second and third stages of the international contract, the fourth stage offers them no objective basis, from behind the veil of ignorance, to assign probabilities to various outcomes: they can turn out to be any society or nation in any generation, and they lack information from behind the veil that would enable them to estimate their chances of being which one in which generation. Similarly, the worst outcomes (such as below-subsistence living standards) are ones they can hardly accept (or endure). These reasons are sufficient for making the use of maximin rational under the circumstances (§ 7.6). Nonetheless, maximin does not require the difference principle, for, first, maximin is a decision rule (for choice under uncertainty), whereas the difference principle is merely a possible object of choice under that rule, and second (and more importantly), the difference principle makes no sense in deciding what justice in savings requires among different generations (§ 9.3). Instead of the difference principle, what maximin requires is simply assessing the situation from the standpoint of the least advantaged, which in this case would mean the least advantaged society or nation.

Combining these results, we get the claim that, in transitioning to the ideal, the collective agents in the international contract would adopt a principle of justice in savings that requires societies and nations in each generation to save and invest enough to improve the standard of living of those societies and nations who are the least advantaged in subsequent generations. However, this saving and investment does not go on without end. It has, as Rawls puts it, a goal or cutoff point, which in this case occurs once we reach the ideal where the least advantaged societies and nations no longer seriously countenance tradeoffs between economic goods and liberal freedoms. The principle, therefore, is transitional to this ideal: it is a principle of nonideal theory.

How much should they save? Again, the structure of the argument is essentially the same as it is with the parties to the domestic contract. Considering matters from the standpoint of the least advantaged society or nation, our collective agents would reason that it is neither rational to save nothing nor rational to save everything short of bare subsistence. Instead, they would elect to save at least the minimum needed to continue making progress toward the ideal, and more than that should their investment make it the case that the economic standard of living, for the subsequent generation's least advantaged society or nation, after subtracting its higher savings contribution, is higher than it would have been, after subtracting its lower savings contribution, had all previous generations saved only the minimum. Meeting this latter condition *hastens* progress toward the ideal. Subject to Rawls's proviso that this amount might vary depending on the burdens borne at each stage of a society's (or nation's) advance, this is as about as precise a formulation of the principle as we may reasonably expect.

Savings and investments, however, are just two relevant vehicles for maintaining and hastening progress toward the ideal. More generally, Rawls speaks of *policies*. If "[s]avings is [to be] achieved by accepting as a political judgment those policies designed to improve the standard of life of later generations of the least advantaged," then, it is fair to ask, what kinds of policies?[22] Rawls mentions "net investment in machinery" as well as "investment in learning and education."[23] He regards "knowledge and culture" too as types of "capital" that societies can accumulate and increase over time through savings and investment.[24] These kinds of examples suggest that there might be other types of policies as well that are justified, derivatively, from the just savings principle.

One broad type of policy, then, that might be justified, derivatively, from the just savings principle is that aspect of a society's *foreign* policy that concerns us: its policy on recognizing states. In fact, we might regard its policy on recognizing states as justified through an intermediate principle that is itself based on the just savings principle. This intermediate principle is the economic development principle.

As we saw earlier, the just savings principle neither requires us to reach the ideal as quickly as we possibly could (by saving maximally) nor permits us to approach it as slowly as we possibly could, consistent with continuing in its direction (by saving minimally). Instead, it requires us to *hasten* attainment of the ideal by saving (and investing) at some intermediate level (§ 9.3). A society's recognition policy should follow these same findings. Just as we are neither required to reach the ideal as quickly as we possibly could, nor as slowly as we possibly could, through our savings policies, neither are we required to reach that ideal as quickly as we could, or as slowly as we could, through our recognition policies. Nonetheless, just as our savings policies require us to hasten progress toward the ideal, so too should our recognition policies. Assuming that the ideal established at the first-stage is broadly liberal, the economic development principle follows. Further political entities (beyond those recognized under the first two principles) are to be recognized as states if and only if recognizing them *hastens* the economic advance of the least well-off entities so that they come closer to the point at which they would no longer seriously countenance tradeoffs between economic goods and liberal freedoms. The least well-off entities, here, may either be societies as a whole, or peoples or nations within a multinational society.

Implementing this principle involves instrumental judgments. Which additional entities, if made members of the international community of states, would make the International Monetary Fund, the World Trade Organization, or the World Bank—to take a few international institutions—better able to hasten the economic advance of the least well-off entities, if, as recognized states, they were eligible to contribute to, or receive from, these institutions? Consider the International Monetary Fund, for instance. Striving to reduce poverty while promoting employment and growth, the IMF charges subscriptions to each of its members based on their size in the world economy, and permits them access to certain levels of financing in times of need. In addition, the IMF has established a Poverty Reduction and Growth Trust. Under the economic development principle, if recognizing an entity as a state would enable the IMF or this Trust to reduce poverty, promote employment, or facilitate growth, hastening the economic advance of the least well-off entities so that they come closer to the point at which they would no longer seriously countenance tradeoffs between economic goods and liberal freedoms, then it should be recognized even if it would be unrecognized under the critical mass principle.

Similar instrumental calculations would inform decisions involving the World Trade Organization. In addition to its role in establishing rules to facilitate international trade, the WTO expedites market access commitments on goods exported by the least-developed countries and provides them with technical assistance. If recognizing an entity as a state would enable the WTO to perform this function better, either because the recognized state possesses the needed technical expertise or because it then is eligible to receive it, it should be recognized under the economic development principle even if it would be unrecognized under the critical mass principle, as long as its recognition hastens the economic advance of the least well-off entities in the manner described.

Whatever the importance of those calculations, the most significant decisions would likely involve the World Bank and its fund for the poorest, the International Development Association. Whether by issuing cash transfers to lift Kenyan children out of poverty, providing health services in Nepal to reduce maternal mortality, maintaining water and infrastructure in Pakistan, expanding access to education for girls in Afghanistan, or offering technical and financial assistance to Benin for developing a social safety net so that families do not have to sell assets or pull children from school in order for them to work, the IDA provides loans and grants for capital programs in developing countries in an effort to boost economic growth, improve living conditions, and meet the UN Millennium Development Goals of slashing poverty, hunger, and disease. As a UN international financial institution, it operates on pledges received from member countries. As in the previous two cases, if recognizing an entity as a state would enable this institution to better fulfill its mission—say, by providing it with greater resources through pledges, with the result that it hastens the economic advance of the least well-off entities in the manner described—then it should be recognized under the economic development principle even if, under the critical mass principle, it would be unrecognized.

By adding the economic development principle to the pragmatic theory of recognition, we expand the theory's reach well beyond the critical mass principle, which requires us to recognize as states only those entities whose recognition is strictly necessary for making some moral progress. Although I have argued previously that the critical mass principle is more expansive than it might at first seem (§ 7.7), it may nonetheless strike people intuitively as being too narrow. Adding the economic development principle is motivated, in part, to fill that intuitive gap. Yet if the argument for it is sound, it also enjoys independent support.

When combined with the critical mass and justifiable secession principles, the economic development principle completes our presentation of the pragmatic theory of international recognition. The hope is that we now have before us a significant result that enables us to address foundational questions in international relations: namely, who should count as a member of the international community, and why? While it may not enable us to address all questions about recognition—such as which *governments* to recognize[25]—if its insights are promising in the area of state recognition, perhaps they can be extended to government recognition and other matters concerning international recognition as well.

Its central insight, of course, is that the basis for recognizing political entities as states comes from a *social contract*. No longer idle, the social contract provides a basis for defending principles that guide us in transitioning toward an ideally just world.[26] As the next chapter shows, these nonideal principles of transitional justice also enable us to evaluate, appraise, and possibly reform our current practice of international recognition.

NOTES

1. For the distinction between the general and special conceptions of justice as fairness, see Rawls, *A Theory of Justice*, §§ 11, 26, 39, and 82.
2. Rawls, *A Theory of Justice*, p. 286.
3. Rawls does this in order to maintain the present-time-of-entry interpretation of the contract doctrine throughout. See Rawls, *A Theory of Justice*, § 24.
4. Rawls, *A Theory of Justice*, p. 292.
5. Rawls, *A Theory of Justice*, p. 140.
6. Rawls, *A Theory of Justice*, p. 292.
7. Rawls, *A Theory of Justice*, p. 289.
8. Rawls, *A Theory of Justice*, p. 287.
9. John Rawls, *Justice as Fairness: A Restatement*, p. 160.
10. Rawls, *A Theory of Justice*, p. 287.
11. Rawls, *A Theory of Justice*, p. 288.
12. Rawls, *A Theory of Justice*, p. 289.
13. Rawls, *A Theory of Justice*, p. 293.
14. See Rawls, *The Law of Peoples*, "Burdened Societies," § 15, which falls under part III, "Nonideal Theory."
15. Rawls, *The Law of Peoples*, p. 107.
16. Rawls, *The Law of Peoples*, p. 107.
17. Rawls, *The Law of Peoples*, p. 106.
18. The duty of assistance "is a principle of *transition*, in much the same way that the principle of real saving over time in domestic society is a principle of transition." Rawls, *The Law of Peoples*, p. 118. Emphasis in original.
19. Rawls recognizes this fact at *A Theory of Justice*, p. 291.
20. Rawls, *A Theory of Justice*, pp. 292–93.
21. Emphasis added. Rawls, *A Theory of Justice*, p. 287.
22. Rawls, *A Theory of Justice*, pp. 292–93.
23. Rawls, *A Theory of Justice*, p. 285.
24. Rawls, *A Theory of Justice*, pp. 288.
25. The one exception is the *negative* result defended in chapter 6 that we should reject the justice-based theory of government recognition.
26. "If processes are so great," writes Robert Nozick, referring to the hypothetical contract procedure that Rawls uses to establish (through an exercise of pure procedural justice) his principles of justice, "Rawls' theory is defective because it is incapable of yielding process principles of justice"—such as Nozick's entitlement principles. "If processes are good enough to found a theory upon, they are good enough to be the possible result of the theory." Robert Nozick, *Anarchy, State, and Utopia* (New York: Basic Books, 1974), pp. 208–9. However, if the argument of this book is sound, then we have answered Nozick's charge. In chapters 7 through 9, the hypothetical contract

argument there shows that, at least when it comes to recognition, principles of transitional justice—those governing the process of transition to the ideal of international justice—are a possible outcome, because they are the actual outcome.

TEN

An Appraisal of International Law

10.1 THREE PRINCIPLES

Ian Brownlie once asserted that there is "room for a whole treatise on the harm caused to the business of legal investigation by theory."[1] With international recognition, moreover, he continued, "theory has not only failed to enhance the subject but has created a *tertium quid* which stands, like a bank of fog on a still day, between the observer and the contours of the ground which calls for investigation."[2] In this chapter, I take up Brownlie's implicit challenge, for if the argument of the preceding four chapters is sound, we get a contractarian defense of a theory of international recognition, a result that will interest philosophers, legal academics, and international relations scholars alike. This is a *normative* theory: its standards and principles are to be used for evaluating, appraising, and possibly reforming the criteria that states and other international bodies use in deciding which entities to count as member states of the international community. In this chapter, I want to explain the relation of this theory to the existing criteria for state recognition, as well as to other kinds of theories that concern state recognition.

Consisting of three principles, the pragmatic theory of international recognition holds:

> The *critical mass* principle: A political entity ought to be recognized as a state if and only if it belongs to the critical mass of entities which, working together, is necessary for making at least some moral progress toward the ideal (chapter 7).

This critical mass establishes an *initial array* of recognized states, which may differ from the actual array of internationally recognized states at any point in time. Possibly, it includes members currently excluded, or excludes members currently included. The pragmatic theory does not guarantee that all and only currently recognized states should continue to be recognized. Very likely, it implies that there should be some changes. This is the sense in which it is normative and reformist. Further, as we saw earlier, the notion of a critical mass should be understood capaciously, as requiring, not just one critical mass for the entire globe, but a series of critical masses for the various regions of the globe. For this reason, it is neither a necessary nor likely consequence of the pragmatic view that it justifies recognizing only a single superpower or a group of great powers. More likely, it requires inclusive subgroups of states working together regionally to advance liberalization in their region—efforts that overlap with those of others outside the region, efforts that improve the condition of the world as a whole.

Once we establish the initial array, the second and third principles allow for adjustments to it, leading to an *adjusted array*. According to the second principle:

> The *justifiable secession* principle: A political entity has the right to secede from its parent state and to receive international recognition as an independent state if and only if it meets two conditions (chapter 8):
>
> > *The consent, plebiscite, or remediation condition*: it receives the consent of its parent state; or it receives the consent of its parent state conditioned on the successful outcomes of plebiscites in both the secessionist territory and the territory that would remain in the parent state (which are both approved); or its inhabitants are victims of persistent, grave human rights abuses committed by the security forces of the parent state and seek recognition as an independent state as a partial remedy; and
> >
> > *The moral progress condition*: its recognition is consistent with continuing to make moral progress toward the ideal.

This principle permits adjustments to the initial array by allowing additions to it. Like the first principle, the second is normative and reformist. In particular, it rejects the status quo under international law, which appears to deny a right of secession as a remedial right (§ 10.3). The adjusted array under the second principle may then be adjusted further by the third principle, which holds:

> The *economic development* principle: Further political entities (beyond those recognized in accordance with the first two principles) ought to be recognized as states if and only if recognizing them hastens the economic advance of the least well-off entities so that they come closer to the point at which they would no longer seriously countenance tradeoffs between economic goods and liberal freedoms (chapter 9).

For reasons of logical parsimony, we may collapse these three principles into a single statement of the pragmatic theory of international recognition as follows:

A political entity ought to be recognized as a state if and only if:

1. it belongs to the critical mass of entities which, working together, is necessary for making at least some moral progress toward the ideal, in which all states meet liberal principles of justice; or
2. it seeks independence from its parent state, meets the consent, plebiscite, or remediation conditions, and its recognition is consistent with continuing to make moral progress toward the ideal; or
3. recognizing it hastens the economic advance of the least well-off entities so that they come closer to the point at which they would no longer seriously countenance tradeoffs between economic goods and liberal freedoms.

I now want to explore the relation between this theory and other kinds of theories of state recognition.

10.2 NONNORMATIVE THEORIES OF STATE RECOGNITION

As a normative theory, the pragmatic theory of international recognition is officially neutral in the longstanding debate between the declarative and constitutive theories of state recognition. According to the declarative theory, a political entity is a member state of the international community if and only if it satisfies the international law definition of statehood, which is typically taken to involve possession of a permanent population, a defined territory, a government, and the capacity to enter into relations with other states.[3] By contrast, according to the constitutive theory, a political entity is a member state of the international community if and only if it receives official recognition from sufficiently many (already acknowledged) member states. The declarative and constitutive theories compete with one another in attempting to explain or account for the members of the set of member states. Since their claims are explanatory, not normative, the pragmatic theory of recognition technically does not contradict them.

Typically, the two theories generate the same results, but they need not, as when a political entity satisfies the international law definition of statehood but does not receive general recognition from other member states, or when one does receive such recognition despite failing to satisfy that definition. Logically, the declarative theory is consistent with the assertion that a political entity is a member state of the international community despite failing to be recognized as such by each and every recognized member state—an implausible implication, according to the theory's critics. It is also consistent with the denial that a political entity is a member state despite being recognized as such by each and every recognized member state, which its critics likewise consider implausible. But then, similarly, the constitutive theory is logically consistent with the assertion that a political entity is a member state of the international community despite failing to possess the features definitive of statehood under international law, an implication that that theory's critics consider implausible. It is also consistent with the denial that a political entity is a member state despite possessing such features, which, again, its critics consider implausible.

In combination, these implications seem to suggest that something more fundamental is at stake in adjudicating this dispute, which it is not my intent to enter.[4] However, as I will suggest in the next section, each of these theories attempts to capture important elements in the history of recognition practice and the criteria for state recognition that have been used. Whereas the declarative theory attempts to capture the historically dominant criteria, the constitutive theory attempts to capture the undeniable fact that there have been many deviations from them. For present purposes, I want to stress two points. First, the main difference between the two theories is that, whereas the constitutive theory makes recognition depend on criteria employed by the entity *conferring* recognition, the declarative theory makes recognition depend on criteria met by the entity upon which recognition is *conferred*. Second, in each case, these criteria can be *evaluated* normatively. The role of a theory of international recognition is to provide the principles for such an evaluation.

What a theory of international recognition evaluates normatively, then, is not the rival explanatory theories themselves, but the criteria they presuppose as the explanatory basis for recognition decisions. However true the declarative theory, for example, as an explanation of recognition practice, we can still evaluate whether recognition should be conferred (prospectively and retrospectively) on all and only entities that satisfy the international law definition of statehood. Since this view contradicts the pragmatic theory's second principle (justifiable secession), which allows the recognition of entities that do not satisfy that definition, as well as the first (critical mass) and third (economic development), which allow the nonrecognition (or derecognition) of some that do, the theory implies that we ought to reject that view. Similarly, however true the constitutive theory as an explanation of recognition practice, we can still evaluate whether recognition should be conferred (prospectively and retrospectively) on all and only entities that generally receive it. Since this view contradicts the pragmatic theory by permitting recognition decisions that violate its principles, the pragmatic theory implies that we ought to reject that view, too. In essence, this view automatically approves the criteria used by (already acknowledged) member states in conferring recognition, whatever their content, which of course runs counter to the normative and reformist role of the pragmatic theory.

Just as the pragmatic theory of international recognition is officially neutral in the debate between the declarative and constitutive theories, so too is it neutral in the debate between those who claim that recognition is obligatory and those who claim instead that it is discretionary (a merely "political" act or decision). These claims are to be understood as legal, not normative, propositions.[5] Since these claims are legal, not normative, the pragmatic theory of recognition technically does not contradict them. However, just as the pragmatic theory can evaluate the criteria presupposed as the *explanatory* basis for recognition decisions, so too can it evaluate the criteria that these rival views presuppose as the *legal* basis for such decisions. Even if it is true, for example, that, as a matter of international law, recognition decisions are discretionary, we can still evaluate whether this should be the case. Since we can always evaluate how discretion is exercised, the pragmatic theory implies that we ought to reject this view, for otherwise we would be approving, no matter what their content, the criteria used by each and every entity on each and every occasion that it exercises its discretion (criteria that may vary by agent and occasion). Given that the pragmatic theory implies that recognition decisions should not be discretionary, it follows, according to that view, that they should be obligatory. This raises the crucial question, though, which is, what should the obligatory criteria be? I'll say more on this in a moment.

Finally, we should note that the pragmatic theory is a normative theory of state recognition, not a normative theory of *government* recognition (much less an explanatory or legal one). It makes no claims about how we should handle rival claims to government authority, as occur, for example, with military coups and the formation of governments in exile. While these are extremely important issues, the pragmatic theory is officially silent with respect to them. Nonetheless, if our contractarian defense of the theory is successful, a logical next step would be to see if we can extend that defense to generate normative principles for government recognition.[6]

10.3 HISTORICAL VIEWS

Even after we establish a theory of international recognition, we face a critical question: what should the (obligatory, legal) criteria for recognition be? The role of the theory then becomes justificatory. Its principles supply the grounds for justifying the specific criteria to be used in granting or denying recognition. By itself, though, the theory does not *entail* these criteria. It does not entail, for instance, that these criteria must be identical with its principles—as if one simply "reads off" the criteria from them. We must also consider the incentive and publicity effects of institutionalizing them (§ 8.5). Therefore, showing which criteria these are requires expert knowledge outside philosophy—in fields like law, political science, and international relations. By combining such knowledge with our principles, we hope to identify the best justified criteria.

To give an idea of the criteria that statesmen and diplomats have found plausible, I give a brief survey in this section of the criteria (or standards) used historically to grant or withhold recognition.[7] This will give us a pool of candidates to consider (at least provisionally). As I hope to show, our existing criteria for state recognition are normatively defective, especially when seen in historical perspective. Then, in the following section, I indicate ways in which our theory of international recognition might enable us to improve this state of affairs.

10.3.A Resisting the Challenge: The Triumph of Parent State Consent in the Aftermath of the American and French Revolutions

While any starting point will be somewhat arbitrary, the American and French revolutions provide useful ones insofar as they posed the first significant challenges to the prevailing criteria or standards of the time.[8] While there was some variation in constitutional arrangement, the dominant mode of social organization for some time had been the hereditary monarchy.[9] Kings possessed their titles to the throne by a grant from God that was transmitted from generation to generation, and only their free consent could transfer sovereignty or territory.[10] Recognition required the consent of the parent country.

The American Declaration of Independence and Revolutionary War challenged this orthodoxy.[11] In the domestic realm, governments were claimed to derive their just powers not from God but from the consent of the governed. Internationally, American emissaries sought recognition from numerous countries. But only France and Holland extended it prior to Britain recognizing the sovereignty and independence of its former colonies.[12] The other major powers insisted upon—and waited for—Britain's consent.

Although the orthodoxy withstood the challenge, some cracks began to emerge. The condition that recognition required consent from the parent country was reaffirmed. However, a competing standard gained traction. While French motivations for recognizing the United States were complex, one of the justifications it cited was that the colonies had effectively established their existence as an independent state.[13] This standard of effectiveness, or de facto statehood, in their view placed an outer limit on their obligation to respect the rights of the British crown. Holland's motivations were even more complicated, combining elements of sympathy for the American cause with self-interest and the expectation that the British would soon recognize the colonies anyway, but the British surrender at Yorktown was undoubtedly a factor. Effective statehood gained traction as a competing standard of recognition.

Just as the American Revolution challenged the orthodoxy requiring consent from the parent country, so too did the French Revolution; and just as the American Revolution initially failed to undermine it, so too did the French Revolution. Like the American Revolution, the French Revolution sought to promote the notions of popular sovereignty and self-determination. But whereas the Americans did not seek to promote them abroad following their revolution, the French did following theirs.[14] Having abolished the monarchy in 1792, the French, under Napoleon Bonaparte, championed the causes of peoples it perceived as being oppressed by theirs—in some cases annexing their territories, in other cases creating new states from the territories of its defeated enemies, Austria, Prussia, and Russia. But with France's defeat in 1814, and the Congress of Vienna the ensuing year, nearly all of the states that were recognized in 1792 were recognized once again, while those states that had been created by France had their recognition annulled. In essence, the anti-French coalition had reaffirmed the condition that recognition requires consent from the parent country by collectively derecognizing those entities created through what it perceived as violations of it.

10.3.B Gaining Strength: The Ascendancy of Effective Statehood Over Parent State Consent in the Aftermath of the Spanish American Revolutions

Whereas the American and French Revolutions saw a reaffirmation of the condition that recognition requires consent from the parent state, the Spanish American revolutions witnessed its denial. If an entity had achieved effective statehood but had not yet received the consent of the parent state—in this case, Spain—it was still recognized as a state by nearly all members of the international community. Effective statehood trumped parent state consent.

The revolt of Spain's American colonies and their declarations of independence began just as Napoleon's army was to incur its final defeat.[15] Within a few years, Spain had suffered significant losses and by 1821 its defeat looked certain. The United States recognized Chile, Colombia, Mexico, and Argentina (Buenos Aires) in 1822.[16] In 1823, Monroe issued his famous Monroe Doctrine, warning the world (and Spain in particular) that any aggression against "the governments who have declared their independence, and maintained it, and whose independence we have, on great consideration, and on just principles, acknowledged" would be looked upon "as the manifestation of an unfriendly disposition towards the United States."[17] If other states followed suit and recognized the independence of these states in Spanish America, the implication seemed clear: following the precedent with France and the nonrecognition of its external conquests, Spain would thereafter be viewed as an external aggressor, whose victories and claims, if any occurred later, would not be honored. The next year, Britain recognized Colombia, Mexico, and Argentina.[18] Soon thereafter, these and the rest of Spain's former colonies were recognized by virtually all of the other major powers. Only during the next decade did Spain itself do so, and only Austria and Russia insisted upon waiting.[19]

Brazil, a Portuguese colony, followed a different trajectory. After its declaration of independence from Portugal in 1815, only the United States recognized it before Portugal itself in 1825, and then only because, in 1823, in the view of the Monroe administration, it had achieved effective statehood.[20] By contrast, the other major powers waited for Portugal's consent. Despite the ascendancy of effective statehood as a ground of recognition, the condition requiring parent state consent still carried some weight.

The main significance of Brazil's recognition, however, lies in two other features. With Brazil's situation, we find, for the first time, extra conditions attached to a state's recognition: normative conditions. Britain insisted that it end its role in the slave trade.[21] Thus, a new kind of standard—one that would later get reformulated, expanded, and embraced by other states—had emerged. We also find reliance on *uti possidetis juris,* which (in its modern incarnation) holds that, absent agreement among them, states inherit their borders as nonsovereign jurisdictions. For South America, what this meant in practice was that the borders of the various states that emerged from their secessionist conflicts with their colonial masters corresponded to administrative divisions established by those very same masters. Other states—and especially neighboring ones contemplating territorial expansion—were under obligations to respect the territorial integrity of the states so defined. Nonetheless, it permitted secession from the newly established parent states. Thus, Brazil was warned against annexing Uruguay, but Uruguay was permitted to secede from Argentina within the borders of its colonial subdivision.[22] Successful homegrown resistance would receive recognition; external conquest would not.

10.3.C Solidifying Control, Finding Limits: Effective Statehood as a Criterion and the Search for its Limits in Nineteenth-Century Europe

While the Congress of Vienna reaffirmed the condition that recognition requires consent from the parent state, the cracks in that consensus that had begun to emerge with the American revolution and that had grown with the Spanish American independence movements now began to expand in the very soil that maintained it. In Europe, we find further support not only for effective statehood as a ground of obligation but also for its prevailing over parent state consent when the two conflict. We also find signs of some misgivings with it.

Between the Congress of Vienna and World War I, Belgium, Greece, Romania, Serbia, and Montenegro all established their effective independence from their parent states—Belgium from Holland, the others from the Ottoman Empire. Belgium declared its independence in 1830 and achieved effective statehood within one month.[23] While formal recognition awaited the outcome of mediation efforts with Britain, France, Austria, Russia, and Prussia over its borders, it was clearly Belgium's effective statehood, not Holland's grudging assent to it, which grounded its 1839 recognition.[24] By contrast, Greece, after revolting in 1821 and declaring its independence from Ottoman rule in 1822, was initially rebuffed when it sought recognition.[25] Upon achieving effective statehood around 1830, however, resistance to its recognition dissipated, and it was generally recognized between 1833 and 1837, simultaneously with Ottoman acquiescence in mediation efforts by Britain, France, and Russia.[26] Finally, between 1875 and 1878, Romania, Serbia, and Montenegro all successfully established their independence from the weakening Ottoman Empire.[27] In this case, however, Ottoman recognition in 1878 preceded recognition by the other major powers at the Congress of Berlin later that year (and, in Romania's case, two years after that).[28] But the requirement of parent state consent apparently played no role in the decisions, as its staunchest defender, the Holy Alliance of Austria, Prussia, and Russia had crumbled two decades earlier, and the Ottoman sultans were no Christian kings.[29]

As we see here, parent state consent could occur simultaneously with and even prior to recognition without it grounding such recognition in the eyes of the states granting it. Both the United States and Serbia were recognized after their parent states had recognized them, yet only in the former case (save for France and Holland) did it ground it. In the latter case, its achievement of effective statehood was the main factor; mediation efforts over borders and other matters only delayed recognition until the parent state could consent to what was otherwise a fait accompli. But other factors were starting to play a role in such decisions, too, as some of the pitfalls of relying on effective statehood were beginning to show.

Effective statehood could be achieved through successful resistance to and secession from the ruler, as the American revolutions against Britain, Spain, and Portugal had shown. But it could also be achieved through annexation and conquest, as Napoleon had shown. The Congress of Vienna annulled the results of the latter, derecognizing the states that had been created. Despite this precedent, the results of Prussia's wars against Denmark, Austria, and France were left to stand—its annexation of various smaller German states producing a unified Germany, which became internationally recognized in 1871.[30] Italy's recognition is perhaps a less clear case, since the various provinces had voted to unify with Sardinia, which had removed its Austrian rulers in the Austro-Sardinian war of 1859.[31] But in the process Sardinia had acquired territory from Austria and had annexed two provinces, and the votes in Sicily and Naples followed an invasion by Garibaldi to liberate them.[32] Nevertheless, Italy became internationally recognized by 1866 even by the states that had protested the glaring inconsistency. While it would be too strong to conclude from this that a new international norm was beginning to emerge, it was clear that, by recognizing de facto states achieved through external conquest, members of the international community were weakening in their resolve to observe the understood limits of effective statehood as a ground of recognition.

If effective statehood found increasing support as a ground of recognition, there were also growing doubts about its sufficiency. Initially, such doubts were captured by the principle requiring parent state consent, but even as support for that principle waned, they were expressed by the restriction (however imperfectly observed) on effective statehood achieved through conquest. Later, they were captured by attaching extra conditions—normative conditions—to the achievement of de facto status, such as Britain's requirement that Brazil cease participating in the slave trade. Now, we find an expansion of such conditions. Recognition of Belgium was conditioned on its agreeing to continue to meet its treaty obligations.[33] Recognition of Greece, Romania, Serbia, and Montenegro were conditioned on their committing to protect religious liberty and equality.[34] Still, if effective statehood was not a sufficient condition for recognition, in the absence of parent state consent it was a necessary one.

10.3.D Adding Normative Conditions: The Paris Peace Conference and its Aftermath

After World War I, this understanding continued. Poland, Czechoslovakia, Yugoslavia, Finland, Lithuania, Latvia, Estonia, Armenia, and Georgia had all achieved effective statehood and were recognized either at the Paris Peace Conference of 1919 or within two years—frequently with extra conditions attached.[35] Having established the borders of Poland, Czechoslovakia, and Yugoslavia, the Paris Peace Conference nonetheless made their recognition conditional on adopting minority conventions to protect linguistic, racial, and religious minorities.[36] Finland was also recognized at the conference, and within two years, so too were Lithuania, Latvia, Estonia, Armenia, and Georgia—the latter two conditional on enacting measures to protect minorities.[37]

The Paris Peace Conference had also given birth to the League of Nations, whose article 10 prohibited wars of conquest as a means of creating newly recognized states.[38] When Japan seized Manchuria in 1931 and set up the puppet state of Manchukuo—trying to portray it as an indigenous uprising—the international community's resolve to observe article 10 was put to the test. Although the United States was not a member of the League of Nations, its secretary of state, Henry Stimson, in the famous Stimson Doctrine, reinforced support for article 10. As a result, the League of Nations bound its members not to recognize Manchukuo.

Just as the period following the Congress of Vienna had witnessed increasing support for effective statehood as a ground of recognition, so too did the period following the Paris Peace Conference; and just as the former supplemented it with normative conditions and a restriction on recognizing effective states created through conquest, so too did the latter. Yet inconsistencies in application remained. The minority conventions that Poland and other states were required to uphold had not been required when Italy—which also had many ethnic and linguistic minorities in its northern provinces—was recognized.[39] Though the international community had withstood the challenge posed by Manchukuo, its record was uneven. Prior to the Manchukuo episode, the Soviet Union had reconquered Armenia and Georgia, whose legal status as independent states then became extinguished.[40] The same fate befell Ukraine—although it had previously been recognized only by Russia, Germany, Austria-Hungary, and the Ottoman Empire.[41] While Azerbaijan, Kuban, and North Caucasus had not been recognized despite achieving effective statehood, the Soviets reconquered them as well.[42] Even if the latter two cases are discounted on grounds that the reconquered states had not been generally recognized, the precedent with German unification could not go unnoticed.

10.3.E Retreating from Effective Statehood: Postwar Decolonization

Whereas the periods following the Congress of Vienna and Paris Peace Conference had witnessed increasing support for effective statehood as a ground of recognition, the period following World War II saw its dilution. Effective statehood ceased to be regarded as a necessary condition for recognition in the absence of parent state consent.

The impetus for the change was decolonization. As late as the 1940s, two decades prior to the main wave of decolonization, effective statehood was still the dominant criterion. Starting with Iraq in 1932, and continuing with Syria, Lebanon, and Transjordan in the midforties, the main consideration was whether these territories—formally mandates under the League of Nations (Iraq) or non-self-governing or trust territories under the United Nations (Syria, Lebanon, Transjordan)—had become effectively independent as states upon the transfer of authority from the colonial powers.[43] In Iraq's case, moreover, there were extra conditions attached (protecting the rights of their minority Kurdish and Assyrian populations)—just as there had been previously with Brazil, Belgium, Greece, Romania, Serbia, Montenegro, Poland, Czechoslovakia, Yugoslavia, Armenia, and Georgia.[44] Israel, too, was recognized in 1948 or 1949, depending on when the recognizing states judged that it constituted a de facto state—whether, for instance, such status could obtain upon its declaration of independence, despite its being attacked by Arab armies immediately afterward, or whether instead it must await the war's outcome.[45]

As colonialism fell into deeper disrepute, though, this began to change. The pace of change accelerated with the 1960 passage of United Nations general assembly resolution 1514—the Declaration on the Granting of Independence to Colonial Countries and Peoples—which condemned colonialism and asserted that "inadequacy of political, economic, social or educational preparedness should never serve as a pretext for delaying independence."[46] For colonial territories, recognition of independent statehood would no longer require de facto status. Despite their ineffectiveness and their plunging immediately into civil war, the Democratic Republic of Congo (then the Republic of Congo) and Rwanda were recognized respectively in 1960 and 1962.[47] Recognition of other African states followed suit, and by the midseventies, even Angola, Mozambique, Guinea-Bissau, and Comoros were generally recognized despite the fact that the colonial powers (Portugal in the first three cases and France in the last) were loathe to withdraw.[48]

Just as effective statehood was no longer necessary for recognizing the independent statehood of former colonies, neither was it sufficient. Possessing effective control of its territory, Southern Rhodesia was condemned nonetheless by Security Council resolution 216 following its 1965 declaration of independence for excluding nonwhites from government, and member states were called upon not to recognize it.[49]

10.3.F Returning to the Scene: Parent State Consent after Decolonization

Besides condemning colonialism and urging its end, however, general assembly resolution 1514 also reaffirmed support for the territorial integrity of the former colonies. In keeping with *uti possidetis juris*, the former African, Asian, and Pacific colonies acceded to sovereign status within their prior juridical borders, just as the former South American colonies had over a century before. But whereas *uti possidetis juris* had protected the newly recognized South and Central American states only from subsequent attempts at external conquest, in Africa, Asia, and the Pacific it was interpreted so as to afford additional protection. Not only would these newly recognized states be protected from attempts at external conquest. They would also be protected against internal challenges as well. As a result, unilateral secession, even if successfully followed by de facto statehood, was no longer a legal means of gaining international recognition.[50]

On this basis, the Baluchis, Biafrans, Eritreans, Tigreans, Ewes, Gandans, Karens, Katchins, Kurds, Moros, Pathans, Sikhs, Tamils were denied recognized statehood even though they had declared their independence; Eritrea, Tamil Eelam, South Sudan, Bougainville, Somaliland were denied even though they had achieved de facto statehood.[51] While Eritrea did eventually receive recognition following a 1993 referendum permitted by Ethiopia, from which it seceded, it had already maintained effective control over its territory for thirty years. Sri Lanka, by contrast, reconquered Tamil Eelam in 2009. Only Bangladesh became internationally recognized in this period through unilateral secession, having achieved de facto statehood in 1971.[52]

If general assembly resolution 1514 outlawed recognized statehood gained through unilateral secession in former colonies, general assembly resolution 2625, enacted in 1970, broadened the prohibition to all United Nations members.[53] Not since the American and French revolutions would parent state consent be required.

Parent state consent clearly had conservative implications. Parent states could be oppressive. The possibility of achieving effective independence through successful revolution gave oppressed peoples a remedy for their condition. The possibility of gaining international recognition upon its success made the remedy legal. When parent state consent was not required, revolutionaries who defeated their oppressors were provided some incentive not to oppress in turn. By requiring parent state consent, this incentive was reduced. Preserving the territorial integrity of existing recognized states took precedence over remedial rights of secession.

This climate enabled Nigeria to maintain its territorial integrity despite its massacres in Biafra. Biafra's subsequent declaration of independence in 1967 was met with general nonrecognition.[54] Similarly, Iraq maintained its territorial integrity despite its brutal suppression of Kurdish resistance in 1991 and Kurdistan's long-known desire for independence; no Kurdish state was recognized.[55] Even Bangladesh's successful independence bid was grounded in its achievement of de facto status, not Pakistan's heavy-handedness.[56] There was no international legal remedial right to secede from a repressive state, and international law and practice reflected this in their recognition practice.[57]

We may pause now to take stock. By this time, international law and practice had come full circle. Parent state consent had been the dominant criterion of recognition at the time of the American and French Revolutions. Afterwards, during the Spanish American revolutions, it had been repudiated in favor of de facto standing. Later, this criterion was refined. De facto standing achieved through domestic revolution would be met with international recognition; de facto standing achieved through conquest or annexation would be denied it. Sometimes, extra conditions—normative conditions—would be attached to de facto standing. Additionally, the recognized territory of a de facto state would conform to *uti possidetis juris*. With decolonization, however, de facto standing itself was repudiated. Nationality gained favor as the dominant criterion. De facto standing was no longer necessary for recognition. As long as a group comprised a nationality—the criteria for which were notoriously difficult to operationalize—and aspired to independent statehood, it would receive international recognition even if that group had not achieved effective statehood. But it would only receive recognition if it emerged from a colony. National groups in preexisting (recognized) states were not eligible. Moreover, the recognized territory of these new, post-colonial, recognized states would conform to *uti possidetis juris* interpreted in novel fashion, so as to protect the emergent entities not only from external conquest but internal challenges as well. Accordingly, secessionist movements, including ones that had essentially established de facto states in portions of the former colonies, went unrecognized. The prohibition was later expanded to protect the territorial integrity of all recognized states. So de facto standing was no longer sufficient either. But then neither was being a national group with aspirations for independent statehood. Not only were national groups outside the context of decolonization shut out from recognition. So too were national groups in the former colonies once the transfer of authority had taken place. As the process of decolonization came to a close, parent state consent became at least the announced criterion of international recognition practice. Parent state consent was necessary and sufficient. Parent state consent would be required even when oppressed groups sought to secede, there being no international legal remedial right to secede. Condemned for its conservative, antirevolutionary, implications for centuries, parent state consent was now defended by former revolutionaries the world over as soon as they had consolidated their power.

If this is the culmination of more than two centuries of recognition practice, then it has reached a rather embarrassing conclusion. Worse still, members of the international community have been rather selective in applying it. Even in the most recent decades, parent state consent would account for perhaps three cases of recognition—Slovakia (1993), the Czech Republic (1993), and South Sudan (2011)—or six if one counts recognition of the Baltic states (Lithuania, Latvia, and Estonia) as retroactively reinstating the legal independence of states whose independence was extinguished in violation of such consent.[58] Despite appearances, not even the states recognized in the aftermath of the breakup of the Soviet Union (the states other than the Baltics) would qualify. While foreign states did not wait for the Soviet Union's consensual dissolution in order to recognize the Baltic states, it was only after this ostensibly occurred that they granted recognition to the remaining members of the republic.[59] In reality, the eleven republics met first, formed the Commonwealth of Independent States, declared the end of the Soviet Union—then presented the federal government with a fait accomplis.[60] As in so many places before, parent state consent there was largely a fiction.[61]

Nor did former Yugoslavia consent to the independence of its constituent republics—but then, according to a ruling by the Badinter Commission, an arbitration panel of jurists established by the European Community to issue nonbinding advisory opinions on the controversy, Yugoslavia had in fact dissolved—obviating the latter's need to consent to the breakup and implying that Slovenia, Croatia, Bosnia, and Macedonia were not unilaterally seceding, since there was no longer any entity from which to secede.[62] The basis for this ruling, apparently, was that late in 1991, the Yugoslav government began to exclude representatives of the four republics from voting on the state's affairs—ostensibly on grounds of national security—and instead relied solely on representatives from Serbia and Montenegro. Regarded by the panel and other states as a "non-functional government," this body, they claimed, ceased to exist, and the state along with it.[63]

However tempting it may have been to regard the rump Yugoslav government as "non-functional," though, facts on the ground indicated otherwise. While its zone of control may have diminished, the Yugoslav government was still firmly in control of Serbia and Montenegro, as well as parts of Croatia and Bosnia—hardly grounds for declaring that the Yugoslav state had "dissolved."[64] Rather than acknowledge that they were recognizing secessions without consent, members of the international community insisted that consent was unnecessary because Yugoslavia no longer existed.

This same sequence would repeat itself with Kosovo's attempt to secede from the "new" Yugoslavia created from the ashes of Serbia and Montenegro[65]—except that this time, without the fiction that Yugoslavia had dissolved to hide behind, members of the international community who recognized Kosovo as a state claimed that they were making an exception warranted by unique circumstances, which they insisted would establish no precedent—exactly the argument Russia would later make in recognizing South Ossetia's and Abkhazia's independence from Georgia.[66]

International law provides neither normatively defensible nor coherently applied criteria for international recognition.

10.4 THE RANGE OF VIEWS

As this survey reveals, historically, the criteria for recognizing states have varied. In fact, even within specified time periods we find different actors applying different criteria. Nonetheless, we can make certain generalizations. The criteria fall into two main categories: genetic criteria and moral quality criteria. These criteria may also be combined, forming a category of mixed criteria.

Genetic criteria make recognition depend on the genesis of the state, that is, how it came to be. For example, one view holds that a political entity ought to be recognized as a state if and only if it has received the consent of the parent state. Another holds that a political entity ought to be recognized as a state if and only if it has achieved effective (de facto) statehood. Some views add the qualification that its de facto status must not have been achieved through annexation or conquest (but permit recognition when de facto status is achieved through successful revolution). Another view asserts that a political entity ought to be recognized as a state if and only if the inhabitants of a geographically defined area constitute a nationality and aspire to independent statehood. Others assert that a political entity ought to be recognized as a state if and only if the inhabitants of a geographically defined area express, through a plebiscite, their desire for independent statehood. These last two views might add the stipulation that the geographically defined area must be consistent with *uti possidetis juris,* and thus take place within borders established previously.

Moral quality criteria make recognition depend on the moral quality of the state. The question then becomes how high to set the bar. One view claims that a political entity ought to be recognized as a state if and only if it agrees to honor the treaty obligations (or a portion thereof) of its predecessor. Another insists that (in addition) it avoid only the most egregious injustices, such as participation in the slave trade. Others require it to adopt minority conventions obligating it to protect the rights and liberties of linguistic, racial, and religious minorities. Still others raise the bar higher, requiring it to respect basic human rights.

Then there are *mixed* views that combine elements of genetic views and views that make recognition depend on the moral quality of the political entity seeking recognition. For example, a view which holds that a political entity ought to be recognized as a state if and only if (a) it received the free consent of its parent state, or (b) it achieved effective statehood through revolution but not conquest or annexation and (c) it protects minority rights, would qualify as such a view.

Naturally, these historical views do not exhaust the logical possibilities, as any of them may be reformulated so as to state a necessary condition only, or a sufficient condition only, and then be combined with one of the others so as to supply necessary and sufficient conditions. With moral quality criteria, moreover, we can raise the bar higher still—requiring adequate respect for the full array of liberal rights and freedoms, and possession of a constitutional democracy—or lower still—not requiring anything beyond meeting genetic criteria.

Consider these views as belonging to the pool of candidates that statesmen and diplomats have found to be plausible. What does the pragmatic theory of international recognition have to say about them? Earlier, we noted that identifying the best-justified criteria requires expert knowledge outside philosophy—in particular, from fields like law, political science, and international relations. So I will not be attempting to identify them, preferring instead to defer to those with expertise in those areas. Nonetheless, we can make certain general statements.

First, we must categorically reject parent state consent as a requirement for recognition. While we may accept it as a sufficient condition, accepting it as a necessary condition violates our second principle, which permits secession, without parent state consent, as a remedy for persistent, grave violations of human rights committed by the security forces of the parent state on the inhabitants of the territory seeking independence, and obligates other political entities to recognize the secessionist entity as an independent state.

Second, we should not refrain from derecognizing certain rogue states—effectively ejecting them from the international community of member states—even if they satisfy the international law definition of a state. Should they fall outside the critical mass, and their inclusion does not hasten the economic advance of the least well-off entities, then we have sufficient grounds for excluding them, according to the pragmatic theory. In other words, we should reject the view that effective statehood is a sufficient condition for recognition. Neither should we regard it as a necessary condition, given that our second principle allows for the possibility that we should recognize a secessionist entity despite its failing to satisfy the international law definition of a state.

Ejecting members clearly raises difficult issues of policy. But if the preceding argument is sound, it would be exercised in limited fashion. The critical mass would likely be capacious (§ 7.7). Further, entities outside the critical mass would be recognized too (chapter 9). For those few that are derecognized, there would have to be some sort of trustee arrangement, where possible, and alternate form of representing the interests of its population, where not. These arrangements would obviously need to be suitably modernized, and I do not mean to minimize the challenges. I only mean to point out that the issues are not without precedent, and that they are best addressed by those with the appropriate expertise.

Third, the pragmatic theory leaves open the possibility—should it be defensible on the basis of expert knowledge outside philosophy—that the right of secession should be extended to secessionist entities that form a nationality and seek independent statehood, irrespective of whether its inhabitants are victims of persistent, grave human rights abuses committed by the security forces of the parent state, and perhaps as well to geographically defined groups that seek independent statehood despite their not constituting a nationality. As we saw earlier (chapter 8), whether the right to secession should be extended beyond the consent, plebiscite, and remediation conditions will depend on whether the assurance condition can be met in further circumstances. If expert knowledge outside philosophy shows that it can, then the right to secession should be extended.

Fourth, the pragmatic theory implies that we should not make minimal justice a necessary condition for recognition either, unless we are sure (based on expert knowledge) that enough entities satisfy that criterion to form the critical mass. As we saw earlier (chapter 6), minimal justice is not full justice. It is something less than full justice that it still makes sense to call just overall (rather than, on balance, unjust). It is also a fixed standard, not an adjustable one. Accordingly, while we may need to relax our moral quality criteria (should we opt to include them, as I believe we should) in order to ensure that we obtain a critical mass (as our first principle requires), we cannot consistently relax our (normative) standard of minimal justice without failing to treat it as a normative minimum. Exactly where to set the bar for our moral quality criteria, though, in order to ensure that we obtain critical mass, requires expert knowledge from other fields.[67]

Of these four implications, clearly the last one is the most conservative, judged against the status quo. Recognition does not and should not require minimal justice, for if it did, scores of recognized states would have to be ejected as members of the international community of states. They would have to be *de*recognized. Nonetheless, as a normative theory—even as a nonideal theory—the pragmatic theory of international recognition will not simply bless the status quo. It will contain a critical edge. It will allow us to derecognize some rogue states (though not quite the wholesale derecognition that making minimal justice a necessary condition would require). It will permit secessions without the parent state's consent (and perhaps at times without government abuses). It embraces these, however, not as lofty ideals, but as normatively defensible, yet pragmatic, transitions. What would such a world be like? Would it be acceptable? Could it work? Would things unravel if we tried?

NOTES

1. Ian Brownlie, "Recognition in Theory and Practice," in Ronald MacDonald and Douglas Johnston (eds.), *The Structure and Process of International Law: Essays in Legal Philosophy, Doctrine and Theory* (Dordrect, NL: Martinus Nijhoff, 1983), p. 627.
2. Ibid.
3. See the Montevideo Convention on the Rights and Duties of States of 26 December 1933.
4. For an excellent discussion of this debate, see Thomas Grant, *The Recognition of States: Law and Practice in Debate and Evolution* (Westport, CT: Praeger Publishers, 1999).
5. The International Law Association's Committee on Recognition/Non-Recognition in International Law maintains that, as there is no international legal duty to recognize a state, recognition is at the discretion of the recognizing state. It also maintains, however, that current law is unclear as to whether there is an international legal duty *not* to recognize a state under certain conditions, and if so, what those conditions are. There is some legal authority for claiming that there is, and some that there is not. Thus, there may be an asymmetry between recognition and nonrecognition on the question of whether recognition is obligatory or discretionary. See http://www.ila-hq.org/en/committees/index.cfm/cid/1032 for the committee's 2014 Washington, DC, conference report.

6. For a legal analysis of government recognition, see Brad Roth, *Governmental Illegitimacy in International Law* (New York: Oxford University Press, 2000). See also Stefan Talmon, *Recognition of Governments in International Law: With Particular Reference to Governments in Exile* (New York: Oxford University Press, 1998).

7. For a fantastic historical treatment of the international practice of recognizing states, see Mikulas Fabry, *Recognizing States: International Society & the Establishment of New States Since 1776* (New York: Oxford University Press, 2010). I will draw from this work in this section. Also, I will use the terms *criteria, standards,* and *conditions,* and the phrase *ground of recognition* interchangeably in this section, and will reserve the term *principles* for the contents of the theory of international recognition.

8. Fabry, *Recognizing States,* p. 25.
9. Fabry, *Recognizing States,* p. 36.
10. Fabry, *Recognizing States,* p. 10.
11. See generally, Fabry, *Recognizing States,* pp. 26–36.
12. This occurred in its 1783 signing of the Treaty of Paris, following its surrender two years earlier at Yorktown.
13. Fabry, *Recognizing States,* p. 35.
14. Fabry, *Recognizing States,* pp. 36–41.
15. Fabry, *Recognizing States,* pp. 51–52, 57.
16. Fabry, *Recognizing States,* p. 57.
17. http://www.ushistory.org/documents/monroe.htm
18. Fabry, *Recognizing States,* p. 60.
19. Fabry, *Recognizing States,* pp. 63, 69.
20. Fabry, *Recognizing States,* pp. 64-5.
21. Fabry, *Recognizing States,* p. 66.
22. Fabry, *Recognizing States,* p. 68.
23. Fabry, *Recognizing States,* p. 81.
24. Fabry, *Recognizing States,* pp. 81–84.
25. Fabry, *Recognizing States,* p. 96.
26. Fabry, *Recognizing States,* p. 98.
27. Fabry, *Recognizing States,* p., 104.
28. Fabry, *Recognizing States,* pp. 104–5, 115 n. 121.
29. Fabry, *Recognizing States,* p. 86.
30. Fabry, *Recognizing States,* pp. 93–95.
31. Fabry, *Recognizing States,* pp. 87–88.
32. Fabry, *Recognizing States,* pp. 89–91.
33. Fabry, *Recognizing States,* p. 84.
34. Fabry, *Recognizing States,* pp. 98, 105–6.
35. Fabry, *Recognizing States,* p. 118.
36. Fabry, *Recognizing States,* pp. 126, 129.
37. Fabry, *Recognizing States,* p. 134.
38. Fabry, *Recognizing States,* p. 135.
39. Fabry, *Recognizing States,* p. 131.
40. Fabry, *Recognizing States,* p. 134.
41. Fabry, *Recognizing States,* p. 132.
42. Fabry, *Recognizing States,* p. 134.
43. Fabry, *Recognizing States,* pp. 151, 155–56.
44. Fabry, *Recognizing States,* pp. 151.
45. Fabry, *Recognizing States,* pp. 156–57.
46. http://daccess-dds-ny.un.org/doc/RESOLUTION/GEN/NR0/152/88/IMG/NR015288.pdf?OpenElement. The vote was 89 to 0 with 9 abstentions. See Fabry, *Recognizing States,* p. 153.
47. Fabry, *Recognizing States,* p., 157–58.
48. Fabry, *Recognizing States,* pp. 158–59.
49. http://daccess-dds-ny.un.org/doc/RESOLUTION/GEN/NR0/222/87/IMG/NR022287.pdf?OpenElement

50. Fabry, *Recognizing States*, p. 149.
51. Fabry, *Recognizing States*, p. 164.
52. Fabry, *Recognizing States*, p. 149, 167.
53. Fabry, *Recognizing States*, p. 160.
54. Fabry, *Recognizing States*, p. 166. Only Tanzania, Gabon, Ivory Coast, Zambia and Haiti recognized Biafra.
55. Fabry, *Recognizing States*, p. 168.
56. Fabry, *Recognizing States*, p. 167.
57. Contrast this with previous practice in Mexico and Colombia, which had both unilaterally seceded from their colonial master, Spain, but then later faced successful unilateral secessionist bids against their own rule: Texas from Mexico in 1836, Panama from Colombia in 1903. See Fabry, *Recognizing States*, p. 161.
58. Fabry, *Recognizing States*, p. 184.
59. Fabry, *Recognizing States*, pp. 185–86.
60. Fabry, *Recognizing States*, p. 185.
61. Recognition was often conditioned on meeting extra normative conditions, too, such as making commitments to honor the rule of law, democracy, and human rights, to guarantee the rights of ethnic and national minorities, and to adhere to nuclear treaties. See Fabry, *Recognizing States*, p. 186 and the Guidelines on the Recognition of New States in Eastern Europe and in the Soviet Union (December 16, 1991). Also, the resulting states were recognized regardless of whether they met the de facto criteria, such as possessing effective control (as Azerbaijan, Moldova, and Georgia apparently did not). Fabry, *Recognizing States*, pp. 187–88.
62. Fabry, 192–93.
63. Paul Szasz, "Discussion on the Fragmentation of Yugoslavia," *American Society of International Law Proceedings* 88 (1994), p. 47. This claim was later reaffirmed in S/RES/757 (1992) and S/RES/777 (1992).
64. See Peter Radan, *The Break-up of Yugoslavia and International Law* (London: Routledge, 2002), ch. 7; Steve Terrett, *The Dissolution of Yugoslavia and the Badinter Arbitration Commission* (Aldershot, UK: Ashgate, 2000); Hurst Hannum, "Self-Determination, Yugoslavia, and Europe: Old Wine in New Bottles?," *Transnational Law and Contemporary Problems* 57 (1993), pp. 6–9; Matthew Craven, "The European Community Arbitration Commission on Yugoslavia," *The British Year Book of International Law* 1995 (Oxford: Clarendon Press, 1996); and Michla Pomerance, "The Badinter Commission: The Use and Misuse of the International Court of Justice's Jurisprudence," *Michigan Journal of International Law* 20 (1998), pp. 31–58.
65. The Federal Republic of Yugoslavia was admitted to the United Nations with A/RES/55/12 on November 10, 2000. It was considered a new state, not the successor state to the Socialist Federal Republic of Yugoslavia that had been declared dissolved in 1991–1992.
66. http://www.nytimes.com/2008/02/19/world/europe/19kosovo.html?pagewanted=1&_r=1
67. For a good discussion from a legal perspective on whether recognition is conditioned on meeting a "democratic entitlement" (as well as some normative discussion of making it so), see the contributions to Gregory Fox and Brad Roth (eds.), *Democratic Governance and International Law* (New York: Cambridge University Press, 2000).

Epilogue

Brian Barry's Encore

By taking the social contract tradition, generalizing from it, and carrying it to a higher level of abstraction, *A Theory of Justice* honored its most famous forebears—Hobbes, Locke, Rousseau, and Kant.

"[I]n my own view and that of many others," writes Rawls in his *Lectures on the History of Political Philosophy*, "Hobbes's *Leviathan* is the greatest single work of political thought in the English language."[1] By "taking . . . its style and its language, its scope and its acuteness and interesting vividness of observation, [and] its intricate structure of analysis and principles," he continues, "the *Leviathan* makes, to me, a very overwhelming impression."[2] Confronting the problem of order during the English Civil War, and concerned (overridingly) with preserving peace, Hobbes "argues that everyone has sufficient rational grounds, rooted in their most basic interests, for creating, by agreement among themselves, a state, or Leviathan, with an effective sovereign with absolute powers, and for supporting such a sovereign whenever one exists," so as to avoid the violence of the state of nature.[3]

Only after spending several chapters attempting, as sympathetically as possible, to reconstruct Hobbes' argument for this position in its best possible light, does Rawls mention criticisms. His main criticism is that, according to Hobbes, "people have no attachment, no desire, etc., to act from principles of reasonable self-restraint or mutuality (fairness) for their own sake. These *reasonable desires* (as you might call them) have no part in his account of human psychology. . . . Hobbes's account of practical reason as rationality has no place for them."[4] People might comply with the Leviathan as they might comply, say, with negotiated articles of peace, but not from a reciprocal sense of fairness that forms the basis of genuine social cooperation.[5] So "[i]f we reject Hobbes's doctrine, one thing we can do is to see how the Social Contract view might be recast so as to provide not merely a perspective from which political institutions can be seen to be collectively rational, but a framework within which the content of the notions essential to social cooperation—reasonable self-restraint and fairness—can be defined or outlined."[6]

For that purpose, Rawls argues, we must consider Locke. Whereas Hobbes' concern was the English Civil War, Locke's was the Exclusion Crisis, the attempt (which Locke supported) to exclude Charles II's younger brother, a Catholic, from succeeding to the throne for fear that he would try to establish a royal absolutism under Catholicism.[7] Therefore, whereas Hobbes was concerned to argue for obedience to the Leviathan in order to avoid the violence of the state of nature, Locke's aim was to prepare "a justification for resistance to the Crown within the context of a mixed constitution" in which the Crown and Parliament shared legislative authority.[8]

With this aim in mind, Locke, in his contract doctrine, as Rawls portrays it, argues not only that individuals in a state of nature "act rationally to advance their legitimate interests," but also that they act "reasonably, that is, in accordance with their duties and obligations under the law of nature."[9] Unlike Hobbes, then, who seems to assume that persons cannot act from principles for their own sake, Locke makes no such assumption. For Locke, unlike Hobbes, a sense of fairness can motivate agents to adhere to principles for their own sake.

Taking this motivation as basic, and coupling it with Locke's claim that life under absolute monarchy is worse than the state of nature, Rawls then reconstructs, as sympathetically as possible, Locke's argument for the view that rational and reasonable persons *could not* contract into absolute monarchy, which is therefore illegitimate (a premise in his argument for justified resistance to the Crown). Only then does he raise a single main criticism against Locke, as he did earlier against Hobbes. Although Locke's view incorporates a duty of charity and a right to a reasonable opportunity to make property from the common (both expressions of "reasonable" motivation),[10] Rawls argues that it still does not guarantee a *democratic* state—a state with universal suffrage—since it is compatible with a *class* state, that is, a state with property qualifications for voting rights.[11] Reasonable and rational individuals, he argues, *could* agree to a class state if they know the particulars of their situations. If those who meet the property qualification are free to form their own state, then those who fail to meet it may decide that it's better to accept a (wealthier) class state with them than to form a (poorer) democratic state by themselves, since they may assess their overall prospects to be better in the former than the latter.[12]

Locke's difficulty, Rawls maintains, arises because "persons enter the compact situation not solely as free and equal, reasonable and rational, but also as in this or that situation with this or that amount of property."[13] Accordingly, "[i]f we want to work out a political conception in which the terms of social cooperation and the form of regime are independent of such contingencies, we must find a way to revise the social contract view."[14] For that purpose, he argues, we must turn to Rousseau and Kant[15]—the "high point of the contractarian tradition."[16]

Rousseau's concern in the years prior to the French Revolution, says Rawls, is the "increasing inequality in political power, in social position, and in wealth and property."[17] He seeks "a form of association that defends and protects the person and goods of each associate with all the common force," while "each one, uniting with all, nevertheless obeys only himself and remains as free as before."[18] Accordingly, Rousseau, in his contract doctrine, as Rawls portrays it, argues that a social contract in which each agrees to be governed by the general will is the solution. The contracting parties are reasonable insofar as they are capable of acting from the general will rather than from their own individual private wills.[19] The general will advances a conception of their common good, which Rawls claims consists in securing their fundamental interests—interests they share.[20] For Rousseau, these fundamental interests are interests in security, property, the development of their potentialities, and a proper self-love[21]—in short, the conditions of their freedom and personal independence.[22] Moved by these fundamental interests, the contracting parties establish laws based on the general will. Since the general will represents a common standpoint from which to determine the terms of their social contract, Rawls suggests, its terms are independent of the various contingencies that affect Locke's view. "Assuming that fundamental laws are properly based on what is required for the common good," Rawls argues, "citizens are [then] free to pursue their aims within the limits laid down by the general will."[23] Therefore, by "following and acting from laws satisfying [the general will], citizens act," as Rousseau had put it, "from a law they give to themselves."[24] According to the terms of their contract, citizens share as equals in their freedom—and participate equally, as voting members, in the sovereign power. There is no class state.[25]

Like Rousseau, and unlike Locke, claims Rawls, Kant too seeks a common standpoint from which to assess principles or (as Kant would say) maxims—one independent of the contingencies that affect our natural desires and inclinations. In his *Lectures on the History of Moral Philosophy*, Rawls outlines the basis for this standpoint.[26]

"[A]ll moral precepts," he claims, "will oppose our settled intentions and plans and natural desires on at least some occasions."[27] Therefore, he argues, if we are to identify, through an act of self-legislation, maxims that can serve as universal laws, "we must specify further the point of view" from which we are to will them.[28] In particular, we must make three assumptions on Kant's behalf. First, so that our maxims do not depend on contingent, variable inclinations, we must identify our *true human needs*—needs that must be met in order to maintain our independence and freedom as rational agents, which will be invariant—and will maxims that guarantee those needs are met.[29] Second, we must accept certain limits on information, ignoring "the more particular features of persons, including ourselves, as well as the specific content of their and our final ends and desires," and reason "as if we do not know what place we may have in that world."[30] Third, we must suppose that there is public knowledge of our maxims, so that no benefits accrue to us through free-riding on the efforts of others who are unaware of them (as for example a deceitful promisor benefits if the promisee is unaware of her maxim of deceit).[31]

If these assumptions sound familiar, they should be, for they describe key features of the choice situation in original position: the reliance on primary goods, the reasoning from behind the veil of ignorance, and the expectation that the principles chosen must meet the publicity condition. Thus, for Kant, according to Rawls, the common standpoint from which to assess principles or maxims is the *original position*. As Rawls puts it in *A Theory of Justice*: "The description of the original position interprets the point of view of noumenal selves, of what it means to be a free and equal rational being."[32] Thus, the argument for the principles of justice "does not assume that the parties have particular ends, but only that they desire certain primary goods"—which in turn implies that acting from those principles "is to act from categorical imperatives in the sense that they apply to us whatever in particular our aims are."[33] Further, because they select principles from behind the veil, those principles "do not depend upon social or natural contingencies, nor do they reflect the bias of the particulars of their plan of life or the aspirations that motivate them."[34] Finally, Rawls maintains, "once we think of moral principles as legislation for a kingdom of ends, it is clear that these principles must not only be acceptable to all but public as well."[35]

The original position, then, is, according to Rawls, that common standpoint, one that embodies Kant's view that "a person [acts] autonomously when the principles of his action are chosen by him as the most adequate possible expression of his nature as a free and equal rational being."[36] Having shed the constraints of their social position and natural endowments, the limitations of their particular society and what they happen to want, and all the other trappings of heteronomy, the autonomous individuals of Rawls's original position are finally free to give themselves laws unburdened by such contingencies. They are *freed*, and for the first time exercise their freedom. In this manner, Rawls concludes, does Kant achieve his "main aim," which is "to deepen and to justify Rousseau's idea that liberty is acting in accordance with a law that we give to ourselves."[37] Famously or notoriously, Rawls will later disown the Kantian heritage of his own social contract view.

Now my objective in rehearsing Rawls's interpretation of the social contract tradition is not to celebrate his reading of it, but to underscore what many readers found striking in *A Theory of Justice* and what they may find even more striking in view of his lectures. Part of the enduring fascination with Rawls, I believe, comes from his devotion to the social contract tradition along with his insistence on being precise. As Rawls sees things, both Rousseau and Kant need a more precise rendering of the generic freedom that they defend. They need to *specify* the basic rights and liberties. They need to *order* them among themselves and against other goods (like wealth and income). They need to *indicate* what the material conditions of personal independence and equality require. All of these Rawls amply provides in *A Theory of Justice*. Equally striking, though, is his devotion to the social contract tradition. Rawls situates himself as a follower of that tradition. He takes his aim to be that of a sympathetic interpreter and developer of it. Only after sympathetically reconstructing the views of Hobbes, Locke, Rousseau, and Kant does Rawls attempt to fill in the gaps that he believed they left open, and to address the problems, philosophical or political, that concerned Rawls when he wrote *A Theory of Justice,* and that continue to concern us today. Rawls takes the social contract seriously.

Given that Rawls takes the social contract seriously, and given that he considers himself to be a social contract theorist, any plausible interpretation of Rawls must take him seriously as a social contract theorist, too. No view can plausibly count as Rawlsian that sacrifices this central commitment to the social contract. Taking Rawls seriously requires taking the social contract seriously.

Yet if we read him as offering a theory of international justice in *The Law of Peoples,* the international contract does no work at all in establishing limits on internal sovereignty—it becomes "an unnecessary shuffle."[38] This fails to take Rawls seriously as a social contract theorist. Reading him as defending a theory of international recognition avoids attributing to him this unnecessary shuffle.

What about the specific theory of international recognition that we defended? Will it work? Having already suggested that the pragmatic theory's specific criteria for recognition requires expert knowledge outside philosophy to develop (§§ 7.5, 8.5, 10.3, 10.4), I nonetheless believe that we can give a general (if partial and tentative) sketch of the kind of world it would endorse. Starting with the status quo, adding entities as recognized states, and derecognizing some currently recognized states, a theory of recognition guides our transition to a more just state of affairs by adjusting the current array of internationally recognized states (§ 7.1). What might some of those adjustments be?

Since the pragmatic theory allows us to derecognize some rogue states, even if they satisfy the international law definition of a state, provided that derecognizing them does not violate the critical mass or economic development principles, it is worth considering what some of those states might be. It seems to me very likely that North Korea would fall into that category, and possibly several others. In general, these would be the very worst of the worst—unlikely to belong to the critical mass (§ 7.7), and unlikely to advance the economic development of the worst-off entities (§ 9.4). While this wouldn't involve the wholesale derecognition of states that the justice-based view would require (in violation of the critical mass principle), it would still do something (nearly) unprecedented in United Nations history by ejecting members even if they qualify as de facto states.[39]

Just as the pragmatic theory allows us to derecognize some rogue states, even if they satisfy the international law definition of a state, so too does it allow us to recognize some de facto states that are generally unrecognized internationally if they belong to the critical mass (in fact, their recognition would be required). For this reason, Taiwan should very likely (indeed, almost certainly) be included as a recognized member of the international community. First, as seems clear, Taiwan is a long-standing de facto state. Although being a de facto state is not a sufficient condition for recognition, Taiwan has, for this reason, a clear track record that can be evaluated (§ 7.7). Were one to rank the de facto states in Asia in terms of their moral quality, Taiwan would likely come out at or near the very top. Its ability to influence moral progress and to promote justice and prosperity both in the region and outside of it are similarly clear. So there is a strong prima facie case for claiming that Taiwan belongs to the critical mass—or more precisely, to one of the overlapping regional critical masses (§ 7.7)—and thus for claiming that it should be recognized. Further, in view of its economic capacity, there is also strong reason for claiming that it should be recognized under the economic development principle. In fact, the case for recognizing it seems strong enough to assert that the burden of proof must shift to those who *deny* that it should be recognized as an independent state and included within international legal institutions such as the United Nations.

The most obvious counterargument is that Taiwanese independence would precipitate war (as threatened by Beijing in its 2005 antisecession law), which would hinder, not promote, moral progress.[40] Against this, however, we should note that even moral requirements call for moral skill in determining how to implement them. In this case, the exercise of moral skill calls for judgments of efficacy and political feasibility. There are options regarding how recognition occurs. Recognition does not require that Taiwan itself declare its independence. It could allow for other states to recognize Taiwan without Taiwan itself issuing a declaration of independence. Nor does it require immediate recognition by all states. It could allow for gradual recognition by some states, followed by some others, and so on. Taiwan would still be entitled to recognition but the implementation of this entitlement could be worked out. Hence, if, as the evidence suggests—there already being states that recognize Taiwan without China fulfilling its threat—the threat is less serious and credible, this may argue for the gradual strategy.

As a remedy for persistent, grave violations of human rights committed by a country's security forces, the pragmatic theory of recognition also permits secession, without parent state consent, and obligates other political entities to recognize the secessionist entity as an independent state. As we saw earlier, formulating the exact language of the remediation condition, for codification within international legal institutions, will require expert skill and care (§ 8.5). Nonetheless, it's fair to claim that, under the pragmatic theory, a number of past secessionist claims would not have been preemptively dismissed on the grounds that they violated parent state consent, and that their claimants would at least have been entitled to a hearing on their remedial basis. These would likely have included at least Biafra, Somaliland, Kurdistan, Tamil Eelam, and Bougainville, which have never obtained recognized statehood;[41] Bangladesh, Eritrea, and South Sudan, which eventually did achieve it, although on other bases, which delayed it; and Kosovo, whose current status is mixed, being neither generally recognized nor generally unrecognized (§ 10.3[F]).

Now that we have this sketch before us of the pragmatic theory in practice, we can return to the question that prompted our drawing of it. Will it work? This question requires interpretation. Does it mean, would it be accepted? If that's the question, then we seem to have our answer already, evidenced by state practice. No, it would not be (generally) accepted. But then, so what? Even nonideal theory will not simply bless the status quo. *Could* it be accepted? What is the force of this "could"? If it means, "Could the pragmatic theory be accepted as the focus of an overlapping consensus?" then we must ask, among whom? While some societies would accept it, others presumably would not. Are all those that reject it necessarily unreasonable? (I would be loath to rest the pragmatic theory on that claim.) Could those societies that reject it ultimately be persuaded—freely, reflectively, and all-things-considered—to endorse it if given enough time for their societies to evolve? The answer to that question is very likely yes. (Does that clinch the case for the pragmatic theory?) What if some of them couldn't? We could go back to the drawing board in that case—reconstruct the contract, generate new results. But then we'd be right back where we started with the same series of questions. What if some societies couldn't freely and reflectively endorse our new results, all-things-considered—ever? What if they were to stick to their guns until time immemorial? What if there were *holdouts*?

At this point, we reach the crux of the issue. Supposing that there are holdouts, should we say, so much the worse for the pragmatic theory—or should we say, instead, so much the worse for the holdouts? The holdouts, after all, are most often going to be the liberal multinational states in the aftermath of decolonization that didn't (and don't) want to get their hands dirty in secessionist crises (many fueled by arbitrary colonial boundaries drawn by themselves). Should we deny remedial rights to secession in that case? Then peoples who suffer under widespread, grave, and persistent human rights abuses at the hands of their government's security forces would be making a tremendous sacrifice just to spare them from having to get their hands dirty (many of whom forcibly assimilated their own national minorities besides). Shouldn't they count as holdouts to any theory that denies remedial rights? We'll have holdouts either way.

If we have confidence in how we constructed our contract, if we find attractive its commitments to fairness and equality, if we find appealing how it models these convictions, if we find persuasive the argument from the original position, and if we find convincing its outcome upon due reflection, then we should find no need to institute any further accommodations for holdouts, and we should reject holding our principles hostage to the mere possibility that some societies might be unable ever to affirm them.

Like Brian Barry, I believe that, as time goes on, *A Theory of Justice* will stand out with increasing clarity as the greatest contribution to political philosophy in the twentieth century. Only two things threaten to obscure that achievement: the publication of *Political Liberalism*, and the publication of *The Law of Peoples*.

NOTES

1. See John Rawls, *Lectures on the History of Political Philosophy*, ed. Samuel Freeman (Cambridge, MA: Harvard University Press, 2007), p. 23.
2. Rawls, *Lectures on the History of Political Philosophy*, p. 23.
3. Rawls, *Lectures on the History of Political Philosophy*, p. 105.
4. Rawls, *Lectures on the History of Political Philosophy*, p. 88.
5. Rawls, *Lectures on the History of Political Philosophy*, p. 87.
6. Rawls, *Lectures on the History of Political Philosophy*, p. 88.
7. Rawls, *Lectures on the History of Political Philosophy*, p. 105.
8. Rawls, *Lectures on the History of Political Philosophy*, p. 105.
9. Rawls, *Lectures on the History of Political Philosophy*, p. 129.
10. Rawls, *Lectures on the History of Political Philosophy*, p. 147.
11. Rawls, *Lectures on the History of Political Philosophy*, pp. 152–55.
12. Rawls, *Lectures on the History of Political Philosophy*, p. 152–55.
13. Rawls, *Lectures on the History of Political Philosophy*, p. 152.
14. Rawls, *Lectures on the History of Political Philosophy*, p. 152.
15. Rawls, *Lectures on the History of Political Philosophy*, p. 155.
16. Rawls, *A Theory of Justice*, p. 252.
17. Rawls, *Lectures on the History of Political Philosophy*, p. 196.
18. Rawls, *Lectures on the History of Political Philosophy*, p. 219.
19. Rawls, *Lectures on the History of Political Philosophy*, p. 224.
20. Rawls, *Lectures on the History of Political Philosophy*, p. 225.
21. Rawls, *Lectures on the History of Political Philosophy*, p. 230.
22. Rawls, *Lectures on the History of Political Philosophy*, p. 243.
23. Rawls, *Lectures on the History of Political Philosophy*, p. 235.
24. Rawls, *Lectures on the History of Political Philosophy*, p. 236.
25. Rawls, *Lectures on the History of Political Philosophy*, p. 222.
26. John Rawls, *Lectures on the History of Moral Philosophy*, ed. Barbara Herman (Cambridge, MA: Harvard University Press, 2000): 143–325 (chapters discussing Kant).
27. Rawls, *Lectures on the History of Moral Philosophy*, p. 173.
28. Rawls, *Lectures on the History of Moral Philosophy*, p. 173.
29. Rawls, *Lectures on the History of Moral Philosophy*, pp. 173–74.
30. Rawls, *Lectures on the History of Moral Philosophy*, pp. 175–76.

31. Rawls, *Lectures on the History of Moral Philosophy*, p. 171.
32. Rawls, *A Theory of Justice*, pp. 255–56.
33. Rawls, *A Theory of Justice*, p. 253.
34. Rawls, *A Theory of Justice*, pp. 252–53.
35. Rawls, *A Theory of Justice*, pp. 252.
36. Rawls, *A Theory of Justice*, pp. 252.
37. Rawls, *A Theory of Justice*, pp. 256.
38. Rawls, *Lectures on the History of Political Philosophy*, p. 170. The reference is to Rawls's characterization of Hume's critique of Locke's social contract view. Hume accuses Locke's view of involving an "unnecessary shuffle," since the principle of fidelity to promises, upon which Locke bases our duty of allegiance to the terms of our contract, can be explained, on Hume's view, by the principle of utility. We can instead appeal directly to the principle of utility to explain our duty to obey government rather than invoking the principle of fidelity. See pp. 169–70.
39. The possible exception is the 1971 ejection of the Republic of China (now Taiwan) and its replacement by the People's Republic of China. This occurred in the United Nations General Assembly with A/RES/2758 (XXVI) of October 25, 1971, which accepted the governing credentials of the authorities representing the People's Republic of China and rejected those from the Republic of China. However, some may regard this as a case of government (rather than state) derecognition, since both the People's Republic of China and the Republic of China claimed authority over the whole of mainland China and the island of Formosa (Taiwan). On this view, China, as a state, was neither derecognized nor ejected from UN membership.
40. It seems problematic, to say the least, to categorize a Taiwanese assertion of independence as a secessionist claim, because the Republic of China's forces did not go on the attack during the Chinese civil war (1928–1949) seeking to establish an independent state. Instead, they were attacked by the People's Liberation Army and retreated to the island of Formosa (now Taiwan).
41. Of these, Somaliland, Tamil Eelam, and Bougainville had at some point already achieved effective statehood. Fabry, *Recognizing States*, p. 164.

Appendix 1

MIDDLE EAST COUNTRIES THAT FAIL THE STRONG STANDARD: SUPPORTING EVIDENCE

The following are mainly excerpts from the US State Department Country Reports on Human Rights Practices issued April 2016 for the year 2015. While there are inevitably variations in a country's human rights performance from year to year, the overall picture remains much the same for appendices 1 through 4.

Algeria

"The government did not take sufficient steps to investigate, prosecute, or punish public officials who committed violations. Impunity for police and security officials remained a problem, and the government rarely provided information on actions taken against officials accused of wrongdoing." (Executive Summary) "women . . . continued to face legal and social discrimination." (Sec. 6)

Bahrain

"Women faced discrimination under the law." (Sec. 6)

Israel

"In the secular criminal and civil courts, women and men enjoy the same rights, but in some matters religious courts—responsible for adjudication of family law, including divorce—limit the rights of Jewish, Christian, Muslim, and Druze women. Women and men who do not belong to a recognized religious group face additional discrimination." (Sec. 6) "Arab citizens . . . faced institutional and societal discrimination." (Sec. 6)

Israel's classification is based on its conduct outside the occupied territories in order to provide the interpretation of its political practices most favorable to the justice-based view. If we consider its conduct in the occupied territories, Israel fails both the weak and the strong standards. See appendix 2.

Kuwait

"Women . . . bidoon [stateless Arabs] and other noncitizens, faced social and legal discrimination." (Executive Summary) "Women . . . do not enjoy the same rights as men under family law, labor law, property law, inheritance law, or in the judicial system." (Sec. 6) "The law requires segregation by gender of classes at all universities and secondary schools, although it was not always enforced. In December the constitutional court ruled that the gender segregation law is constitutional but that separate facilities are not required to enforce gender segregation. The court ruled that separate sitting areas in the classroom met the law's requirement." (Sec. 6)

Oman

"In some personal status cases, such as divorce, a woman's testimony is equal to half that of a man. The legal provision that allows men to divorce their wives with the signature of two witnesses is not accorded to women. The law favors male heirs in adjudicating inheritance." (Sec. 6)

Qatar

"Legal, institutional, and cultural discrimination against women limited their participation in society." (Executive Summary)

United Arab Emirates (2015)

"Legal and cultural discrimination, however, existed and went unpunished. The law does not prohibit discrimination based on sex, political opinion, national origin. . . . Women faced legal and economic discrimination." (Sec. 6)

Appendix 2

MIDDLE EAST COUNTRIES THAT FAIL THE WEAK STANDARD: SUPPORTING EVIDENCE

Unless otherwise indicated, the excerpts below are from the US State Department Country Reports on Human Rights Practices issued April 2016 for the year 2015. Since occasional human rights abuses (committed by a few rogue cops, say) do not seem sufficient for declaring a country to be a human rights violator, some judgment inevitably had to be exercised. Evidence that human rights abuses were frequent, widespread, or systematic was taken as sufficient for declaring a country to be a human rights violator. So, for example, evidence that extrajudicial killings, torture or harsh interrogation methods, arbitrary arrest, or prolonged detention were widespread or occurred within an environment of impunity was taken to indicate that a country systematically violates the basic human right to personal security. When UN Security Council or General Assembly resolutions are cited, they substantiate failures to meet the weak standard. (Similar remarks apply to appendices 3 and 4.)

Egypt

"Many aspects of the law discriminate against women and religious minorities, and the government did not effectively enforce prohibitions against such discrimination." (Sec. 6)

"The government inconsistently punished or prosecuted officials who committed abuses, whether in the security services or elsewhere in government. In most cases either the government did not comprehensively investigate human rights abuses, including most incidents of violence by security forces, or investigations resulted in acquittals, contributing to an environment of impunity." (Executive Summary) "There were numerous reports that the government or its agents committed arbitrary or unlawful killings while making arrests, dispersing demonstrators, or holding persons in custody. There were also reports of civilians killed during military operations in the Sinai. Impunity was a problem." (Sec. 1a)

Iran

See A/Res/70/173 (2015), recalling A/Res/69/190 (2014).

Iraq

"Severe human rights problems were widespread. Da'esh committed the overwhelming number of serious human rights abuses, including attacks against civilians, especially Shia but also Sunnis who opposed Da'esh; members of other religious and ethnic minorities; women; and children. Some Shia PMF reportedly committed human rights violations. Numerous reports continued during the year of Shia PMF killing, torturing, kidnapping, and extorting civilians. Simultaneously, to a much lesser extent, government forces reportedly engaged in abuses against civilians in liberated areas, such as arbitrary detentions and limits on freedom of movement. Sectarian hostility, widespread corruption, and lack of transparency at all levels of government and society weakened the government's authority and worsened effective human rights protections." (Executive Summary)

Israel

See A/Res/70/90 (2015), recalling A/Res/69/93 (2014). From the 2015 US DOS Country Report: "NGOs continued to accuse Israel of using disproportionate force and indiscriminate fire to counter the threat posed by rockets launched from the Gaza Strip, resulting in unnecessary and excessive civilian casualties." (Sec. 1a) "NGOs reported that impunity among Israeli security forces remained a problem, in part because mechanisms for investigating allegations were not effective. Reports of abuse go to the Attorney General's Office; PCATI in June 2013 reported that authorities systematically disregarded abuse allegations. . . . Throughout the year there were reports Israeli security forces in East Jerusalem and in the West Bank arbitrarily arrested and detained numerous Palestinian protesters and activists, particularly those participating in demonstrations against the separation barrier or against killings of Palestinians." (Sec. 1d) From the 2014 US DOS Country Report annex on the Occupied Territories: "There were numerous reports that Israeli security forces killed Palestinians during demonstrations. . . . During the year there were a significantly higher number of Palestinian deaths at the hands of Israeli security forces than in past years as a result of Israeli military operations between July 8 and August 26 [2013]. Israeli security forces killed at least 2,222 Palestinians in Gaza, including 2,205 during military operations associated with Operation Protective Edge. . . . [T]he Israeli government estimated half of those killed were civilians and half were combatants, while the United Nations reported that 69 percent of those killed were civilians. According to the United Nations, more than 500 minors and nearly 300 women were killed." (Sec. 1a)

Jordan

"Impunity remained widespread." (Executive Summary) "International and local nongovernmental organizations (NGOs) continued to report incidents of torture and widespread mistreatment in police and security detention centers." (Sec. 1c)

Lebanon

"The law does not specifically prohibit all forms of torture or cruel, inhuman, or degrading treatment or punishment, and there were reports security officials employed such practices. The penal code prohibits using acts of violence to obtain a confession or information about a crime, but the judiciary rarely investigated or prosecuted allegations of such acts. According to domestic and international human rights groups, security forces abused detainees and used torture to obtain confessions or encourage suspects to implicate other individuals." (Sec. 1c) "The law requires judicial warrants before arrests except in cases of active pursuit. Nonetheless, the government arbitrarily arrested and detained persons. . . . Authorities failed to observe many provisions of the law, and government security forces . . . continued the practice of extrajudicial arrest and detention, including incommunicado detention." (Sec. 1d)

Libya

See S/Res/2095 (2013), recalling 1970 (2011), 1973 (2011), 2009 (2011), 2016 (2011), 2017 (2011), 2022 (2011), 2040 (2012).

Morocco

"A variety of sources reported other human rights problems. These included security forces committing human rights abuses on multiple occasions, including reports of torture in detention. Prison and detention conditions were substandard. The judiciary lacked independence, and pretrial detention frequently exceeded what the law allows. Domestic and international nongovernmental organizations (NGOs) asserted there were political prisoners, many of whom were detained under the antiterrorism law. . . . There were few examples and no high-profile reports of investigations or prosecutions of abuse or corruption, whether in the security services or elsewhere in the government, contributing to the widespread perception of impunity." (Executive Summary) "An August 2014 report from the UN Working Group on Arbitrary Detention stated it had received accusations 'from sources deemed to be credible' that disappearances continued to occur in direct violation of the constitution, which provides for human treatment of prisoners and detainees." (Sec. 1b) "A May 19 report by Amnesty International (AI), Shadows of Impunity: Morocco and the Western Sahara, claimed that, based on more than 150 interviews between 2010 and 2014, while torture may no longer be an officially state-sanctioned practice, 'an array of torture techniques are used by Moroccan security forces to extract confessions to crimes, silence activists, and crush dissent.' The report concluded that police and security forces over this period routinely inflicted beatings, asphyxiation, stress positions, simulated drowning, and psychological and sexual violence. An AI representative went on to say, 'there is a gap between what's on paper and what's in practice. Torture is not systematic but common. The safeguards that exist currently are not being implemented.' Additionally, the report noted that a lack of investigations into, and prosecutions of, individuals accused of torture contributes to a 'climate of impunity.'" (Sec. 1c)

Saudi Arabia

"The law provides that no entity may restrict a person's actions or imprison a person, except under provisions of the law. Legally, authorities may not detain a person under arrest for more than 24 hours, except pursuant to a written order from a public investigator. Authorities must inform the detained person of the reasons for detention. Nonetheless, the Ministry of Interior, to which the majority of forces with arrest power reported, maintained broad authority to arrest and detain persons indefinitely without judicial oversight, notification of charges against them, or effective access to legal counsel or family. Authorities held persons for months and sometimes years without charge or trial, and reportedly failed to advise them promptly of their rights, including their legal right to be represented by an attorney." (Sec. 1d) "Lengthy pretrial detention was a problem. In the past, local unlicensed nongovernmental organizations (NGOs), such as the Saudi Association for Civil and Political Rights (ACPRA) and the Adala Center for Human Rights, challenged the Ministry of Interior publicly and in court on cases considered to involve arbitrary arrest or detention. The two NGOs ceased operating in 2013 and 2014, respectively, after authorities disestablished them. ACPRA claimed the ministry sometimes ignored judges' rulings; judges appeared powerless to take action against the ministry." (Sec. 1d)

Syria

S/Res/2258 (2015), recalling 2042 (2012), 2043 (2012), 2118 (2013), 2139 (2014), 2165 (2014), 2175 (2014), 2191 (2014), 2209 (2015), 2235 (2015), 2254 (2015).

Tunisia

"Although the law prohibits such practices, police reportedly subjected many detainees to harsh physical treatment, according to first-hand accounts provided to international organizations. Several prominent local human rights lawyers have decried the practice of torture in police stations and detention centers. Human rights NGOs criticized the government for reluctance to investigate torture allegations." (Sec. 1c) "Civilian authorities maintained control over police, although international organizations, such as Amnesty International and Human Rights Watch, reported instances of detainees being subjected to harsh physical treatment. The government lacked effective mechanisms to investigate and punish abuse, corruption, and impunity by police and prison officials, and there was little transparency in internal investigations." (Sec. 1d) "A January report entitled Justice in Tunisia: Year Zero, by the anti-torture French NGO ACAT in collaboration with three Tunisian human rights associations, detailed the dysfunctional mechanisms for complaining of torture during custody, detention, and imprisonment." (Sec. 1d)

Yemen

"The most significant human rights problems were arbitrary killings, disappearances, kidnappings, and other violence committed by various groups, as well as a corrupt judicial system that did not provide for the rule of law, further weakened after the Houthi-Saleh takeover. The internationally recognized government-in-exile lacked the capacity to enforce laws protecting against human rights abuses, particularly after its exile in March. . . . Impunity was persistent and pervasive. Security forces remained essentially immune from civilian oversight." (Executive Summary) "During the period September 2014 to August 15, Houthi and pro-Saleh forces and their allies arbitrarily detained 5,894 persons." (Sec. 1b) "Prior to its exile, there were reports that the government's security officials committed abuses. Human rights NGOs, former detainees, and prisoners alleged that torture and mistreatment occurred frequently during arrests or detentions. There were also reports of abuses by elements of the Houthi-Saleh security forces and in institutions under their control. Torture and other forms of mistreatment were common in Houthi-Saleh detention facilities, according to the YCMHRV, which documented 796 cases in 16 of the country's 21 governorates and the capital Sana'a from September 2014 to August 15." (Sec. 1c)

Appendix 3

AFRICAN COUNTRIES THAT PASS THE WEAK STANDARD: SUPPORTING EVIDENCE

The following are drawn from the US State Department Country Reports on Human Rights Practices issued April 2016, for the year 2015:

Benin

While there was evidence that security forces committed extrajudicial killings (Sec. 1a), tortured suspects (Sec. 1c), and made arbitrary arrests (Sec. 1d), these were not widespread enough to support the claim that Benin fails the weak standard.

Botswana

There was no evidence that security forces committed extrajudicial killings (Sec. 1a), politically motivated disappearances (Sec. 1b), or torture (Sec. 1c). The government generally observed prohibitions on arbitrary arrest and detention (Sec. 1d).

Burkina Faso

Aside from a failed coup attempt and killings of individuals protesting the coup, there was general observation of human rights requiring respect for the integrity of the person (Sec. 1).

Cabo Verde

There was no evidence that security forces committed extrajudicial killings (Sec. 1a), politically motivated disappearances (Sec. 1b), or torture (Sec. 1c). The government generally observed prohibitions on arbitrary arrest and detention (Sec. 1d).

Comoros

There was no evidence that security forces committed extrajudicial killings (Sec. 1a), politically motivated disappearances (Sec. 1b), or torture (Sec. 1c). The government generally observed prohibitions on arbitrary arrest and detention (Sec. 1d).

Gabon

There was no evidence that security forces committed arbitrary or unlawful killings (Sec. 1a), or politically motivated disappearances (Sec. 1b). While the law prohibits torture (Sec. 1c) and arbitrary arrest and detention (Sec. 1d), government security forces did not always observe the prohibitions. However, there was no evidence that the violations were widespread or systematic. Applying the principle of charity, Gabon passes.

Lesotho

Although there were credible reports that the security forces committed arbitrary or unlawful killings, there was no evidence that the violations were widespread of systematic (Sec. 1a). Similarly, although there were reports that the security forces committed torture or cruel treatment of suspects, there was no evidence that the violations were widespread of systematic (Sec. 1c). There was no evidence implicating security forces in politically motivated disappearances (Sec. 1b), and the government generally observed prohibitions against arbitrary arrest or detention (Sec. 1d). Applying the principle of charity, Lesotho passes.

Namibia

There was no evidence that security forces committed arbitrary or unlawful killings (Sec. 1a), or politically motivated disappearances (Sec. 1b). There were "almost no" reported cases of torture (Sec. 1c), and government security forces generally observed prohibitions on arbitrary arrest and detention (Sec. 1d).

Niger

While there were some reports that security forces committed arbitrary or unlawful killings (Sec. 1a), beat or abused citizens (Sec. 1c), or violated prohibitions against arbitrary arrest or detention (Sec. 1d), there was no evidence that these practices were widespread or systematic. There were no reports of politically motivated disappearances perpetrated by security forces (Sec. 1b).

Sao Tome and Principe

There was no evidence that security forces committed extrajudicial killings (Sec. 1a), politically motivated disappearances (Sec. 1b), or torture (Sec. 1c). The government generally observed prohibitions on arbitrary arrest and detention (Sec. 1d).

Senegal

There were no reports of security forces committing arbitrary or unlawful killings (Sec. 1a), or politically motivated disappearances (Sec. 1b). While there were occasional reports that security forces employed torture or physical abuse (Sec. 1c), or that they did not always observe prohibitions on arbitrary arrest or detention (Sec. 1d), there was no evidence that these violations were widespread or systematic.

Seychelles

There were no reports of security forces committing arbitrary or unlawful killings (Sec. 1a), or politically motivated disappearances (Sec. 1b). While there were reports that security forces beat and abused persons (Sec. 1c), or that they did not always observe prohibitions on arbitrary arrest or detention (Sec. 1d), there was no evidence that these violations were widespread or systematic.

Sierra Leone

While there were some reports that security forces committed arbitrary or unlawful killings (Sec. 1a), and while there were occasional violations of prohibitions on arbitrary arrest or detention (Sec. 1d), their occurrence was not widespread of systematic. In addition, there were no reported politically motivated disappearances (Sec. 1b).

Tanzania

While there were reports that security forces committed unlawful killings (Sec. 1a) or abused civilians (Sec. 1c), there was no evidence that these violations were widespread of systematic. There were no reports of politically motivated disappearances (Sec. 1b). The government generally observed prohibitions on arbitrary arrest and detention. (Sec. 1d)

Togo

There was no evidence that security forces committed extrajudicial killings (Sec. 1a), politically motivated disappearances (Sec. 1b), or torture (Sec. 1c). The government generally observed prohibitions on arbitrary arrest and detention (Sec. 1d).

Appendix 4

AFRICAN COUNTRIES THAT FAIL THE WEAK STANDARD: SUPPORTING EVIDENCE

The following are excerpts from the US State Department Country Reports on Human Rights Practices issued April 2016, for the year 2015:

Angola

"The government took some steps to prosecute or punish officials who committed abuses; however, accountability was weak due to a lack of checks and balances, lack of institutional capacity, a culture of impunity, and widespread government corruption." (Executive Summary) "The law prohibits arbitrary arrest and detention; however, security forces often did not respect these prohibitions." (Sec. 1d) "According to several NGO and civil society sources, police arbitrarily arrested individuals without due process and routinely detained individuals who participated, or were about to participate, in antigovernment protests, despite this right being protected by the constitution." (Sec. 1d) "Unlawful arrest and detention remained serious problems." (Sec. 1d)

Burundi

S/Res/ 2279 (2016), recalling 2248 (2015).

Cameroon

"During the year terrorist group Boko Haram's strategy in the country evolved to include using knives, sophisticated weapons, improvised explosive devises, and child soldiering. This had unprecedented consequences in affected regions as killings of civilians, abductions, looting, and destruction of property increased in frequency. In response the government increased security measures, but its efforts often failed to prevent excesses, which led to additional human rights abuses, including arbitrary arrests and detentions, and avoidable loss of life. The most important human rights problems were Boko Haram killings and other abuses in the Far North Region, including child soldiering, abductions, beheadings, and immolations; security force (police and/or gendarmerie) torture and abuse, primarily of Boko Haram suspects; denial of fair and speedy public trial; and life-threatening prison conditions. . . . Although the government took steps to punish and prosecute officials who committed abuses in the security forces and in the public service, these actors often continued to act with impunity." (Executive Summary)

Chad

"There were reports that the government or its agents committed arbitrary and unlawful killings, including by torture. Human rights groups credibly accused the security forces of killing and torturing with impunity, according to Freedom House." (Sec. 1a) "In its Annual Report 2013, AI noted that 'cruel, inhuman, or degrading punishments, including beatings, continued to be widely practiced by security forces and prison guards with almost total impunity.'" (Sec. 1c)

Central African Republic

S/Res/2262 (2016), recalling 2121 (2013), 2127 (2013), 2134 (2014), 2149 (2014), 2181 (2014), 2196 (2015), 2212 (2015), 2217 (2015).

Congo, Democratic Republic of the

S/Res/2277 (2016), recalling 2211 (2015), 2198 (2015), 2147 (2014), 2136 (2014), 2098 (2013).

Congo, Republic of the

"The most significant human rights problems included arbitrary or unlawful killings by security forces; arbitrary arrests, beatings, and torture of detainees by police; and refugee abuse. . . . The government seldom took steps to prosecute or punish officials who committed abuses, whether in the security services or elsewhere in the government, and official impunity was a problem." (Executive Summary) "There were numerous reports the government or its agents committed arbitrary or unlawful killings." (Sec. 1a) "There were numerous credible reports of politically motivated disappearances." (Sec. 1b) "The constitution bans torture and the law contains a general prohibition against assault and battery, but there is no legal framework specifically banning torture under the criminal code. There were widespread reports of cases of government-led torture and other cruel, inhuman, and degrading treatment." (Sec. 1c)

Côte D'Ivoire

S/Res/2112 (2013), recalling 1933 (2010), 1942 (2010), 1951 (2010), 1962 (2010), 1967 (2011), 1968 (2011), 1975 (2011), 1980 (2011), 1981 (2011), 1992 (2011), 2000 (2011), 2062 (2012), 2101 (2013).

Djibouti

"There were reports that the government or its agents committed arbitrary or unlawful killings. According to political opposition members and domestic human rights organizations, security force use of excessive force resulted in deaths. . . . Authorities took no known action to investigate reported cases of arbitrary or unlawful killings from previous years or to punish suspected perpetrators. Impunity was a problem." (Sec. 1a). "The law prohibits arbitrary arrest and detention, but the government did not respect these prohibitions." (Sec. 1d) "During the year government officials arbitrarily arrested journalists, opposition members, academics, and demonstrators, often without warrants." (Sec. 1d) "Lengthy pretrial detention was a problem, and approximately 20 percent of the prison population was in pretrial detention. Prisoners often waited two, three, or more years for their trials to begin." (Sec. 1d)

Eritrea

S/Res/ 2244 (2015), recalling 733 (1992), 1844 (2008), 1907 (2009), 2036 (2012), 2023 (2011), 2093 (2013), 2111 (2013), 2124 (2013), 2125 (2013), 2142 (2014), 2182 (2014).

Equatorial Guinea

"The law prohibits such practices, but torture and excessive force by police occurred 'routinely,' according to Human Rights Watch and Amnesty International." (Sec. 1c)

Ethiopia

"According to NGO reports, thousands of ethnic Oromos, whom the government accused of terrorism, were arbitrarily arrested and in some cases reportedly tortured." (Sec. 1c) "Although the constitution and law prohibit arbitrary arrest and detention, the government ignored these provisions. There were many reports of arbitrary arrest and detention by police and security forces throughout the country." (Sec. 1d)

Gambia

"The constitution and law prohibit such practices; however, there were reports security forces tortured, beat, and mistreated persons in custody. In November 2014 the government prevented UN special rapporteurs from investigating reports of torture and extrajudicial execution. The team's preliminary findings, however, indicated the National Intelligence Agency (NIA) consistently practiced torture. Police reportedly tortured individuals suspected of common crimes. The UN findings indicated the NIA tortured detainees for days or weeks; methods included severe beatings, electric shock, asphyxiation, and burning. According to Human Rights Watch, methods of torture also included water torture, rape, and simulated burial." (Sec. 1c)

Ghana

"While the constitution and law prohibit such practices, there were credible reports police beat, raped, and otherwise abused suspects, prisoners, and other citizens. Beatings of suspects and other citizens occurred throughout the country but were generally unreported in official channels because victims were reluctant to file formal complaints. Police generally denied allegations or claimed the level of force used was justified. Military officials also reportedly mistreated persons. Two years after his initial visit in 2013, Juan E. Mendez, the UN special rapporteur on torture and other cruel, inhuman, or degrading treatment or punishment, conducted a follow-up assessment in October and stated that torture at the point of apprehension, which mostly takes the form of coercive methods used by police officers, remained pervasive." (Sec. 1c) "The constitution and law provide for protection against arbitrary arrest and detention, but the government frequently disregarded these protections." (Sec. 1d)

Guinea

"Impunity persisted for grave abuses perpetrated by state actors in years past, including security force killings of at least 150 opposition demonstrators and the rape of more than 100 women and girls in the 2009 stadium massacre. Only one person—a lower-level gendarme—was tried and convicted of rape during the stadium massacre." (Sec. 1a) "The government took no action against perpetrators of the 2007 killings of between 137 and 186 demonstrators." (Sec. 1a) "Although the constitution and law prohibit torture and other cruel, inhuman, or degrading punishments, government officials continued to employ such practices with impunity. According to Freedom House, 'security forces continue to engage in arbitrary arrests, torture of detainees, and extrajudicial executions with impunity.'" (Sec. 1c) "Abuse of inmates in prisons reportedly declined, but abuse in judicial police and gendarme detention centers continued at previous levels. Gendarmes and police designated as 'judicial police officers' (OPJs) routinely abused detainees to coerce confessions." (Sec. 1c)

Guinea-Bissau

S/Res/2103 (2013), recalling 1876 (2009), 2030 (2011), 2048 (2012), 2092 (2013).

Kenya

"Several organizations documented alleged extrajudicial killings or disappearances committed by security force members. In September a draft of a preliminary report by the Kenya National Commission on Human Rights (KNCHR), a government-supported body, was leaked to the press. The report described human rights abuses allegedly committed by security forces in the crackdown against terrorism. According to the report, more than 120 cases of human rights violations, including 25 extrajudicial killings and 81 enforced disappearances occurred, and these types of violations were 'widespread, systematic, and well-coordinated.' In many cases the report attributed the human rights abuses to the Kenya Defense Forces." (Sec. 1a) "While the constitution and law prohibit torture, the legal code does not define torture and provides no sentencing guidelines for violating the constitutional and legal prohibitions. These gaps functionally prevent prosecution for torture. Police reportedly used torture and violence frequently during interrogations as well as to punish both pretrial detainees and convicted prisoners. According to Amnesty International and other NGOs, physical battery, being tied up in painful positions, and suspension from the ceiling were the most common methods of torture used by police. A range of human rights organizations and the media reported cases of torture and indiscriminate police beatings committed with impunity. The draft KNCHR report leaked to the press in September included accounts of use of torture by security forces. . . . The accounts included allegations of torture through beatings, waterboarding, genital mutilation, electric shocks, exposure to extreme cold or heat, hanging from trees, mock executions, exposure to stinging ants, and denial of sleep and food. Amnesty International documented 41 cases of alleged police torture in 2014; in May 2014 it released a survey indicating that 58 percent of citizens feared being tortured." (Sec. 1c) "Police, however, frequently arrested and detained citizens arbitrarily or accused them of more severe crimes than they had committed." (Sec. 1d)

Liberia

"Police officers or magistrates frequently detained citizens for simply owing money to a complainant. There was little distinction between trying these cases in criminal or civil courts when they were not under the purview of specialized tribunals. The government often used police as a low-level dispute mechanism to settle minor issues." (Sec. 1d) "Impunity remained a serious problem despite intermittent and limited government attempts to investigate, prosecute, and punish officials who committed violations, whether in the security forces or elsewhere in the government." (Executive Summary) "The constitution prohibits practices such as torture and inhuman treatment; nonetheless, police officers and other security officials allegedly abused, harassed, and intimidated persons in police custody to extort money, out of personal animosity, or for other reasons." (Sec. 1c)

Madagascar

"The most important human rights abuses included the inability of the government to provide rule of law, which resulted in security force abuse, including unlawful killings and mob violence. . . . The government did not always prosecute or punish officials who committed abuses, whether in the security forces or elsewhere in the government, and impunity remained a problem." (Executive Summary) "Although no official statistics were available, there were numerous reports security forces killed criminal suspects, both while in pursuit and during arrest." (Sec. 1a) "The constitution and law provide for the inviolability of the person and prohibit such practices, but security forces subjected prisoners and criminal suspects to physical and mental abuse, including torture, according to nongovernmental organizations (NGOs) and media reports. Security personnel used beatings as punishment for alleged crimes or simply as a tool of coercion. Off-duty and intoxicated members of the armed forces assaulted civilians. In most cases investigations announced by security officials did not result in prosecutions or sentences." (Sec. 1c) "The government did not have effective control over matters relating to rule of law outside the capital. Security forces at times failed to prevent or respond to societal violence, particularly in rural areas." (Sec. 1d)

Malawi

"The Malawi Human Rights Commission (MHRC) and NGOs working in prisons expressed concern regarding the human rights of detained persons. The MHRC cited overcrowding, poor sanitation, and inadequate food and health care as major problems in prisons and detention centers. It also observed that torture was widespread and most prisoners and detainees lived in degrading and inhuman conditions." (Sec. 1c)

Mali

"The constitution and law generally prohibit arbitrary arrest and detention. Nevertheless, government security forces and Platform and CMA forces detained and arrested numerous individuals in relation to the ongoing northern conflict, particularly in the wake of clashes in Menaka and Anefis, and terrorist attacks in Misseni and Fakola." (Sec. 1d) "Impunity also continued to be a problem in cases concerning both government and nongovernment actors accused of perpetrating crimes." (Executive Summary) "Human rights organizations reported widespread allegations of arbitrary arrest and detention." (Sec. 1d) "The military, rebel groups, northern militias whose interests aligned with the government, and terrorist organizations killed persons throughout the country, but primarily in the north. Violent confrontations ensued between the military and rebel forces in the north before the June signing of the peace accord, resulting in numerous civilian deaths." (Sec. 1g)

Mauritania

"The constitution and law prohibit arbitrary arrest and detention, but authorities did not observe these prohibitions." (Sec. 1d) "Malnutrition, particularly among foreign inmates, prisoners without familial support, and sick inmates, was widespread." (Sec. 1c) "Corruption and impunity were serious problems. Police regularly demanded bribes at nightly roadblocks in Nouakchott and at checkpoints between cities. There were numerous reports that police at such roadblocks arbitrarily detained individuals." (Sec. 1d) "Although the government made advances toward ending slavery, such as the adoption of the Roadmap for the Eradication of the Vestiges of Slavery, its efforts to enforce the 2007 antislavery law were widely seen as inadequate, given the severity of the problem. . . . Some former slaves reportedly continued to work for their former masters or others under exploitative conditions to retain access to land that they traditionally farmed. Although the law provides for distribution of land to the landless, including to former slaves, authorities rarely enforced it." (Sec. 1c)

Mauritius

"The constitution and law prohibit such practices [torture or cruel, inhuman, or degrading treatment or punishment], but there continued to be widespread reports of police abuses." (Sec. 1c)

Mozambique

"[T]orture in police stations remained a problem as poorly trained police frequently used excessive force when apprehending, interrogating, and detaining criminal suspects and handling prisoners." (Sec. 1c)

Nigeria

"The most serious human rights abuses included those committed by Boko Haram, which conducted numerous attacks on government and civilian targets that resulted in thousands of deaths and injuries, widespread destruction, the internal displacement of an estimated 1.8 million persons, and the external displacement of 220,000 Nigerian refugees to neighboring countries. In its response to Boko Haram attacks, and at times to crime and insecurity in general, security services perpetrated extrajudicial killings, and engaged in torture, rape, arbitrary detention, mistreatment of detainees, and destruction of property. The country also suffered from widespread societal unrest, including ethnic, regional, and religious violence. . . . The government took few steps to investigate or prosecute officials who committed violations, whether in the security forces or elsewhere in the government, and impunity remained widespread at all levels of government." (Executive Summary) "The government and its agents committed numerous arbitrary and unlawful killings." (Sec. 1a) "Reports indicated security service personnel regularly tortured, beat, and abused demonstrators, criminal suspects, militants, detainees, and convicted prisoners." (Sec. 1c)

Rwanda

"The constitution and law prohibit such practices, but there were numerous reports of abuse of detainees and prisoners by police, military, and National Intelligence and Security Services (NISS) officials. . . . HRW and domestic observers reported the abuse of detained street vendors, commercial sex workers, and beggars at the Gikondo Transit Center, a detention facility in Kigali (locally known as 'Kwa Kabuga'), by police and other detainees. The HRW report cites beatings and ill-treatment of detainees by police or other detainees by order or approval of police were commonplace." (Sec. 1c) "The constitution and law prohibit arbitrary arrest and detention, but SSF personnel regularly arrested and detained persons arbitrarily and without due process." (Sec. 1d)

Somalia

S/Res/ 2244 (2015), recalling 733 (1992), 1844 (2008), 1907 (2009), 2036 (2012), 2023 (2011), 2093 (2013), 2111 (2013), 2124 (2013), 2125 (2013), 2142 (2014), 2182 (2014).

South Africa

"Police use of lethal and excessive force, including torture, resulted in numerous deaths and injuries, according to the Independent Police Investigative Directorate (IPID), Amnesty International, and other nongovernmental organizations (NGOs). Politically motivated killings by ANC members and members of opposition political parties also occurred. The country had a high crime rate." (Sec. 1a) "During the year IPID received 5,879 complaints ranging from killings to assault, recommended prosecution in 983 cases, and arrested 983 police officers. Of the cases recommended for prosecution, the NPA prosecuted 52 resulting in one guilty verdict." (Sec. 1a) "Watchdog groups noted deaths in custody often resulted from physical abuse combined with a lack of medical treatment or neglect." (Sec. 1a) "In its 2014–15 annual report, IPID reported 145 torture cases, up from 78 cases the previous year. Qualitative studies by monitoring organizations found victims in many communities did not report police abuse due to a 'normalization' or public acceptance of police torture and brutality." (Sec. 1c) "The constitution and law prohibit arbitrary arrest and detention, but security forces arbitrarily arrested numerous persons during the year." (Sec. 1d)

South Sudan

S/Res/2280 (2016), recalling 2057 (2012), 2109 (2013), 2132 (2013), 2155 (2014), 2187 (2014), 2206 (2015), 2241 (2015), 2252 (2015), 2271 (2016).

Sudan

S/Res/2113 (2013), recalling 1265 (1999), 1296 (2000), 1674 (2006), 1738 (2006), 1894 (2009), 1612 (2005), 1882 (2009), 1998 (2011), 2068 (2012).

Swaziland

"During the year there were numerous reports the government or its agents committed arbitrary or unlawful killings. Police investigated unlawful killings and referred cases to the Directorate of Public Prosecutions as appropriate, but there was no evidence suggesting the state prosecuted perpetrators." (Sec. 1a) "Although the constitution and law prohibit arbitrary arrest and detention, police arbitrarily arrested and detained numerous persons, primarily to prevent their participation in public protests." (Sec. 1d)

Uganda

"There were numerous reports of torture and abuse in police detention facilities." (Sec. 1c) "Although the constitution and law prohibit such practices, security forces often arbitrarily arrested and detained persons, including opposition leaders, politicians, activists, demonstrators, and journalists." (Sec. 1d) "Arbitrary arrests during police sweeps remained a problem, as were arbitrary arrests allegedly based on preventive action, suspicion of treason, disobeying lawful orders, and incitement of violence charges." (Sec. 1d)

Zambia

"The government took selective and halting steps to prosecute or punish officials who committed abuses, targeting mostly those who opposed the ruling party. Impunity remained a problem, as ruling party supporters were either not prosecuted for serious crimes or, if prosecuted, released after serving small fractions of prison sentences." (Executive Summary) "There were reports police frequently used excessive force, including torture, and cruel, inhuman, or degrading treatment when apprehending, interrogating, and detaining criminal suspects." (Sec. 1c) "Although the constitution and law prohibit arbitrary arrest and detention, the HRC reported the authorities frequently violated these prohibitions." (Sec. 1d) "According to human rights groups, arbitrary or false arrest and detention remained problems. In a change from prior stated policy on police independence, the Inspector General of Police Stella Libongani on August 10 announced the president had the right to order police to investigate or arrest anyone. Police arbitrarily summoned family members of criminal suspects, often for questioning. Authorities often arrested criminal suspects based on uncorroborated accusations or as a pretext for extortion. Human rights groups reported police routinely detained citizens after midnight, a practice only legal during a state of emergency." (Sec. 1d)

Zimbabwe

"ZANU-PF used intimidation and targeted violence to retain some parliamentary seats during 2015 by-elections. . . . The most important human rights problems remained the government's targeting members of non-ZANU-PF parties and civil society activists for abduction, arrest, torture, abuse, and harassment; partisan application of the rule of law by security forces and the judiciary; and restrictions on civil liberties. There were many other human rights problems. . . . The government generally failed to investigate or prosecute state security or ZANU-PF supporters responsible for violence. . . . The government continued to evict citizens; invade farms, private businesses and properties; and demolish informal marketplaces and settlements." (Executive Summary) "There were reports the government or its agents committed arbitrary or unlawful killings. Progress in cases from previous years was slow, and most cases remained open. Police units sometimes organized or participated in political violence. Security sector impunity stemming from politically motivated abuses remained a problem." (Sec. 1a) "Human rights groups reported the continuance of physical and psychological torture perpetrated by security agents and ZANU-PF supporters. Reported torture methods included beating victims with sticks, clubs, whips, cables, and sjamboks (a heavy whip); burning; falanga (beating the soles of the feet); use of electric shocks; solitary confinement; and sleep deprivation. According to one NGO, from January through September, 155 persons sought treatment for injuries and trauma sustained from security force abuse, compared with 169 persons in 2014. During the same period, the NGO reported that 165 persons sought treatment for injuries and trauma sustained from abuse by ZANU-PF supporters, compared with 88 persons in 2014. . . . ZANU-PF supporters—often with tacit support from police—continued to assault and mistreat scores of persons, including civil society activists and known Movement for Democratic Change (MDC) members and their families, especially in Harare neighborhoods and nearby towns." (Sec. 1c) "The government continued to use arbitrary arrest and detention as tools of intimidation and harassment, especially against political activists, civil society members, journalists, and ordinary citizens asserting their rights." (Sec. 1d)

Bibliography

Alexander, Yonah, and Robert Friedlander, eds. *Self-Determination: National, Regional, and Global Dimensions* (Boulder, CO: Westview Press, 1980).

Altman, Andrew, and Christopher Heath Wellman. *A Liberal Theory of International Justice* (New York: Oxford University Press, 2009).

Aristotle. *Nicomachean Ethics* (transl. Terence Irwin) (Indianapolis: Hackett, 1985).

Armitage, David. "Hobbes and the Foundations of Modern International Thought," in *Rethinking the Foundations of Modern Political Thought*, edited by Annabel Brett and James Tully (New York: Cambridge University Press, 2006).

Avila, Mitchell. "Defending a Law of Peoples: Political Liberalism and Decent Peoples," *The Journal of Ethics* 11, no. 1 (March 2007): 87–124.

———. "Human Rights and Toleration in Rawls," *Human Rights Review* 12, no. 1 (March 2011): 1–14.

Barry, Brian. "Review of J. H. Wellbank, Dennis Snook, and David Mason, *John Rawls and His Critics: An Annotated Bibliography* (New York: Garland Publishing, 1982)," *Ethics* 94, vol. 2 (January 1984): 351–53.

———. *Theories of Justice* (Berkeley: University of California Press, 1989).

———. "John Rawls and the Search for Stability," *Ethics* 105, vol. 4 (July 1995): 874–915.

Beitz, Charles. *Political Theory and International Relations* (Princeton, NJ: Princeton University Press, 1979).

———. "Rawls's Law of Peoples," *Ethics* 110, no. 4 (July 2000): 669–96.

Bernstein, Alyssa. "A Human Right to Democracy? Legitimacy and Intervention," in *Rawls's Law of Peoples: A Realistic Utopia?* Edited by Rex Martin and David Reidy (Malden, MA: Blackwell Publishing, 2006), ch. 16.

———. "Justifying Universal Human Rights via Rawlsian Public Reason," *Human Rights and Ethics/Derechos Humanos y Ètica: Proceedings of the 22nd IVR World Congress* (Granada, Spain, 2005), Volume III: 90–103.

———. "Human Rights, Global Justice, and Disaggregated States: John Rawls, Onora O'Neill, and Anne-Marie Slaughter," *American Journal of Economics and Sociology* 66, no. 1 (January 2007): 87–112.

Blake, Michael. *Justice & Foreign Policy* (New York: Oxford University Press, 2013).

Brooks, Thom and Fabian Freyenhagen, eds. *The Legacy of John Rawls* (London and New York: Continuum, July 2005).

Brownlie, Ian. "Recognition in Theory and Practice," in *The Structure and Process of International Law: Essays in Legal Philosophy, Doctrine and Theory*, edited by Ronald MacDonald and Douglas Johnston (Dordrect, NL: Martinus Nijhoff, 1983).

Buchanan, Allen. "Recognitional Legitimacy and the State System," *Philosophy & Public Affairs* 28, no. 1 (Winter 1999): 46–78.

———. "Rule-governed Institutions versus Act-Consequentialism: A Rejoinder to Naticchia," *Philosophy & Public Affairs* 28, no. 3 (Summer 1999): 258–70.

———. "Rawls's Law of Peoples: Rules for a Vanished Westphalian World," *Ethics* 100, no. 4 (July 2000): 697–721.

———. "Justice, Legitimacy, and Human Rights," in *The Idea of a Political Liberalism: Essays on Rawls*, edited by Victoria Davion and Clark Wolf (Lanham, MD: Rowman & Littlefield, 2000), 73–89.

———. *Justice, Legitimacy, and Self-Determination: Moral Foundations for International Law* (New York: Oxford University Press, 2004).

Caney, Simon. "Cosmopolitanism and the Law of Peoples," *Journal of Political Philosophy* 10, no. 1 (2002): 95–123.

Carr, E. H. *The Twenty Years' Crisis 1919–1939* (London: Macmillan, 1939).

Cassese, Antonio. *Self-Determination of Peoples: A Legal Reappraisal* (Cambridge: Cambridge University Press, 1995).

Cohen, Joshua. "A More Democratic Liberalism," *Michigan Law Review* 92, no. 6 (May 1994): 1503–46.

Copp, David. "The Idea of a Legitimate State," *Philosophy & Public Affairs* 28, no. 1 (Winter 1999): 15.

Cordesman, Anthony. "Symposium on Dual Containment: U.S. Policy Toward Iran and Iraq," *Middle East Policy* (Fall 1994): 11–13.

Craven, Matthew. "The European Community Arbitration Commission on Yugoslavia," *The British Year Book of International Law* 1995 (Oxford: Clarendon Press, 1996).

Crawford, James. *The Creation of States in International Law* (Oxford: Oxford University Press, 1979).

Davion, Victoria, and Clark Wolf. *The Idea of a Political Liberalism: Essays on Rawls* (Lanham, MD: Rowman & Littlefield, 2000).

Dworkin, Ronald. *Law's Empire* (Cambridge, MA: Harvard University Press, 1986).

———. "The Threat to Patriotism," *New York Review of Books* 28 (February 2002): 44–49.

English, Jane. "Justice between Generations," *Philosophical Studies* 31, no. 2 (1977): 91–104.

Exdell, John. "Feminism, Fundamentalism and Liberal Legitimacy," *Canadian Journal of Philosophy* 24 (1994): 441–63.

Fabry, Mikulas. *Recognizing States: International Society & the Establishment of New States Since 1776* (New York: Oxford University Press, 2010).

Fox, Gregory, and Brad Roth, eds. *Democratic Governance and International Law* (New York: Cambridge University Press, 2000).

Freeman, Samuel. "Political Liberalism and the Possibility of a Just Democratic Constitution," *Chicago-Kent Law Review* 69 (1994): 619–68.

———, ed. *John Rawls: Collected Papers* (Cambridge, MA: Harvard University Press, 1999).

———. "Congruence and the Good of Justice," in *The Cambridge Companion to Rawls*, edited by Samuel Freeman (New York: Cambridge University Press, 2003), ch. 7, pp. 281–82.

———, ed., *The Cambridge Companion to Rawls* (New York: Cambridge University Press, 2003).

Gazit, Shlomo. "Israel and the Palestinians: 50 Years of War and Turning Points," *Annals of the American Academy of Political & Social Science* (January 1998): 82–97.

General Assembly Resolution 2625 of 24 October 1970. *Declaration on Principles of International Law concerning Friendly Relations and Cooperation among States in accordance with the Charter of the United Nations*, A/RES/25/2625.

Grant, Thomas. *The Recognition of States: Law and Practice in Debate and Evolution* (Westport, CT: Praeger Publishers, 1999).

Guidelines on the Recognition of New States in Eastern Europe and in the Soviet Union, December 16, 1991.

Hamdan al-Alkim, Hassan. "The Gulf Subregion in the Twenty-First Century: U.S. Involvement and Sources of Instability," *American Studies International* (February 2000): 72–95.

Hannum, Hurst. "Rethinking Self-Determination," *Virginia Journal of International Law* 34 (1993): 1–69.

———. "Self-Determination, Yugoslavia, and Europe: Old Wine in New Bottles?," *Transnational Law and Contemporary Problems* 57 (1993): 6–9.

———. "The Right of Self-Determination in the Twenty-First Century," *Washington & Lee Law Review* 55 (1998): 773–80.

Hart, H. L. A. "Are There any Natural Rights?" *Philosophical Review* 64, no. 2 (April 1955): 175–91.

Higgins, Rosalyn. *Problems and Process: International Law and How We Use It* (Oxford: Oxford University Press, 1994).
Hobbes, Thomas. *Leviathan* (1651) ed. C.B. Macpherson (New York: Penguin Books, 1985).
Hoffman, Stanley. *The State of War* (New York: Praeger, 1965).
Horowitz, Donald. "The Cracked Foundations of the Right to Secede," *Journal of Democracy* 14, no. 2 (2003): 5–17.
———. "A Right to Secede?" *Nomos* 45 (2003): 50–76.
Hume, David. "Of the Original Contract," in *Hume: Political Essays*, edited by Knud Haakonssen (New York: Cambridge University Press, 1994): 186–201.
Johnson, L. M. *Thucydides, Hobbes, and the Interpretation of Realism* (DeKalb: Northern Illinois University Press, 1993).
Kavka, Gregory. *Hobbesian Moral and Political Theory* (Princeton, NJ: Princeton University Press, 1986).
Kennan, George. *Realities of American Foreign Policy* (New York: Norton, 1966).
Korsgaard, Christine. *Creating the Kingdom of Ends* (New York: Cambridge University Press, 1996).
Kymlicka, Will. *Liberalism, Community, and Culture* (New York: Oxford University Press, 1989).
———. *Multicultural Citizenship* (New York: Oxford University Press, 1995).
Laden, Anthony Simon. "The House That Jack Built: Thirty Years of Reading Rawls," *Ethics* 113, vol. 2 (January 2003): 367–90.
MacDonald, Ronald, and Douglas Johnston, eds. *The Structure and Process of International Law: Essays in Legal Philosophy, Doctrine and Theory* (Dordrect, NL: Martinus Nijhoff, 1983).
Machiavelli, Niccolò. *The Prince* (1532) (transl. Christian Detmold) (New York: Washington Square Press, 1963).
MacIntyre, Alasdair. *After Virtue: A Study in Moral Theory* (Notre Dame: University of Notre Dame Press, 1981).
Malcolm, Noel. "Hobbes's Theory of International Relations," in *Aspects of Hobbes*, edited by Noel Malcolm (New York: Oxford University Press, 2002).
Margalit, Avishai, and Joseph Raz. "National Self-Determination," *Journal of Philosophy* 87, no. 9 (Sept. 1990): 439–61.
Martin, Rex, and David Reidy, eds. *Rawls's Law of Peoples: A Realistic Utopia?* (Malden, MA: Blackwell Publishing, 2006).
Middle East Report (November/December 1990).
Miller, David. "The Ethical Significance of Nationality," *Ethics* 98, no. 4 (July 1988): 647–62.
———. *On Nationality* (New York: Oxford University Press, 1995).
Moellendorf, Darrel. "Constructing the Law of Peoples," *Pacific Philosophical Quarterly* 77, no. 2 (June 1996): 132–54.
Montevideo Convention on the Rights and Duties of States, December 26, 1933.
Morgenthau, Hans. *Politics Among Nations* (New York: Knopf, 1948).
Murphy, John. "Self-Determination: United States Perspectives," in *Self-Determination: National, Regional, and Global Dimensions*, edited by Yonah Alexander and Robert Friedlander (Boulder, CO: Westview Press, 1980) 43–61.
Naticchia, Chris. "Human Rights, Liberalism, and Rawls's Law of Peoples," *Social Theory and Practice* 24, no. 3 (Fall 1998): 345–74.
———. "Recognition and Legitimacy: A Reply to Buchanan," *Philosophy & Public Affairs* 28, no. 3 (Summer 1999), 242–57.
———. "Recognizing States and Governments," *Canadian Journal of Philosophy* 35, no. 1 (March 2005), 27–82.
———. "The Law of Peoples: The Old and the New," *Journal of Moral Philosophy* 2, no. 3 (November 2005), 353–69, reprinted in *The Legacy of John Rawls*, edited by Thom Brooks and Fabian Freyenhagen (London and New York: Continuum, July 2005), 177–94.

Nozick, Robert. *Anarchy, State, and Utopia* (New York: Basic Books, 1974).
Okin, Susan Moller. *Justice, Gender, and the Family* (New York: Basic Books, 1989).
———. "Political Liberalism, Justice, and Gender," *Ethics* 105 (1994): 23–43.
O'Neill, Onora. "Ethical Reasoning and Ideological Pluralism," *Ethics* 98 (1988): 705–22.
Patten, Alan. *Equal Recognition: The Moral Foundations of Minority Rights* (Princeton, NJ: Princeton University Press, 2014).
Pennock, J. Roland, and John W. Chapman, eds. *Ethics, Economics, and the Law: Nomos XXIV* (New York: New York University Press, 1982).
Phillips, Michael. "Reflections on the Transition from Ideal to Non-Ideal Theory," *Nous* 19, no. 4 (1985): 551–70.
Plato. *Meno* in Plato, Five Dialogues (transl. G.M.A. Grube) (Indianapolis: Hackett, 1981).
Pogge, Thomas. *Realizing Rawls* (Ithaca, NY: Cornell University Press, 1989).
———. "An Egalitarian Law of Peoples," *Philosophy & Public Affairs* 23 (1994): 195–224.
———. "Rawls on International Justice," *Philosophical Quarterly* 51, no. 203 (April 2001): 246–53.
Pomerance, Michla. "The Badinter Commission: The Use and Misuse of the International Court of Justice's Jurisprudence," *Michigan Journal of International Law* 20 (1998): 31–58.
Quong, Jonathan. *Liberalism without Perfection* (New York: Oxford University Press, 2011).
Radan, Peter. *The Break-up of Yugoslavia and International Law* (London: Routledge, 2002).
Ratner, Steven. *The Thin Justice of International Law: A Moral Reckoning of the Law of Nations* (New York: Oxford University Press, 2015).
Rawls, John. *A Theory of Justice* (Cambridge, MA: Harvard University Press, 1971).
———. "The Independence of Moral Theory," *Proceedings and Addresses of the American Philosophical Association* XLVIII (1974–1975): 5–22, reprinted in *John Rawls: Collected Papers*, edited by Samuel Freeman (Cambridge, MA: Harvard University Press, 1999), ch. 15.
———. "Kantian Constructivism in Moral Theory," *Journal of Philosophy* 77 (1980): 515–72, reprinted in *John Rawls: Collected Papers*, edited by Samuel Freeman (Cambridge, MA: Harvard University Press, 1999), ch. 16.
———. "Justice as Fairness: Political not Metaphysical," *Philosophy & Public Affairs* 14 (1985): 223–52, reprinted in *John Rawls: Collected Papers*, edited by Samuel Freeman (Cambridge, MA: Harvard University Press, 1999), ch. 18.
———. *Political Liberalism* (New York: Columbia University Press, 1993).
———. "The Law of Peoples," *On Human Rights: The Oxford Amnesty Lectures, 1993*, edited by Stephen Shute and Susan Hurley (New York: Basic Books, 1993): 41–82, 220–30, reprinted in *John Rawls: Collected Papers*, edited by Samuel Freeman (Cambridge, MA: Harvard University Press, 1999), ch. 24.
———. "The Idea of Public Reason Revisited," *University of Chicago Law Review* 64 (Summer 1997): 765–807, reprinted in *John Rawls: Collected Papers*, edited by Samuel Freeman (Cambridge, MA: Harvard University Press, 1999), ch. 26.
———. *The Law of Peoples* (Cambridge, MA: Harvard University Press, 1999).
———. *Lectures on the History of Moral Philosophy*, edited by Barbara Herman (Cambridge, MA: Harvard University Press, 2000).
———. *Justice as Fairness: A Restatement* (Cambridge, MA: Harvard University Press, 2001).
———. *Lectures on the History of Political Philosophy*, edited by Samuel Freeman (Cambridge, MA: Harvard University Press, 2007).
Reidy, David. "Rawls on International Justice: A Defense," *Political Theory* 32, no. 3 (June 2004): 291–319.

———. "Political Authority and Human Rights," in *Rawls's Law of Peoples: A Realistic Utopia?* Edited by Rex Martin and David Reidy (Malden, MA: Blackwell Publishing, 2006), ch. 10.
———. "A Just Global Economy: In Defense of Rawls," *The Journal of Ethics* 11, no. 2 (June 2007): 193–236.
———. "Human Rights: Institutions and Agendas," *Public Affairs Quarterly* 22, no. 4 (October 2008): 381–404.
Richards, David A. J. "International Distributive Justice," in *Ethics, Economics, and the Law: Nomos XXIV*, edited by J. Roland Pennock and John W. Chapman (New York: New York University Press, 1982), pp. 275–99.
Roth, Brad. *Governmental Illegitimacy in International Law* (New York: Oxford University Press, 2000).
Safty, A. "Sadat's Negotiations with the United States and Israel: Camp David and Blair House," *American Journal of Economics & Sociology* (October 1991): 473–85.
Sandel, Michael. *Liberalism and the Limits of Justice* (New York: Cambridge University Press, 1982).
———. "The Procedural Republic and the Unencumbered Self," *Political Theory* 12, no. 1 (February 1984): 81–96.
Scheffler, Samuel. *The Rejection of Consequentialism* (New York: Oxford University Press, 1982).
———. "The Appeal of Political Liberalism," *Ethics* 105 (1994): 4–22.
Sen, Amartya. *The Idea of Justice* (Cambridge, MA: Harvard University Press, 2009).
Simma, Bruno. *The Charter of the United Nations: A Commentary* 3d. ed., vol. 1 (Oxford: Oxford University Press, 2012).
Simmons, A. John. *Moral Principles and Political Obligations* (Princeton, NJ: Princeton University Press, 1979).
———. *On the Edge of Anarchy: Locke, Consent, and the Limits of Society* (Princeton, NJ: Princeton University Press, 1993).
———. "Justification and Legitimacy," *Ethics* 109 (1999): 739–71.
———. "Ideal and Nonideal Theory," *Philosophy & Public Affairs* 38, no. 1 (Winter 2010): 5–36.
Szasz, Paul. "Discussion on the Fragmentation of Yugoslavia," *American Society of International Law Proceedings* 88 (1994).
Talmon, Stefan. *Recognition of Governments in International Law: With Particular Reference to Governments in Exile* (New York: Oxford University Press, 1998).
Tan, Kok-Chor. "The Problem of Decent Peoples," in *Rawls's Law of Peoples: A Realistic Utopia?* Edited by Rex Martin and David Reidy (Malden, MA: Blackwell Publishing, 2006), pp. 76–94.
Taylor, Charles. *Philosophy and the Human Sciences: Philosophical Papers, Vol. 2* (New York: Cambridge University Press, 1985).
Telhami, Shibley. "From Camp David to Wye: Changing Assumptions in Arab-Israeli Negotiations," *Middle East Journal* (Summer 1999): 380–82.
Terrett, Steve. *The Dissolution of Yugoslavia and the Badinter Arbitration Commission* (Aldershot, UK: Ashgate, 2000).
Thucydides. *History of the Peloponnesian War* (431 BC) (transl. Rex Warner) (London: Penguin Books, 1954).
United Nations Development Program. *Human Development Report 2015*.
von Glahn, Gerhard. *Law Among Nations: An Introduction to Public International Law*. 6th ed. (New York: Macmillan, 1992).
Walzer, Michael. *Spheres of Justice* (New York: Basic Books, 1983).
———. *Interpretation and Social Criticism* (Cambridge, MA: Harvard University Press, 1987).
———. *On Toleration* (New Haven, CT: Yale University Press, 1997).
———. *The Paradox of Liberation: Secular Revolutions and Religious Counterrevolutions* (New Haven, CT: Yale University Press, 2015).

Weithman, Paul. *Why Political Liberalism? On John Rawls's Political Turn* (New York: Oxford University Press, 2010).

Wellman, Christopher Heath. *A Theory of Secession: The Case for Political Self-Determination* (New York: Cambridge University Press, 2005).

Wenar, Leif. "Political Liberalism: An Internal Critique," *Ethics* 106, no. 1 (October 1995): 32–62.

———. *Blood Oil: Tyrants, Violence, and the Rules that Run the World* (New York: Oxford University Press, 2016).

Zunes, Stephen. "The Israeli-Jordanian Agreement: Peace or *Pax Americana*?" *Middle East Policy* (April 1995): 57.

———. "The Strategic Functions of U.S. Aid to Israel," *Middle East Policy* (October 1996): 90–91.

Index

absolutist prohibitions, 17, 166–167, 171, 172, 173
adjusted array, 216
Africa, 137–138, 140, 141, 177, 196, 226
alien rule, 188–190, 191–192, 193, 196
almost-liberal objection, 7, 17, 45, 55, 57, 62, 63, 108–110, 164
American Revolution, 220–221, 222, 227
anarchy, 22–23
annexation, 188–189, 191, 222, 223, 227, 229, 230
Arab-Israeli conflict, 135–136, 225
Arab Spring uprisings, 147
assurance problem, 191, 192–194, 231
atomism, 8, 67–68, 69, 71
autonomy, 74, 75
Avila, Mitchell, 95–96

Badinter Commission, 228–229
Barry, Brian, 12, 97–103, 104–105, 108, 242; explanatory aim, 104–105; normative versus explanatory aim, 104
basic human rights: alien rule, and, 191; as condition of international tolerance, 112, 148, 230; as considered moral judgment, 35; as outcome of original position, 31, 32, 34, 67; Bernstein, and, 96; cosmopolitan defense of, 94; empirically contingent support, 59; entailed by common good conception of justice, 37, 38, 56; imposition of, 64; minimal justice, and, 15, 129; penalty for violating, 142; precondition, and, 39; Rawls's conception of, 5, 30, 64; reflective equilibrium, and, 48; Reidy, and, 96; secession, and, 240; strong standard, 130, 131–137; weak standard, 130, 131, 137–138
benevolent absolutisms, 58, 109
Bernstein, Alyssa, 95, 96
Blake, Michael, 62, 63, 164
blameless wrongdoing, 147–148
Brownlie, Ian, 215
Buchanan, Allen, 86, 127, 191
burdened societies, 109, 205
burdens of judgment, 97

Camp David Accords, 135
Carr, E. H., 23
Cassese, Antonio, 19
characteristics of the parties, 68, 169–170, 182, 183–184
China, 240
citizens as free and equal, 107
closed societies, 11, 46, 71, 86–87, 181
collective agents: as representing peoples, 85, 87; as representing societies, 85, 87; as representing states, 85; communitarian concession, result of, 7, 8, 10, 67, 79, 87; inability to generate internal restrictions, 5, 40, 161; *The Law of Peoples*, role in, 34; nation as, 188; reconstructed social contract, role in, 18, 85, 121, 169, 170, 171, 184, 185, 186, 187, 192, 202, 207–209; representation of, 10, 11, 85, 86, 87, 93, 182–183; retention of, 7, 13, 94, 110; substitute for, 7, 12, 94
colonialism, 188–189, 191, 196, 222, 226
commensurability, 161–162, 163
common good, interpretations of, 37–38, 43, 58, 59, 62, 96
common questions, 4
comprehensive doctrines, 70, 74, 94, 95, 98, 102, 103, 104, 106, 164, 184, 208;

content-based criterion of reasonableness, 98; content-free criterion of reasonableness, 99; relationship to political conception, 100–101, 105
comprehensive views. *See* comprehensive doctrines
conception of the self, 8, 9, 67, 68, 69, 75, 77
conceptions of the good. *See* comprehensive doctrines
Congress of Berlin, 223
Congress of Vienna, 221, 222–223, 225
congruence, problem of, 98, 104
connected criticism, 72–74
conquest, 188–189, 191, 222, 223, 224, 225, 226, 227, 228, 229, 230
consent theory, 188, 220
considered moral judgments, 35, 36, 46, 47, 48
consociation, 182
constitutive attachments, 69
consultation hierarchy, 42, 43, 44, 58, 61, 183
context of choice, 9, 75, 76, 80
cosmopolitanism, cosmopolitan strategy, 7, 12, 13, 94, 97, 108, 110
Crawford, James, 19
critical mass, nature of, 175–177, 216, 231
critical mass (principle), 15, 18, 19, 24, 159–177, 181, 197, 201, 207, 210–211, 215, 218, 231, 239; statement of, 165
cultural membership, 9, 75, 76

Declaration on the Granting of Independence to Colonial Countries and Peoples. *See* United Nations Resolution 1514
decent societies, 6, 11, 31, 46, 56, 57, 58, 95, 96, 109, 110, 111, 169
decolonization, 177, 225–226, 227, 228, 241
de facto statehood, 21, 22, 176, 177, 196, 197, 220–227, 229, 230, 231
derecognition, 14, 18, 21, 177, 215, 218, 221, 223, 231, 232, 239
difference principle, 30, 205, 208
discovery, morality of, 71, 72
duty of justice, 136–137, 138, 204
Dworkin, Ronald, 60

economic development (principle), 18, 19, 24, 197, 201–212, 218, 231, 239, 240; statement of, 201, 210, 216
effective statehood. *See* de facto statehood
English, Jane, 5
equal justice for women, 6

Fabry, Mikulas, 20, 188
feminist criticisms, 5
four-stage sequence, 15, 17–18, 24, 163, 197, 201, 202, 207; stage-one, 164, 197, 202, 210; stage-two, 164, 167–171, 186, 197, 202, 207, 208; stage-three, 164, 185–187, 190–194, 202, 207, 208; stage-four, 164, 201, 202, 207, 208; thickness of veil of ignorance, 163–164
foreign policy, 111, 209
Freeman, Samuel, 104, 105, 107, 108
freestanding principles, 70
French Revolution, 220–221, 227, 236
full Rawlsian reply, 35–39

gender discrimination, 59, 60, 61, 64, 130, 131
Gramsci, Antonio, 72

Hannum, Hurst, 19
hereditary monarchy, 220
hierarchical societies. *See* decent societies
Higgins, Rosalyn, 19
Hobbes, Thomas, 23–24, 235–236, 239
Hoffman, Stanley, 23
Holy Alliance, 223
Horowitz, Donald, 19
Human Development Report, 140
Hume, David, 46

"The Idea of Public Reason Revisited," 6
ideal versus nonideal theory: critical edge, 20, 21, 232, 241; departure from Rawls, 16, 160, 193; distinction between, 16, 159–160; economic

development principle, and, 210; first-stage entitlement, 202; general conception, and, 203; just savings principle, and, 204–205, 206, 208, 209; maximin, and, 173; realism, and, 23, 24; secession, and, 17, 181, 185–186, 188–189; Sen, and, 161–163; Simmons, and, 160; social contract, and, 212; substitute ideal in theory of recognition, 16, 17, 161, 164, 201
idealism in international relations, 23, 24
idle-contract objection, 5, 6, 7, 11, 14, 39–42, 48, 55, 67, 93, 94, 97, 113, 175, 212
individual self determination, 80, 82
individuals as parties, 5, 7, 67, 85, 94, 110, 170, 207, 208
initial array, 215, 216
interests of the parties, 170–171
International Atomic Energy Agency, 134
international community, 111, 112, 122, 131, 132, 136, 146, 148, 151, 167, 210, 211, 217, 224, 225, 228, 231, 232
international legal system, goals of, 128, 131
International Monetary Fund, 134, 140, 141, 210
interpretation, morality of, 8, 46, 72, 73
invention, morality of, 71, 72, 73, 83
Iraq-Kuwait conflict, 134–135, 136

just savings principle, 6, 18, 203–207, 208, 209–210; statement of, 201
justice as fairness, 103, 105, 106, 203, 205; as local account, 73; Kantian interpretation of, 98, 104, 105
justice-based view, 15, 121, 122, 127–130, 133, 138, 160, 165; amendments to, 123, 139–143
justifiable secession (principle), 17, 19, 24, 181–197, 201, 207, 211, 218, 231, 240; conditional right to secede, 188, 190–194, 216; general right to secede, 185–187, 188, 189, 191, 202; independence from institutional considerations, degree of, 189, 190, 192–194; infinite secession, 195; nationality as basis for, 185, 190, 196–197; normative priority of claimants, 190–192; objections to, 194–197; primary right to secede, 192; remedial right to secede, 185, 189, 190, 192, 194, 216, 227, 231, 241; right to secede implying right to recognition, 196; statement of, 216

Kant, Immanuel, 4, 8, 235, 237–239
Kazanistan, 58, 97
Kennan, George, 23
Kosovo, 229, 241
Kymlicka, Will, 8, 9, 10, 11, 75–77, 79–80, 84, 85, 86

The Law of Peoples: article version, 6, 55, 109; as defense of theory of international justice, 13, 31, 94, 110, 239; as defense of theory of recognition, 13, 14, 15, 17, 111–112, 113, 161, 239; limited interests, 32; thinner veil, 32, 33; three main features, 5, 94
League of Nations, 224, 225
Lectures on the History of Moral Philosophy, 237–238
Lectures on the History of Political Philosophy, 235–236
legitimacy, political, 96, 98; as correlate of political obligation, 148–151; Lockean accounts of, 149; Kantian accounts of, 149
liberal foreign policy, 13, 24, 111
liberal individualism, 12, 64, 94, 97, 188
liberal self-inquiry, 96
libertarianism, 74
Locke, John, 4, 235–237, 239

Machiavelli, Niccolò, 23
MacIntyre, Alasdair, 8, 67, 68, 70, 71
Manchukuo, 224–225
Marx, Karl, 72
maximin, 34, 171–174, 186, 191, 205, 208
membership, 11, 13, 19, 94, 110–112, 131, 137, 140, 141, 183, 196, 211, 215, 217, 221, 231, 232
Meno, 98
Middle East, 131, 134–137, 141

Mill, John Stuart, 74
Miller, David, 8, 9, 10, 11, 75, 77–79
minority nations, 11, 18, 86, 87, 93, 169, 181, 182, 185, 191, 196
minority rights, 79
modus vivendi, 101
Monroe Doctrine, 221
moral skepticism, 23–24
Morgenthau, Hans, 23
multinational states, 11, 172, 182, 183, 185, 210, 241
Murphy, John, 19

narrative unity of self, 68, 69, 70
nationality, ethical significance of, 9, 10, 75, 77, 79–84, 85, 87, 93, 169; as basis for recognition, 227, 230, 231; fundamental value of, 9, 10, 77–79, 188; instrumental value of, 9, 10, 75–77
national self-determination. *See* self-determination of peoples
necessity of moral progress, 17, 166–167, 186, 202
neutrality of aim, 70
neutrality of effects, 81
neutrality of treatment, 81
nonintervention, 5, 13, 30, 31, 34, 41, 62, 96, 111, 112, 150
nonliberal societies. *See* decent societies
nonparticipant objection, 6
normative advice, 21
normative conditions. *See* recognition, minimal justice, and
North Korea, 239

obligation to belong to society, 67, 71
Okin, Susan Moller, 5
outlaw regimes, 33, 34, 35
overlapping consensus: almost-liberal objection, and, 110; as second of two stages, 47, 95; as unnecessary for justification, 12, 97–103, 104, 108; Avila, and, 96; Barry, and, 97–103; Freeman, and, 105; human rights, focus on, 7; *Political Liberalism*, role in, 94; political liberal strategy, role in, 12, 94, 97, 103; practical aim, 60, 83, 105; pragmatic theory, and, 241; Quong, and, 107–108; Weithman, and, 106

paradox of liberation, 82–84
parent state consent, 19, 20, 22, 185, 190–191, 192, 193–194, 220–224, 225, 226–229, 230, 231, 232, 240–241
Paris Peace Conference, 224–225, 225
particularism, 10, 77, 79
paternalism, 41, 42
Patten, Alan, 79–82, 84
peacekeeping operations, 137, 138, 148
peoples, 10, 64, 95, 183, 186, 187, 202, 210; conception of themselves, 184, 185, 187, 192, 202, 207; versus societies, 10, 85–87, 182–183
plebiscite, 185, 190, 193, 230, 231
pluralism, 8, 98, 105
Pogge, Thomas, 31–33, 35, 39, 49
political conception, 12, 94, 97
political liberal strategy, 12, 13, 94–97, 103, 108
Political Liberalism, 4, 7, 8, 69, 73, 94, 95, 97–103, 104, 242
political not metaphysical, 8, 69
political values, 107
pragmatic theory, 16, 17, 20–21, 23, 24, 121–122, 127–130, 133, 139–140, 151, 164, 196, 211, 239–241; and accomplices in injustice, 145–146, 166; consequentialism, relation to, 145; deontology, relation to, 145; final statement of, 215–217; justificatory role of, 219; main objections to, 143–151; normative criteria, role of, 144; understanding of as normative and reformist, 215, 216, 217, 218, 219
precondition on contract, 36–39, 42–44, 45, 46, 47, 48, 56, 60, 109
preliminary Rawlsian reply, 33–35
priority of individual to society, 68
public reason, 7, 12, 94, 95, 96, 97, 108

Quong, Jonathan, 104, 107–108

range of options, 80
Ratner, Steven, 19

Rawls fatigue, 3
Rawls, John, 3–4
realism in international relations, 22–24
realpolitik, 23–24, 144, 169
reasonableness, 94, 95, 96, 97, 99, 100, 101, 110, 241
reciprocity, 95, 96
recognition, 13; *as-if*, 142–143; asymmetry, 14, 20, 21, 22; automatic, 144; backward-looking, 14, 21, 112; constitutive theory, 217–218; contrast with secession, 13, 14, 20, 112; criteria, 13, 15, 18, 111, 112, 128, 130, 215, 218, 219, 220, 229–232, 239–240; declarative theory, 217–218; discretionary, as, 218; forward-looking, 14, 21; governments, of, 123, 141–142, 211, 219; historical account of, 188, 218, 220–229; limited to new states, 13, 19, 20, 21; minimal justice, and, 15, 23, 121–127, 128–129, 130, 133, 136, 137, 139, 143, 144, 165, 222, 224, 225, 227, 230, 231, 232; obligatory, as, 218; political acts pursuant to, 146, 147; pragmatic considerations, role of, 122–123, 126–127, 128–129, 140, 144, 151; stakes, 122; status quo as starting point, 14, 16, 18, 112, 159, 239
reflective equilibrium, 36, 46–47, 48, 242
regulative principle of nonideal theory. *See* necessity of moral progress
Reidy, David, 95–96
relativism, 72
religious freedom, 56, 57, 58, 59, 60, 61
remainder, 183, 184, 185, 187, 202, 207
right to emigrate, 44–46, 57, 109
Rousseau, Jean-Jacques, 4, 235, 236–237, 238–239
rules for negotiation, 168

Sandel, Michael, 8, 67, 69, 71, 75, 77
Scanlonian motivation, 104
secession as remedial right, 17, 19, 20, 21
Security Council Resolution 216, 226
self-determination of peoples, 19, 96, 127, 188, 221
Sen, Amartya, 161–163
sense of duty, 104, 105
shared understandings, 8, 9, 72, 73, 74, 75, 79, 87, 93
skepticism toward Law of Peoples, 29
Simmons, A. John, 160
social meanings. *See* shared understandings
society as a fair system of social cooperation, 107
Society of Peoples, 11, 93, 110, 111
Soviet Union, 225, 228
Spanish American Revolutions, 221–222, 226, 227
stability, 94, 105, 106
statehood, rights and powers of, 122, 128, 133, 141, 142, 143, 150
states of affairs, ranking of. *See* commensurability
Stimson Doctrine, 224
strains of commitment, 192, 193, 194, 195, 241

Taiwan, 177, 240
target of negotiations, 168
Taylor, Charles, 8, 67, 68, 71, 75, 77
telos, 8, 70–71
territorial integrity, right to, 19, 20, 122, 136, 138, 150, 222, 226, 227
theoretical consistency, 14, 112
A Theory of Justice, 3, 4, 69, 73, 99, 104, 105, 159, 163, 165, 171, 203, 204, 235, 238–239, 242
Thucydides, 23
tolerance, general, 74, 101, 187
tolerance, international, 5, 6, 7, 11, 32, 35, 40, 49, 55, 63, 93, 96, 109, 110, 111, 182
transaction costs, 185, 186, 190
trusteeship, 231
two stages, 7, 47, 95, 104, 105, 107
two-stages objection, 7, 55, 61, 108

unilateral right to secede, 19, 226–227
United Nations Resolution 1514, 226
United Nations Resolution 2625, 19, 20, 227

universal liberalism, 16, 24, 45, 62, 63, 109, 110, 164, 201, 203
unrecognized entities, permissible relations with, 132–134
utilitarianism, 15, 74, 165
uti possidetis juris, 222, 226, 227, 228, 230

Walzer, Michael, 8, 9, 67, 71, 71–73, 73–74, 79, 82–84, 87
Weithman, Paul, 104, 105–107, 108
Wenar, Leif, 147
World Bank, 134, 140, 141, 210, 211
World Trade Organization, 134, 140, 210
World War I, 222, 224
World War II, 225

Yugoslavia, 228–229

About the Author

Chris Naticchia is professor of philosophy at California State University, San Bernardino, and specializes in moral, political, and legal philosophy.

CPSIA information can be obtained at www.ICGtesting.com
Printed in the USA
BVOW08*0358211016

465496BV00004B/3/P

9 781498 526135